CONSTITUTIONAL CHANGE AND TRANSFORMATION IN LATIN AMERICA

Over the past 30 years, Latin America has lived through an intense period of constitutional change. Some reforms have been limited in their design and impact, while others have been far-reaching transformations to basic structural features and fundamental rights. Scholars interested in the law and politics of constitutional change in Latin America are turning increasingly to comparative methodologies to expose the nature and scope of these changes, to uncover the motivations of political actors, to theorise how to better execute the procedures of constitutional reform, and to assess whether there should be any limitations on the power of constitutional amendment. In this collection, leading and emerging voices in Latin American constitutionalism explore the complexity of the vast topography of constitutional developments, experiments and perspectives in the region. This volume offers a deep understanding of modern constitutional change in Latin America and evaluates its implications for constitutionalism, democracy, human rights and the rule of law.

Constitutional Change and Transformation in Latin America

Edited by
Richard Albert
Carlos Bernal
and
Juliano Zaiden Benvindo

•HART•
OXFORD • LONDON • NEW YORK • NEW DELHI • SYDNEY

HART PUBLISHING

Bloomsbury Publishing Plc

Kemp House, Chawley Park, Cumnor Hill, Oxford, OX2 9PH, UK

HART PUBLISHING, the Hart/Stag logo, BLOOMSBURY and the Diana logo are trademarks of Bloomsbury Publishing Plc

First published in Great Britain 2019

A catalogue record for this book is available from the British Library.

Library of Congress Cataloging-in-Publication data

Names: Albert, Richard (Law professor), editor. | Bernal Pulido, Carlos, editor. | Benvindo, Juliano Zaiden, editor.

Title: Constitutional change and transformation in Latin America / edited by Richard Albert, Carlos Bernal and Juliano Zaiden Benvindo.

Description: Oxford, UK ; Chicago, Illinois : Hart Publishing, 2019. | Includes bibliographical references and index.

Identifiers: LCCN 2019007696 (print) | LCCN 2019009137 (ebook) | ISBN 9781509923519 (EPub) | ISBN 9781509923502 (hardback)

Subjects: LCSH: Constitutional law—Latin America.

Classification: LCC KG548 (ebook) | LCC KG548 .C664 2019 (print) | DDC 342.803—dc23

LC record available at https://lccn.loc.gov/2019007696

ISBN: HB: 978-1-50992-350-2
ePDF: 978-1-50992-352-6
ePub: 978-1-50992-351-9

Typeset by Compuscript Ltd, Shannon

To find out more about our authors and books visit www.hartpublishing.co.uk. Here you will find extracts, author information, details of forthcoming events and the option to sign up for our newsletters.

FOREWORD

The Life and Death of Constitutions in Latin America: Constitutional Amendments, the Role of Courts and Democracy

LUÍS ROBERTO BARROSO[1]

Richard Albert, Carlos Bernal and Juliano Zaiden Benvindo have assembled, in this book, some of the most representative names of contemporary Latin American constitutionalism. Their texts create a mosaic of distinct tones, convening analysis and thoughts on the institutional order of several countries, such as Bolivia, Brazil, Chile, Colombia, Ecuador and Mexico. The reader who is less familiar with Latin American reality must know that, despite the many common difficulties, it is not an easy task to crosscut the continent's multifarious constitutional experiences to build a unified narrative. For this reason, one of the great merits of this book of exceptional theoretical quality is to establish a dialogue between scholars from different countries and conceptions. This is an achievement in itself, given that the interaction between Latin American jurists is much less common than one would suppose and desire.

The following texts discuss various related themes, including the transition to democracy, the constitution-making process, constitutional reforms, the possibilities and limits of judicial review of constitutional amendments and the challenging consolidation of democracy in Latin America. The high quality texts of this book, as well as a constant dialogue with its editors, inspired the reflections that I make hereinafter, in an exchange that has brought me great benefit and intellectual pleasure. I am honoured by the invitation to preface this work.

I. Some Common Vicissitudes of Latin American Constitutionalism

Latin American constitutionalism has undergone several phases since the first half of the nineteenth century. Over these 200 years, amidst varied arrangements

[1] Justice at the Brazilian Supreme Court. Professor of law, Rio de Janeiro State University. LLM, Yale Law School. Senior Fellow, Harvard Kennedy School.

between conservatives and liberals, some factors have been ubiquitously present, influencing and conforming the continent's multiple constitutional experiences. Among them, we can highlight: (i) *Authoritarianism and institutional instability*, manifested in civilian or military dictatorships, coups d'état and the permanent ghost of military intervention, as well as in hyperpresidentialism; (ii) *Patrimonialism and corruption*, consequences of the poor separation between the public and private spheres, one of the legacies of Iberian colonisation, and the antecedents of a culture of private appropriation of the state by extractive elites, of crony capitalism, and of the existence of structural and systemic corruption, omnipresent in Latin America; (iii) *Social inequality*, an indelible mark of Latin American societies, fostered during a long time by measures such as the requirement of minimum income to vote or the ban on political participation of illiterates. More recently, many constitutions included social rights in their texts, making the limits of their enforceability one of the most intricate issues of contemporary constitutional law.

II. The Endurance of Constitutions in Latin America

In a troubled history, many countries in the region experienced a high rate of demise in their constitutional orders, and currently live under very recent constitutions.[2] This is the case of the Dominican Republic, which has had 31 constitutions (setting the world record in this matter), with the current one dating from 2015; of Venezuela, with 26 constitutional texts (the current one dating from 1999); and of Ecuador, with 20 constitutions (the current one dating from 2008). Brazil followed the Latin American fate and had eight constitutions, with its current one dating back to 1988. Colombia was not any different: it had nine constitutions and is currently governed by its 1991 charter. Chile had 10 different constitutions, and now lives under the 1980 constitution. In all, from independence until today, Latin American countries edited over 250 constitutions, in an inflation of short-lived texts.

Comparatively, in North America and Europe the substitution rate of constitutions is, in general, significantly lower. Throughout its history, the US has had only one constitution (amended many times) and Canada has had two major texts. In Europe, countries like Belgium, Denmark, Netherlands and Italy have also been ruled by a single constitution. France, on the other hand, is the European country with the greater number of constitutional texts: 16 in total, although the current constitution, which dates back to 1958, has been in force for over 60 years.

[2] See Jose Luis Cordeiro, *Constitutions Around the World: A View from Latin America*, IIDE Discussion Paper n 164.

The project of a European Constitution did not become a reality. Although the lifespan of a constitution is not a safe indicator of success, it does directly affect the constitution's ability to promote the objectives for which it has been enacted: the limitation of state power within the framework of the rule of law,[3] and the protection of fundamental rights. Furthermore, if constitutions live at the mercy of political winds, citizens do not develop the indispensable *constitutional sentiment* that nourishes democracy.

III. The Constitutional Amendment Power

Constitutions, therefore, need to have a predisposition for permanence. Ideally, they regulate issues that, because of their relevance and transcendence, should be shielded from ordinary politics. The constitutionalisation of certain fundamental decisions removes them from the influence of casual majorities. Nonetheless, constitutions are not eternal and cannot claim to be entirely immutable. Some flexibility is imperative for constitutional stability itself, in order to allow for the correction of eventual defects of the original text and for their adaptation to new realities. A generation cannot subordinate the next generations to its decisions. The dead cannot rule over the living.[4]

To survive and not succumb to time, there are formal and informal mechanisms of constitutional change that guarantee the flexibility required to face new realities and social demands. Along with informal changes by means of interpretation (constitutional mutation),[5] constitutional amendments arise as a necessary tool to preserve the durability of the constitution. Nonetheless, the freedom to amend the constitutional text, although through a more demanding procedure, can be used to radically change the document or to suppress its essential rules and principles.[6] The amendment power has, therefore, an ambivalent character: at the same time that it guarantees the Constitution's survival, preventing it from becoming obsolete, it can represent its death decree, because it may allow for structural changes of precepts that give the Constitution its meaning and identity.

[3] Gabriel Negretto, *The Durability of Constitutions in Changing Environments: Explaining Constitutional Replacements in Latin America.* Working paper n 350, The Helen Kellogg Institute for International Studies.

[4] See Thomas Paine, *The Rights of Man* (1969); Norman Dorsen, Michel Rosenfeld, András Sajó and Susanne Baer, *Comparative Constitutionalism* (2003).

[5] Bruce Ackerman, *We the People: Foundations* (1995); Bruce Ackerman, *We the People: Transformations* (1998); Georg Jellinek, *Reforma y mutación de la Constitución* (1991).

[6] Ulrich K Preuss, '"The Implications of 'Eternity Clauses": The German Experience' (2011) 44 *Israel Law Review* 429.

IV. Preserving the Essential Core of Constitutions: Immutable Clauses

The power to reform the Constitution should not be the power to deform it, by depriving it of its essential elements. In order to justify its maintenance, a constitution must retain the essence of its original identity, the core political decisions and the fundamental values that justified its creation. In some countries, the Constitution's essential core is protected by explicit material limits to the amendment power. The clauses protected by these limits are called the immutable or eternity clauses: they cannot be altered or affected in their essence, not even by a qualified majority.

These restrictions on the majority rule can serve multiple functions.[7] One of them is precisely to preserve essential constitutional provisions in light of history, tradition and local culture, especially of those more vulnerable to abuse.[8] In Latin America, for example, it is not surprising that the ban on re-election of the chief executive is one of the most frequent immutable clauses in the region's constitutions, seeking to avoid authoritarian abuses and ruptures by successive presidents. Several countries that did not protect the clause of non-re-election against amendments had their constitutions changed on this matter, such as Peru (1993), Argentina (1994), Brazil (1996), Venezuela (in 1999 and then in 2009) Colombia (2004), Ecuador (2008) and Bolivia (2009).

Nonetheless, there is invariable tension between immutable clauses and democracy, to the extent that those clauses impose a significant limit on political majorities' ability to govern. Because of this counter-majoritarian and potentially anti-democratic trait, immutable clauses must be strictly interpreted, without broadening their meaning and scope. Along these lines, the Venice Commission recommends that they be limited to the protection of the basic principles of democratic order, and be interpreted and applied strictly and cautiously. The Brazilian Supreme Court has a precedent along these lines. In doctrine, and even in some countries' practice (such as India and Colombia), it has already been argued that even without explicit immutable clauses, constitutional amendments cannot modify the text's core, for that would entail the replacement of the constitution itself.

V. Judicial Review of Constitutional Amendments

The existence of immutable clauses does not necessarily mean that constitutional amendments will be subject to judicial review. In France, for example,

[7] Richard Albert, *Constitutional Handcuffs* (2010) 42 *Arizona State Law Journal* 663; Yaniv Roznai, *Unconstitutional Constitutional Amendments* (2017).

[8] ibid.

on more than one occasion, the Constitutional Council has declared it has no jurisdiction to rule on the validity of constitutional amendments. In the US and in some European countries, despite the fact that judicial review of amendments is admissible, in practice there are no precedents. In countries like Austria, Bulgaria and the Czech Republic there have been cases, but they are exceptional and quite rare.

In Latin America, circumstances are utterly different. With some frequency, the region's Supreme Courts and Constitutional Courts have recognised their prerogative to review the constitutionality of amendments, invalidating them for formal and substantial reasons. That is to say: they recognised the existence of explicit or implicit substantial limits to the scope of reforms. Brazil has a handful of precedents. An emblematic example is that of Colombia. According to the country's constitution, the Constitutional Court's jurisdiction is restricted to reviewing procedural errors in the genesis of amendments. Since 2003, however, the Court has been expanding its competence to review not only formal, but substantial, defects. The Court has stated that the power of constitutional reform does not amount to the full replacement of the constitution (substitution theory). The substitution theory has been applied in more than a dozen occasions, including the paradigmatic cases of Uribe's re-elections.[9]

VI. Conclusion

Time to move out of the way. Several intricate questions arise from the discussion on the scope, groundings and limits of constitutional change. The chapters contained in this volume advance multiple answers to these questions and have greatly enriched the literature on the matter. I am sure that the reader who dedicates his time to exploring the dense and thoughtful pages of this excellent collection will be enlightened by Latin American constitutional experiences and will be able to better understand some of the challenges the region faces in a plural, polarised and changing world, where the risks brought by authoritarianism, populism and tribalism cannot be neglected.

[9] In 2005, the Court validated a constitutional amendment allowing for presidential re-election. However, it held unconstitutional an amendment that would authorise a third term, on grounds that it would violate the separation of powers clause and the democratic principle.

TABLE OF CONTENTS

LIST OF CONTRIBUTORS

Fernando José Gonçalves Acunha is a Professor of Constitutional Law at Centro Universitário de Brasília (UniCEUB), Brazil.

Richard Albert is the William Stamps Farish Professor in Law at the University of Texas at Austin.

Diego Werneck Arguelhes is an Associate Professor of Law at Insper – Institute of Education and Research, in São Paulo, Brazil, and a former Associate Professor of Law at the Getulio Vargas Foundation (FGV) Law School in Rio de Janeiro.

Leonardo Augusto de Andrade Barbosa is a Law Professor in the Master's Degree Program in Legislative Studies at the Center for Continuing Education and Professional Development (CEFOR, Chamber of Deputies, Brazil).

Vicente F Benítez-R is a Constitutional Law Professor at Universidad de La Sabana (Colombia) and JSD Candidate at New York University (NYU) School of Law.

Juliano Zaiden Benvindo is a Professor of Constitutional Law at the University of Brasília in Brazil and a Research Fellow at the Brazilian National Council for Scientific and Technological Development.

Carlos Bernal is a Justice at the Colombian Constitutional Court.

Carolina Alves das Chagas is a PhD Candidate and Research and Teaching Assistant at the University of Graz, Austria.

Francisca Pou Giménez is a Professor of Constitutional Law at the Law Department of the Instituto Tecnológico Autónomo de México (ITAM) in Mexico City.

Juan F González-Bertomeu is an Assistant Professor at ITAM University (Law Department), Mexico.

Magdalena Inés Correa Henao is the Director of Constitutional Law Department at the Externado University.

Andrea Pozas Loyo is an Associate Professor at the Institute of Legal Research (IIJ) of the National University of Mexico (UNAM).

Breno Baía Magalhães is a Constitutional Law Professor at the Universidade Federal do Pará (UFPA), Brazil.

Mariana Velasco Rivera is a JSD candidate at Yale Law School.

Yaniv Roznai is a Senior Lecturer at the Harry Radzyner Law School, Interdisciplinary Center (IDC) Herzliya.

Eneida Desiree Salgado is a Constitutional Law Professor at Universidade Federal do Paraná, Brazil.

Sergio Verdugo is an Associate Professor of Law at the Universidad del Desarrollo, Chile.

Introduction: Facts and Fictions in Latin American Constitutionalism

JULIANO ZAIDEN BENVINDO, CARLOS BERNAL AND RICHARD ALBERT

Latin America is usually depicted as a region whose democracies are fragile,[1] where political and economic instability has long spurred institutional breakdowns,[2] and where constitutions are replaced at an unusually rapid pace.[3] In the popular imagination, the region's hallmarks include coups, dictatorships, guerilla movements, persistent authoritarian legacies, deep social inequality and corruption infiltrating all branches of government, but the most well-known may be the regularity of constitutional change. As Peter Smith has observed, 'there were 155 regime changes over the 101-year period from 1900 through 2000 – a rate of 1.53 per year'.[4]

Consider some examples. The Dominican Republic has had 34 constitutions. Venezuela has had 26 constitutions so far, and Ecuador is not too far behind: the 2008 Constitution was its twentieth. Since their independence, Latin American countries have written, in total, 197 constitutions, most of them from 1900 onwards, although this pace has waned in the last decades (from 1978 to 2017, there have been 18 new constitutions in the region).[5] The constitutional amendment rate is also high, though it does not differ much from most established

[1] See Terry Lynn Karl, 'Dilemmas of Democratization in Latin America' (1990) 23 *Comparative Politics* 1, 12.

[2] See, eg, Aníbal Pérez-Liñán, *Presidential Impeachment and the New Political Instability in Latin America* (Cambridge University Press, 2007); Adam Przeworski. *Democracy and the Market: Political and Economic Reforms in Eastern Europe and Latin America.* (Cambridge University Press, 1991); K Remmer, 'The Political Impact of Economic Crisis in Latin America in the 1980s' (1991) 85 *American Political Science Review* 777.

[3] See Przeworski, nn 2, 82.

[4] Peter H Smith, *Democracy in Latin America: Political Change in Comparative Perspective* (OUP, 2005) 42.

[5] See Gabriel L Negretto, 'Replacing and Amending Constitutions: The Logic of Constitutional Change in Latin America' (2012) 46 *Law & Society Review* 748, 752. The data were updated using information available from the Constitute.

democracies if we exclude Brazil and Mexico,[6] home to two of the most amended constitutions worldwide.[7]

The dynamics of constitutional change in the region have been shaped by conflicts among political elites. Zachary Elkins, Tom Ginsburg and James Melton argue that nineteenth century Latin America 'experienced this roller coaster, with constitutions marking the rise and fall of groups on opposite sides of issues such as the degree of centralisation, the structure of executive-legislative relations, or ideology'.[8] Gabriel Negretto observes that notwithstanding the increasing constitutional stability by means of greater adoption of 'inclusive institutions, more flexible amendment procedures, and strong mechanisms for constitutional adjudication, it is likely that constitutional crises will continue to provide incentives for the constant renegotiation of constitutional agreements'.[9] These analyses of strategic behaviour predominate in assessing how constitutions endure, change, and perform.[10]

Latin America raises important questions in constitutional change. Constitutional politics in the region have historically presented challenges to institutionalisation. Extraconstitutional means of change are not uncommon, nor is recourse to abusive or informal procedures.[11] The region invites questions about how constitutions can and should cope with internal conflict, trauma, stress, inequality and extreme poverty in the midst of fragile institution-building. Centuries of experience in constitutionalism offer fertile ground for research and learning.

Comparative constitutional scholars outside of the region, however, have not yet fully discovered Latin America. Political scientists, historians and economists have long seen the region as one of the most appealing sites of study. They have inquired into the historical determinants of regime breakdowns, the forces and processes of democratisation, the difficulty of building inclusive democracies, and the enormous problems of poverty and inequality. One particular problem continues to recur: the trade-offs between consolidating democracy and distributing economic prosperity in a region where resources are scarce and not often shared. This itself is a cause for instability. No wonder populism is common

[6] See Detlef Nolte and Almut Schilling-Vacaflor, 'Introduction: The Times They Are a Changin': Constitutional Transformations in Latin America Since the 1990s' in Almut Schilling-Vacaflor and Detlef Nolte (eds), *New Constitutionalism in Latin America Promises and Practices* (Routledge, 2012) 4.

[7] See Tom Ginsburg and John Melton, 'Does the Constitutional Amendment Rule Matter at All? Amendment Cultures and the Challenges of Measuring Amendment Difficulty' (2015) 13 *International Journal of Constitutional Law* 686, 689.

[8] Z Elkins et al, *The Endurance of National Constitutions* (Cambridge University Press, 2009) 24.

[9] Negretto, nn 5, 750.

[10] See Elkins et al, nn 8, 73; D Levinson, 'Parchment and Politics: The Positive Puzzle of Constitutional Commitment' (2010) 124 *Harvard Law Review* 690.

[11] D Landau, 'Abusive Constitutionalism' (2013) 47 *University of California-Davis Law Review* 191; Laurence Whitehead, 'Latin American Constitutionalism: Historical Development and Distinctive Traits' in Schilling-Vacaflor and Nolte, nn 6, 130.

in Latin America: it calls for higher resource redistribution and inclusive policies, but brings with it increased risk of democratic collapse.

Existing analyses of the region are quite fascinating but they pay too little attention to constitutional design and performance. Existing analyses moreover tend to elide over important differences among the countries of the region. What is more, the conventional approach to Latin American constitutions features a pessimist forecast, as though Latin America, marked by high levels of social inequality, characterised by political clientelism, and defined by legal mutability, is doomed to failure. Latin America thus becomes the paradigm for identifying the other America that has not thrived and whose history has been, unlike the North, a succession of both external and self-inflicted injuries that, even with recent democratic achievements, is always at the verge of falling apart.

Latin America can bring a distinct narrative to public law and in particular to the study of constitutional change. The volatile though increasingly democratic political environments in the region highlight how political agents and institutions find ways to adapt to difficult realities, sometimes by circumventing constitutional rules. Concepts such as abusive constitutionalism,[12] stealth authoritarianism,[13] constitutional dismemberment,[14] democratic decay[15] and others offer, in Latin America, a plethora of examples. Most Latin American countries now operate mature democratic institutions and they have developed constitutional strategies to contain sparks of instability, namely supreme and constitutional courts, flexible systems of formal change and mechanisms to encourage popular engagement. There remains a long way to go to become fully formed democracies but it is no longer appropriate to take for granted the traditionally pessimistic narratives about the region.

I. Latin American Style of Constitutional Change?

A. Presidentialism

Constitutional change in Latin America is often linked to the presidential system of government. Observers have commonly pointed to presidentialism in the region as the proximate cause of recurring crises, which has in turn led to a high rate of constitutional replacement and amendment. Yet more than a cause of instability, presidentialism in contemporary Latin American democracies may turn out to be an important engine for legitimating constitutional reforms and introducing

[12] Landau, nn 11.

[13] Ozan Varol, 'Stealth Authoritarianism' (2015) 100 *Iowa Law Review* 1678.

[14] Richard Albert 'Constitutional Amendment and Dismemberment' (2018) 43 *Yale Journal of International Law* 1.

[15] Tom Gerald Daly, 'Democratic Decay in 'Keystone' Democracies: The Real Threat to Global Constitutionalism?' (10 May 2017) *International Journal of Constitutional Law Blog*.

a measure of popular will into how constitutions change. Of course, there is a thin line between calls for participatory constitutionalism and populist appeals.

Although many Latin American constitutions today feature an executive power-concentrating design, they have developed means and mechanisms to manage the dangers of presidentialism, including an expanded role for courts, a culture of constitutional amendment that sees change not as an extraordinary phenomenon, and distinct strategies by political actors to moderate change so as to avoid having to resort to constitutional replacement as a first option. There are politically expedient reasons for some of these developments but they are useful all the same for constraining the excesses of presidentialism. Empowering constitutional and supreme courts, normally seen as guardians of the constitution, can serve as a 'convenient refuge for politicians to avoid or delay unwanted political outcomes'.[16] A more positive attitude toward constitutional amendment may reflect a desire to have the option to rein in some of the rights provisions in contemporary constitutional texts.[17] And informal constitutional change keeps the constitutions current, although the ease of informal change comes at the cost of keeping untouched those institutions and structures that can be altered only by formal procedures.

B. Constitutional Replacement

This leads us to question whether there exists a unique Latin American style for constitutional change. The new democratic context of rising supreme courts, increasing constitutional flexibility for formal change, and the possibility of informal institutions do not on their own distinguish the region from other parts of the globe. Yet there might be some common ground that brings together the various Latin American constitutional systems despite the evident methodological challenges of cross-cultural analyses. The high rate of constitutional replacement and amendment, which has always been one of the most prominent hallmarks of Latin American constitutionalism, is a good place to start. The question presents itself: is there a Latin American style to constitutional replacement?

Constitutional replacements have waned in the last decades, particularly after the wave of new constitutions since the transitions to democracy in the late 1970s onwards. Even so, from the 1990s onwards, constitutional replacement occurred in several Latin American countries: Bolivia (2009), Colombia (1991), the Dominican Republic (1994, 2002–03, 2010, 2015), Ecuador (1998, 2008),

[16] R Hirschl, *Towards Juristocracy: The Origins and Consequences of the New Constitutionalism* (Harvard University Press, 2004) 15.

[17] See LA Barbosa, *História Constitucional Brasileira: Mudança Constitucional, Autoritarismo E Democracia No Brasil Pós-1964* (Biblioteca Digital da Câmara dos Deputados, 2012) 252 (revealing how Brazilian political actors have long attempted to ease the constitutional amendment rules 'to correct the excesses of a Constitution that grants too many rights').

Paraguay (1992), Peru (1993), and Venezuela (1999). Other countries have lived distinct but related phenomena: instead of replacement, their constitutions have endured a substantive overhaul of some of its main parts, as in Argentina (1994), Chile (2005), and Mexico (2011).

The number of constitutional replacements, though still high, however, does not lead by itself to a definition of a Latin American style for constitutional change. Despite some constitutional replacements in one country or another, Latin America is simply following a worldwide trend: the more stable the country is, the less it experiences constitutional replacements. Even though most countries in the region are geographically and historically connected and have endured many similar constitutional challenges and changes, the differences in the way Latin American countries have dealt with constitutional replacement reveal no single overriding pattern. An investigation into some of these experiences across the region appears to confirm this conclusion.

Consider Chile, long a stable country. In the nineteenth century, its 1833 Constitution was one of the most enduring on the continent. In the twentieth century, the Constitution continued to endure with very few major changes, most notably the replacement of its 1925 Constitution in 1980, during Augusto Pinochet's dictatorship. Despite the transition to democratic civil government in 1990 and the many amendments since then, the 1980 Constitution remains in force today.

Chile is largely praised as a country whose transition to democracy was one of the most successful in Latin America,[18] but much of this success rests with an informal institution based on a 'two-coalition competition' between the centre-left (the Concertación) and centre-right (the Alianza por Chile).[19] This informal institution has fostered a trade-off between democratisation and stability, keeping some of the longstanding benefits among political actors virtually untouched,[20] though there has been gradual progress towards democratisation over the years.[21] Despite the recent movement to launch a constituent process to replace the 1980 Constitution,[22] this 'two-coalition competition' framework is a serious obstacle to this end.[23] Chances are that Chile may still keep seeing its originally authoritarian constitution for a long time and instead make use of its amendment procedure – as it has done so far – as a simpler way out to 'adapt' its content to the new times.

[18] See Peter Siavelis, 'Accommodating Informal Institutions and Chilean Democracy' in S Levitsky and G Helmke (eds), *Informal Institutions and Democracy: Lessons From Latin America* (The John Hopkins University Press, 2006) 33.

[19] ibid.

[20] See W Hunter, 'Negotiating Civil-Military Relations in Post-Authoritarian Argentina and Chile' (1998) 42 *International Studies Quarterly* 297.

[21] Nolte and Schilling-Vacaflor, nn 6, 9.

[22] See Alberto Coddou Mc Manus, 'The Chilean Constituent Process: A Long and Winding Road' (4 May 2016) *International Journal of Constitutional Law Blog*.

[23] See Oya Yegen, 'Chile's Constitutional Moment?' (13 November 2013) *International Journal of Constitutional Law Blog*.

It is worth stressing that the Chilean Constitution does not include any provision for its own replacement.

When Chile is compared with other contemporary dictatorships in the region, it is difficult to outline a similar pattern of constitutional replacement. Argentina, despite its many revisions, is home to the oldest Latin American constitution in force. Its 1853 Constitution has endured all sorts of crises and regime breakdowns. Dictatorships – not to mention its many *coups d'état* in the twentieth century (1930, 1943, 1955, 1962, 1966, and 1976) – have spawned supra-constitutional legislation or constitutional amendments, molding the Constitution to their ends.[24] Once democracy was reinstated in 1983, the 1853 Constitution, which was, in fact, suspended by means of the authoritarian supra-constitutional legislation of the previous regime, regained its strength in a typical case of 'restoration constitution-making'.[25] Since a major reform in 1994, the Constitution has remained formally intact. Yet the way Argentinians treat constitutional change stands out in Latin America. Their amendment procedure, which is open to an entire revision of the Constitution, demands a constitutional convention. Article 30 of the 1853 Constitution states that 'the Constitution may be amended in its entirety or in any of its parts. The need for its amendment must be declared by the Congress by a vote of at least two-thirds of its members, but the amendment shall not be accomplished except by a Convention called for such a purpose.'[26] The requirement of a constitutional convention naturally makes for a much more rigid the procedure for constitutional amendment.

Uruguay is also an interesting case for discussion. While its 1830 Constitution was also one of the longest enduring constitutions in Latin America at 86 years, the twentieth century was marked by many crises and constitutional replacements. After the replacement of the 1830 Constitution in 1918, Uruguay had a sequence of short-lived constitutions: 1934, 1942, 1952 and 1967, the latter still in force today. As happened in Argentina, the 1967 Constitution, during the 1973–85 dictatorship, was constrained by typical supra-constitutional legislation, then titled 'institutional acts'.[27] The military government that ruled Uruguay from 1973 to 1985 even attempted to establish a new authoritarian constitutional document in 1980. But in an interesting movement that managed to fuse authoritarianism with popular participation, this proposal was subject

[24] See L Rosas et al, *Historia Constitucional Argentina* (Astrea, 1996). During the 1976–83 dictatorship, the following supraconstitutional acts conditioned the functioning of the 1853 Constitution: Acta para la Reorganización Nacional (24 March, 1976), Acta fijando el Propósito y los Objetivos Básicos del Proceso de Reorganización Nacional (24 March, 1976); Estatuto para la Reorganizacion Nacional (29 March, 1976); Reglamento para el funcionamiento de la Junta Militar, Poder Ejecutivo y Comisión de Asesoramiento Legislativo (26 March, 1976).

[25] W Partlett, 'Restoration Constitution-Making' (2015) 9 *ICL Journal* 527 (defining 'restoration constitution-making' as 'a process of constitutional change that is governed by the partial or full restoration of a pre-existing constitution as well as its associated laws and institutions').

[26] Constitution of Argentina of 1853, Art 30.

[27] See F Aguero, 'Legacies of Transitions: Institutionalization, the Military, and Democracy in South America' (1998) 42 *Mershon International Studies Review* 387.

to a referendum and was ultimately rejected by the people; this is what precipitated the country's transition to democracy.[28] After the end of the dictatorship in 1985, those authoritarian provisions were abolished, and the 1967 Constitution was effectively reinstated, and then amended in 1989, 1994, 1996, and 2004. Like the Argentinian Constitution, the Uruguayan Constitution sets out procedures for amendment and replacement, but, unlike its neighbour, it features even more participatory procedures. One of the possibilities for fully or partially amending the Constitution does not require the participation of Congress: 'Upon the initiative of ten percent of the citizens inscribed in the National Civil Register, by presenting a detailed proposal which shall be referred to the President of the General Assembly, to be submitted for popular decision at the next election.'[29] Uruguay has become regarded as the most advanced Latin American country in developing solid liberal democratic institutions and fostering the rule of law. It is largely perceived as the least corrupt and most democratic country in the region.

Brazil adds more complexity to defining a single Latin American style for constitutional replacement. Brazil has had seven constitutions in its history. Each coincides with a regime breakdowns. In the nineteenth century, Brazil had both an imperial (1824) and a republican (1889) constitution. Brazil's twentieth century was marked by a series of regime breakdowns, and the constitutions pretty much reflected the continuous transitions from dictatorships to democratic moments, and vice versa. The 1934 Constitution, drafted during the provisional government led by Getúlio Vargas from 1930 to 1934, resulted from the need to adapt the constitutional framework to the interests of ascendant industrial elites and the new middle class. It was the product of the Revolution of 1930 and the Constitutionalist Revolution of 1932, and it brought an end to the so-called 'Old Republic' where rural elites from the states of São Paulo and Minas Gerais controlled the government. It also paved the way for the rise of Getúlio Vargas's authoritarian rule and the drafting of the 1937 Constitution. In 1945, Getúlio Vargas' authoritarian government ended and was ultimately replaced by the 1946 Constitution. This Constitution did not last long, though. The advent of the civil-military dictatorship in March 1964 resulted in the 1967 authoritarian constitution, later revised in 1969.

After the transition to democracy in 1985, a largely participatory process of constitution-making gained momentum during the Constituent Assembly of 1987/1988, the result of which was the most democratic constitution ever in Brazilian history. The 1988 Constitution, which remains in force today, has been celebrated as the mark of a rising democratic nation. History has proven that Brazilians interpret constitutional transitions as the natural outcome of regime transitions. No wonder that constitutions have not historically laid down

[28] See ibid, 390.
[29] Constitution of Uruguay of 1966, Art 331(a).

a particular procedure for replacement, unlike most of the Latin American constitutions.[30] Brazil has since been a relatively stable country, even though, more recently, a severe political crisis resulted in the impeachment of then President Dilma Rousseff.

Argentina, Brazil, Chile, and Uruguay are intimately connected by history, geography and social and economic developments. They all have endured contemporary dictatorships and their transitions to democracy took place at around the same time in the 1980s and 1990s. Yet they are significantly distinct in many important respects. Chile has shown no immediate correlation between regime breakdown and constitutional replacement, a contrast with Brazil. Argentina has not replaced its 1853 Constitution despite the many crises it has endured over the years. The Constitution has been revised many times, sometimes significantly, but its constitutional structure and some of its content differ substantially from the constitutions of its neighbours. Uruguay, like Argentina, also reinstated its constitution once the dictatorship came to an end, but unlike Argentina the political system has complied with the Constitution in a way that has fostered a much greater degree of political stability. We could point to many more differences among these four constitutions. The question, to us, is obvious: on what basis can we identify a 'Latin American style' for constitutional change when it appears that there is not one single style but rather various styles, often pointing in opposite directions?

Other countries in Latin America add still more variables to this equation. Mexico, with its 1917 Constitution, is a clear example of how a hegemonic party – the Institutional Revolutionary Party (PRI) – has played a significant role in changing the Constitution through amendments but did not see the need to replace it. The Dominican Republic is an outlier when it comes to constitutional replacement, though Ecuador, Venezuela, Bolivia, and Peru come right behind it. Nevertheless, even the sequence of replacements in these countries does not necessarily entail effective change, since there is a high similarity between their new constitutions and those that preceded them.[31] In Central America, the last wave of constitutional replacements took place in the 1980s: Honduras (1982), El Salvador (1983), Guatemala (1985), and Nicaragua (1987). When we add Costa Rica (1949), Panamá (1972), and Cuba (1976) to the list, it becomes clear that constitutional replacements are a rarer phenomenon than normally depicted.

In South America, then, most countries have not replaced their constitutions for more than 20 years. Only recently has the advent of the so-called 'New Latin American Constitutionalism' – which embraces left-leaning politics of social integration but also an even greater centralisation of the executive branch – heralded

[30] See Nolte and Schilling-Vacaflor, nn 6, 6 (listing Brazil, Chile, the Dominican Republic, El Salvador, Peru and Honduras as the Latin American constitutions with no provision for total revision or replacement).

[31] See Elkins et al, nn 8, 57.

a new wave of constitutional replacement in Bolivia (2009), Ecuador (2008) and Venezuela (1999). This 'New Latin American Constitutionalism' even exposes remarkable differences among Venezuela, Ecuador and Bolivia.[32]

The search for a Latin American style for constitutional replacement may be possible but only at a high level of abstraction in light of the many variants in constitutional design and history. But at a lower level of specificity, it would be difficult to identify a regional style in constitutional replacement because there are several distinct types of constitutional practices that have taken root in the region. As Whitehead puts it, 'there is a 'kaleidoscopic' pattern of alternative democratic models and experiments underway in today's Latin America.'[33]

C. Constitutional Amendment

The same conclusion may hold for constitutional amendment in the region. The rate of constitutional amendments has been on the rise.[34] But why? Amendment may be perceived as a profitable means of averting more radical changes, like constitutional replacements. And as democracy gains strength, regime breakdowns become rarer and amendments are used as the natural mechanism for constitutional change alongside judicial interpretation.

The larger point, for our purposes of answering the question whether there is a Latin American style of constitutional amendment, is that there seems to be no cross-country pattern in how amendment frameworks are codified in constitutions or in how Latin American countries have made use of amendments as a 'typical' mechanism for constitutional change.

Some countries, like Brazil and Mexico, have a high rate of constitutional amendment that places them clearly as outliers not only in Latin America but in the world. The 1988 Brazilian Constitution is one of the longest across the globe, has its origins in a strong culture of popular participation, and is characterised by its quite detailed public policies. From 1988 to 2017, the Brazilian Constitution was amended 97 times for an average of 3.34 per year. Most of these amendments were minor changes, not ones that affected the core of the Constitution.[35] Brazil has learned to use constitutional amendments as a normal procedure that does

[32] See Fernando José Gonçalves Acunha, 'Continuity and Change in Latin America: The Ever-Present Authoritarianism and the Democratic Capacities of the New Latin American Constitutions' in this volume; Alberto Noguera Fernández, 'What do We Mean When We Talk about 'Critical Constitutionalism?' Some Reflections on the New Latin American Constitutions' in Schilling-Vacaflor and Nolte, nn 6, 116.

[33] Laurence Whitehead, 'Latin American Constitutionalism: Historical Development and Distinctive Trends' in Schilling-Vacaflor and Nolte, nn 6, 134.

[34] See Nolte and Schilling-Vacaflor, nn 6, 7 (reporting that 'the annual rate of amendments has increased in most of the countries of the region in the decade 2000–2009 compared to the 1990s').

[35] See Juliano Zaiden Benvindo, 'The Brazilian Constitutional Amendment Rate: A Culture of Change?' (10 August 2016) *International Journal of Constitutional Law Blog.*

not entail a disruption of the constitutional system.[36] Political elites might have taken the country in this direction as a gradual strategic move to manage the Constitution according to their own interests, as Leonardo Barbosa argues in this volume. Federalism also plays an important role insofar as the country's subnational constitutions and their governments do not provide much of a check on national amendments, as Breno Baía Magalhães suggests in his contribution to this collection.

In contrast, the Mexican Constitution – amended more than 700 times since its creation in 1917 – is a reformist constitution that has been dramatically transformed over the years, and particularly in the decades following the country's democratisation. As Francisca Pou-Giménez and Andrea Pozas-Loyo argue in this book, constitutional amendment and democratisation have gone hand in hand, though for them hyper-reformism has been an obstacle to democratic consolidation. Mariana Velasco Rivera observes in her own contribution to this volume that hyper-reformism has been used as a 'tool for hegemonic preservation', with the rising number of amendments in the last 16 years signalling a strategy of multiparty accommodation and concession.

It is hard to find a common narrative in constitutional amendment that joins together Brazil and Mexico. The only common ground may be that political actors in both countries use the means of constitutional change strategically to serve their own ends, yet this would not be unique to Latin America.

Consider Chile once again. Political compromise has been the country's hallmark for institutional stability. Constitution amendments have been adopted to gradually overcome the authoritarian legacies of its 1980 Constitution. This adaptive behaviour has been a more suitable vehicle for constitutional change than replacing the Constitution, and in any case it is consistent with the practices of 'two-coalition competition' that have predominated in the country since democratisation. Although this has made constitutional change more manageable and it has warded off the instability of radical change, the consequence has been to keep the country under the rule of a constitution drafted during Pinochet's authoritarian years.

Other countries, such as El Salvador, Honduras, Colombia and Costa Rica, have amended their constitutions practically every year or so. Still others have taken other routes to channel such strategies. Argentina has never amended its 1853 constitution since the 1994 revision; Paraguay amended its 1992 Constitution in 2011, after a referendum to allow Paraguayans who live abroad to participate in national elections.[37] Various causes may explain these different behaviours when it comes to constitutional amendment. But whatever the explanation, the result is to undermine if not defeat the claim that there exists a Latin American style

[36] Yet, recently, Brazil has approved a constitutional amendment that limits public spending for the next 20 years, strongly affecting the exercise of social rights. Richard Albert, eg, has described this reform as a case of 'constitutional dismemberment'. See Albert, nn 14, 36.

[37] Enmienda Constitucional nº 1, 8 November 2011.

for constitutional amendment. Although most countries in the region trace their origins to common sources, the developments across the region have driven actors to the use of mechanisms of formal change in different ways, suggesting that there are more differences than commonalities among the countries of Latin America when it comes to constitutional amendment.

D. Informal Constitutional Change

As for informal mechanisms of constitutional change, namely through judicial interpretation of a constitution, there are no simple connections among the Latin American countries that would allow us to define a Latin American style for this form of constitutional change either.

Judicial review has been central to the development of constitutions in the region. The Chilean experience is an interesting case of how a strong legislative branch 'can provide the courts with the necessary political backing to assert themselves against [the president]'.[38] Colombia, which features possibly the most well-known Latin American high court, is the paradigm of judicial review aiming at implementing transformative constitutionalism after years of 'institutional decay and crisis of the political order'.[39] Brazil, whose Supreme Court is still very much underexplored in comparative constitutional law,[40] is quite possibly the strongest court in the world, though it does reveal evidence of dysfunction.[41] And in Costa Rica, the creation of the Constitutional Chamber in 1989 has grown from hearing 380 cases to 18,000 cases per year – often decided within the same year – offering the people a responsive forum for their grievances.

Interesting doctrines have emerged from the region. From the Colombian Constitutional Court's substitution of the constitution doctrine, which Juan F Gonzales Bertomeu describes in his chapter for this volume, or the adoption of the unconstitutional constitutional amendments doctrine in Brazil, which Eneida Desiree Salgado and Carolina Alves das Chagas critique in this volume, certain courts in the region have made a name for themselves. The judgments of high courts in the region could be fascinating case studies for what Ran Hirschl has called the 'judicialization of mega-politics'.[42] Yet one important country lags behind in the region: Mexico. The Institutional Revolutionary Party's (PRI) more

[38] Javier Couso, 'Judicial independence in Latin America: The lessons of History in the Search for an Always Elusive Ideal' (2005) 20 *Institutions and Public Law: Comparative Approaches* 204.

[39] Manuel José Cepeda Espinosa and David Landau, *Colombian Constitutional Law: Leading Cases* 1, 2 (Oxford University Press, 2017).

[40] See LR Barroso, JZ Benvindo and A Osorio, 'Developments in Brazilian Constitutional Law: the Year 2016 in Review' (2017) 15 *International Journal of Constitutional Law* 495.

[41] See DW Arguelhes and LM Ribeiro, 'O Supremo Individual: Mecanismos De Atuação Direta Dos Ministros Sobre O Processo Político' (2015) 46 *Revista Direito, Estado e Sociedade* 121; DW Arguelhes and IA Hartmann, 'Timing Control Without Docket Control' (2017) 5 *Journal of Law and Courts* 105.

[42] See Hirschl, n 16.

than seven decades (1929–89) of hegemonic power has deeply affected the behaviour of the Supreme Court, which has long acted as an immediate collaborator of the government. Despite the major constitutional reform of 1994, which expanded the scope of judicial review through a direct and centralised action of unconstitutionality, a more relatively independent and active Court emerged only after 2000, when the PRI lost its hegemony in the executive and legislative branches.[43] Interestingly enough, there is a temporal coincidence between the rise of the Court and the increasing rate of constitutional amendments, which suggests a direct relation between pluralist fragmentation and the use of mechanisms of constitutional change.

And yet there are connections among Latin American high courts. One prominent example is the widespread adoption of concrete judicial review, the increasing adoption of abstract judicial review, and the peculiarity of a mixed concrete and abstract system of judicial review in the region. However, even this development entails different paths and outcomes, and distinct models have been implemented.[44]

Latin American high courts do indeed share some important similarities. Yet we cannot claim that they share the same degree of influence in their respective jurisdictions nor that they have similarly strong or weak protections for basic rights, nor even that they take the same or similar approaches for settling inter-branch conflicts. There is therefore no overriding Latin American style of informal constitutional change through courts. In fact we have witnessed courts taking at times more active and at others more passive approaches to the resolution of disputes. There appears to be more difference than similarity in the practices of informal constitutional change in the region.

II. Studying Change and Transformation in Latin America

This book is an effort to interpret and situate constitutional change in Latin America. All of the chapters begin from the same three propositions: that Latin American constitutions must be understood in all their nuances, that it is long past time to move beyond the conventional wisdom that there exists a one-size-fits-all 'Latin American constitutionalism,' and that Latin American constitutions must be brought into conversation with the rest of the world.

The volume begins with a Foreword by Luís Roberto Barroso, a justice of the Supreme Court of Brazil. A giant in the country and the larger region,

[43] Julio Ríos-Figueroa, 'Fragmentation of Power and the Emergence of an Effective Judiciary in Mexico, 1994–2002' (2007) 49 *Latin American Politics and Society* 36.

[44] See A Tschentscher and C Lehner, 'The Latin American Model of Constitutional Jurisdiction: Amparo and Judicial Review' (19 July 2013) (working paper on file).

Justice Barroso has been at the forefront of the development and interpretation of Brazil's 1988 Constitution.

The book is then divided into three main Parts.

Part I is entitled *Popular and Populist Constitutional Democracy*. The authors consider the role of the people and constituent power in constitutional change.

In *Constitution-Making (without Constituent) Power: On the Conceptual Limits of the Power to Replace or Revise the Constitution*, Carlos Bernal makes a case against the widespread conception of the constitution-making power as constituent power. He argues that a conceptual analysis of the power to replace or revise the Constitution shows that this understanding is incorrect. Instead, he advances a socio-ontological conception of the power to replace or revise a written constitution, as a limited deontic power of citizens' political proxy-agents, who are collectively intentionally recognised as having the status of constitution makers for performing the function of institutionalising constitutionalism. This conception illuminates a clearer approach to understand the constitution-making power, and to evaluate the legitimacy of its exercises.

In *Continuity and Change in Latin America: The Ever-Present Authoritarianism and the Democratic Capacities of the New Latin American Constitutions*, Fernando José Gonçalves Acunha argues that although constitutionalism in Latin America is seen as a succession of detrimental changes to stability, this is a misperception of Latin American constitutional history. The development of its constitutionalism is characterised by a paradoxical combination of an enduring concentration of power with constant constitutional changes. This chapter seeks to explain this connection through an exposition of the institutional arrangements that have helped elites keep their grip on power and the effects of various constitutional modifications conceived as means to respond to social demands, though with limited impact in distribution of power. From the perspective of the new constitutions, which promise reconfiguration of power, the challenge seems daunting, since a renewed threat is posed by contemporary authoritarianism even in countries whose constitutions are committed with an institutional change. In this chapter, he studies those threats as a contribution to the development of the capacities of modern constitutional design to resist concentration of powers and other undemocratic settlements.

The next chapter – *Constitutional Moments and Constitutional Thresholds in Brazil: Mass Protests and the 'Performative Meaning' of Constitutionalism* – is authored by Juliano Zaiden Benvindo. This chapter explores the nuances in how institutional constraints and constitutional thresholds, such as amendment procedural rules, behave in moments of crisis in a country like Brazil, which is neither in an environment such as those stable Western industrialised constitutional democracies, nor in the same social context of some of its neighbours in Latin America. He explores how recent Brazilian constitutional history might have yielded a 'performative meaning' that paved the way for some democratic gains over the years. By placing special emphasis on the recent developments of Brazilian constitutional history, this chapter concludes that Brazil has provided mechanisms to empower interactions among distinct institutions and individuals, to strengthen institutional constraints and constitutional thresholds, and in particular to enhance pluralism.

In the final chapter in this Part, Yaniv Roznai argues in *Constitutional Unamendability in Latin America Gone Wrong?* that constitutional unamendability has become a characteristic feature of Latin American constitutions, with implications for constitutional design, judicial interpretation and the resilience of democracy. Roznai focuses on a central tension in unamendability: on the one hand, it holds promise for helping to protect democratic values but on the other hand it is susceptible to misuse.

In Part II, the book shifts focus to the informal mechanisms of constitutional change. Titled *Judicial Review of Constitutional Amendment*, its chapters assess the role of the judiciary in facilitating and inhibiting constitutional change in Latin American states.

In *The Colombian Constitutional Court's Doctrine on the Substitution of the Constitution*, Juan F Gonzales-Bertomeu explains that the defence of substantive limits on constitutional change has taken two roads. One has been to claim that certain constitutional provisions cannot ever be changed. A second has been to claim that, ex ante, any provision can be amended, though the constitution's essential structure cannot; a 'normal' process of constitutional change cannot 'substitute' the Constitution. The notion of substitution has been invoked by judges in politically salient decisions by the Colombian Constitutional Court – the most recent important one in May 2017 in a case involving the government (FARC agreement) – and this chapter brings to bear critical analysis to it. The Court has presented the 'substitution' doctrine on procedural grounds. Yet the doctrine deals with substantive questions about the nature and content of the Constitution, the limits of constituent power, and judicial review in a democracy. Given the Court's current use of the doctrine and the renewed discussions of constituent power in the region, these are timely inquiries.

In *We the People, They the Media: Judicial Review of Constitutional Amendments and Public Opinion in Colombia*, Vicente Benitez-R analyses the influence of public opinion on the Colombian Constitutional Court's decisions pertaining the judicial review of salient constitutional amendments. He seeks to demonstrate that when there has been a shift in the people's and the media's perceptions on the Court or on its decisions, there has also been a change in the Court's approach to the judicial review of constitutional amendments. More specifically, when the Court is perceived as an impartial institution its constitutional credibility increases and this situation probably promotes judicial creativity and boldness, as well as the enforcement of its rulings. He argues the contrary: that where the Court is not deemed as a credible player, the Court has embraced a self-censored stance when interpreting the Constitution and, moreover, political actors have complied with some reluctance with its judgments.

In the following chapter, *'Resistance by Interpretation': Supreme Court Justices as Counter-Reformers to Constitutional Changes in Brazil in the 90s*, Diego Werneck Arguelhes and Mariana Mota Prado explore the idea that a court of law, empowered to strike down or review legislation, may use the power of judicial review to advance its preferences and reverse institutional changes. The novelty in their analysis lies in its focus on the judicial review of reforms of the powers of the court deciding the case – reforms on which the members of the court had revealed their views and preferences during the lawmaking process. In such a scenario, the court can be seen as a self-interested actor who is using legal interpretation as a tool to disguise and promote its own preferences. They argue that when the judges who now interpret the Constitution had previously expressed their views in the democratic process (as political actors) on how the Constitution should have been written, scholars have a smoking gun. Specifically, their analysis builds on a case during the Brazilian democratic transition, where Supreme Court judges employed judicial interpretation to actively resist reforms that had been explicitly enshrined in the new Constitution of 1988.

In *The Judicial Review of Constitutional Amendments in Brazil and the Super-Countermajoritarian Role of the Brazilian Supreme Court: The Case of the 'ADI 5017'*, Eneida Desiree Salgado and Carolina Alves de Chagas focus on formal constitutional changes in court. More specifically, they note that in many cases the rigidity of the constitutional reform process has led to the increased participation of the judiciary. Countries such as India, Colombia, Turkey and in this chapter, Brazil, are known for this behaviour. In their chapter, the authors argue that what may be seen as an obstacle for the creation of unconstitutional amendments can be seen as an appropriation by the judiciary of prerogatives that are not their a priori role – that is, making changes in the constitutional text. They argue that the constitutional text should be respected since it has a normative force. To deny the normative character of the Constitution, they say, is to see it as an occasional compromise by political groups, which could be substituted at any time. On their view, courts should assure the integrity of the constitutional text and refrain from going beyond its boundaries.

The final chapter in this Part is authored by Sergio Verdugo. In *The Role of the Chilean Constitutional Court in Times of Change*, Verdugo justifies the lack of a judicial doctrine restricting constitutional reform with substantive limits – as opposed to procedural limits – in Chile. He examines the recent Chilean constitutional history and the few relevant Constitutional Court decisions, to argue that lacking such a judicial doctrine was desirable because it allowed constitutional amenders to gradually and incrementally democratise the Chilean Constitution. Nevertheless, he adds, there may be good reasons for restricting future constitutional reforms if those reforms aim to reverse the democratic achievements of the post-authoritarian era.

The volume closes with Part III entitled *Constitutional Reform and Stability*. These chapters examine the impact of constitutional change and amendment on political stability, and they also evaluate the role of the court as an engine for reform.

In *The Paradox of Mexican Constitutional Hyper-Reformism: Enabling Peaceful Transition while Blocking Democratic Consolidation*, Francisca Pou-Giménez and Andrea Pozas-Loyo argue that, after delivering gains for quite a long time, Mexican reformism is reaching a point of exhaustion. The country, they claim, is currently trapped in a pattern they call 'hyper-reformism', which is a particular species of reformism that has become self-sustaining and that is now closely associated to the obstacles the country faces to install a recognisable version of the rule of law and to achieve democratic consolidation. In their chapter, they demonstrate how constitutional amendment once supported the gradual completion of the largely peaceful process of democratic transition but that hyper-reformism is today closely associated with many of the difficulties the country confronts in consolidating democracy under the rule of law. Their analysis contributes to a fundamental debate on the advantages and disadvantages of constitutional longevity.

The next chapter, by Mariana Velasco Rivera, considers *The Political Sources of Constitutional Amendment (Non)Difficulty in Mexico*. She argues that, traditionally, constitutional law scholars have considered that amendment difficulty can be read off the text. That is to say one may have an idea of how easily and often a constitution would be amended by reading the constitutional entrenchment rules only. Moreover, constitutional amendments are often considered both as means by which popular sovereignty and self-government are most effectively exercised as well as the mechanism that distinguishes higher and ordinary law. She argues that these assumptions are insufficient to understand formal constitutional change. In fact, she says, they have obscured the study of other, and perhaps more important, factors that play an essential role in determining amendment difficulty. Her chapter analyses Mexico's constitutional amendment dynamics in the last century as a case study showing that amendment difficulty is politically constructed rather than institutionally determined. Amendment difficulty, she shows, is the result of the interplay between constitutional culture and party politics rather than the result of the design of the amendment mechanism. All along Mexican history, constitutional amendment has played a prominent role for political entrenchment; thus, despite providing a stringent amendment process, the Constitution has frequently been amended. She insists that this situation should not be considered problematic ex ante in that it may suggest the presence of a healthy democracy and a living constitution. She concludes, however, that a closer look at amendment processes in Mexico in the last three decades suggests trends that seem to be responding to oligarchic rather than democratic values.

In *Subnational Constitutionalism and Constitutional Change in Brazil: The Impact of Federalism in Constitutional Stability*, Breno Baía Magalhães argues that the absence of constitutional values in subnational constitutions may be one of the reasons why the Brazilian constitution is so often amended. He suggests that without either the capacity of a polity to make independent decisions or the power of a regional political community to engage on equal footing in disputes with the federal government, the national constitution becomes the main forum for the discussion of political and social changes.

In *Legislative Process and Constitutional Change in Brazil: On the Pathologies of the Procedure for Amending the 1988 Constitution*, Leonardo Augusto de Andrade Barbosa analyses constitutional amendment in Brazil. In the last 27 years, he explains, the Brazilian Constitution has been amended nearly 100 times. Contrary to conventional belief, this chapter suggests that blaming the burgeoning of constitutional amendments solely on the breadth of the constitutional text is misleading. Instead, he suggests that in order to understand the rhythm of formal constitutional change in Brazil, we must also factor into consideration the gradual process through which the rules governing the amendment procedure – originally designed to make it difficult – were 'softened' (and sometimes circumvented) – by both legislative practice and judicial interpretation. Those changes amount to pathologies in the process of constitutional reform because they seriously hinder the transparency of the procedures through which the Constitution is amended, creating potential gaps in accountability and responsiveness. The apparent collapse of constitutional politics into the everyday political struggle in Brazil, the chapter suggests, is not an inescapable result of the all-encompassing breadth of the Brazilian Constitution. It is also a consequence of legislative and judicial practices that make the Constitution increasingly more available to normal politics. Hence, those aiming at developing a better understanding of formal constitutional change in Brazil should pay closer attention to the legislative process involved in the enactment of the constitutional amendments.

The last chapter in this Part and in this volume is entitled *Transformative Constitutionalism and Extreme Inequality: A Problematic Relationship*, authored by Magdalena Correa Henao. She begins her argument by showing, quite clearly, that constitutions in Latin America make extreme inequality a central concern. She surveys constitutions across the entire region, with a particular focus on Bolivia, Brazil, Colombia, Ecuador and Peru, and demonstrates the strength of these constitutional commitments to combating inequality. She also examines the tools these constitutions give constitutional actors to ameliorate these conditions. She subsequently explores how well constitutional actors have lived up to their constitutionally-mandated commitment to combat inequality, and she offers a comparative analysis of the institutional capacity of courts and legislatures to make good on the promises their constitutions make.

III. The Prospects for Latin American Comparative Constitutional Law

If indeed there exists a Latin American style for constitutional change, it is less pronounced than commonly depicted. Latin American constitutionalism therefore raises a challenge for comparative constitutional law: scholars must examine distinct constitutions in all of their specificities and nuances rather than bundling all of them together as though they were one and the same. Scholarship in comparative constitutional law should take care not to overstate conclusions about the region. It should instead seek to understand and appreciate the richness of the constitutional histories across the region. This volume is a first step in the direction of showing that the 'other America' is well worth studying. We hope the chapters in this volume will contribute to bringing new eyes and perspectives on the region, and that comparative constitutional law will ultimately discover that there is not a single Latin American constitutionalism but rather many different and quite fascinating Latin American constitutionalisms.

PART I

Popular and Populist Constitutional Democracy

1

Constitution-Making (without Constituent) Power: On the Conceptual Limits of the Power to Replace or Revise the Constitution

CARLOS BERNAL[1]

I. Introduction

Some scholars and judges claim that people can only make, replace or revise a constitution when they exercise the constituent power, that is, a power that is foundational, legally boundless, and sovereign. They identify the constitution-making power with the constituent power,[2] or characterise it as one of its instances.[3]

This chapter argues against that view. It holds that the theory of the constituent power is only a conception or an understanding of the concept of the constitution-making power,[4] and that such conception is incorrect, because of the characterisation of the constitution-making power as unlimited.

[1] Justice of the Colombian Constitutional Court. I would like to thank Virgilio Afonso da Silva, Robert Alexy, Rosalind Dixon, Jeff King, José Luis Martí, José Juan Moreso, Rebecca Pendleton, Silvia Suteu, María José Viana, and Juliano Zaiden Benvindo for valuable feedback that I received from them, in particular, in seminars held at the University College London, the University of New South Wales (Sydney), the University Pompeu Fabra (Barcelona), and the 2016 Global Symposium on Constitutional Amendment and Replacement in Latin America (Brasilia). I am in great debt to Richard Albert, Jose I Colón-Ríos, Denise Meyerson, and Sergio Verdugo for detailed comments and suggestions to previous versions of this manuscript.

[2] See Joel I Colón-Ríos, 'Rousseau, Theorist of Constituent Power' (2016) 1 *Oxford Journal of Legal Studies* 'Constituent power [...] is the legally unlimited power of creating (and re-creating) constitutions'.

[3] According to Martin Loughlin, in constitutional thought, 'constituent power expresses the generative aspect of the political power relationship'. See 'The Concept of Constituent Power' (2014) 13(2) *European Journal of Political Theory* 231. Constitution-making is an instance in which there is generation of the political power.

[4] On the distinction between a concept and its conceptions – as understandings of the concept – see Maite Ezcurdia, 'The Concept-Conception Distinction' (1998) 9 *Philosophical Issues* 187–92.

To justify this claim, this chapter carries out a conceptual analysis of a core instance of the constitution-making power, namely, the power to replace or revise constitutional texts. For this purpose, while 'replacement' will refer to the substitution of a constitutional text by another, 'revision' will designate the modification of the basic structure of a constitution by means of constitutional amendment. The analysis of this phenomena shows that the constitution-making power cannot be conceptually unlimited. Therefore, it cannot be understood according to the theory of the constituent power. Instead, this chapter advances an alternative conception of the constitution-making power, as a limited power, one that is based on recent developments in the field of social ontology.

This chapter proceeds in the follow way. Section II narrows down the scope of the analysis as the project to understand the nature of the constitution-making power. Section III accounts for the theory of the constituent power, and its judicial and doctrinal use as an attempt to justify constitutional replacements and revisions, and to ground substantive limitations to constitutional amendments. Then, as Section IV elaborates, a conceptual analysis of the power to replace or revise the Constitution shows that it is conceptually incorrect to conceive this core instance of the constitution-making power as unlimited or boundless. Instead, Section V advances a socio-ontological conception of the power to replace or revise the constitution, which characterises it as a limited deontic power of certain citizens' political proxy-agents, who are collectively intentionally recognised as having the status of constitution-makers for performing the function of institutionalising constitutionalism. This conception is generalisable as an appropriate understanding of the constitution-making power.

II. On the Nature of the Constitution-Making Power

Written constitutions come into existence by virtue of a foundational act. As Loughlin and Walker explain, that foundational act 'purports to establish a polity by creating a framework of government and defining the essential form of the political bond between the people (the citizens of the state) and its governing authorities'.[5] Constitution-making is instantiated in the enactment of new constitutions by foundational acts of that kind, but also at least in constitutional replacements and revisions.

Scholars study constitution-making from different perspectives. Historians and political scientists account for the intricacies of constitution-making processes in single jurisdictions.[6] Political philosophers discuss how to plan and carry out

[5] Martin Loughlin and Neil Walker, 'Introduction' in id (eds), *The Paradox of Constitutionalism* (Oxford, Oxford University Press, 2007) 3.

[6] See eg Laurel E Miller (ed), *Framing the State in Times of Transition: Case Studies in Constitution Making* (Washington DC, United States Institute of Peace, 2010).

these processes,[7] and what outcomes they should produce in order to achieve legitimacy.[8] Constitutional designers endeavour to discover the theoretical and empirical relationships between processes of constitution-making and their outputs.[9] Finally, comparatists analyse different models of constitution-making, and assess what are the best practices, and how to follow them.[10]

In contrast, this chapter is about the nature of the constitution-making power. Its approach is conceptual and normative. It undertakes a conceptual analysis of the power to replace or revise a constitution[11] – as a core instance of the constitution-making power – with the purpose of accounting for its essential properties.[12] This strategy is analogous to the jurisprudential elucidation of the nature of law by stating a set of 'propositions about the law which are necessarily true',[13] or asserting 'necessary truths about the law'.[14] The reference of those truths is a set of properties conferring to the law its essence,[15] its 'identity'.[16] *Mutatis mutandi*, this chapter asks two questions. First, whether the conception of the constituent power succeeds in explaining the essential properties – the nature of the power – to replace or revise a constitution. If not, secondly, what might be a sound alternative conception?

This conceptual analysis necessarily encompasses normative considerations. Elucidating the nature of the constitution-making power, and whether an act is an instance of it, implies taking a standpoint to justify or criticise that act or

[7] See eg Angela M Banks, 'Expanding Participation in Constitution Making: Challenges and Opportunities' (2008) 49 *William & Mary Law Review* 1046; Andrew Arato, *Post Sovereign Constitution Making. Learning and Legitimacy* (Oxford, Oxford University Press, 2016).

[8] See Claude Klein and András Sajó, 'Constitution-Making: Process and Substance' in Michel Rosenfeld and András Sajó, *The Oxford Handbook of Comparative Constitutional Law* (Oxford, Oxford University Press, 2012) 419–25.

[9] See Tom Ginsburg, Zachary Elkins, and Justin Blount, 'Does the Process of Constitution-Making Matter?' (2009) 5 *Annual Review of Law and Social Science* 201–23; Todd A Eisenstadt, A Carl LeVan and Torigh Maboudi, 'When Talk Trumps Text: The Democratizing Effects of Deliberation during Constitution-Making, 1974–2011' (2015) 109(3) *American Political Science Review* 592–612.

[10] Xenophon Contiades (ed), *Engineering Constitutional Change: A Comparative Perspective on Europe, Canada and the USA* (London, Routledge, 2012).

[11] This conceptual analysis is different from what Mattias Kumm calls the 'sociological' question, in 'Constituent power, cosmopolitan constitutionalism, and post-positivist law' (2016) 14(3) *International Journal of Constitutional Law* 698 f. While an answer to the sociological question will account for the facts connected to an actual exercise of the constitution-making power, the conceptual question asks about the essential properties of the concept of constitution-making power. On the difference between conceptual, empirical (or sociological), and normative analysis in constitutional theory, see Robert Alexy, *A Theory of Constitutional Rights* (Oxford, Oxford University Press, 2002) 5 f.

[12] On the methodological features of this sort of conceptual analysis, see Kenneth Einar Himma, 'Reconsidering a Dogma: Conceptual Analysis, the Naturalistic Turn, and Legal Philosophy' in Michael Freeman and Ross Harrison (eds), *Law and Philosophy. Current Legal Issues* (Oxford, Oxford University Press, 2007) 4.

[13] Joseph Raz, 'Can There Be a Theory of Law?' in Martin P Golding and William A Edmundson (eds), *The Blackwell Guide to the Philosophy of Law and Legal Theory* (Oxford, Blackwell, 2005) 324–25.

[14] Robert Alexy, 'On the Concept and the Nature of Law' (2008) 21(3) *Ratio Juris* 284.

[15] Joseph Raz, 'Can There Be a Theory of Law?' in Martin P Golding and William A Edmundson (eds), *The Blackwell Guide to the Philosophy of Law and Legal Theory* (Oxford, Blackwell, 2005) 324–25.

[16] Scott Shapiro, *Legality* (Cambridge Mass, Belknap Press of Harvard University Press, 2011) 10.

its effects.[17] For example, analysing whether an extra-constitutional constituent assembly is endowed with constitution-making power, is necessarily connected to the question of whether it is justified to recognise its outputs as a constitution. Also, assessing whether the power to amendment the Constitution encompasses the power to modify its basic structure, necessarily implies taking a stand on the justifiability of undertaking structural constitutional changes by means of amendment procedures. The question on the possibility of normatively neutral conceptual analysis is indeed contested.[18] Notwithstanding, the adscription of the constitution-making power to an authority implies a judgement that encompasses not only conceptual and empirical but also normative elements.[19] Therefore, Dworkin's view that the description of any phenomenon central to the law cannot be normatively neutral,[20] and that it rather is an 'interpretation' grounded in moral judgements and beliefs,[21] applies here.

A widespread conception of the nature of the constitution-making power is the theory of the constituent power.[22] There are several versions of this theory.[23] However, their common element is the thesis that the constitution-making power is foundational, legally boundless, and sovereign.[24] I will refer to this conception as the argument from the constituent power.

[17] See Carlos Santiago Nino, 'El concepto de poder constituyente originario y la justificación jurídica' in Eugenio Bulygin, Martín Diego Farrell, Carlos Santiago Nino and Eduardo Rabossi (eds), *El lenguaje del derecho: homenaje a Genaro R. Carrió* (Buenos Aires, Abeledo-Perrot, 1983) 353.

[18] See Andrei Marmor, 'Legal Positivism: Still Descriptive and Morally Neutral' (2006) 26(4) *Oxford Journal of Legal Studies* 683–704. For a broader discussion, see Jordi Ferrer Beltrán, José Juan Moreso, and Diego M Papayannis (eds), *Neutrality and Theory of Law* (Dordrecht, Springer, 2013).

[19] Mattias Kumm is right when he emphasises that the point of the theory of the constituent power is to 'legitimate legal change that can't be legitimated with reference to existing legal norms'. He claims that: 'the point of constituent power within the tradition of eighteenth-century constitutionalism is normative and justificatory, not sociological and explanatory'. See 'Constituent power, cosmopolitan constitutionalism, and post-positivist law', n 11, 698–99, and 701. However, Kumm's claim seems too extreme in ruling out the sociological – and perhaps also the conceptual – dimension of the theory of the constituent power. The correctness of an '*ex*-post interpretative adscription' (701) of the constituent power to an authority depends indeed on the correctness of normative reasons, but also on the truth of conceptual and empirical propositions. While the relevant conceptual propositions relate to the issue of what are the sufficient and necessary conditions for a power to amount to an instance of the constituent power, the empirical propositions concern the question of whether the authority under consideration meets those conditions. Nino's concept of 'judgments of normative adherence' seems to encompass all the three dimensions: normative, conceptual, and empirical. See Carlos Santiago Nino, 'El concepto de poder constituyente originario y la justificación jurídica' (Buenos Aires, Abeledo-Perrot, 1983) 361.

[20] Ronald Dworkin, *Justice in Robes* (Cambridge Mass, Belknap Press of Harvard University Press, 2006) 140–41.

[21] Ronald Dworkin, *Justice for Hedgehogs* (Cambridge Mass, Belknap Press of Harvard University Press, 2011) 404.

[22] There are other instances of exercise of the constituent power beyond constitution-making. An example is the absolute authority of the English Parliament to represent the British people. See Martin Loughlin, 'Constituent Power Subverted: From English Constitutional Argument to British Constitutional Practice' in *The Paradox of Constitutionalism* (Oxford, Oxford University Press, 2007) 27–48.

[23] Antonio Negri, *Insurgencies. Constituent Power and the Modern State* (Minneapolis and London, University of Minnesota Press, 1999) 4 f.

[24] See Joel I Colón-Ríos, *Weak Constitutionalism. Democratic legitimacy and the question of constituent power* (London and New York, Routledge, 2012) 7. Although the concept of constituent power

The constituent power is foundational – it is argued – for it is the primary source of legal authority.[25] This characterisation attempts to break the circularity implicit in the foundations of legal authority: an authority is legal if and only if a legal norm empowers it, and a norm is legal if and only if it has been created by a legal authority.[26] Assuming the existence of a constituent power as a primary, pre-legal authority, that creates the constitution, breaks that circularity without giving rise to an infinite regress.[27] With this aim Carl Schmitt claimed that the foundation of the validity of the Constitution rests upon the constituent power,[28] understood as a 'decision' or a 'political will' defining the 'type and form' of the political entity in which the people constitute themselves.[29] Moreover, from the foundational character it follows that all constituted powers derive their legal authority from the constituent power, and that they should abide by the legally binding formal and material limitations of their specific empowerments.[30]

Secondly, as a constituent power, the constitution-making power is boundless.[31] Sieyés highlighted this property when he stated that that power 'is not and cannot be bound by the constitution',[32] for it is the source of all legality. The constituent power can neither be subject to formal nor to material limitations. It is free to create, replace or revise a constitution by means of any procedure and with any content.

Finally, the argument from the constituent power portrays the constitution-making power as sovereign arguing that it holds the ultimate authority to create legal norms.[33] No other authority can invalidate its decisions.[34]

arose in the English law of the XVII century (see Martin Loughlin, 'Constituent Power Subverted: From English Constitutional Argument to British Constitutional Practice' in *The Paradox of Constitutionalism* (Oxford, Oxford University Press, 2007) 27–48), the understanding of the people's power to create a constitution as a kind of constituent power began with the French revolution. See Joel I Colón-Ríos, 'Five Conceptions of Constituent Power' (2014) 130 *Law Quarterly Review* 307.

[25] Martin Loughlin, 'The Concept of Constituent Power' (2014) 13(2) *European Journal of Political Theory* 219.

[26] Alf Ross stated this problem in *On Law and Justice* (Berkeley CA, University of California Press, 1959) 80; and 'On Self-Reference and a Puzzle in Constitutional Law' (1969) 78 *Mind* 1.

[27] HLA Harts' rule of recognition attempts to play the same role. See *The Concept of Law* (Oxford, Clarendon Press, 1994) 91 f.

[28] Carl Schmitt, *Verfassungslehre*, 5th edn (Berlin, Duncker & Humblot, 1970) 22.

[29] ibid, 82.

[30] See Renato Cristi, 'The Metaphysics of Constituent Power: Schmitt and the Genesis of Chile's 1980 Constitution' (1999–2000) 21 *Cardozo Law Review* 1749.

[31] Erst-Wolfgang Böckenförde, 'Die verfassunggebende Gewalt des Volkes. Ein Grenzbegriff des Verfassungsrechts', in id, *Staat, Verfassung, Demokratie: Studien zur Verfassungstheorie und zum Verfassungsrecht* (Frankfurt am Main, Suhrkamp, 1991) 90–112.

[32] Emmanuel-Joseph Sieyès, *Qu'est-ce que le Tiers-Etat?* (Paris, Pagnerre, 1839) (1789) 132. According to Sieyès, the nation – and not the people – is the holder of the constituent power.

[33] Martin Loughlin, 'Why Sovereignty?' in Richard Rawlings, Peter Leyland and Alison L Young, *Sovereingy and the Law. Domestic, European, and International Perspectives* (Oxford, Oxford University Press, 2013) 45 and 48.

[34] Giorgio Agamben, *Homo Sacer* (Stanford, Stanford University Press, 1998) 43. Some scholars consider boundlessness as an aspect of sovereignty. See, for instance, the 'negative side' of Parliamentary Sovereignty of Albert Venn Dicey, *Introduction to the Study of the Law of the Constitution* (London, Macmillan, 1939) 40.

Andreas Kalyvas[35] highlighted that this characterisation implied a mutation of the concept of sovereignty as drafted by Jean Bodin as the 'higher power to command'.[36] As a constituent power, the sovereignty of the constitution-making power[37] grounds the highest authority to create legal norms.[38]

III. Constitutional Replacement, Constitutional Revision, and the Argument from the Constituent Power

The argument from the constituent power has often been used to justify constitutional replacements and constitutional revisions. Constitutional replacements and constitutional revisions are special cases of formal structural constitutional changes. A constitutional change is a modification in the set of valid constitutional norms. Constitutional changes can be formal or informal. The difference between constitutional provisions and constitutional norms facilitates the understanding of these modalities.[39] Constitutional provisions are the statements of a written constitution. In the case of written constitutions, constitutional norms are the set of meanings expressed by the constitutional provisions. Those meanings can be articulated in prescriptive propositions, which state that something is constitutionally commanded, prohibited or permitted, or that a constitutional power or immunity is granted to someone.

Formal constitutional changes imply a modification in one or more constitutional provisions whose effect is a modification in the set of valid constitutional norms. Constitutional enactment, replacement, revision, amendment, and explicit

[35] Andreas Kalyvas, 'Popular Sovereignty, Democracy, and the Constituent Power', (2005) 12(2) *Constellations* 223–44, at 225. However, in contrast to Sieyés, Kalyvas suggests that the people can only exercise the constituent power by means of participatory procedures.

[36] Jean Bodin, *Les six livres de la République* (Paris, Librairie générale française, 1993) (1583) 74.

[37] Andreas Kalyvas, 'Constituent Power' in *Political Concepts: A Critical Lexicon*. Available online at: www.politicalconcepts.org/constituentpower/ (20.02.2015).

[38] The distinction between command and legal rule that was at the core of HLA Hart's criticisms to John Austin's theory of law might illustrate the difference between these two conceptions of sovereignty. I will understand here 'rule' as synonym of 'norm'. Austin maintained that the law is a set of commands. A command is the expression of a wish of the sovereign that someone shall do or forbear from some act, backed by the threat of a sanction in case of lack of compliance. See Wilfrid E Rumble (ed), *The Province of Jurisprudence Determined* (Cambridge, Cambridge University Press, 1995) 21. In contrast, according to Hart, the existence of a rule implies that deviation from the standard of conduct it sets, gives rise to criticism and imposition of sanctions; that criticism for deviation and imposition of sanctions is regarded as legitimate, justified or made with good reason; and the so-called internal aspect of rules, that is, that agents 'must look upon the behavior in questions as a general standard to be followed by the group as a whole'. See *The Concept of Law* (Oxford, Clarendon Press, 1994) 55–66. The attribution of sovereignty to the constituent power implies acknowledging its capacity to set rules.

[39] On the distinction between provision and norm in Constitutional Law, see Vezio Crisafulli, 'Disposizione (e norma)' (1964) *XIII Enciclopedia del Diritto* 165, 203. Also, within the field of Constitutional Rights, see Robert Alexy, *A Theory of Constitutional Rights* (Oxford, Oxford University Press, 2002) 32.

derogation are kinds of formal constitutional changes. In contrast, an informal constitutional change is a modification in the set of valid constitutional norms that takes place without a modification in the set of constitutional provisions. Constitutional mutation by interpretation,[40] infra-constitutional mutation[41] and constitutional desuetude,[42] are types of informal constitutional change.

Only formal constitutional changes are relevant for the scope of this chapter. The differences and relationships between the concepts related to formal constitutional change, that is, enactment, replacement, revision, and amendment, are subject to debate.[43] For instance, for the purposes of their 2009 empirical study, Zachary Elkins, Tom Ginsburg and James Melton endorsed a procedural distinction between amendment and replacement: while in the former 'the actors claim to follow the amending procedure of the existing constitution', in the latter 'they undertake revision without claiming to follow such procedure'.[44]

In contrast, according to Richard Albert, while 'an amendment should be understood as an effort to continue the constitution-making project that began at the founding moment', 'a revision should be understood as an effort to unmake the Constitution by introducing an extraordinary change that is inconsistent with the fundamental presuppositions of the constitution'.[45] The Colombian Constitutional Court follows a similar functionalist approach to the difference between amendment and – in its terminology – 'substitution'. A clear case of constitutional amendment implies a minor change in one or more non-essential elements of the Constitution. An undisputable instance of constitutional substitution is a modification of 'great transcendence and magnitude',[46]

[40] This concept refers to the case in which judges attribute a new meaning to an old constitutional provision. Concerning a non-state related context, Julian Arato has shown how informal constitutional change can take place in any legislative and political practice of constitutional interpretation, in addition to the practice of interpretation by the judges. See Julian Arato, 'Treaty Interpretation and Constitutional Transformation: Informal Change in International Organizations' (2013) 38 *Yale Journal of International Law* 304.

[41] This concept refers to change that occurs by the enactment of ordinary legislation, ratification of international treaties, the undertaking of executive action or the *mise-en-scène* of political practices that, despite being inconsistent with the constitution, is neither challenged in the courts nor judicially declared unconstitutional. On this concept, see Carlos Bernal, 'Informal Constitutional Change' (2014) 62 *American Journal of Comparative Law* 495.

[42] On constitutional desuetude, see Richard Albert, 'Constitutional Amendment by Constitutional Desuetude' (2014) 62 *American Journal of Comparative Law* 641.

[43] For an illuminating discussion on the differences between constitutional revision and constitutional amendment, see Richard Albert, 'Amendment and Revision in the Unmaking of Constitutions' in David Landau and Hanna Lerner (eds), *Handbook on Comparative Constitution-Making* (Cheltenham, Edward Elgar, forthcoming). Available online at: https://papers.ssrn.com/sol3/papers2.cfm?abstract_id=2841110 (13.2.2017).

[44] Zachary Elkins, Tom Ginsburg, and James Melton, *The Endurance of National Constitutions* (Cambridge, Cambridge University Press, 2009) 55.

[45] Richard Albert, 'Amendment and Revision in the Unmaking of Constitutions' in David Landau and Hanna Lerner (eds), *Handbook on Comparative Constitution-Making* (Cheltenham, Edward Elgar, forthcoming).

[46] See Colombian Constitutional Court, Judgments C-551/2003 and C-1200/2003. Also, Gonzalo A Ramírez Cleves, 'El control material de las reformas constitucionales mediante acto legislativo a

in one or more essential elements of the state's architecture[47] or the basic structure of the constitution.[48] A constitutional amendment preserves the identity and continuity of the existing constitution. Conversely, a constitutional substitution undermines the existing constitution. A constitutional substitution is, in this sense, anti-constitutional.[49]

Scholars also use the concept of constitutional replacement to refer to the change of the whole constitutional text, that is, of the entire set of constitutional provisions. According to Negretto, this usually takes place when the governance structure enshrined in a constitution fails to achieve its goals, and political actors lack the 'capacity to implement changes by means of amendments or judicial interpretation'.[50] In this sense, a constitutional replacement is the derogation of the existing written constitution as consequence of the enactment of a new one. A constitutional replacement might be the result of procedures that the existing constitution foresees and regulates – for instance, a constituent assembly or a referendum – or the output of extra-constitutional strategies,[51] often of popular geneses.[52] This strategy of formal constitutional change is frequently employed,

partir de la jurisprudencia establecida en la Sentencia C-551 de 2003' (2006) 18 *Revista de Derecho del Estado* 10.

[47] The thesis that a modification of an essential element of the Constitution is a constitutional substitution and not an amendment lies at the core of the constitutional substitution doctrine of the Colombian Constitutional Court. See Judgments C-970/2004, C-971/2004, C-1040/2005, C-588/2009, C-141/2010, C-397/2010, C-574/2011, C-170/2012, C-249/2012, C-288/12, C-317/2012, C-1056/2012, C-010/2013, C-579/2013, and C-577/2014. For a critical explanation of this doctrine, see Carlos Bernal, 'Unconstitutional constitutional amendments in the case study of Colombia: An analysis of the justification and meaning of the constitutional replacement doctrine' (2013) 11(2) *International Journal of Constitutional Law* 339–57.

[48] Since *Kesavananda Bharati v State of Kerala*, AIR 1973 SC 1461, the Indian Supreme Court has held that the Parliament's amending power does not encompass the authorisation to change the basic structure of the Constitution. In *Minerva Mills Ltd v Union of India*, AIR 1980 SC 1789, that Court linked the concept of basic structure to the identity of the Constitution. A disputed question is still: What elements do belong to the basic structure? See Sudhir Krishnaswamy, *Democracy and Constitutionalism in India: A Study of the Basic Structure Doctrine* (Oxford, Oxford University Press, 2011) 71 f. Also, Madhav Khosla, 'Constitutional Amendment', in Sujit Choudhry, Madhav Khosla, and Pratap Bhanu Mehta, *The Oxford Handbook of the Indian Constitution* (Oxford, Oxford University Press, 2016) 232–50, at 235 f. On the doctrine of the basic structure in comparative perspective, see Aharon Barak, 'Unconstitutional Constitutional Amendments' (2011) 44 *Israeli Law Review* 321–41.

[49] See Richard Albert, 'Nonconstitutional Amendments' (2009) 22(1) *Canadian Journal of Law and Jurisprudence* 10.

[50] Gabriel Negretto, 'Replacing and Amending Constitutions: The Logic of Constitutional Change in Latin America' (2012) 46(4) *Law and Society Review* 749.

[51] Richard Albert, 'Nonconstitutional Amendments' (2009) 22(1) *Canadian Journal of Law and Jurisprudence* 10–11: 'Extraconstitutional constitutional change relies on strategies that derive their legitimacy from sources external to the text of the constitution', such as popular appeals to self-determination.

[52] See Gavin W Anderson, 'Societal Constitutionalism, Social Movements, and Constitutionalism from Below' (2013) 20(2) *Indiana Journal of Global Legal Studies* 881–906. The Arab spring offers examples of constitutional replacements of popular geneses. See William Parlett, 'The Dangers of Popular Constitutional Making' (2012) 38(1) *Brooklyn Journal of International Law* 1–46. See also Catherine Turner, 'Transitional Constitutionalism and the Case of the Arab Spring' (2015) 64(2) *International and Comparative Law Quarterly* 267–91.

in particular, in the global south. During the last 40 years, only in Latin America, there have been constitutional replacements in Bolivia (2009), Brazil (1988), Chile (1980), Colombia (1991), Ecuador (1998 and 2008), Guatemala (1985), Honduras (1982), Nicaragua (1987), Panama (1972), Paraguay (1992), Peru (1979 and 1993), El Salvador (1983), the Dominican Republic (2015), and Venezuela (1999) for a variety of reasons. These include the transition to democracy (in Chile),[53] the efforts to end a situation of anomie (in Colombia),[54] and attempts by incumbent presidents and governments to enact constitutions that allow them to remain perpetually in power or to diminish political and legal controls (Venezuela, Bolivia and Ecuador).[55]

Following Albert and Negretto, I will understand that a constitutional amendment implies a minor change that does not modify the structure of the Constitution, a constitutional revision and a whole constitutional replacement – for the sake of brevity I will just use 'replacement' – are changes in the structure of the Constitution. In this sense, revisions and replacements are two kinds of formal structural constitutional changes. Both modify the structure of the Constitution and, in Albert's words, they attempt to 'unmake' the valid constitution. However, while a replacement entails a modification in the entire set of constitutional provisions, a revision only implies modifying some of them.[56]

There is support for the claim that constitutional replacements and revisions should demand more democratic participation than constitutional amendments.[57] More controversial is the issue of whether from the conceptual distinction between

[53] See Renato Cristi, 'The Metaphysics of Constituent Power: Schmitt and the Genesis of Chile's 1980 Constitution' (1999–2000) 21 *Cardozo Law Review* 1749. For an alternative narrative of the genesis of Chile's 1980 Constitution, see Fernando Atria, 'Sobre la soberanía y lo político' (2006) 12 *Derecho y humanidades* 47–93.

[54] On the concept of anomie as lack of norms or the unsuitability of existing norms for guiding society, see Émile Durkheim, *Le suicide. Étude de sociologie (1897)*, 2nd edn (Paris, Les Presses Universitaires de France, 1967) Book 1, chapter V. Also, on anomie in the circumstances of the enactment of the 1991 Colombian Constitution, see Jorge Andrés Hernández, 'La Constitución de Colombia de 1991 y sus enemigos. El fracaso del consenso constitucional' (2013) 79 *Colombia Internacional* 49–76 at 56.

[55] See David Landau, 'Abusive Constitutionalism' (2013) 47 *University of California Davis Law Review* 189–200, at 195.

[56] A relevant case of constitutional revision in Latin America is the 1994 amendment to the Constitution of Argentina. See Alberto A Natale, 'La reforma constitucional argentina de 1994' (2000) 2 *Cuestiones constitucionales* 219–37. On the debate on the nature of this amendment, see Miguel Shor, 'The Once and Future Democracy: Argentina at the Bar of Constitutionalism' in Denis J Galligan and Mila Versteeg (eds), *Social and Political Foundations of Constitutions* (Cambridge, Cambridge University Press, 2013) 574.

[57] On the discussion of this claim, see Carlos Bernal, 'Unconstitutional constitutional amendments in the case study of Colombia: An analysis of the justification and meaning of the constitutional replacement doctrine' (2013) 11(2) *International Journal of Constitutional Law* 355 f; Richard Albert, 'Amendment and Revision in the Unmaking of Constitutions', in David Landau and Hanna Lerner (eds), *Handbook on Comparative Constitution-Making* (Cheltenham, Edward Elgar, forthcoming) 1. A different question is whether participation, in contrast to representation, is the best way to replace and revise a constitution. On this complex issue, see Xenophon Contiades and Alkmene Fotiadou (eds), *Participatory Constitutional Change. The People as Amenders of the Constitution* (London, Routledge, 2017).

constitutional amendment, on the one hand, and constitutional replacement and revision, on the other, it follows that while the former is and ought to be limited, the latter is not, and ought not to be. According to a version of the theory of the constituent power, only the power to amend the Constitution can, is, and ought to be limited, because the amending power (or derivative constituent power) is a legal competence created by the (original) constituent power. Given that every legal competence can only be exercised within the boundaries of the actions authorised by it, if the derivative constituent power violates the boundaries of the competence to amend the constitution, the corresponding amendment is unconstitutional.[58] According to the argument from the constituent power, this is not the case concerning constitutional replacements. The original constituent power knows no limits to replace the constitution.

During the last few decades, political actors and state institutions – such as some apex courts in Latin America[59] – have appealed to this claim linked to the argument from the constituent power, with the purpose of justifying extra-constitutional constituent assemblies and ruling out limits to their procedures and outputs. Scholars, such as Joel Colón-Ríos, have welcomed this line of argument. According to Colón-Ríos, allowing an unlimited constituent power to manifest from time to time creates the possibility of a 'democratic re-constitution' of a society in a crisis infusing 'democratic legitimacy' to its constitutional regime.[60] In a weaker manner, Yaniv Roznai argued that: 'Unamendability thus limits the delegated amendment power but it cannot block the [] constituent power – the "sovereignty at the back of the Constitution" – from its ability to amend even the basic principles or structure of the constitutional order'.[61] However, Roznai seems to acknowledge that there are certain procedural limitations to constitutional replacements and revisions, when he agrees that: 'what unamendability means is that certain amendments establishing a "new constitution" or a new "constitutional identity" cannot be achieved through the regular amendment procedure but require a different constituent process'.[62]

However, as Dixon and Landau have highlighted, autocrats or strongmen could employ both formal ways of constitutional change – structural and non-structural – for purposes related to abusive constitutionalism, that is,

[58] See Mark Tushnet, 'Peasants with pitchforks, and toilers with Twitter: Constitutional revolutions and the constituent power' (2015) 13 *International Journal of Constitutional Law* 639–54, at 646.

[59] Francisco Soto Barrientos, 'Asamblea Constituyente: La experiencia latinoamericana y el actual debate en Chile' (2014) 12(1) *Estudios Constitucionales* 397–428, at 403.

[60] See Joel I Colón-Ríos, 'The Legitimacy of the Juridical: Constituent Power, Democracy, and the Limits of Constitutional Reform' (2010) 48(2) *Osgoode Hall Law Journal* 199–245; and Allan Hutchinson and Joel I Colón-Ríos, 'Constituciones Duraderas – Una Crítica Democrática' (2011) 1 *Anuario de Derecho Público* 437–60.

[61] Yaniv Roznai, 'The Spectrum of Constitutional Amendment Powers' in Richard Albert, Xenophon Contiades and Alkmene Fotiadou, *The Foundations and Traditions of Constitutional Amendment* (Oxford, Hart Publishing, forthcoming) 4. Available online at: http://papers.ssrn.com/sol3/papers.cfm?abstract_id=2649816 (14.02.2016).

[62] ibid.

for perpetuating themselves in power or undermining checks on the exercise of their competencies.[63] The deeper concern is not that they unmake the Constitution but that, via revision or replacement, they unmake constitutionalism. Furthermore, in a constitutional crisis there is an increased risk of authoritarian and unilateral exercises of power that should be avoided.[64] Powerful political actors can manipulate popular majorities for unmaking constitutionalism by imposing manufactured structural fundamental laws, window-dressed as constitutions.[65] Hence, the same normative and conceptual reasons that justify the limitation of the constitutional amendment power ground general constraints to the constitution-making power, which also apply to constitutional revisions and replacements.

An analysis of the judgments by the Colombian and Venezuelan Supreme Courts, which justified the empowerment of extra-constitutional constituent assemblies for enacting the current constitutions of those countries, will help to underscore the point.[66] In judgment 138 of 9 November 1990, the Colombian Supreme Court reviewed the constitutionality of Decree 1926/1990, which enabled the people to elect an extra-constitutional constituent assembly for replacing the then existing 1886 National Constitution. The Supreme Court upheld the constitutionality of the creation of the assembly. The key argument of the judgment was that 'the people [...] are the primary constituent power, from whom all constituted or derivative powers follow'.[67] 'As primary constituent power, the Colombian nation can give to itself a new constitution at any time without being bound by the requirements of the previous constitution'.[68] 'As sovereign primary constituent power, from which all other powers derive, the nation cannot have limits other than the constraints it imposes to itself. No constituted power has the authority to review the decisions made by the nation.'[69] Thus, by exercising its sovereign and boundless primary constituent power, the people could replace the 1886 National Constitution by means of an extra-constitutional procedure.[70]

The Venezuelan Supreme Court displayed a similar argument in its Judgment N° 17 of 19 January 1999. After his election in 1998, President Hugo Chávez

[63] See Rosalind Dixon and David Landau, 'Constraining Constitutional Change' (2015) 50 *Wake Forest Law Review* 859–90, at 862.

[64] See David Landau, 'Constitution-Making gone wrong' (2013) 64(5) *Alabama Law Review* 923–80.

[65] See David Landau, 'The Importance of Constitution-Making' (2011–2012) 89(3) *Denver University Law Review* 611–33.

[66] For a critical analysis of the judgments concerning Venezuela, see David Landau, 'Abusive Constitutionalism' (2013) 47 *University of California Davis Law Review* 203; David Landau, 'Constitution-Making gone Wrong' (2013) 64(5) *Alabama Law Review* 938–48; and Joel I Colón-Rios, 'Carl Schmitt and Constituent Power in Latin American Courts: The Cases of Venezuela and Colombia' (2011) 18(3) *Constellations* 365–88, at 369–73.

[67] See Corte Suprema de Justicia de Colombia, Judgment 138, 9 November 1990.

[68] ibid.

[69] ibid.

[70] For an analysis of this aspect of the judgment, see Gonzalo Andrés Ramírez Cleves, *Límites de la reforma constitucional en Colombia: el concepto de constitución como fundamento de la restricción* (Bogotá, Universidad Externado de Colombia, 2005) 437 f.

proposed the creation of an extra-constitutional constituent assembly for replacing the then valid 1961 Constitution.[71] A group of citizens requested the Venezuelan Supreme Court to interpret Article 181 of the 1997 Act on Elections and Political Participation. That Article empowered the President to 'call a referendum for consulting the electors on decisions of special national importance'.[72] The key question was whether the President had the power to call a referendum on the creation of an extra-constitutional constituent assembly.

In Judgment 17 of 19 January 1999,[73] the Supreme Court delivered a positive answer supported by the argument from the constituent power. The Court held that the people are sovereign,[74] and 'never surrender their constituent power to the constituted powers'.[75] The constituent power is the 'original competence of the political community for creating a constitutional organization'.[76] Unlike the amending power, 'it precedes the legal order and is higher than it'. It is 'severing, unlimited, original, and cannot be bound' by the amending procedures that the Constitution regulates.[77] After that, on 2 February 1999, President Chávez enacted Decree Number 3 calling for a referendum that allowed the people to decide on the creation of a Constituent Assembly. The Supreme Court issued several judgments on the methodology for electing the Assembly, its limits, and the respect for the terms of the political authorities that, at the time, exercised the constituted powers.[78] The Court used again the argument from the constituent power to claim that the Constituent Assembly enjoyed an unlimited 'supra-constitutional' power to change the structure of the constituted powers.[79] On this basis the Constituent Assembly illegitimately terminated the terms of the main incumbent political authorities, even the judges of the Supreme Court. It also drafted a Constitution that enabled President Chávez to dismantle democracy, gain control over the legislative and the judiciary, and to perpetuate himself in power until the day of his death and beyond by installing Nicolas Maduro as his successor.[80]

[71] On the context of this constitution-making process, see Carlos M Ayala Corao, 'Venezuela: De la constituyente de 1999 a la reforma constitucional de 2007', in José María Serna de la Garza (ed), *Procesos constituyentes contemporáneos en América Latina. Tendencias y Perspectivas* (México, Universidad Nacional Autónoma de México, 2009) 333–405.

[72] *Organic Law on Voting and Political Participation*, Gaceta Oficial No. 5200, 30 December 1997.

[73] Supreme Court of Venezuela, judgment No. 17 of 19 January 1999.

[74] Section 4 of the 1961 Constitution allocated the sovereignty to the people.

[75] Supreme Court of Venezuela, judement No. 17 of 19 January 1999.

[76] ibid.

[77] ibid.

[78] See Allan R Brewer-Carías, *Poder Constituyente Originario y Asamblea Nacional Constituyente* (Caracas, Editorial Jurídica Venezolana, 1999) 117.

[79] Supreme Court of Venezuela, *Vicepresidente del Congreso de la Republica vs Asamblea (Decreto 25-8-99)*, 14 October 1999, published at (1999) 77–80 *Revista del Derecho Público* 111. The Court displayed a non-conventional version of the argument from the constituent power according to which not only the power of the people but also the power of a constituent assembly is unlimited.

[80] Allan R Brewer-Carías, 'La configuración judicial del proceso constituyente o de cómo el guardián de la Constitución abrió el camino para su violación y para su propia extinción' (1999) 77–80 *Revista de Derecho Público* 502. Also, Allan R Brewer-Carías, *Dismantling Democracy in Venezuela. The Chávez Authoritarian Experiment* (Cambridge, Cambridge University Press, 2010) 59.

The examples from Colombia and Venezuela show two dimensions of the use of the argument from the constituent power. On the one hand, the Colombian example is a clear case of what Colón-Ríos calls a 'democratic re-constitution' of society. On the other hand, the illustration from Venezuela is an instance of authoritarian manipulation of a constitutional replacement, as feared by Landau and Dixon. Is it possible to conceptualise the constitution-making power, as instantiated in the power to replace or revise the constitution, in a way that grounds a democratic re-constitution of the society in times of crisis while, at the same time, making it unjustifiable for autocrats and strongmen to hijack constitution-making?

IV. A Critique of the Argument from the Constituent Power as a Justification for Constitutional Replacements and Revisions

Legal theorists have revealed several flaws in the theory of the constituent power. Carlos Santiago Nino, for instance, claimed that the theory of the constituent power was the source of a 'serious conceptual disorder that negatively impacted scholars' and judges' thought processes'.[81] More recently, David Dyzenhaus argued that 'legal and constitutional theory should avoid the idea of constituent power' for it results 'in a deep ambivalence about whether authority is located within or without the legal order'.[82] I do not purport to advance a diatribe against this theory but only to highlight why employing the argument from the constituent power for justifying the unlimited undertaking of constitutional replacements and revisions – in cases like the whole extra-constitutional constitutional replacements Colombia and Venezuela – and, in doing so, for understanding the nature of the constitution-making power, is conceptually incorrect. The incorrectness arises from the characterisation of the constitution-making power as 'unlimited'. The arguments from the outcome and from the competence reveal why the constitution-making power cannot be conceptually unlimited.

A. The Argument from the Outcome

The argument from the outcome states that the constitution-making power is a legal competence to institutionalise constitutionalism. The function of

[81] Carlos Santiago Nino, 'El concepto de poder constituyente originario y la justificación jurídica' (Buenos Aires, Abeledo-Perrot, 1983) 40.

[82] David Dyzenhaus, 'Constitutionalism in an old key: Legality and constituent power' (2012) 1(2) *Global Constitutionalism* 229–60, at 229; and id, 'The Question of Constituent Power' in Martin Loughlin and Neil Walker (eds), *The Paradox of Constitutionalism* (Oxford, Oxford University Press, 2007) 143–45.

constitution makers is limited to the enactment of a constitution. They cannot put in place an institutional arrangement of some other kind. From this perspective, the key question is: What is a constitution within this context? Or, in other words, what elements must an institutional arrangement bear for counting as a constitution?

There are two possibilities at stake: a purely empirical conception of constitution, and a normative/empirical conception of constitution.[83] According to a purely empirical conception, any institutional arrangement of the state, as a framework of governmental relationships between the citizens and their authorities, which is authoritatively enacted and socially recognised, counts as a constitution.[84] The above-mentioned necessary connection between the conceptual and normative dimensions of the constitution-making power shows why this conception cannot be sound. Were it true, every formal structural constitutional change would be justified, even the replacement of a liberal and democratic constitution by a set of rules entrenching a rogue political regime that an autocrat manages to impose against its opponents.

Instead, according to the normative/empirical conception that I endorse here, an institutional arrangement of the state can count as a constitution if and only if it is authoritatively enacted and socially recognised as a constitution, and encompasses certain essential elements related to the purpose of constitutionalism.[85] In brief, there cannot be a constitution without constitutionalism.[86] In this regard, the concept of a constitution, which we use in both ordinary and technical language, implies, at least, four essential elements: the rule of law, the principle of the separation of powers, some sort of protection to individual rights or – at least – interests that are guaranteed by the Constitution or the legislation,[87] and an entrenchment of the democratic idea that the legitimacy of government

[83] In a similar way, in: 'The Cult of Constitutionalism' (2012) 39 *Florida State University Law Review* 379–80, Richard Albert introduces the distinction between 'functional' and 'aspirational' constitutionalism. While the former points 'to something recognizable as a constitution', the latter 'sets a higher standard for a constitution'. It 'seeks to breathe into it values coherent with the larger project of liberal democracy'.

[84] The material conception of the Constitution endorsed by Carl Schmitt in his *Verfassungslehre* (Berlin, Duncker & Humblot, 1970) is a sort of the purely empirical conception. On Schmitt´s material conception, see Martin Loughlin, *Foundations of Public Law* (Oxford, Oxford University Press, 2010) 211.

[85] Interestingly, in 'Constituent Power and Carl Schmitt's Theory of Constitution in Kenya's Constitution-Making Process' (2011) 9(3–4) *International Journal of Constitutional Law* 587–614, Richard Stacey offers an interpretation of Schmitt's view on the constituent power that is constrained for the purposes of institutionalising the rule of law.

[86] On the problem of constitutions without constitutionalism, in some African countries, see HWO Okoth-Ogendo, 'Constitutions Without Constitutionalism: An African Paradox' in Douglas Greenberg, Stanley N Katz, Steven C Wheatley and Melanie Beth Oliviero (eds), *Constitutionalism and Democracy: Transitions in the Contemporary World* (Oxford, Oxford University Press, 1993) 65 f; and in China: Qianfan Zhang, 'A constitution without constitutionalism? The paths of constitutional development in China' (2010) 8(4) *International Journal of Constitutional Law* 950–76.

[87] Despite that the constitutions of Australia, Canada, and New Zealand lack a list of fundamental rights, they do protect individual rights. Furthermore, the conception of rights or interests endorsed here also allows for a statutory protection that is constitutionally possible. This renders it compatible

rests on the consent of its subjects.[88] Constitutionalism is a means to instantiate the rule of law. It is a strategy that creates incentives for political authorities to act in accordance to the law,[89] by submitting all governmental action 'to the structures, processes, principles, and values of a constitution'.[90] Furthermore, constitutions implement and interconnect the ideas that government should be in the service of the rights of the individuals, and that legitimacy of government rests on the consent of those individuals subject to it.[91] The constitutional entrenchment of a charter of fundamental (liberal, political and, even, social) rights is a possible – yet, not a necessary – strategy to accomplish that aim.[92] Finally, a mechanism of separation of powers enables accountability of political authorities for securing that they behave according to the law and observing individual rights and democratic institutions.[93] The normative/empirical conception of a constitution highlights the goal of constitutionalism consisting in the institutionalisation of a form of government in which the power of the state is controlled, limited, and restrained, people are democratically empowered to control the sources of law, and the apparatus of government is harnessed to the aspirations of the people.[94]

If this conception is employed to assess the justifiability of a constitutional replacement or revision, a constitutional change of this kind would be justifiable if and only if the new or revised constitution somehow incorporates all the four essential constitutional elements, in a way in which they can fulfil

even with weak conceptions on the relationship between the Constitution and the protection of individuals, such as the one defended by Jeremy Waldron since his seminal article: 'A Rights-Based Critique of Constitutional Rights' (1993) 13(1) *Oxford Journal of Legal Studies* 18–51.

[88] This concept underpins Articles 2 and 16 of the French Declaration of the Rights of Man and of the Citizen. Article 2 states that the aim of all political associations [that are created by means of a constitution] is the preservation of the rights of human beings. Article 16 states that a 'society in which the observance of the law is not assured, nor the separation of powers defined, has no constitution at all'.

[89] As Philip Selznick has pointed out, there are several conceptions of the rule of law (see 'Democracy and the Rule of Law' (2005) 33 *Syracuse Journal of International Law and Commerce* 29). Brian Tamanaha classifies them in formal (thin) and substantive (thick) conceptions; see *On the Rule of Law. History, Politics, Theory* (Cambridge, Cambridge University Press, 2004) 91–113. However, the different conceptions share at least two core elements: control of power and legality. See Geranne Lautenbach, *The Concept of the Rule of Law and the European Court of Human Rights* (Oxford, Oxford University Press, 2013) 19 f.

[90] See Martin Loughlin, 'What is Constitutionalisation?' in Petra Dobner and Martin Loughlin (eds), *The Twilight of Constitutionalism?* (Oxford, Oxford University Press, 2010) 47.

[91] See Dieter Grimm, 'The Achievement of Constitutionalism' in Petra Dobner and Martin Loughlin (eds), *The Twilight of Constitutionalism?* (Oxford, Oxford University Press, 2010) 8.

[92] There are also constitutions with implicit constitutional rights, such as the Australian Constitution. On this issue, see Adrienne Stone, 'Australia's Constitutional Rights and the Problem of Interpretive Disagreement' (2005) 25 *Sydney Law Review* 29–48.

[93] Cheryl Saunders, 'Separation of Powers and the Judicial Branch' (2006) 11(4) *Judicial Review* 337–47. On the connection between the separation of powers and the rule of law, see Friedrich A Hayek, *The Constitution of Liberty* (London and Henley, Routledge & Kegan Paul, 1976) 210. I separate here both concepts because there are thin conceptions of the rule of law that do not specifically encompass the separation of powers.

[94] Jeremy Waldron 'Constitutionalism – A Skeptical View' in Thomas Christiano and John Christman (ed), *Contemporary debates in political philosophy* (Oxford, Wiley-Blackwell, 2009) 270 and 279.

their function.[95] The four essential elements are independently necessary and jointly sufficient for constitutionalism. Moreover, their instantiation allows a margin of discretion to the constitution-making power. For instance, a constituent assembly of a traditional presidential political regime could instantiate the separation of powers in the new constitution in the form of semi-presidentialism. However, that assembly would trespass the conceptual limits of the constitution-making power if the new constitution concentrates all powers in the executive. Constitution-makers can institutionalise abstract constitutional concepts in different ways, but the institutionalisation cannot infringe the semantic limits of those concepts.

As applied to the examples from Colombia and Venezuela, while this conception would understand the enactment of the 1991 Colombian Constitution as an exercise of the constitution-making power, it would interpret as something else – such as a sole exercise of ultimate authoritarian power – the enactment of the 1999 Venezuelan Constitution, due to its deficiencies concerning the institutionalisation of the rule of law and the separation of powers.[96] Because of the centralisation of political powers in the executive, and the changes concerning the President's ability to nominate and have ascendency over the judiciary, the 1999 Venezuelan constituent process ended up unmaking constitutionalism.

It is possible to raise an objection against the normative/empirical conception. It would rule out the classification as constitutions of many constitutional texts that do not instantiate the four essential constitutional elements. Then, it would overlook the fact that even those 'constitutions' fulfil some functions. The argument from the constituent power would not face this objection.

Indeed, Graham Walker speaks about 'non-liberal' constitutions for referring to constitutional texts grounding despotic or arbitrary political regimes.[97] In the same vein, Li-Ann Thio suggests a taxonomy of current constitutionalism in illiberal polities, encompassing mixed regimes with liberal and illiberal domains, theocratic constitutional systems, and political power structures – such as those based on so-called 'Asian values' – in which communitarian cultural priorities entrenched in constitutional law outweigh individual rights.[98] Moreover, Mark Tushnet conceives the possibility of authoritarian constitutionalism and claims

[95] These four elements are a conception of what Dixon and Landau call: 'some notion of an international constitutional "minimum core", or core set of constitutional provisions that are common to all truly functional constitutional democracies'. See Rosalind Dixon and David Landau, 'Constraining Constitutional Change' (2015) 50 *Wake Forest Law Review* 888.

[96] See Allan R Brewer-Carías, *Dismantling Democracy in Venezuela. The Chávez Authoritarian Experiment* (Cambridge, Cambridge University Press, 2010); Phoebe King, 'Neo-Bolivarian Constitutional Design: Comparing the 1999 Venezuelan, 2008 Ecuadorian, and 2009 Bolivian Constitutions' in Denis J Galligan and Mila Versteeg (eds), *Social and Political Foundations of Constitutions* (Cambridge, Cambridge University Press, 2013) 375.

[97] Graham Walker, 'The Idea of Nonliberal Constitutionalism' in Ian Shapiro and Will Kymlicka (eds), *Ethnicity and Group Rights* (New York, NYU Press, 1997) 169.

[98] Li-Ann Thio, 'Constitutionalism in Illiberal Polities' in Michel Rosenfeld and András Sajó, *The Oxford Handbook of Comparative Constitutional Law* (Oxford, Oxford University Press, 2012) 137 f.

that pluralising our understanding of constitutionalism may enhance conceptual clarity.[99] Even in illiberal societies or authoritarian political regimes, constitutions are foundational instruments that articulate the political identity of a society, its core values,[100] a normative architecture allowing social coordination,[101] and the agreements and compromises between rivals in power.[102] They also outline the 'structural distribution of power, defining inter-institutional and government–citizen relations'.[103] Despite that authoritarian rulers ordinarily are forced to make some concessions to enact illiberal constitutions, this strategy enables them to adopt enduring reforms and protect their personal and corporate interests while exercising and after leaving power.[104]

It is undeniable that all constitutions fulfil these structural functions. However, they are not sufficient for linking structural foundational laws with the goals of constitutionalism, as explained above. The issue is that the use of the term 'constitution' for referring to authoritarian constitutions is not normatively neutral. This use generates an illusion of legitimacy about government actions grounded in the constitutional text. This can be called the window-dressing argument. This defect is to be found not only in illiberal but also in non-democratic constitutional texts. Attributing the denomination of 'constitution' only to structural fundamental laws that also encompass the four essential constitutional elements contributes to prevent the effect highlighted by the window-dressing argument.[105]

Finally, the four essential constitutional elements can be entrenched in different degrees. The rule of law, the protection of individual rights, democratic institutions, and the separation of powers are normative ideals that can be institutionalised and implemented with a higher or weaker strength.[106] For present purposes, it is appropriate to conceive them as a minimal conceptual constrain of

[99] Mark Tushnet, 'Authoritarian Constitutionalism. Some Conceptual Issues' in Tom Ginsburg and Alberto Simpser, *Constitutions in Authoritarian Regimes* (Cambridge, Cambridge University Press, 2013) 36 f.

[100] On constitutions as expressions of values, see Denis J Galligan and Mila Versteeg, 'Theoretical Perspectives on the Social Foundations of Constitutions' in Denis J Galligan and Mila Versteeg (eds), *Social and Political Foundations of Constitutions* (Cambridge, Cambridge University Press, 2013) 8 f.

[101] Russel Hardin, *Liberalism, Constitutionalism and Democracy* (Oxford, Oxford University Press, 1999) 133; id, 'Why a Constitution?' in Denis J Galligan and Mila Versteeg (eds), *Social and Political Foundations of Constitutions* (Cambridge, Cambridge University Press, 2013) 59 f.

[102] Ran Hirschl, 'The Strategic Foundations of Constitutions' in Denis J Galligan and Mila Versteeg (eds), *Social and Political Foundations of Constitutions* (Cambridge, Cambridge University Press, 2013) 167 f.

[103] Li-Ann Thio, 'Constitutionalism in Illiberal Polities'in Michel Rosenfeld and András Sajó, *The Oxford Handbook of Comparative Constitutional Law* (Oxford, Oxford University Press, 2012) 133.

[104] Gabriel L Negretto, 'Authoritarian Constitution Making. The Role of the Military in Latin America' in Tom Ginsburg and Alberto Simpser, *Constitutions in Authoritarian Regimes* (Cambridge, Cambridge University Press, 2013) 83.

[105] In a similar sense, Aiofe O'Donoghue rejects 'a very broad concept of constitutional order as a system of governance [... that] simply reduces constitutionalism to a mere set of organizational rules'. See *Constitutionalism in Global Constitutionalisation* (Cambridge, Cambridge University Press, 2014) 16.

[106] See, for instance, interesting analyses concerning the entrenchment of these ideals in Islamic constitutions in Reiner Grote, 'Models of Institutional Control: The Experience of Islamic Countries'

constitution-making, in the sense that if a constitutional replacement or revision eliminates one of them or makes it void or irrelevant, it would not be justified. Under these circumstances, the new or revised constitution would only window-dress a dismemberment of constitutionalism.[107] It could not be considered as an outcome of the constitution-making power.

B. The Argument from the Competence

To explain the argument from the competence I will focus on the enactment of a new constitution. However, the results of the analysis can apply, *mutatis mutandi*, to other cases of constitution-making. The enactment of a new constitution is a declaration. A declaration is a kind of illocutionary speech act. An illocutionary speech act is an act that is performed 'in saying something'.[108] Agents exercising the constitution-making power enact the Constitution – that is attribute legal validity to a written constitutional text – by solemnly declaring that they enact the constitution.[109] A declarative speech act – the declaration that 'Peter and Amy are married' – is successful, if it makes it the case that Peter and Amy are married.[110] Accordingly, the enactment of a constitution is successful, if it makes the case that the Constitution is enacted.

All illocutionary speech acts must meet some conditions concerning what must be fulfilled for a successful and non-defective performance of the act. For instance, 'all acts whose point is to get the hearer to do something – orders, requests, commands, etc – have as a preparatory condition that the hearer is able to do the act directed'.[111] Regarding these conditions, an agent or a group of agents can only successfully enact a constitution if they are empowered to do so. Hence, a condition of the enactment of the Constitution is that political agents enacting the Constitution have a competence to do so. Declarations have at least a world-to-word direction of fit. Their point is 'to bring the world to match their contents'.[112] No one can transform the legal world by enacting a

(221–38) – concerning the limitation of power – and Tilmann J Röder, 'The Separation of Powers in Muslim Countries: Historical and Comparative Perspectives' (321–72) – concerning the separation of powers – both in Reiner Grote and Tilmann J Röder, *Constitutionalism in Islamic Countries. Between Upheaval and Continuity* (Oxford, Oxford University Press, 2012).

[107] Richard Albert has crafted the concept of constitutional dismemberment for referring to a 'deliberate effort to disassemble one or more of the constitution's constituent parts'. See *Constitutional Dismemberment*, manuscript, p 1.

[108] See John L Austin, *How to do Things with Words* (Oxford, Oxford University Press, 1976) 98.

[109] See, on declaratives, John Searle, *Speech Acts* (Cambridge, Cambridge University Press, 1969) 31f., and 64 f.

[110] In speech act theory, this is called 'illocutionary point'. See Daniel Boisvert and Kirk Ludwig, 'Semantic for Nondeclaratives', in Ernest Lepore and Barry C Smith (eds), *The Oxford Handbook of the Philosophy of Language* (Oxford, Oxford University Press, 2006) ch 34.

[111] John Searle and Daniel Vanderveken, *Foundations of Illocutionary Logic* (Cambridge, Cambridge University Press, 1985) 17–18.

[112] John Searle, *Making the Social World* (Oxford, Oxford University Press, 2010) 12. According to Searle, declarations also have a word-to-world direction of fit. In a successful declaration, we

valid constitution, that is, by means of the declaration that a constitution is valid, if they lack the legal competence to do so.

In the next section I will elucidate some of the properties of the competence to enact a constitution. For now, I will state the argument from the competence: if for enacting a constitution it is necessary to have the competence to do so, then each exercise of the (constitution-making) power to enact a constitution is limited by the boundaries of the competence to do so. In this respect, despite their differences, the power to enact a constitution shares a feature with the power to amend the constitution, namely, that both are limited.[113] Both can only be legally exercised within the confines of their respective competences. This is also the case with regards to all other instances of the constitution-making power.

If this is true, then the argument from the constituent power is not an appropriate conception of the constitution-making power. It fails to account for an essential property of this power, namely, that it is a legal competence, and that, like any other legal competence, it can only be validly exercised within the limits of its boundaries. The argument from the constituent power soundly reflects some empirical aspects of the constitution-making power. No agent lacking real political power can enact a constitution. However, this conception overlooks that the constitution-making power is a legal authority, that is, a 'normative power to change another's normative relations'.[114] It mistakenly reduces the constitution-making power to facts: coercion and factual power. Nevertheless, from a factual power cannot derive a normative power to change normative relations.[115] Only an agent empowered with a normative competence to change normative relations of other people can do so.

Finally, there is a conceptual and a normative connection between the argument from the competence and the argument from the outcome. On the one hand, the constitution-making power is instantiated in the competence to enact, revise or replace a constitution – that includes the above-mentioned four essential constitutional elements – and not a set of structural fundamental law entrenching other types of institutional arrangements. Hence, enacting, revising or replacing a constitution with another constitutional arrangement are the only actions conceptually authorised by the constitution-making empowerment. On the other hand, the understanding that all legal competences are necessarily limited is a core normative strategy to protect individual rights from arbitrary exercises of political power. While individual freedom is unlimited, legal powers are limited in their scope and aims, as they can only purport to protect the

change the world to match the content of the speech act (world-to-word direction of fit) only because 'we represent the reality as being so changed'.

[113] An open question is what are the differences between their limits. I cannot address this question here.

[114] Scott Shapiro, 'Authority' in Scott Shapiro and Jules Coleman, *The Oxford Handbook of Jurisprudence and Philosophy of Law* (Oxford, Oxford University Press, 2002) 398.

[115] See Nicole Roughan, *Authorities. Conflicts, Cooperation and Transnational Legal Theory* (Oxford, Oxford University Press, 2103) 24.

rights of others,[116] and achieve the common good.[117] As Hohfeld illuminated, beyond its powers, private individuals and authorities have a 'disability'. Within that scope, correlatively, everyone has an immunity, that is, the 'freedom from the legal power or 'control' of another with regards to some legal relation'.[118] From the connection between the argument from the outcome and the argument from the competence it follows that citizens are immune against employments of the constitution-making power purporting aims that are different to the goal of institutionalising constitutionalism.

Furthermore, individual and collective competences of individuals and groups related to constitution-making are also limited. Individuals participating in constitutional referenda or electing members of constituent assemblies enjoy the limited competence of voting for the options and candidates at stake under valid electoral rules. Moreover, constituent assemblies sometimes have a definite mandate with thematic and sometimes temporal constraints, such as the Colombian 1991 Constituent Assembly, which ought to enact the Constitution by 4 July 1991. In addition, the empowerment of constituent assemblies is limited to the action of enacting a constitution and not a text entrenching an institutional arrangement of some other kind. Last but not least, the limited nature of legal competences enables accountability. Political authorities are accountable for exercising political powers within their scope. Thus, it would be paradoxical that the highest and most powerful authority of law and state, namely, the constitution-making power, should be conceived as an unaccountable power, given that making accountability of authorities possible is precisely one of the aims of creating a state and a legal system by enacting a constitution.[119] Constitution-makers act on behalf of the citizens.[120] Hence, constitution-makers also must be accountable if they overstep their competences.

V. The Constitution-making Power as Deontic Power for Institutionalising Constitutionalism

On the basis of the previous critical analysis, I will advance an alternative socio-ontological conception of the constitution-making power, which characterises it

[116] Immanuel Kant, 'On the Common Saying: "This May be True in Theory, but it does not Apply in Practice"' in Hans Reiss (ed), *Kant: Political Writings* (HB Nisbet (translator)) (Cambridge University Press, Cambridge, 1991) 75–76.

[117] John Locke, *Two Treatises of Government: Book II* (Cambridge University Press, Cambridge, 1988) 357.

[118] NWL Hohfeld, *Fundamental Legal Conceptions, As Applied in Judicial Reasoning* (1919, New Jersey, The Lawbook Exchange, 2010).

[119] See Nicholas Bramforth and Peter Leyland, 'Introduction: Accountability in the Contemporary Constitution' in Nicholas Bramforth and Peter Leyland, *Accountability in the Contemporary Constitution* (Oxford, Oxford University Press, 2013) 2 f.

[120] On the link between accountability and acting on behalf of others, see Annie CL Davies, *The Public Law of Government Contracts* (Oxford, Oxford University Press, 2008) 67.

as a limited deontic power exercised by certain political proxy-agents, who are collectively intentionally recognised as having the status of constitution-makers for performing the function of institutionalising constitutionalism.

This conception encompasses several terms: social ontology, proxy-agents, status, functions, deontic power, limitations, and collective intentional recognition.

A. Social Ontology

Social ontology is an approach to a branch of analytical philosophy that John Searle called 'the philosophy of society', whose aim is 'the study of human society itself', or, in other words, 'the mode of existence of social entities such as governments, families, cocktail parties, summer vacations, trade unions, baseball games and passports'.[121] Studies on the nature of social entities by Michael Bratman, Margaret Gilbert, Seumas Miller, John Searle, and Raimo Tuomela[122] have laid down in the last four decades the foundational principles of social ontology. Increasingly, more and more philosophers and social scientists have been discussing these principles,[123] and applying them to account for the ontological structure of a great variety of entities: from communication, technology, music, art, language, emotions, and violence, to values, the concepts of citizenship, human rights, government, legislation, corporations, and other political, and legal institutions.[124]

Social ontology is based on the intuition that social entities depend on the ability that we, as human beings, have to act collectively, that is to say, as members of groups or plural subjects. This ability is called sociality.[125] Social entities are epistemologically 'objective' but ontologically 'subjective'. They are no less objectively knowable than natural and physical objects, yet their existence depends on the subjectivity of human minds and on certain subjective attitudes

[121] John Searle, *Making the Social World* (Oxford, Oxford University Press, 2010) 5.

[122] See especially, Michael Bratman, *Faces of Intention: Selected Essays on Intention and Agency* (Cambridge, Cambridge University Press, 1999); Michael Bratman, *Shared Agency. A Planning Theory of Acting Together* (Oxford, Oxford University Press, 2013); Margaret Gilbert, *On Social Facts* (Princeton, Princeton University Press, 1992); Seumas Miller, *Social Action: A Teleological Account* (Cambridge, Cambridge University Press, 2001); John Searle, *The Construction of Social Reality* (New York, Simon and Schuster, 1995); John Searle, Making the Social World (Oxford, Oxford University Press, 2010); Raimo Tuomela, *The Philosophy of Social Practices: A Collective Acceptance View* (Cambridge, Cambridge University Press, 2002); and Raimo Tuomela, *The Philosophy of Sociality* (Oxford, Oxford University Press, 2007).

[123] See, for instance, Kirk Ludwig (ed), *The Routledge Handbook of Collective Intentionality* (London and New York, Routledge, 2017).

[124] The most refined socio-ontological account of law is the one presented by Scott Shapiro in *Legality* (Cambridge Mass, Belknap Press of Harvard University Press, 2011).

[125] On the concept of sociality, see Margaret Gilbert, *Living Together. Rationality, Sociality and Obligation* (Lahman, Boulder, New York and London, 1996) 6 and 263 f; Margaret Gilbert, *Sociality and Responsibility* (Lahman 2000), 1 f.; and Raimo Tuomela, *The Philosophy of Sociality* (Oxford, 2007) 11 and 66.

(such as intentions) of agents participating in practices in which they are grounded.[126] For instance, the fact that the 1949 *Grundgesetzt* is the current German Constitution is no less objectively knowable than the fact that there are trees in the *Schwarzwald*. But the validity *qua* existence of the *Grundgesetz* depends on certain subjective attitudes and actions of certain relevant individuals involved in a practice in which they recognise it as the German Constitution, and accord certain status and functions to it.[127]

B. Proxy Agents and Status-Functions

From a socio-ontological perspective, the constitution-making power is a social entity that depends on subjective attitudes and actions of a plurality of individuals. One of the biggest ontological hurdles of the argument from the constituent power is that it presupposes the existence of a super-agent, namely, 'the people' or 'the nation', which is supposedly able to have a 'will' – as Schmitt puts it.[128] However, there are no super-agents in the world, endowed with a super-mind with the capacity of having attitudes. Even if there were such a thing as a super-agent – called the people – it would lack a mind. Thus, sentences such as 'the belief of the people is …' or 'the intention of the people is …' are rather odd. They lack actual reference, since the 'people' does not have a mind in which beliefs, desires or intentions could be found.

The socio-ontological perspective renders it clear that constitution-making is usually a set of coordinated actions and speech acts carried out by several groups of individuals, and that it is successful if and only if certain subjective attitudes are present in relevant individuals belonging to those groups. In this sense, when we talk about a group of people doing something, we are in fact talking about its members individually contributing to bringing that something about. In a basic scenario of constitution-making at least two groups are present. I will call them: constitution-makers and the people.

The group of constitution-makers is the relatively small group of individuals that draft, and sometimes enact, a written constitution.[129] They are political proxy-agents of the people. Given that not all the individuals belonging to the people

[126] John Searle, *Making the Social World* (Oxford, 2010) 1 f.

[127] In 'Ontology of the Constituent Power' (2015) 22(2) *Constellations* 166, Hans Lindahl introduces a collective intentional view of the constituent power. His main claim is that the legal order 'can be best described' as an 'authoritative collective action'. However, his view is very different from the one that I endorse in this chapter.

[128] In: 'Three arenas of struggle: A contextual approach to the constituent power of "the people"' (2014) 3(2) *Global Constitutionalism* 200–35, Zoran Oklopcic undertakes a critical analysis of the political strategies – often manipulative – which can be associated with the exploitation of the belief on the existence of the people as a collective entity.

[129] There are cases in which the people enact the Constitution by means of a referendum or participate in drafting the constitutional text. On this latter phenomenon, see Carlos Bernal, 'How Constitutional Crowddrafting can enhance Legitimacy in Constitution-Making?' manuscript. For the following

can participate in drafting and enacting the Constitution – and that it might also be undesirable that they do it – they usually agree that some representatives draft and enact the Constitution in the name of the people. By means of this kind of proxy-agency the people act through the constitution-makers. In proxy agency, 'one person or subgroup's doing something *counts* as or *constitutes* or is *recognized* as (tantamount to) another person or group's doing something'.[130]

Kirk Ludwig outlined a model of proxy-agency in five steps that is helpful for the present purposes. It is possible to summarise Ludwig's model as follows. Let '*PA*' stand for a proxy agent, let '*G*' stand for a group that may include the proxy agent, and let '*A*' stand for an 'audience' (an individual or group with whom '*G*' is to potentially interact).[131]

The first step is recognising that proxy agency implies two agreements. On the one hand, the members of '*G*' agree with each other and with '*PA*' that '*PA*' will act on their behalf. On the other hand, the members of the audience '*A*' agree with the members of '*G*' to acknowledge that '*PA*' will act on behalf of the members of '*G*'.

The second step is noting that, because of these agreements, '*PA*' has a particular status-function as an agent authorised to act on behalf of the members of '*G*'.[132] A person has this status-function if it is generally accepted in the community as having the function of an authorised agent for certain social transactions.[133] Because of the agreement between the members of '*A*' and '*G*', '*PA*' is regarded as an authorised agent of the members of '*G*' with respect to '*A*'. This recognition enables '*PA*' to fulfil this function.

The third step is recognising that the members of '*G*' can confer on '*PA*' its status-function by means of following what in social-ontology is called: a constitutive rule. A constitutive rule constitutes a type of behaviour, in the sense that the rule defines the behaviour, and the behaviour occurs when the rule is intentionally followed.[134] For instance, a constitutive rule of chess creates the behaviour called 'checkmate'. Checkmate happens when a player intentionally puts the other player's king in check, and there is no way to remove the threat. In proxy-agency the relevant behaviour is empowering someone as a proxy agent. A constitutive rule defines empowering someone as a proxy agent as the action by means of which the agents of a group authorise an agent to act on their behalf. Following this rule, the members of '*G*' bring about the empowering of '*PA*' by authorising him as proxy agent. This authorisation implies the acceptance by the members of '*G*' that '*PA*' will act on their behalf, and that *PA's* action will be attributed to '*G*'.

reflections I will employ a model of constitution-making in which the people empower the constitution-makers to draft and enact the Constitution in their name.

[130] Kirk Ludwig, 'Proxy Agency in Collective Action' (2013) 31(1) *Noûs* 76.

[131] What follows is an adaptation of Ludwig's construction from ibid, 89–92.

[132] On the concept of status function, see: John Searle, *The Construction of Social Reality* (New York, Simon and Schuster, 1995) 41.

[133] Kirk Ludwig, 'Proxy Agency in Collective Action' (2013) 31(1) *Noûs* 77.

[134] ibid, 83, though see sections 3–4 for some qualifications with respect to the second clause.

The fourth step relates to the concept of constitutive agency. This concept subsumes certain individual actions by means of which an agent, following one or more constitutive rules, 'does something that both (a) contributes to instantiating a type of collective action by being partially constitutive of it and (b) is constitutive of a particular type of action that is a component of that collective action'.[135] In expressing his agreement with the appointment of '*PA*' as proxy agent, each of the members of '*G*' performs an individual action that contributes to instantiate a collective action (the empowerment of '*PA*' by '*G*') and is a component of it.

In the fifth step, '*PA*' performs his action *as* a proxy agent in relation to '*A*', and '*A*' and '*G*' for that reason both count what '*PA*' does as falling under a type that expresses the agency of the members of '*G*' and not just '*PA*'.

It is possible to employ Ludwig's five steps framework to understand the role of constitution-makers – such as a constituent assembly – as proxy agents of the people. In this instance, the five steps are the following. Let '*CA*' stand for a constituent assembly, let '*P*' stand for the people, a group that include the sub-group of the constituent assembly, and let '*A*' stand for an audience (both, the domestic audience: the people, and the international audience: other peoples, their governments, and international institutions).

Step one: The members of '*P*' agree with each other and with '*CA*' that '*CA*' will act on their behalf to make a constitution. This can be called the agreement on constitution-making representation. Naturally, it is too demanding to require in this step the agreement of all the members of '*P*'. I will return to this issue below. However, for now, let me use John Austin's concept of 'the bulk'[136] of the people for referring to the set of a relevant number of individuals whose agreement is necessary for empowering a group of constitutional-makers.

Step two: Because of these agreements, '*CA*' has the status of a constitution-maker for carrying out the function of entrenching constitutionalism in a written constitutional text as an authorised agent of '*P*'.

Step three: The bulk of '*P*' can confer on '*CA*' its status function as constitution-maker by means of each member of '*P*' following a constitutive rule. The content of the constitutive rule is the following: the agreement between the bulk of the members of '*P*' in empowering '*P*' to draft and enact the Constitution counts as '*P*' authorising '*CA*' to draft and enact the Constitution in the name of '*P*'.

Step four: Because of the authorisation by the bulk of the members of '*P*' that '*CA*' drafts and enacts the Constitution in the name of '*G*', '*CA*' is an agent of '*P*' for drafting and enacting the constitution.

Step five: '*CA*' drafts and enacts the Constitution as a proxy agent in relation to '*A*'. Thus, '*A*' and '*P*' count what '*CA*' does or has done as '*P*' having drafted and enacted its constitution.

[135] ibid, 85.

[136] John Austin, *The Province of Jurisprudence Determined* (Cambridge, Cambridge University Press, 1995) 169. Austin talks about the 'bulk of the members of the society' for referring to the population whose allegiance to the Sovereign is necessary for the validity of law.

The role of the political proxy-agents as constitution-makers is necessary in a mass society in which there is division of labour. From a normative point of view, it might also strengthen democratic participation – because it requires for the members of '*G*' to somehow express their agreement about the empowerment of '*CA*' –. It also enhances deliberative democracy. It encourages two levels of deliberation. Deliberation among the members of '*P*' about the content of the empowerment of '*CA*', and expert political discussions among the members of '*CA*' about the content of the Constitution to be drafted and enacted in the name of '*P*'.[137]

C. Deontic Powers

The third element of the socio-ontological conception of the constitution-making power endorsed here, is the concept of deontic powers. Concerning this concept, the people empower constitution-makers '*CM*', such as '*CA*', with the deontic power to draft and enact a constitution.

A deontic power is a structure of a power relationship.[138] The constitution-making deontic power is a structure in which the bulk of members of '*P*' confers authority to '*CM*' to change the constitution, and in doing so, to change the legal status of all the members of '*P*'. Given that the members of '*P*' are subject to the constitution, a constitutional change implies a change in their legal status. What is characteristic of the constitution-making empowerment is that the members of the bulk of '*P*' recognise the competence of '*CM*' to enact the Constitution and agree that all the members of '*P*' will be subject to that new or revised constitution, despite their actual or future desires about obeying the new constitutional norms.[139]

D. Limits

The people have conceptual and normative limits to empower constitution-makers and constitution-makers have conceptual and normative limits for exercising their deontic power. As explained above, the entrenchment of the four elements of constitutionalism is the core conceptual limit. According to the literature, there might be further normative limitations, usually connected to the procedural or substantial legitimacy of the new constitution. I cannot explore this issue further here. Nonetheless, these limitations may be drawn

[137] On the significance of expertise in deliberative democracy, see Mark B Brown, 'Expertise and Deliberative Democracy' in Stephen Elstub and Peter McLaverty, *Deliberative Democracy. Issues and Cases* (Edinburgh, Edinburgh University Press, 2014) 50, 66 and 67.

[138] John Searle, 'What is an Institution?' (2005) 1(1) *Journal of Institutional Economics* 11.

[139] This is a specific instance of the point of deontic powers, which is creating desire-independent reasons for actions. On this matter, see, ibid, 12.

from the respect to international human rights, the entrenchment of democratic institutions widespread across transnational law,[140] the degree of democratic participation in the constitution-making process, and the compliance with provisions regulating constitutional replacement,[141] eternity clauses, agreed constitutional principles, or supranational law.[142] The strength, scope and binding force of these limitations should be analysed with regards to each particular legal system and instance of constitutional replacement and revision.[143]

E. Collective Intentional Recognition

According to David Dyzenhaus, the concept of constituent power is subject to what he calls 'the paradox of authorship': 'for a people to act as author of the legal forms of constituted power, it must already exist as an author – an entity capable of authorising. But an entity capable of so authorising is an artificial entity, not just a random assemblage of individuals. Hence, it must itself be identifiable by legal forms'.[144]

This paradox refers to the concept of 'the people'. As explained above, the people cannot be conceived as a super-agent that is different from its members.[145] However, 'the people' is also different from a mob or a random group of individuals without any connection among them. The socio-ontological conception of the constitution-making power provides a way out of the paradox of the authorship by defining the people as a group, which empowers the constitution-makers for institutionalising constitutionalism in a written constitution.

Three questions arise here. Who are the members of '*P*'? The agreement of how many members of '*P*' is required for a successful empowerment of the constitution-makers? And what is the structure of the agreement of the members of '*P*' in empowering the constitution-makers?

Answering these questions implies taking a conceptual and a normative stand, whose appropriateness for assessing specific cases of constitutional replacement

[140] See Rosalind Dixon and David Landau, 'Transnational Constitutionalism and a Limited Doctrine of Unconstitutional Constitutional Amendment' (2015) 13(3) *International Journal of Constitutional Law* 630.

[141] Rosalind Dixon and David Landau, 'Constraining Constitutional Change' (2015) 50 *Wake Forest Law Review* 880.

[142] See Yaniv Roznai, 'The Theory and Practice of 'Supra-Constitutional' Limits on Constitutional-Amendments' (2013) 62(3) *International and Comparative Law Quarterly* 557–97.

[143] An open separate question is whether judges – usually constitutional courts – should be empowered to enforce these limitations. I cannot address this question here.

[144] David Dyzenhaus, 'Constitutionalism in an Old Key: Legality and Constituent Power' (2012) 1(2) *Global Constitutionalism* 229–60, at 233–34.

[145] Denis J Galligan seems to endorse a different view when he claims: 'By "the people" I mean the members of a society as a collective entity' […] the people 'as distinct from the notion of individual persons'. See 'The People, the Constitution, and the Idea of Representation' in Denis J Galligan and Mila Versteeg (eds), *Social and Political Foundations of Constitutions* (Cambridge, Cambridge University Press, 2013) 134.

or revision is also contextual. Nevertheless, it is possible to introduce some general conceptual claims about these questions. For instance, concerning the question: who are the members of '*P*'? A *prima facie* conceptual assumption is: the citizens. As Ackerman claimed, revolutions and constitutional replacement usually take place from a 'non-conventional adaptation' of an already existing institutional framework.[146] The fact that *all* citizens and *only* the citizens should be considered as members of '*P*' is a relevant fact of the institutional framework of every country. However, this *prima facie* assumption can be defeated by relevant normative contextual considerations. For instance, if the point of a constitutional replacement is to include into the political discussion a minority that has been denied the citizenship in the current institutional framework, this provides a good reason to include the members of that minority as members of '*P*' for the purpose of the constitution-making empowerment. Also, if secession is the point of a constitutional replacement, then it might be reasonable to confine '*P*' to the individuals of the region that will separate from the existing state.

Similar remarks should be made concerning the question about the number of members of '*P*' whose agreement is required for a successful empowerment of the constitution-makers. A *prima facie* conceptual assumption is that the agreement of the bulk of the citizens is required. A relevant conceptual and normative question is: What does the 'bulk' stand for? Certainly, Austin's concept of the bulk expresses a sound intuition, namely, that the validity of a constitution presupposes the allegiance of a significant number of the members of the society. A quality of the concept of 'the bulk' lies in its indeterminacy. In this respect, it is superior to the concept of the majority. There might be a constitution whose validity rests on the allegiance of a number of citizens that is less than the majority but is more politically powerful. Also, a constitution backed by the majority of the least influential citizens of a country could easily lose its validity. Moreover, within the bulk of the citizens, a successful empowerment of the constitution-makers usually requires the allegiance of the bulk of the legal officials, who will be in charge of implementing and enforcing the new constitution.[147]

The final question is: What is the structure of the agreement of the members of '*P*' in empowering the constitution-makers? Due to the varieties of forms of human collaboration and expression of agreement, allegiance or conformity, the answer to this question is highly complex. I will only state three claims here:

First, the agreement of the members of '*P*' in empowering the constitution-makers is a collective intentional action of the members of '*P*'. There are at least

[146] Bruce Ackerman, *We the People: Transformations* (Cambridge, Mass, Harvard University Press, vol 2, 2000) 11–13.

[147] On the importance of the agreement by the legal officials, see HLA Hart, *The Concept of Law* (Oxford, Clarendon Press, 1994) 116.

two necessary conditions that are common to the most emblematic accounts of collective intentional actions:[148] (1) the action must be performed by several individual agents acting together as a group. Because of that, the action can be attributed to the group; (2) individual agents acting together must act in accordance with, and because of, some appropriate we-intentions. We-intentions are intentions with a special content. Their content entails that the group performs the relevant action by means of the appropriate individual actions of its members.[149]

Secondly, in the case of constitution-making, members of '*P*' can bring about the collective empowerment of the constitution-makers by actions, such as voting in the election of an extra-constitutional constituent assembly or in a constitutional referendum, or participating in deliberations hosted by the constitution-makers about the content of the future constitution. Those are types of individual intentional actions contributing to the collective intentional action of '*P*'. The content of the we-intentions of the members of '*P*' that accompany those actions is that '*P*', as a group, agrees to the empowerment of the constitution-makers '*CM*' and to be subject to the Constitution that '*CM*' will draft and enact, if the new or revised constitution institutionalises constitutionalism. This subjection is accepted regardless of future actual desires of the members of '*P*' regarding obedience or allegiance to the new constitutional norms.

Thirdly, the agreement of the members of '*P*' concerning the constitution-making empowerment can be *ex-ante* – such as in the voting concerning the call for a constituent assembly – or *ex post* – like in voting to approve the constitutional text in a referendum. It might also be explicit – like in these two examples of actions *ex-ante* and *ex-post* – or implicit. Concerning the latter possibility, the validity of a constitution necessarily presupposes the *ex-post* implicit agreement by the bulk of the legal officials in implementing and enforcing the constitution. This is a necessary condition for a successful exercise of the constitution-making power.

To sum-up, the power to replace or revise a constitution is: (i) a limited deontic power to change the legal status of the members of the people; (ii) held by the constitution-makers; (iii) in virtue of – and limited by – an empowerment in which the bulk of the people appoint them as proxy agents for replacing or revising the constitution, and agree to subject to the new or revised constitution if it institutionalises the four essential constitutional elements; (iv) the proxy-agents are collectively intentionally recognised (ex-ante or ex-post, implicitly or explicitly, by the bulk of the people and the legal officials) as having the status of constitution-makers for performing the function of institutionalising constitutionalism.

[148] On these elements, and their relevance for the purpose of accounting for the nature of law, see Rodrigo Sanchez Brígido, 'Collective Intentional Activities and the Law' (2009) 29 *Oxford Journal of Legal Studies* 305–06.

[149] See, Kirk Ludwig, *Understanding Collective Action*, unpublished manuscript in file (2016) 168.

This conceptual structure can be used to achieve a more transparent assessment of the legitimacy of concrete constitutional replacements or revisions. Such an assessment will depend on the stronger or weaker standards that can be required concerning the number of the members of the people, the characteristics of the constitution-making empowerment and the collective intentional recognition of the constitution-makers, and the quality of the institutionalisation of constitutionalism.

2

Continuity and Change in Latin America: The Ever-Present Authoritarianism and the Democratic Capacities of the New Latin American Constitutions

FERNANDO JOSÉ GONÇALVES ACUNHA*

I. Introduction

Common knowledge portrays Latin American constitutionalism as a continuum of formal and informal detrimental changes to constitutional stability. Notwithstanding some facts that point in that direction, such representation does not fully grasp Latin America's complex constitutional history. Indeed, the development of constitutionalism in Latin American countries is characterised by a paradoxical combination of *continuity* (a perceived regularity in the organisation of societies that allowed a persistent concentration of powers) and *change* (mostly through modifications of provisions related to constitutional rights) that this chapter aims to explore in connection with recent constitutional novelties in the region and their potential implications to the young democracies of Bolivia and Ecuador.

The most known aspect of Latin American constitutionalism is the fairly regular structure of the polity widely perceived as authoritarian and anti-democratic,[1]

* Professor of Constitutional Law at Centro Universitário de Brasília (UniCEUB), Brasília, Brazil. PhD in Constitutional Law at University of Brasília (UnB), Brasília, Brazil. MsC at University of Brasília (UnB), Brasília, Brazil. Graduated from Federal University of Paraná (UFPR), Curitiba, Brazil. Email: fernandojgacunha@gmail.com. Acknowledgements: I would like to thank Professor Juliano Zaiden Benvindo, who was my PhD supervisor at University of Brasília (UnB). This work would not be possible without his help. I would also like to thank John J Liolos for reading and reviewing this chapter. His contribution greatly improved its final version.

[1] Various accounts of democracy stress that one of its most important characteristics is the possibility of alternation of power, exactly what centralised political systems aim to prevent. In that sense,

which pervades institutions (the 'constitutional machinery') throughout the region, commonly through an organisational arrangement that works in favour of strong Executives purporting to maintain power and help those in command retain their authority. The most common formula has been a powerful Presidency – what we shall call *hyper-presidentialism*[2] – conjoined with friendly Legislatures and Judiciaries. In order to promote such a centralised structure, many Latin American Constitutions have been prone to grant their Presidents a broad range of legislative capacities, budgetary competences, extensive emergency powers, long-term mandates and, recently, expanded possibilities of reelection.

These presidential powers either are not matched by correspondent checks or grant the Executive a large amount of influence over accountability institutions, leaving an open field for almost uncontrolled exercise of power.[3] This model of state has spread throughout the region in different countries (despite national peculiarities that cannot be overlooked).

From this perspective, for many years, the number one priority of political elites in Latin America was to prevent 'The People' – those considered 'unfit', like poor workers, women, black and indigenous people, among others – from claiming any real political participation. In order to assure the prevalence of this model, constant changes have been necessary: some institutions and even Bills of Rights have been continuously reformed, enlarged and reinterpreted; coups have occurred; and other institutional settings have been built with the goal of providing the means to cope with growing demands from lower levels of society. All of these changes have been designed without causing substantial modifications to the distribution of political and economic power. In other words, this particular 'rights-based' type of reform has been the golden formula to reassure continuity in power and to avoid reconfiguration of social roles and statuses.

The past two centuries witnessed plenty of such modifications. Even though the history of Latin America is not homogenous, it is correct to say that most countries have witnessed civilian and military coups often followed by populist governments and even some democratic periods. Many of those very different regimes have enacted, altered or reinterpreted Constitutions to promote their

see Samuel Issacharoff: 'Democracy is, first and foremost, the ability to contest established governmental authority and claim a mandate for a new ruling coalition, one that in turn will be subject to subsequent contestation by new rivals vying for the support of the electorate.' (Samuel Issacharoff, 'Constitutional Law and Consolidated Power' (2014) 62/3 *American Journal of Comparative Law* 18 https://ssrn.com/abstract=2438932, accessed 10 February 2018).

[2] See Roberto Gargarella, *Latin American Constitutionalism, 1810–2010: The Engine Room of the Constitution* (Oxford, 2013). Gargarella and others base their analyses on the critics to hyper-presidentialism in Latin America originally made by Carlos Santiago Nino, *Fundamentos de Derecho Constitucional: Análisis filosófico, jurídico y politológico de la práctica constitucional* (Astrea, 2013).

[3] Bolívar's thesis about the necessity of strong Executives exemplifies a political thinking that defined much of the constitutional design in Latin America. And Frank Safford mentions the idea of a 'Napoleonic State' as an extreme form of conservative centralisation. See Frank Safford, 'Política, Ideologia e Sociedade na América Espanhola do Pós-Independência in Leslie Bethell' (org), *História da América Latina: Da Independência a 1870*, vol III (EDUSP, 2014) 344.

leaders' agenda. It is important to note that those Constitutions have established a great variety of institutions and have been successful in the task of enlarging their citizens' rights. The drawback is that, with few exceptions, they have failed badly in changing the lives of their populations, precisely because most of the reforms have not been aimed at addressing inequality regarding the distribution of political and economic power.

The enactment of changes that do not substantially alter the distribution of power seem to continue in the twenty-first century and their prolonged effects may put in danger the future of constitutional projects that were born out of radical demands for transformation, like in Bolivia and Ecuador. These Constitutions (often deemed as examples of the 'new Latin American constitutionalism') bring new normative demands and present themselves as opportunities for the long-term disadvantaged majority of the population to take a real role in the political decisions of their societies.

Bolivian and Ecuadorian Constitutions, first and foremost, are lavish in granting new rights for the people, especially to those who have been historically neglected, like indigenous and black communities. The Bolivian Constitution is the first Latin American Constitution that offers a tentative alternative to the traditional structure of powers, inasmuch as it has been planned to empower local communities and historical indigenous nations that have long been marginalised. And the Ecuadorian Constitution is as innovative with respect to women's rights and to the new normative regulation of the Nature (*Pachamama*).

Nevertheless, both countries now face renewed authoritarian challenges that may jeopardise the intended transformation and full implementation of democracy. In Ecuador,[4] former President Correa took executive actions and continuously supported legislation and constitutional reforms to concentrate power; though President Lenín Moreno – who took the oath of office in May 2017 – is partially reversing this course,[5] a concentrated structure with a powerful Presidency

[4] Bartolomé Clavero points to the fact that the institutional arrangement that followed the enactment of the 2008 Ecuadorian Constitution was not consistent with the rights protected by the text. He also makes severe critics to the 'Bolivarian heritage' he thinks Ecuador is importing from Venezuela. See Bartolomé Clavero, 'Estado Plurinacional: Aproximação de um novo Paradigma Constitucional Americano' in César Augusto Baldi (coord), *Aprender desde o Sul: Novas Constitucionalidades, Pluralismo Jurídico e Plurinacionalidade Aprendendo desde o Sul* (Fórum, 2015) 111–31.

[5] For example, President Moreno convoked a referendum about the constitutional amendment on the presidential reelection that was held in February 2018. By a wide margin (around 65% of the votes), the Ecuadorian electorate revoked the possibility of indefinite reelections. See Francesco Manetto, 'Ecuador elimina la reelección indefinida y pone fin a la era Correa' *EL PAÍS*, https://elpais.com/internacional/2018/02/04/america/1517770527_944169.html accessed 18 January 2019. He also sent to Congress a draft bill to completely overhaul the Comunications Law, which was approved on 19 December 2018 and was being examined by the Executive at the time of writing. See 'Proyecto de reforma a la Ley de Comunicación al Ejecutivo', *EL UNIVERSO*, https://www.eluniverso.com/noticias/2018/12/20/nota/7105776/proyecto-reforma-ley-comunicacion-ejecutivo accessed 18 January 2019.

remains in place. For his part, Bolivian President Evo Morales insists on seeking a fourth consecutive mandate and was also taking steps to concentrate power.

These 'missteps' are understood as new episodes of a well-known threat, represented by *hyper-presidentialism* in its contemporary formula as a new expression of the ongoing force even in countries where factual conditions exist for some sort of real change.

In order to accomplish its purposes, in the first part, this chapter will examine the above-mentioned *continuity* through a general exposition of the *authoritarian Latin American structure based on a centralised presidential regime*, and through a description of the most common parameters that have guided constitutional changes and amendments, especially in the twentieth century.

In the second part, the origins and goals of the new Constitutions of Bolivia and Ecuador will be studied, emphasising some tools embedded in those constitutional texts as means to achieve a real transformation of their societies.

Thereafter, in the third part, this chapter will explore the renewed threats represented by the long-lasting Latin American authoritarianism in order to understand the stakes involved and the potential burden to modern constitutional design, which needs to resist tendencies of concentration of powers and give the transformative initiatives a chance of altering the institutional arrangements of Latin America.

A. The Authoritarian Structure of the Latin American Constitutionalism

In the forthcoming paragraphs, authoritarianism will be depicted as a *permanent force* that operates throughout Latin American political and constitutional landscapes and helps sustain its unequal balance of economic, political and social resources. Nonetheless, regional history cannot be simply understood as a homogeneous set of events blurring existing particularities of a continent so diverse.

Frank Safford[6] emphasises this point. For him, differences concerning ethnicity, geography, society and economy gave birth to experiences particular to each country, which advises us not to fuse unlike events as if they were the same.

Once the precaution is taken and the similarities are not exaggerated, it is possible to look for *some common regularities*. The past two centuries are prone in examples of institutional breakdowns in the region. Therefore, there was almost no Latin American country that did not pass through a coup, as well as a succession of Constitutions (adopted, modified or reinterpreted) to accommodate the interests of those in power. Likewise, Latin American Constitutions, especially after the innovative Mexican Constitution of 1917, have been eager to defy economic odds and obstacles in favour of granting large amounts of rights to their citizens

[6] Safford (n 3).

(they are known worldwide for their generosity in matters of rights, not evenly matched by their counterparts in more economically developed regions of the world), whereas they have not been fully as successful in the task of altering the lives of their citizens.

With this depiction, we want to emphasise the possibility of identifying some common features from Latin American political experiences, noting that *similarities* cannot be seen as historical blunders. In fact, there is a shared colonial past and similar independence fights[7] that have produced some analogous institutions and political practices from Mexico to Argentina. An example is widely illustrative: the presidential system of government with increased presidential powers[8] that prevails in the region.[9]

This is the aforementioned *hyper-presidentialism*, through which Latin American Constitutions have often adopted a model of separation of powers that is not effectively balanced, inasmuch as they have commonly given much more institutional leverage and political strength to the Executive relative to the Judiciary or the Legislative.[10] And it is important to realise that, even though there have been plenty of democratic breakdowns and coups in the past 200 years (partly responsible for economic turmoil[11]), it is possible to recast hyper-presidentialism as a *permanent force* deeply rooted in Latin American history.

A historical perspective is needed. The authoritarian arrangement lays its foundations in the early phase of Latin American independent life. Mauricio García Villegas and César A Rodríguez identify the origins of Latin American

[7] Besides Brazil, almost all Latin American countries were colonies of Spain and needed to wage a war in the beginning of the 19th century in order to free themselves from Spanish dominion.

[8] An analysis of Latin American presidentialism can be found in Héctor Fix-Fierro and Pedro Salazar-Ugarte, 'Presidentialism' in Michel Rosenfeld and András Sajó (ed), *The Oxford Handbook of Comparative Constitutional Law* (Oxford University Press, 2012) 628–49.

[9] Adam Przeworski and others researched several regimes in order to address the relationship among institutions, the economy and democracy. Their analysis of 135 countries showed that 50 were Presidentialist democracies; only 9 of them stayed outside the American continent. Accordingly, there were only 2 Parliamentarian experiences in America. See Adam Przeworski and others, 'O que Mantém as Democracias?' (1997) 40–41 *Lua Nova* 113.

[10] Recent literature emphasises that it is not possible to underline institutional design as the only (or even the most important) feature of a political system. Stephen Gardbaum stresses that government is at least as much influenced by the way electoral and party systems operate: 'Whatever the formal institutional arrangements on the separation or 'fusion' of executive and legislative powers – whether presidential, parliamentary, or semi-presidential – the way any constitutional system operates in terms of concentrating or dispersing political power is significantly a function of the party system in place and electoral outcomes at any given time. In other words, in addition to the branches of government, political parties are a key site of political competition and a central factor in the relative concentration or dispersal of power in all systems. They can not only fuse what a constitution's executive-legislative relations provisions separate, but also separate what they fuse. As a result, the same set of institutional relations can function quite differently in separation of powers terms depending on the party political and electoral context.' (Stephen Gardbaum, 'Voting Systems, and the Separation of Powers' (2017) 65 *American Journal of Comparative Law, Estados Unidos* 2 https://ssrn.com/abstract=2774419, accessed 31 January 2018.

[11] William Glade, 'A América Latina e a Economia Internacional' in Leslie Bethell (org), *História da América Latina: De 1870 a 1930*, vol IV (Geraldo Gerson de Souza tr, 1st edn 1st reprint, EDUSP, 2009) 20–82.

authoritarianism in Spanish conservativism mixed with a peculiar reading of the Illustration made by the regional elite during the Independence fight.[12] That was a time of conflict and disruptive successions in power of opposite groups (mainly liberals and conservatives, then fierce enemies[13]) that used the political apparatus to protect their own interests. Since that moment, Presidents have been conceived as centrepieces of the political structure, hardly matched or made accountable by equally independent public organs or powers.[14]

Succeeding periods in Latin American history presented different contexts; nevertheless, the role of the Executive and the centralisation of political power remained in place. During the second half of the nineteenth century – the period that saw the emergence of what Roberto Gargarella calls *fusion constitutionalism*,[15] when the repressive apparatus of the state was constantly used by the alliance between liberals and conservatives against groups that stayed outside the limited circle of political elites – the President continued to accumulate power to prevent a social revolt that could agitate the political sphere and hurt the economy. Later, when industrialisation gave birth to a new urban working class and other organised groups started fighting for political and economic equality, the right to vote and work, among others, restricted reforms allowed the elites to retain power while the 'social question' received a treatment designed only to provide rights to the people. Indeed, rights-based changes were enacted, but the political basis was almost entirely left untouched.

Afterwards, the crisis made inevitable the fallout of classical economic liberalism,[16] but nascent *social constitutionalism* and the various reforms adopted under its ideology did not alter the distribution of power as well. Since the end of World War II, different Latin American countries have been ruled by elected Presidents, dictators, populist leaders and so forth; though they have enacted

[12] See Mauricio García Villegas and César A Rodríguez, 'Derecho y sociedad en América Latina: propuesta para la consolidación de los estudios jurídicos críticos' in Mauricio García Villegas and César A Rodríguez (ed), *Derecho y Sociedad en América Latina: un debate sobre los estudios jurídicos críticos* (ILSA, 2003), 30–32.

[13] For Roberto Gargarella, there are three models of constitutionalism in Latin America: (a) *republicanism or radicalism* (whose main ideals are *political majoritarianism* and *moral populism*, both aimed to enable society to be governed by a democratic will based on majoritarian deliberation); (b) *conservatism* (centered on *political elitism* and *moral perfectionism*, by which society should not be governed by an enlarged and inclusive citizenry; instead, it should be guided by an enlightened elite, adopt religious values and adapt its practices accordingly); and (c) *liberalism* (based on *individual autonomy* that should bar the state from interfering in particular choices, like religion, while would also align itself with the position of a society not governed by all). Since of the end of the conflicts that popped up in the first decades of Latin American independent period, liberals and conservatives settled an unwritten but stable agreement aimed to prevent completely that radicals/republicans could exercise political power. See more at Gargarella (n 2) 7–17.

[14] For Safford (n 3) 344–46, the first decades after Independence were loaded with Constitutions committed to a model that assured Presidents several emergency powers.

[15] Gargarella (n 2) 32–33.

[16] A brief exposition can be found in Eric J Hobsbawm, *Era dos Extremos: O breve século XX (1914–1991)* (Marcos Santarrita tr, São Paulo, 2003).

hundreds or even thousands of constitutional changes that expanded their respective Bills of Rights or modified some institutional arrangements, the exclusionary design of the polity has been preserved, which is to say that the undemocratic feature of a centralised hyper-presidential system with few opportunities of effective participation or share of political power has continued to prevail.[17]

Part of the literature concerned with Latin American constitutional affairs emphasises that the reforms and amendments adopted throughout the region have always been pretty much centred on the *dogmatic part* of the Constitution, that is, the norms enacted to discipline constitutional rights and guaranties.[18] Bartolomé Clavero gives an example from the Ecuadorian Constitution of 2008: despite its radical affiliation and its transformational character, it has not been able to *make powers instruments of rights*;[19] in other words, for him, the Ecuadorian Constitution has not changed the distribution of power to attribute full efficacy to the new fundamental rights. The author also argues that state powers do not seem willing to cooperate in the implementation of these fundamental rights, since the latter could be used as tools to thwart powers invested in sitting public agents and officeholders.[20]

Such an outcome is in full display when legislation enacted in Ecuador until recently is examined. Most of the statutes and executive measures enacted by the administration of former President Rafael Correa happened to be aimed to concentrate public powers instead of implementing the constitutional mandate to share them. Once this development is understood alongside with the undemocratic composition of public organs – such as the Transparency and Social Control branch[21] – the problems that emerged from the concentration of powers can be figured out. We will return to this point.

[17] The paradoxical relation between *more presidential powers* and *more rights* is apprehended by Gargarella (n 2) 162 in the following terms: 'In sum, hyper-presidentialism is, according to our view, consistent with the creation and enforcement of new rights but at the same time consistent with the non-application and undermining of those rights. Moreover, we suggested that hyper-presidentialism tends to normally work against rights – particularly when the enforcement of certain rights contributes to the empowerment of social sectors that can challenge the authority of those in power.'

[18] This classification comes from Roberto Gargarella, whose theoretical hypothesis about two separate but interconnected parts of the Constitution is adopted here. For Gargarella (n 2) 132–39, the Constitution may be split between an *organic* and a *dogmatic* part. The organic part contains norms and dispositions responsible for the *structure of power and the State* (Constitution's *engine room*), while the dogmatic part is composed by norms and dispositions that regulate fundamental rights and guaranties.

[19] Clavero (n 4) 125–27.

[20] García Villegas and Rodríguez (n 12) 41–42 also stress that constant reforms that convert disputes not settled through the channels of political representation into judicial questions can be a political power, since they put the Judiciary in a central position and do not tackle the unbalance of political distribution in society.

[21] Catherine M Conaghan explains that this 'fifth power' represents an innovation of the new Constitution. The power to examine and approve presidential appointees to judicial and executive functions was stripped from the Legislative and attributed to this newly created public organ. The main reason of concern, in Conaghan's words, is that 'while autonomous in theory, the TSC is subject to elaborate procedures requiring the participation of representatives from various government entities; this gives the president significant influence in the TSC branch.' See more in Catherine M Conaghan, 'Ecuador: Rafael Correa and the Citizens' Revolution' in Steven Levitsky and Kenneth M Roberts (ed),

These institutional arrangements laid bare the relatively superficial (though not altogether irrelevant) impact of constitutional rights, when they are not complemented by a reconfiguration of power to buttress them.

The importance of the way power is allocated[22] (especially to preserve democracy from unilateral seizing) is described in the following terms by David Landau:

> This in turn suggests that an important goal of modern constitution-making should be to control unilateral or imposed exercises of power by particular groups or individuals. Experience across regions has shown that both strongmen and individual parties, unchecked by either institutions or other moments, will often take steps to consolidate their own power by weakening nascent democratic institutions. These steps are sometimes taken in the text of the constitution, where strongmen, for example, create strong presidencies, but as I show in the case of Venezuela, they are also often undertaken via more informal means linked to reconfigurations of political power that surround the political process. Further, attempts to unilaterally impose constitutions on unwilling oppositions may create a near breakdown or total breakdown of order, as I show in the example of Bolivia below.[23]

Most of the time, constitutional changes in Latin America have been inefficient to alter the distribution of power, partly due to the prolonged influence exerted by the most powerful political groups. The main consequence is that damages are not evenly distributed. Given the relative heavier weight of the organic part of the Constitution and its potential to shrink the scope and effectiveness of rights, what Latin American societies have been experiencing for many years is a permanent condition that has not been fundamentally altered by successive legal modifications. The conservative-liberal political project has maintained its grip on power, and, with it, the elitist character of our polities remains fundamentally unchanged.

The Resurgence of the Latin American Left (Johns Hopkins, 2011) 260–82. It is worth noting that the composition of the main organ of the TSC, the Council of Citizen Participation and Social Control (in Spanish, *Consejo de Participación Ciudadana y Control Social*) was also subject of a question in the referendum of February 2018, whereby 63% of the electorate voted to end the mandates of all incumbents of the *Consejo* (whose terms would end in 2020), which constituted another victory for President Lenín Moreno. Notwithstanding that, the TSC remains a highly controversial organ within the Ecuadorian government.

[22] Stephen Holmes, 'Superpresidentialism and its Problems' (1993) 2 *East European Constitutional Review* 123 seems to agree with this view in a work dedicated to *superpresidentialism* in Russia. In his words: 'Institutions can make a difference even if they do not make all of the difference. Fine-sounding rights and liberties, for instance, can be inscribed piously into a national charter. But Yeltsin's newly ratified constitution will actually protect individual rights better than Brezhnev's constitution only if it organizes the government in a self-limiting way. So without exaggerating the importance of institutional design, we have good reason to examine closely the sort of political system established by the new Russian Constitution.'

[23] David Landau, 'Constitution-Making Gone Wrong' (2012) 64/5 *Alabama Law Review* 923, 937 www.law.ua.edu/pubs/lrarticles/Volume%2064/Issue%205/1%20Landau%20923-980.pdf, accessed 27 December 2017.

B. New Constitutional Projects in Latin America: Origins and Objectives

Although the region has lived through the fairly stable pattern discussed above for most of its history, it has also achieved some degree of innovation. Since the 1980s, dozens of new Constitutions have replaced old systems in countries that freed themselves from dictatorships or elitist regimes. The question that emerges is this: do these developments represent any sign of real change?

Despite the many constitutional solutions adopted across the continent, this chapter is concerned with the more recent Constitutions of Ecuador and Bolivia, enacted in 2008 and 2009, oftentimes depicted by the literature as representatives of a broader movement, the 'new Latin American constitutionalism,'[24] which would be concerned with some fundamental goals. Two of these goals are to achieve:

a) a change in the material basis of the considered societies through a transformation of the socioeconomic reality of their populations; and
b) a democratic reconfiguration in the exercise of power and the production of law through changes in institutions that should open themselves to forms of participation by subordinated groups that have long stayed on the peripheries of the political system.

How would these objectives be achieved? How do the 'new Latin American constitutionalism' and the Constitutions moulded by its ideas propose to accomplish such a huge task?

An answer to these questions may start with an overview that takes into consideration some of the dispositions aimed to offer an appropriate solution to the social problems posed. Whereas that certainly does not represent the full story – since the *constitutional practice* is more valuable and richer than the *constitutional text* itself – it may bring some contributions to the argument that will be explored in the next section, which aims to highlight deviations and dangers to the full implementation of these Constitutions.

First, Catherine Walsh makes a point worth mentioning: the real innovation coming from these Constitutions are not the new institutions created, but instead 'a new logic and a new way of thinking under radically distinct parameters.'[25]

[24] There are disputes about the existence of something 'new' about these Constitutions. Defending the innovative character of these Constitutions, Joel Colón-Ríos writes that these Constitutions have some common features, like their highly participatory democratic processes, the inclusion promoted by their constituent bodies, the new set of economic relations created, and the enactment of long lists of fundamental rights (including collective rights and rights of nature). See in Joel Colón-Ríos, 'The Rights of Nature and the New Latin American Constitutionalism' (2015) 13 *New Zealand Journal of Public and International Law* 107, 108–9. For a distinct analysis, see Roberto Gargarella, *Too much 'Old' in the 'New' Latin American Constitutionalism* www.law.yale.edu/system/files/documents/pdf/SELA15_Gargarella_CV_Eng_20150512.pdf accessed 7 January 2018.

[25] Catherine Walsh, 'Carta do Equador é intercultural e pedagógica' *CONJUR* (César Augusto Baldi tr, Brazil, 27 June 2009) www.conjur.com.br/2009-jun-27/carta-equador-aspecto-interculturalizador-pedagogico accessed 20 January 2018 (free translation).

This means that it is more relevant to take the texts in their full extension and implement the transformation they propose than to analyse isolated parts that may not be all that innovative in comparison to the entire set of norms.

Regarding the Bolivian constitutional experience, it is possible to say that since the end of the 1990s popular movements formed by urban and rural workers, indigenous nations and other marginalised groups started to fight for a new order that could move the country towards a more inclusive social structure that could deal with the heterogeneity of the population.[26] Galvanised by their common resistance to neoliberal policies, mainly those concerning natural resources (the Water and Gas Wars of 2000 and 2003 were important driving factors), they achieved an electoral coalition that elected the country's first indigenous President in 2005, Evo Morales, the leader of leftist MAS (*Movimiento al Socialismo*).[27]

The forces that elected President Morales had always had as an objective the enactment of a new Constitution. For that reason, in 2006, the constitution-making process started, and it tried to mobilise the entire country (especially those who historically had been left behind) around a new project with an aspiration to empower the whole society.

Since the beginning of the project, the succession of events that led to the 2009 Constitution was a long and tortuous one, which almost gridlocked the political system when political parties seemed to disrupt procedures that were taking place in Sucre. That is the reason why the first draft approved by the Constituent Assembly was immediately rejected and denounced by the opposition, which demanded comprehensive modifications to agree to a vote. Segregationist threats emerged in the half-moon part of the country (the *Departamentos* that constitute its Eastern part – Pando, Bandi, Santa Cruz and Tarija – were politically aligned with the opposition) and a divided political context made urgent that the text approved by the Assembly was amended before it was subjected to a popular referendum.

[26] According to data from Instituto Nacional de Estadística, *Bolivia: Características de Poblacións y Vivienda: Censo de Población y Vivienda 2012* (2012) www.bivica.org/upload/censo-resultados.pdf, accessed 30 January 2018, in 2012, there were 6,916,732 people at ages 15 years or more in Bolivia, of which 2,806,592 belonged to indigenous nations or were African-Bolivian. The rest of the population was constituted of white people, various kinds of *mestizos* (much speaking indigenous languages) and other ethnic groups. Despite the fact that the indigenous nations comprise a large portion of the Bolivian population, history demonstrates that they never had proportional leverage in political and economic affairs.

[27] An explanation about the political process that led President Morales to power can be found in Raúl Madrid, 'Bolivia: Origins and Policies of the Movimiento al Socialismo', in Steven Levitsky and Kenneth M Roberts (ed), *The Resurgence of the Latin American Left* (Johns Hopkins, 2011) 239–59. A detailed account can be found in Gladstone Leonel Junior, *O Novo Constitucionalismo Latino-Americano: um estudo sobre a Bolívia* (Lumen Juris, 2015) and Pedro Brandão, *O Novo Constitucionalismo Pluralista Latino-Americano* (Lumen Juris, 2015). From a different perspective, see also Landau (n 23) 949–58.

In the end, more than 140 articles were altered, and the final text was approved by more than 60 per cent of the electorate. The Constitution took effect in January 2009.[28]

Meanwhile, Ecuador – also an ethnically complex country, with a mixed population formed by indigenous peoples, African-Ecuadorians, European descendants and many kinds of *mestizos*[29] – had its own turbulences to deal with. Focusing on the period immediately prior to the new Constitution, the last two decades of the twentieth century – especially since the administration of President León Febres Cordero – were marked by unstable governments and the implementation of neoliberal measures. Even the Constitution of 1998, already enacted under pressure from the indigenous movement, was considered right-wing in economic matters, despite being at the same time an important tool to advance an agenda of equality and recognition in matters of gender and ethnic affairs.[30]

The Constitution of 1998 had a short life. Six Presidents came to power during the 10 years that followed the deposition of President Abdala Bucaram in 1997 until the election of Rafael Correa in 2006 – the leader of leftist *Movimiento Alianza PAIS* (*Patria Altiva i Soberana*) – who immediately convoked a referendum to

[28] Distinct perspectives about this process can be extracted from Landau (n 23) and Leonel Junior (n 27). The former says that a compromise between MAS and the opposition concerning the constitutional text prior to its ratification was important to calm the country. See Landau (n 23) 958: 'Once the agreement occurred, however, it appears to have had a calming effect. Politically, the agreement helped to unify the country and to reduce regional tensions. Morales, for example, won a far higher percentage of the vote in the half-moon region in 2009 than he had initially in 2005. Moreover, the process appears to have taught Morales and his supporters a considerable amount about governing – the tortured process of getting the new constitution approved helped MAS evolve from a radical opposition movement that was accustomed to protesting on the streets to a more reformist movement that was willing to cut meaningful deals with the opposition'. On the other hand, the latter, relying on the opinion of authors like Boaventura de Sousa Santos, believes that the agreement was essentially a loss to the revolution that lied in the core of the constitutional process. Leonel Junior (n 27) 113–14 (free translation) says that 'the version of the constitutional text that had been produced in Oruro was much more advanced in terms of rights and structural changes', reason why 'the agreement settled in Cochabamba, which added [to the new constitutional text] points defended by the opposition, may be seen as a delegitimizing element'.

[29] According to the available data from Instituto Nacional de Estadísticas y Censos, *Resultados del Censo 2010* (2010), www.ecuadorencifras.gob.ec/resultados/ accessed 30 January 2018, 71.9% of the Ecuadorian population was formed by *mestizos*, 7.4% are *montubios*, 7.2% are African-Ecuadorians, 7.0% are indigenous, 6.1% are whites and 0.4% is classified as 'others'. In a way similar to what happened elsewhere in the region, though profoundly diverse, the largest part of Ecuadorian population has never truly exercised power.

[30] Enrique Ayala Mora says that different Presidents bowed to the formula conceived by the IMF and the Reagan administration of a reduced role of government in economy, privatisations and cuts in welfare programs. This hatched the resistance from certain groups, mainly the indigenous population, since the beginning of the 1990s, which also explains the contradictory character of the 1998 Constitution. See at Enrique Ayala Mora, 'Equador, 1930 – c. 1990' in Leslie Bethell (org), *História da América Latina: A América Latina após 1930: México, América Central, Caribe e Repúblicas Andinas*, vol IX (Geraldo Gerson de Souza tr, EDUSP, 2015) 529–83. Similarly, Raquel Yrigoyen Fajardo depicts the Constitution of 1998 as an example of the *second cycle of the pluralist constitutional horizon*, based on a pluricultural (not yet *plurinational*) paradigm, and designed to mix its cultural background with a neoliberal economic origin.

obtain popular support for a new Constitution.[31] The referendum occurred on 15 April 2007, and 81.72 per cent of the electorate approved the proposal.

The text was drafted with great governmental support (*Alianza PAIS* had 80 of the 130 constituents) and was subject to a new referendum, which took place on 28 September 2008. The Constitution was approved by 63.93 per cent of the electorate.

Both Constitutions are contemporary, and both are conceived out of a new theoretical basis established by a *plurinational paradigm*. It is important to take a closer look at them in order to fully apprehend the change they (intend to) represent.

There are mixed opinions about the Constitutions. There is widespread consensus that they are innovative compared to prior Bolivian and Ecuadorian Constitutions. Some of them are regarded as much desired developments (eg, concerning indigenous and collective rights); others are understood as tools to concentrate political power in the hands of their presidents. Most of the advances are concentrated on a pure normative element, and the perceived drawbacks come mostly from practical and political aspects.

Starting with the norms and dealing with the well-regarded dispositions of these different Constitutions,[32] it is possible to notice that they do not seem to embrace the old formula of a *single nation* with a *single culture* as the core of a centralised State. Article One of the Bolivian Constitution declares that Bolivia is a *Plurinational State* whose fundamentals lie on an *intercultural basis* expressed through ideas of political and juridical *pluralism*, and Article One of the Ecuadorian Constitution also embraces the principle of *plurinationality*.

These dispositions aim to sustain a fundamental principle that pervades the Constitutions. In the Bolivian case, that comes along with the norms that regulate Legislative and Judicial powers (both with a *plurinational* proportional representation, as can be seen in Articles 147 and 197) and goes through to the norms that discipline a deliberative democracy that intends to fuse elements of the cultures involved (an example is the disposition of Article 11, Section II, that organises the democratic procedures officially recognised by the Constitution). The Ecuadorian Constitution has a norm that establishes a territorial autonomy based on plurinationality (Article 257), among others.

[31] A detailed account about the election of Correa is presented in Conaghan (n 21).

[32] They offer different approaches in many subjects. For example, the Bolivian Constitution emphasises its *plurinational* character, since the Constitution of Ecuador, per Walsh (n 25), has a stronger focus on norms that could ensure an intercultural exchange among several different populations, and does not put much weight on the plurinational reformulation. In order to exemplify these limitations, as long as the Bolivian Constitution guarantees a proportional indigenous representation in the Constitutional Court or in the Legislative Assembly, the Ecuadorian Constitution does not have a similar disposition. However, it is important to notice that the Ecuadorian text has many other advanced provisions even in comparison to the Bolivian Constitution in regard to women's rights, African-Ecuadorians and so forth.

The impact of *pluralism* and *plurinationality* constitute the unique character of those Constitutions. Raquel Yrigoyen Fajardo writes that there are examples of Constitutions that used to accept the importance of *multi-* and *pluriculturalism* (like the Brazilian Constitution of 1988, as well as several Latin American Constitutions of the 1990s) in a limited way, since they do not completely break the unified character of a national law based on Western constructions, like the single-nation axiom, the anthropocentric paradigm, the centrality of forms of codified and written law and so forth. Nevertheless, she stresses that the Bolivian Constitution of 2009, as well as the Ecuadorian Constitution of 2008, represent a new era – *the third cycle of the pluralist constitutional horizon* – whose main character would precisely be the importance given to the recognition that their populations are comprised of diverse peoples, with unambiguous histories and traditions (in other words, diverse *nations*), and that *all* those cultures should be equally considered.[33]

That assumption emphasises the notion that the state shall be (re)founded out of a *plurinational basis*, and that alternative forms of jurisdictional adjudication (based on oral traditions and forms of intercultural dialogue) must be regarded as equally binding law.[34] Antonio Carlos Wolkmer writes that the pluralistic view of law (or juridical pluralism) acknowledges the intrinsic value of principles as *diversity* and *difference*, inasmuch as its theory works with 'the existence of more than one single reality, of multiple forms of practical action and of the diversity of social and cultural fields with their own particularities, which means that it comprises the set of autonomous phenomena and heterogeneous elements that do not fuse into each other'.[35]

There are other innovations as well, regarding elements as diverse as the *good way of living* (*vivir bien*, or *suma qamaña*) or the *harmonious way of living* (*vida armoniosa*, or *ñandereko*) in Article 8 of the Bolivian Constitution; or the whole chapter (Chapter Seventh, Title Second, Articles 71 to 74) dedicated to regulating the rights of the *Nature* (*Pacha Mama*) in the Ecuadorian Constitution. For Joel Colón-Ríos, the innovations regarding the environment are so important that he

[33] See more at Raquel Yrigoyen Fajardo, 'Pluralismo Jurídico y Jurisdicción Indígena en el Horizonte del Constitucionalismo Pluralista' in César Augusto Baldi (coord), *Aprender desde o Sul: Novas Constitucionalidades, Pluralismo Jurídico e Plurinacionalidade Aprendendo desde o Sul* (Fórum, 2015) 35–57.

[34] There is also a substantive difference between Bolivia and Ecuador in this point, since the former embraced a new vision that breaks away with a subordinated form of pluralism (through which traditional European-based law would have the final word in contradictions with indigenous law), a task not fulfilled by the Ecuadorian Constitution, whose Article 171 still limits the range of indigenous law and sacrifices it whether it is considered contrary to the Constitution or international human rights. Similarly, the Ecuadorian Constitution does not impose proportional composition of the Constitutional Court. See more at Brandão (n 27) 199–201.

[35] Antonio Carlos Wolkmer, 'Constitucionalismo e Pluralismo na Trajetória do Direito Brasileiro' in César Augusto Baldi (coord), *Aprender desde o Sul: Novas Constitucionalidades, Pluralismo Jurídico e Plurinacionalidade Aprendendo desde o Sul* (Fórum, 2015) 254 (free translation). The author enlists six principles that would guide a pluralistic theory: (a) autonomy, (b) decentralisation, (c) participation, (d) localism, (e) diversity, and (f) tolerance.

argues that these Constitutions recognise as legitimate democracies only those that respect nature.[36]

It is undeniable that these Constitutions have innovative provisions. Their attempt to address historical issues must be praised. The problem worth considering from now on stands on the practice that surrounds them to comprehend the challenges that they must face.

C. Authoritarianism and Threats to the New Constitutions

The new Constitutions of Bolivia and Ecuador must cope with their contradictions. Although they aim at a social transformation and offer some tools to achieve it, it is also evident that they walk on the verge of authoritarianism.

David Landau notices some similarities in recent Constituent Assemblies that took place in regions as diverse as Latin America, the Middle East and Eastern Europe. These assemblies, the argument goes, are often driven by short-term interests that may compromise the entire constitutional system.[37] The author focuses specifically onto the Venezuelan constitutional process and showcases it as an illustration of the negative outcomes that can be produced once pluralism and long-term national interests are not taken as central concerns by those in charge of making the Constitution.

Another shortcoming is that countries that contemporarily need to enact Constitutions often have limitations that stem from the absence of strong institutions.[38] These institutions could act as counterweights to prevent the

[36] Colón-Ríos (n 24) 109–10.

[37] This is the vision he offers about which should be the main objectives of a constituent process: 'The design of constitutional politics must often be aimed at avoiding these worst-case scenarios rather than in reaching best-case outcomes. In these cases, the central question in our theories of constitution-making is not how do we achieve a truly deliberative constitutional process so as to achieve a first-best, transformative outcome? It is instead: how do we manage to reach a second-best in lieu of the two worst-case scenarios outlined above? This second-best outcome is likely to be some variant of competitive democracy; a constitution written under such conditions is unlikely to be transformative in the South African sense, but it will at least avoid either a breakdown of order or an authoritarian or quasi-authoritarian regime.' (Landau (n 23) 936).

[38] Though we do not fully agree with the thesis, it is important to notice that Douglass North explains differences in economic development in part due to the divergent institutional landscapes that can be seen in the US and in Latin America. In his words, '[t]he divergent paths established by England and Spain in the New World have not converged despite the mediating factors of common ideological influences. In the former, an institutional framework has evolved that permits complex impersonal exchange necessary to political stability as well as to capture the potential economic benefits of modern technology. In the latter, "personalistic" relationships are still the key to much of the political and economic exchange. They are the consequence of an evolving institutional framework that has produced erratic economic growth in Latin America, but neither political nor economic stability, nor realization of the potential of modern technology.' Douglass North, 'Institutions' (1991) 5/1 *The Journal of Economic Perspectives* 97 www.jstor.org/stable/1942704 accessed 20 December 2017. On the other hand, there are notable contemporary works that intend to lower the weight attributed to institutions for a functioning

usurpation of power promoted by strong leaders that temporarily enjoy great public acceptance and are willing to use it as a way to accumulate as much power as possible.

Unfortunately, this is not a problem that only affects regimes that are blatantly authoritarian or evidently elitist, as there is a growing number of originally popular regimes that veer into some form of authoritarianism.[39] The legitimation of authoritarian projects by democratic credentials is part of a tactic called *stealth authoritarianism* (a nuanced form of domination that does not embrace an openly autocratic way of governing).[40]

Plenty of similar tools have been used in Latin America, as discussed in the studies conducted by Santiago Basabe-Serrano and Catherine M. Conaghan (Ecuador), or Gretchen Helmke and Steven Levitsky,[41] or David Landau (Venezuela). Unfortunately, this problem is partly the reality in Ecuador and Bolivia, where powerful Presidents concentrate enormous amount of influence

democracy. See Adam Przeworski, 'Institutions Matter?' (2004) *Government and Opposition* 527 www.politics.as.nyu.edu/docs/IO/2800/go_2004.pdf accessed 3 January 2018.

[39] See at Ozan O Varol, 'Stealth Authoritarianism' (2014–15) 100 *Iowa Law Review* 1673 https://ilr.law.uiowa.edu/print/volume-100-issue-4/stealth-authoritarianism accessed 28 December 2017. David Landau means something resembling when he uses the expression *abusive constitutionalism* (a form of uncontrolled Constitution-making power that could impend democracy and pluralism). See David Landau, 'Abusive Constitutionalism' (2013) 47/1 *UC Davis Law Review* 189 http://lawreview.law.ucdavis.edu/issues/47/1/Articles/47-1_Landau.pdf accessed 27 December 2017. Unmistakably, this kind of misleading has historical roots. Edmund Morgan writes about the origin of the principle of *sovereignty of the people* – which replaced the *divine right of the kings* as the foundation for the legitimate exercise of power in the Anglo-American tradition – and explains how the *will of the people* was used by an absolute regime as a source of legitimacy. For Morgan, the *sovereignty of the people* would be another *fiction* – an invention crafted to deceive – that would allow *the few govern over the many*. See more at Edmund Morgan, *Inventing the People* (WW Norton & Company, 1988).

[40] Varol (n 39) 1679: 'For example, instead of jailing journalists or shutting down media outlets, incumbent politicians sue them for libel, which raises the costs of critical commentary. Rather than imprisoning political opponents without due process, they prosecute them for violations of the existing criminal laws. They employ seemingly legitimate and neutral electoral laws, frequently enacted for the purported purpose of eliminating electoral fraud or promoting political stability, to create systematic advantages for themselves and raise the costs to the opposition of dethroning them. Often with the backing of international organizations, they adopt surveillance laws and institutions with the purported purpose of combatting organized crime and terrorism, but use those laws to blackmail or discredit political opponents. They rely on judicial review, not as a check on their power, but to consolidate power. To shape perceptions and deflect attention from anti-democratic practices, they frequently enact democratic reforms and invoke rule-of-law rhetoric. These practices permit the incumbents to retain their seats even in the face of changing political preferences by the electorate. That, in turn, undermines a core component of democracy: competitive, multi-party elections and the resulting alternation in government power.'

[41] Gretchen Helmke and Steven Levitsky, 'Informal Institutions and Comparative Politics: A Research Agenda' (2003) *Working Paper* 307 www3.nd.edu/~kellogg/publications/workingpapers/WPS/307.pdf accessed 25 December 2017, 5, 6 write about the domination by the President over the Supreme Court in Argentina in the following terms: 'Judicial Politics. In the realm of judicial politics, Helmke's study of executive-court relations in Argentina found that notwithstanding constitutional guarantees of tenure security and judicial independence, Supreme Court justices responded with greater regularity to an informal institution of tenure insecurity, according to which incoming (democratic and non-democratic) governments were widely expected to stack the court. The result was a pattern of judicial behavior that departed significantly from that stipulated by the formal rules.'

all over the political spectrum, with the help of their new Constitutions,[42] threatening the innovative measures proposed by the reforms aforementioned.

In Ecuador, President Lenín Moreno parted ways with former President Rafael Correa soon after he took the oath of office in May 2017. He adopted measures that partially reversed the politics of his predecessor (the most pronounced one being the referendum[43] that reverted the authorisation to indefinite reelections), apparently abiding by some basic features of constitutionalism. Nevertheless, many authors denounce the risks still posed to the new Constitution by hyper-presidentialism in Ecuador (irrespective of incumbency),[44] which seems to try to make an expansion of presidential powers compatible with an increase in terms of rights attributed to its citizenry. This is possible because the 2008 Constitution did not reassess the country's organic structure to restrain the President's capacities; actually, notwithstanding a few limitations – such as the power of the National Assembly to convoke an anticipated election for both Executive and Legislative[45] (Article 130, Item 2), or a recall of mandates by the population (Article 61, Item 6, and Article 105), etc – it did the opposite, as long as the President was awarded with enormous powers, not evenly matched by the scarce limitations whatsoever.[46]

[42] For Clavero (n 4) 129 there would be a *continuum* from the Venezuelan Constitution to Bolivian and Ecuadorian ones, markedly by an exacerbation of presidentialism, which would be apparently paradoxical to their projects of plurinational States. This hyper-presidentialism is a challenge that must be properly addressed by these Constitutions, according to the author.

[43] It is worth noting that the referendum was convoked in clear defiance to the Judiciary. A more detailed explanation of recent events in Ecuador can be found at Mauricio Guim & Augusto Verduga, 'Is Ecuador Heading Towards a Constitutional Crisis', *Int'l J Const. L Blog* 1 November 2017, at: www.iconnectblog.com/2017/11/is-ecuador-heading-towards-a-constitutional-crisis/, and Mauricio Guim & Augusto Verduga, 'Ecuador's "Unstoppable" Constitutional Referendum', *Int'l J. Const. L. Blog*, 16 December 2017 at: www.iconnectblog.com/2017/12/ecuadors-unstoppable-constitutional-referendum, accessed 2 January 2018.

[44] Gargarella (n 2) 245 testifies about a personal experience. Endnote no 4 of ch 9 of his book tells us that he had been invited, during the work of the Constitutional Assembly, 'to lecture about the citizens' rights of participation in light of the many reforms that had been put forward during the convention.' He mentions that he had alerted the constituents that, in order to effectively promote the participation, they should 'act in a way different from what they have done; that is, they should have first reformed the organic part of the Constitution, in which the bases of powers were established and which reaffirmed the traditional hyper-presidential character of the Ecuadorian political system.' He indicates that that was not the pathway followed by the constituents, which led to current problems.

[45] The President has a similar right enshrined in Article 148 of the Constitution. Gargarella (n 2) 245 (endnote 3) also stresses the burdens imposed on the Assembly to use this tool, saying that 'the *sudden death* escape clause can only be used once; it is a dramatic extreme, requiring an enormous percentage of votes (two-thirds of the Assembly members), and it involves the "death" of the posts of its own promoters.'

[46] Conaghan (n 21) adds another point: President Correa gave little importance to popular participation and acted in a way that openly contradicted the Constitution. According to Conaghan (n 21) 275, 'Correa's stiff resistance to what he often refers to as the "infantile left" (encompassing indigenous, environmental, and gender rights groups) reveals an important tension in the Citizens' Revolution. Correa led the country to embrace a constitution enshrining citizen participation and multitudinous rights for every imaginable group in society. Nonetheless, in the course of policy conflicts, the government has balked when groups demand active participation. Through its Secretaria de Pueblos, Movimientos Sociales y Participación Ciudadana, the government opted for a top-down approach aimed at co-opting

A notorious example of the scope of the President's authority is his power to veto laws approved by the National Assembly, as disciplined by Article 138 of the Constitution. Under this provision, the President has the ability to veto a whole draft, in which case the Assembly can only propose the measure again after one year, and it will only prevail if the presidential veto is overturned by a two-thirds majority. In a partial veto, the President himself can propose his own version for the law, in which situation the National Assembly has two options: it can either agree with the President (by a single majority), or it can disagree with him (once more, by a two-thirds majority). Moreover, if the National Assembly does not take a vote in 30 days, the President's opinion becomes stable, and his draft (in case of a partial veto) is signed into law.

Using his powers, former President Rafael Correa partially vetoed the Law of Citizen Participation (*Ley de Participacion Ciudadana*) and approved other measures aimed to restrict constitutional clauses of democratisation.[47]

A brief synthesis of the stakes involved in the Ecuadorian situation – with special emphasis on the troubles brought about by the concentration of powers in the hands of the President to the many advances regarding the rights of indigenous nations – is in a text of Bartolomé Clavero, in the following terms:

> The Ecuadorian Constitution does not stand behind the Venezuelan one, since it really exacerbates presidentialism. The relations between Legislative and Executive functions are unbalanced to a point in which the decision that may be taken by the President can prevail over an agreement settled by the National Assembly even in legislative matters. Furthermore, there are ways of civic participation that demand a prior action by the President of the Republic. Regarding to the plurinationality, it relates to decision-making processes on behalf of the nation identified with the State, postponing the nations composed by indigenous peoples. It not only does not help articulate national diversity, but it can also easily contribute to its de-structuration. For example, Ecuadorians women and men – which means, the female and male citizens with no specific mention to their nations – have the right to be consulted (article 61.4). This consultation, in general terms, means only a proposition to the Presidency (articles 104 and 147.14). It ignores the specific indigenous right to be consulted, apparently intending to subsume the latter in the former, aiming at a constitutional semblance.

grassroots organisations and marginalising those that dared to defy the president's agenda. Alberto Acosta, one of the original architects of PAIS, openly broke ranks with Correa over the absence of "citizens" in the revolution when the president insisted on abbreviating consultations with social movements during the drafting of the new constitution.'

[47] One of them is the Communications Law, that severely restricted the capacity of media outlets to criticise the president. President Moreno is vying to undo many provisions of this law, as can be seen in the project aimed to overhaul the Communications Law that recently passed Congress (n 5). Reflecting about problems of democracy within the Constitution, Agustín Grijalva, 'Principales innovaciones en la Constitución de Ecuador de 2008' in César Augusto (coord), *Aprender desde o Sul: Novas Constitucionalidades, Pluralismo Jurídico e Plurinacionalidade Aprendendo desde o Sul* (Fórum, 2015) 133–40 writes that the full implementation of the model thought of by the Constitution could only been correctly evaluated after the approval of norms required by the text and an ensuing analysis of following practices in terms of politics, policy, law and institutions.

> What matters here is not that the current Ecuadorian President may be prone to use it in an anti-plurinational way, but that the Constitution has been projected in such a manner that allows it to happen.[48]

Bolivia also flirts with danger. For example, there are some similarities with the Ecuadorian case as regards to the approval of economic projects in confrontation with indigenous rights of consultation (the *TIPNIS* case is the most well-known in this respect and opposed the Morales administration and some indigenous groups over road construction), something that is partially eroding popular support for the President.

In the political sphere, President Morales proposed a referendum aimed to change the constitutional norm that prohibits the President to seek a second consecutive reelection, which would have given him the possibility to run for the fourth time (he has held office since 2006 and is now on his third term, the second under the current Constitution). Although Morales's proposal was defeated by a thin margin (51.3 per cent to 48.7 per cent), in December of 2016 he accepted a new nomination handed to him by the Congress of the MAS to become the party's candidate in the 2019 election. He also managed to obtain, on 28 November 2017, a judicial decision issued by the Plurinational Constitutional Court (*Tribunal Constitucional Plurinacional*) that declared the constitutional norms that prohibited a new reelection for him not applicable, because limiting the possibility of reelections would violate candidates' fundamental rights and the American Convention on Human Rights.[49] On 4 December 2018, the Supreme Electoral Court of Bolivia accepted President Morales' candidacy and allowed him and Vice-President Alvaro Garcia Linera to take part of the primaries that would be held in January 2019.[50]

The very idea of a sitting President remaining in power for 15 or 20 years, regardless of his normative credentials or his intentions, only emphasises the dangers inherent in the concentration of powers, especially so in places where democracy is so young and still unstable.[51] It also shows that new Constitutions, despite their popular origin, their advanced formulas and their innovative rights, still face a huge challenge to address long-lasting political inequality and centralisation of powers.

[48] Free translation.

[49] The decision is assessed in further detail at Sergio Verdugo, 'How the Bolivian Constitutional Court Helped the Morales Regime to Break the Political Insurance of the Bolivian Constitution', *Int'l J. Const. L. Blog*, 10 December 2017, at: www.iconnectblog.com/2017/12/how-the-bolivian-constitutional-court-helped-the-morales-regime-to-break-the-political-insurance-of-the-bolivian-constitution/ accessed on 2 January 2018.

[50] See 'Evo Morales: El Tribunal Electoral de Bolivia lo habilita como candidato presidencial tras haber perdido reréndum por la reelección' *BBC*: www.bbc.com/mundo/noticias-america-latina-46450251 accessed 18 January 2019.

[51] Landau (n 23) reaches similar conclusions in his analysis about a similar move attempted in Colombia in the past decade, through which President Álvaro Uribe wanted to run for a third term.

II. Conclusion

This chapter explored some of the constitutional challenges currently facing Latin America, many of them coming from the exclusionary tradition that comprises Latin American constitutionalism and neglects huge portions of the citizenry in political and economic affairs.

Ecuador and Bolivia tried to address part of those concerns through innovative constitutional proposals. They brought about new rights, proposed new formulas of participation (mainly in the Bolivian case), broke with the single nation axiom, embraced juridical pluralism, showed a renewed respect for the nature and intended to empower the excluded. These new propositions of rights and institutions must be praised as steps in the right direction.

Nevertheless, there is a long path to travel before the possibilities embedded in the new Constitutions are fully implemented. They are still heirs of the *hyper-presidential* tradition of the region's constitutionalism, enshrining a powerful Presidency and advancing little in terms of democratic relations in their societies. The enunciation of revolutionary intentions becomes an empty statement if it is not complemented by institutions that effectively grant the people real leverage in political, economic and social issues.

The work of advancing the democratic capacities of these Constitutions is unfinished. New powers related to democratic deliberation, new forms of political representation and new ways to exercise democracy on a daily basis are needed. It is unconceivable that *plurinational* projects supposed to end centuries of exclusion still grant unmatched lists of prerogatives to their President without correspondent levers to the people.

We think these cases confirm the thesis outlined in the first section of this chapter. There is a strong *continuity* in Latin American constitutionalism, represented by the central place occupied by the Executive in our political systems. This feature needs to be understood if our systems are to work in a democratic way and allow Latin American populations to effectively engage in political decisions. We think that the first steps have already been taken, since the new Constitutions have plenty of innovative norms with potential to advance the aspirations of proportional representation (in the Bolivian case), fundamental rights, cultural background and juridical pluralism, among others. It is time, now, to mould the reality out of the possibilities these norms allow.

3

Constitutional Moments and Constitutional Thresholds in Brazil: Mass Protests and the 'Performative Meaning' of Constitutionalism

JULIANO ZAIDEN BENVINDO*

I. Introduction

In June 2013, Brazil was faced with an interesting but intriguing phenomenon. During the FIFA Confederations Cup that June, more than one million people thronged the streets of many cities all over the country with a wide variety of grievances and agendas.[1] Mass protests became suddenly a routine without any leadership or specific demand. Amorphous and diffuse agendas, many clearly at cross-purposes, dominated the scenario, from calls for justice for oppressed social groups to banning gay marriage; from specific claims such as the hike in bus fares to generalities like traditional politics or corruption.[2] It was a social catharsis that

* Professor of Constitutional Law at the University of Brasília, Brazil. CNPq Research Fellow (Process n. 308733/2015-0). PhD, 2009, Humboldt University of Berlin, Germany; MSc, 2005, University of Brasilia; LLB, 2003, University of Brasilia. Email: juliano@unb.br. Portions of this chapter were previously published in 'The Seeds of Change: Popular Protests as Constitutional Moments' (2015) 99 *Marquette Law Review* 364–426. For helpful comments and conversations, I am grateful to Richard Albert, Carlos Bernal, David Landau, Andreas Fischer- Lescano, Sofia Ranchordás, Yaniv Roznai, Marcelo Neves, Cristiano Paixão, Leonardo Barbosa, and to the panelists and participants of the 4th YCC Conference of the American Society of Comparative Law, held at the Florida State University College of Law in April 2015, the Workshop on Comparative Constitutional Amendments, held at Boston College in May 2015, and the Global Symposium on Constitutional Amendment and Replacement in Latin America, held at the University of Brasília in September 2016. I have also benefitted from a visiting position as a post-doctoral fellow at the Centre for European Law and Politics (ZERP) of the University of Bremen, in Germany. I am especially indebted to all the staff of the Centre for European Law and Politics (ZERP) of the University of Bremen for giving me all the support necessary during my stay in Germany. John James Liolos copyedited this chapter.

[1] See Paulo Prada and Maria Carolina Marcello, 'One Million March Across Brazil in a Biggest Protest Yet' (*Reuters*, 2013) www.reuters.com/article/2013/06/21/us-brazil-protests-idUSBRE95J15020130621 accessed 3 February 2018.

[2] See Juliano Zaiden Benvindo, 'Brazilian Elections and Demonstrations of June 2013: The Rise of Conservatism?' (*International Journal of Constitiutional Law Blog*, 1 November 2014) www.iconnectblog.

caught the attention of many in Brazil and different parts of the globe by surprise, which rapidly came under the spotlight of the international media. A phenomenon that intrigued many that viewed Brazil as a relevant example of a rising democracy that bore good fruits in recent decades, and which has achieved relevant goals virtually unthinkable before.

The immediate consequence of those protests was an attempt by the federal government to draw up a national pact that would outline some measures focusing, especially, on five priority areas: (a) to assure economic stability and to combat inflation; (b) to develop a national plan on urban mobility; (c) to assign 100 per cent of oil royalties and 50 per cent of pre-salt oil resources to education; (d) to expand the numbers of foreign doctors in order to improve public medical services in needy areas; and (e) to further a political reform that would deepen popular participation and make Brazilian politics more representative.[3] In this last specific area, then President Dilma Roussef stated, on national TV, that she would 'propose a debate on convening a popular plebiscite that would authorise the functioning of a specific constituent process in order to bring about the political reform the country very much needs'.[4] By taking advantage of the massive popular support for change (68 per cent according to a Datafolha survey),[5] President Dilma Roussef attempted to push for a political reform through a sort of 'fast track' procedure of constitutional amendment that would, nevertheless, circumvent the strict amendment rules set out in Article 60 of the Brazilian Federal Constitution of 1988.[6] Through a plebiscite,[7] the amendment proposal to the Constitution

com/2014/11/brazilian-elections-and-demonstrations-of-june-2013-the-rise-of-conservatism/ accessed 3 February 2018.

[3] Dilma Roussef, 'Discurso da Presidenta da República, Dilma Roussef, durante reunião com governadores e prefeitos de capitais' (*Palácio do Planalto*, 24 June 2013) www2.planalto.gov.br/acompanhe-o-planalto/discursos/discursos-da-presidenta/discurso-da-presidenta-da-republica-dilma-rousseff-durante-reuniao-com-governadores-e-prefeitos-de-capitais accessed 3 February 2018.

[4] Roussef (n 3), para 10; see also Anthony Boadle, 'Brazil's Roussef pushes political reform to quell discontent' (*Reuters*, 2 June 2013) www.reuters.com/article/2013/07/02/us-brazil-politics-plebiscite-idUSBRE96115A20130702 accessed 3 February 2018.

[5] Boadle (n 4).

[6] Article 60. The Constitution may be amended on the proposal of: I – at least one-third of the members of the Chamber of Deputies or of the Federal Senate; II – the President of the Republic; III – more than one half of the Legislative Assemblies of the units of the Federation, each of them expressing itself by the relative majority of its members. Paragraph 1. The Constitution shall not be amended while federal intervention, a state of defense or a state of siege is in force. Paragraph 2. The proposal shall be discussed and voted upon in each House of the National Congress, in two readings, and it shall be considered approved if it obtains in both readings, three-fifths of the votes of the respective members. Paragraph 3. An amendment to the Constitution shall be promulgated by the Directing Boards of the Chamber of Deputies and the Federal Senate with its respective sequence number. Paragraph 4. No proposal of amendment shall be considered which is aimed at abolishing: I – the federative form of State; II – the direct, secret, universal and periodic vote; III – the separation of the Government Powers; IV – individual rights and guarantees. Paragraph 5. The matter dealt with in a proposal of amendment that is rejected or considered impaired shall not be the subject of another proposal in the same legislative session.

[7] See Anthony Boadle, 'After Post-Protest Flurry, Brazil's Politicians Resist Reform' (*Reuters*, 2013) www.reuters.com/article/us-brazil-politics-corruption/after-post-protest-flurry-brazils-politicians-resist-reform-idUSBRE96L0MS20130722 accessed 3 February 2018.

would be discussed and voted on in a single-chamber parliament and considered approved if it obtained a simple majority of the aggregate number of all senators and representatives. The requirement of three-fifths of the votes of the members of each House in two readings, as Article 60 determines, would be thereby relaxed for the specific purpose of that political reform.

The academic backlash to this proposal was significant. The attempt to push for a political reform through a plebiscite would authorise what scholars called 'an exclusive constituent assembly,'[8] because it would soften the strict rules for constitutional amendment. By directly comparing this proposal to the Constituent Assembly of 1987/1988, for instance, Cristiano Paixão, Juliana Neunschwander Magalhães, Marcelo Cattoni, and Vera Karam de Chueiri, all very prestigious professors from different universities in Brazil, argued that 'it is a fallacious argument to affirm that the convening of a revising assembly, or even a mini-constituent assembly, whose works would be authorised by a plebiscite or put to a referendum, would be the expression of popular sovereignty despite being contrary to the Constitution.'[9] Gustavo Binenbojm, professor of constitutional law at the Rio de Janeiro State University, in an interview for *Consultor Jurídico*, also presented a similar view. According to him, those protests could not be compared to the Constituent Assembly of 1987/1988, because, in this case, there is no break with the legal order and Brazil lives in a democratic regime.[10]

There is, accordingly, a very interesting debate over the ability of Brazilian institutional constraints and constitutional thresholds to respond to such moments of crisis. This chapter seeks to explore how constitutionalism, especially during such moments, is directly challenged in a country like Brazil. After all, it is not an ordinary aspect of Brazilian political life to observe this kind of event: streets crowded with people from everywhere in the country, as the government's approval rating dropped from over 57 per cent the week prior to 30 per cent right afterwards.[11] Moreover, Brazilian institutions were, at least until recently, believed to be quite stable, unlike some other countries in Latin America.[12] True, that relative stability has been severely challenged since President Dilma Rousseff's second

[8] See Cristiano Paixão et al, 'Constituinte Exclusiva: Inconstitucional e Ilegítima' (*Consultor Jurídico*, 27 June 2013) www.conjur.com.br/2013-jun-27/proposta-constituinte-exclusiva-inconstitucional-ilegitima?imprimir=1 accessed 3 February 2018.

[9] Cristiano Paixão et al (n 8).

[10] See Rafael Baliardo & Rodrigo Haidar, 'Constituinte Exclusiva é Desnecessária e Perigosa' (*Consultor Jurídico*, 24 June 2013) www.conjur.com.br/2013-jun-24/constituinte-reforma-politica-desnecessaria-perigosa accessed 3 February 2018.

[11] See 'Popularidade de Dilma cai 27 Pontos após Protestos' (*Folha de S. Paulo*, 29 June 2013) www1.folha.uol.com.br/poder/2013/06/1303541-popularidade-de-dilma-cai-27-pontos-apos-protestos.shtml accessed 3 February 2018.

[12] See David Landau, 'Abusive Constitutionalism' (2013) 47 *UCD L Rev* 189; Steven Levitsky and Kenneth M Roberts, 'Introduction: Latin America's 'Left Turn': A Framework of Analysis' in Levitsky Steven and Roberts Kenneth M (eds), *The Resurgence of the Latin American Left* (The John Hopkins University Press, 2011).

term, when a rising movement against her government gained momentum.[13] The following events could point out that a sort of 'democratic decay'[14] has since been underway: a very controversial impeachment – some would even call it a 'parliamentary coup'[15] – toppled President Dilma Rousseff's government in August 2016;[16] a corruption probe involving President Michel Temer, a large number of politicians, and political parties revealed how widespread the stench of graft is among public officials and the private sector;[17] and even the former President Luiz Inácio Lula da Silva, the most popular President since redemocrasation,[18] was convicted on graft charges in a criminal investigation marked by controversy[19] and which some have argued that it was aimed at preventing him from running for presidency once again.[20] More importantly, Brazil is currently under visible polarisation, which, as Levitsky and Ziblatt argue, is a decisive cause for '[wrecking] even established democracies,'[21] let alone young ones like Brazil's. The 2018 national elections, in which Brazilians ended up choosing the far-right candidate Jair Bolsonaro as President, reveals much of this disturbing scenario Brazil is enduring nowadays.[22]

[13] See Pedro Paulo Zahluth Bastos, 'Ascensão e Crise do Governo Dilma Rousseff e o Golpe de 2016: Poder Estrutural, Contradição e Ideologia' (2017) 21 *Rev. Econ. Contemp.* 1; Eugênio Bucci, *A Forma Bruta dos Protestos: Das Manifestações de Junho de 2013 à Queda de Dilma Rousseff em 2016* (Companhia das Letras, 2016).

[14] See Tom Gerald Daly, 'Public Law and the Puzzle of Democratic Decay in Brazil' (unpublished manuscript, on file with the author).

[15] Fabiano Santos & Fernando Guarnieri, 'From Protest to Parliamentary Coup: An Overview of Brazil's Recent History' (2016) 25 *Journal of Latin American Cultural Studies* 485.

[16] See Simon Romero, 'Dilma Rousseff is Ousted as Brazil's President in Impeachment Vote' (*The New York Times*, 31 August 2016) www.nytimes.com/2016/09/01/world/americas/brazil-dilma-rousseff-impeached-removed-president.html?_r=0 accessed 3 February 2018.

[17] See Jonathan Watts, 'Operation Car Wash: Is this the biggest Corruption Scandal in History? (*The Guardian*, 1 June 2017) www.theguardian.com/world/2017/jun/01/brazil-operation-car-wash-is-this-the-biggest-corruption-scandal-in-history accessed 3 February 2018.

[18] See Tom Philpis, Lula era comes to an end in Brazil (*The Guardian*, 31 Dec 2010) www.theguardian.com/world/2010/dec/31/brazil-lula-era-ends acessed 27 January 2018.

[19] See Igor Suzano Machado, 'O Julgamento de Lula envolve divergências genuinamente jurídicas' (*JOTA*, 26 January 2018) www.jota.info/stf/supra/julgamento-de-lula-envolve-divergencias-genuinamente-juridicas-26012018 accessed 3 February 2018.

[20] See Mark Weisbrot, Brazil's Democracy Pushed into Abyss (*The New York Times*, 23 January 2018) www.nytimes.com/2018/01/23/opinion/brazil-lula-democracy-corruption.html accessed January 25 2018; Fernando Fontaimha, 'O Julgamento de Lula: O Ocaso do Direito Brasileiro' (*JOTA*, 2 February 2018) www.jota.info/opiniao-e-analise/colunas/judiciario-e-sociedade/o-julgamento-de-lula-o-ocaso-do-direito-brasileiro-02022018 accessed 3 February 2018;

[21] See Steven Levitsky & Daniel Ziblatt, How Wobbly is Our Democracy? (*The New York Times*, 27 January 2018) www.nytimes.com/2018/01/27/opinion/sunday/democracy-polarization.html?action=click&pgtype=Homepage&clickSource=story-heading&module=opinion-c-col-left-region&region=opinion-c-col-left-region&WT.nav=opinion-c-col-left-region accessed 27 January 2018.

[22] See Juliano Zaiden Benvindo, 'Brazil's "False Consciousness of Time": The Rise of Jair Bolsonaro' (*International Journal of Constitutional Law Blog*, 10 November 2018): www.iconnectblog.com/2018/11/brazils-false-consciousness-of-time-the-rise-of-jair-bolsonaro/ accessed 12 January 2019.

Yet the difficulty in understanding this scenario is that, at least up until now and despite the blurred future landscape in the country,[23] there is no cataclysm going on. On the other hand, the periodic uproar that naturally arises among the polarised groups has been a recurrent phenomenon.[24] Disagreement among scholars is also mounting and some, unlike those who stress the signs of 'democratic decay',[25] posit that, though a period of instability lies ahead, 'democracy is not at risk in Brazil'.[26] Others would go even further and sustain that 'the crisis revealed the strength of the country's law-enforcement and judicial institutions'.[27] These and other viewpoints have flourished, despite remaining doubts whether such analyses have overvalued the judicial system's impartiality and undervalued the longstanding and entrenched practices of political and economic agents in Brazil.[28]

Reinhart Koselleck once wrote that 'as a growing temporal distance increased the prospects of knowledge of the past, so a history written up on the basis of day-to-day events lost its methodological dignity'.[29] The pace of the events currently in Brazil is thereby a serious challenge for any interpreter of the reality who is living this very moment. Time is needed to better assess these events. Still these are moments that contribute even further to understanding the resilience of a democracy, and, more specifically, of a constitutional framework.[30] They certainly cause severe stress on the foundations of a democracy achieved with great difficulty, but, as such, they should be part of a broader analysis that aims to investigate the broader picture and lay emphasis on a more diachronic dimension of Brazilian democracy.

In this regard, although there are signs of democratic regression[31] as the current events reveal and also a great deal still remains to be done, it would be incorrect not to acknowledge that years of democratic life, centralisation, inclusive

[23] See Juliano Zaiden Benvindo, 'We Should Learn from Historians: Seeing the Future in Brazil's Political Landscape' (*International Journal of Constitutional Law Blog*, 31 December 2018): http://www.iconnectblog.com/2018/12/we-should-learn-from-historians-seeing-the-future-in-brazils-political-landscape/ accessed 12 January 2019.

[24] See Vanessa Barbara, 'Banging Pots and Beating Dogs ina Polarized Brazil' (*The New York Times*, 25 March 2016) www.nytimes.com/2016/03/26/opinion/banging-pots-and-beating-dogs-in-a-polarized-brazil.html accessed 28 January 2018; Oriana van Praag, 'Safeguarding Democracy and Preventing Polarization in Brazil' (*Brown Political Review*, 26 March 2016) www.brownpoliticalreview.org/2016/03/safeguarding-democracy-preventing-polarization-brazil/ accessed 28 January 2018.

[25] Daly (n 14).

[26] Felipe Nunes & Carlos Ranulfo Melo, 'Impeachment, Political Crisis and Democracy in Brazil (2017) 37 *Revista de Ciência Política* 205.

[27] Marcus André Melo, 'Crisis and Integrity in Brazil' (2016) 27 *Journal of Democracy* 50.

[28] See Fernando Limongi, 'Um brasileiro como os outros?' (*Valor Econômico*, 29 January 2018) www.valor.com.br/politica/5287325/um-brasileiro-como-os-outros; Weisbrot (n 20).

[29] Reinhart Koselleck, *Futures Past: On the Semantics of Historical Time* (CUP, 1985) 243.

[30] Zachary Elkins, Tom Ginsburg and James Melton, *The Endurance of National Constitutions* (CUP, 2009).

[31] See Oscar Vilhena Vieira, 'Em defesa da democracia' (*Folha de S Paulo*, 3 February 2018) www1.folha.uol.com.br/cotidiano/2018/02/em-defesa-da-democracia.shtml accessed 3 February 2018.

institutions, and some lucky contingencies[32] have brought some valuable political, social, and economic achievements in Brazilian constitutionalism. This scenario is attractive from a comparative perspective. Brazil, after all, is a young democracy in consolidation process, with institutional achievements and a reasonable level of pluralism despite the serious social inequality and growing levels of intolerance among social and political actors. This complex nature turns it into an appealing focal point to investigate how constitutionalism, particularly through institutional constraints and constitutional thresholds, can cope with the inherent difficulties of such critical moments. Countries like the United States, Canada and many others from Western Europe have already faced – and naturally still face – many of these complexities. But Brazil faces them as a country that is, step by step, striving to develop institutionally and democratically while the ladder to development, if not kicked away,[33] still has rungs to climb. Brazil, within this context, provides a special flavor for research: it is neither in an environment of historically stable constitutional democracies nor in a context of 'abusive constitutionalism'[34] or 'stealth authoritarianism'.[35] It is somewhere in between, which leads to another question: is its constitutionalism also in between?

This chapter will focus on how institutional constraints and constitutional thresholds have evolved since Brazilian transition to democracy in 1985. For this purpose, it will primarily delve into those mass protests of June 2013 in order to discuss how constitutionalism reacts to some attempts to change the constitution without following the rules of the game. Those protests, after all, provide interesting insights about how they could somehow cohere with the learning curve of democratic life Brazil has experienced since the promulgation of the Constitution of 1988. The effects of this learning curve on how institutional constraints and constitutional thresholds have behaved in this context are noticeable. After examining distinct episodes of Brazilian democratic history, especially the Constituent Assembly of 1987/1988, this chapter concludes that, although Brazilian democracy is currently under considerable stress, there are signs pointing out that the country has reached some positive turning points at the institutional and constitutional levels. This conclusion, nonetheless, does not deny that the events following President Dilma Rousseff's impeachment may reveal a serious setback to Brazilian democracy and can even lead to a serious disruption of the democratic credentials Brazil has so hardly achieved. It understands, though, that there exists a learning curve of living constitutionalism that has become stronger over the years

[32] See Daron Acemoglu and James A Robinson, *Why Nations Fail: The Origins of Power, Prosperity, and Poverty* (Crown Business, 2012) 436, 457–60.

[33] See Ha-Joon Chang, *Kicking Away the Ladder: Development Strategy in Historical Perspective* (Anthem, 2002) 10 (arguing that 'the developed countries [try] to 'kick away the ladder' by which they have climbed up to the top, by preventing developing countries from adopting policies and institutions that they themselves used').

[34] Landau (n 12).

[35] Ozan O Varol, 'Stealth Authoritarianism' (2015) 100 *Iowa Law Review* 1673.

of democratic life and which, especially now, must defend the country from its inherent vulnerabilities and the remaining deep-rooted extractive institutions[36] that have long plagued the Brazilian reality.

II. Brazil and the Dilemmas of Constitution-Making

A. The Constituent Assembly of 1987/1988: Effects on the Mass Protests of June 2013?

It might sound like a historiographical sin to compare these two distinct moments of Brazilian reality, which are separated by approximately 25 years and by completely different purposes. The Constituent Assembly of 1987/1988 was a transition from a dictatorship to a democracy. The mass protests of June 2013 were a kind of social catharsis without, at least in the end, any specific agenda but an expression of general dissatisfaction with politics, economy, public services, and so on. However, if we compare side-by-side the specific features of both moments, we may observe some interesting parallels between them. In particular, we may discern some relevant conditions to better understand how institutional constraints and constitutional thresholds behave in a country like Brazil.

The Constituent Assembly of 1987/1988 is the result of a bumpy road towards democracy. Until 1987, the military regime, although having left office in 1985, was relatively successful in controlling how the transition would take place.[37] The motto was 'safe, slow, and gradual opening.' Democracy, according to this motto, was then a simple achievement after 21 years of military regime, which was responsible for laying the groundwork for this new future. In the final years of dictatorship, the military could, among other things: (a) pass an amnesty law that 'forgave' those members of the regime who perpetrated serious human rights violations;[38] (b) retain the majority of parliamentarians in power until the final days of the dictatorship; and (c) ensure that the first civil president and vice-president indirectly elected by the electoral college would be sponsored by the dictatorship despite the expressive popular mobilisation for direct presidential elections in 1984. The Constituent Assembly of 1987/1988 was also convened as the result of a constitutional amendment to the dictatorial Constitution of 1967/1969,

[36] Acemoglu & Robinson (n 32) 161.

[37] See Leonardo Augusto de Andrade Barbosa, *História Constitucional Brasileira: Mudança Constitucional, Autoritarismo e Democracia no Brasil Pós-1964* (Biblioteca Digital da Câmara dos Deputados, 2012); Cristiano Paixão, 'Past and future of authoritarian regimes: constituiton, transition to democracy and amnesty in Brazil and Chile' (2015) 30 *Journal of Constitutional History* 89; Juliano Zaiden Benvindo, 'The forgotten people in Brazilian constitutionalisms: Revisiting behavior strategic analyses of regime transitions' (2017) 15 *International Journal of Constitutional Law* 333.

[38] Brasil, Lei n 6.683, de 28 de Agosto de 1979.

although this fact might have paradoxically sparked broader public participation during the proceedings.[39]

Everything seemed to be heading towards an appeasing transition controlled by the regime and its supporters. Frances Hagopian, for example, argues that the transition took place as a 'negotiated settlement on the part of the political elites'.[40] It was not an effective process of liberalisation and rupture, but rather a 'series of political pacts'.[41] They could, after all, best cope with a civil society eager for change and that was increasingly promoting wide-spread mass protests, while the military and the elites could not lose privileges and positions. Political bargains[42] characterised that transition, with serious impacts on the future of the Brazilian democracy. According to her, in a country where traditional politics 'is based on three pillars of clientelism, regionalism, and personalism',[43] many of the privileges of the old regime were kept untouched in the new institutional framework, clearly compromising the consolidation of democracy in Brazil. In her words, Brazil would not have a 'vibrant democracy, but a perverted one skewed toward the representation of elite interests',[44] especially where there existed until then a frail democratic framework.[45]

Nevertheless, history might have proven more nuanced and less daunting, at least if we look at those events from today.[46] The Constituent Assembly of 1987/1988, though marked by distinct forms of political bargaining, also brought something unprecedented in Brazilian history: It was not framed from above by a group of experts representative of those elites.[47] Instead, it resulted from the work of some congressmen (most of them without legal skills), the major influence of public opinion,[48] institutional mechanisms of popular participation, and

[39] Naturally, this might have frustrated the idea of a real rupture with the authoritarian past, but, in reality, it did not seem a great deal at that time despite some dissenting voices. On the contrary, the proposal for amendment to the Constitution of 1967/1969 might have, paradoxically, created the environment for public participation, especially due to the pressure Congress received while discussing that amendment. Besides, it also anticipated some relevant discussion of the main constitutional subjects. See Barbosa (n 37) 187–91.

[40] Frances Hagopian, '"Democracy by Undemocratic Means"?: Elites, Political Pacts, and Regime Transition in Brazil' (1990) 23 *Comparative Political Studies* 149.

[41] Hagopian (n 40) 149.

[42] Hagopian (n 40) 149.

[43] Frances Hagopian, *Traditional Politics and Regime Change in Brazil* (CUP, 1996) 16.

[44] Hagopian (n 40) 160; see also Frances Hagopian and Scott Mainwaring, 'Democracy in Brazil: Problems and Prospects' (1987) 4 *World Policy Journal* 486.

[45] Hagopian (n 40) 148.

[46] Most of Hagopian's papers on Brazil discussed here were written during the transition to democracy and the 1990s. Over this time, naturally, Brazil has changed at the institutional and social levels.

[47] See Cristiano Paixão, 'Direito, Política, Autoritarismo e Democracia no Brasil: Da Revolução de 30 à Promulgação da Constituição da República de 1988' (2011) 26 *Araucária* 164.

[48] From 1977 to 1985, there was an increasing pressure of distinct social groups to make the Constituent Assembly a reality. Unions, the Catholic Church, civil associations, grassroots movements, the Brazilian Bar Association, the MDB political party, groups from the business community, among many others, were everywhere claiming this new future. See Bernardo Kucinsky, *O Fim da Ditadura Militar: O Colapso do 'Milagre Econômico', a Volta aos Quartéis, a Luta pela Democracia* (Contexto, 2001) 75; Barbosa (n 35) 165–74.

a decentralised dynamic of numerous theme committees and subcommittees on distinct matters working simultaneously without any preliminary draft of a constitutional text.[49] Pluralism was, therefore, somewhat visible during those preparatory efforts. It was, quoting Leonardo Barbosa, 'an authentic polyphony'.[50] In a sense, this 'polyphony' disputes Hagopian's premise that 'in Brazil the traditional political elite blocked the transformation of political institutions and arrangements in a way that perpetuated a less than democratic traditional politics'.[51] After all, if elites still maintain substantial responsibility over perpetuating many of their privileges and positions, it does not follow that institutions and the very project of constitutionalism will necessarily perpetuate this logic.[52] Despite its permanent risk of regression, democracy is, after all, also a 'self-correcting learning process'.[53]

The pluralistic feature of the Constituent Assembly might thus bring relevant insights about how Brazilian institutions and constitutionalism have evolved over time. The idea of pacific transition and not of a rupture with the past has indeed echoed as a motto and been employed as an argument to hamper some changes in Brazil, especially those related to events and acts committed by the dictatorship.[54] After all, it is quite symptomatic that the Constituent Assembly of 1987/1988 was installed by Supreme Court Chief Justice Moreira Alves saying that, at that moment, 'the final term of the period of transition is reached, whereby, without constitutional rupture and via conciliation, the revolutionary cycle comes to an end'.[55]

Beneath this discourse, however, the popular pressure, through mass protests and a great involvement of organised civil society, was largely present.[56] Furthermore, the Constituent Assembly's internal works were treated as a public issue, and the discussions and procedural rules of the Constituent Assembly were marked by an effort to extend the dialogue to society,[57] while creating some institutional constraints on Congress in order to lower the risks of a hegemonic bloc controlling its results.[58] After years of mass protests and public mobilisation, especially from

[49] See Barbosa (n 37)164.
[50] ibid, 147.
[51] Hagopian (n 40) 6.
[52] As Vermeule argues, 'Institutions are systems that aggregate the desires, beliefs, and choices of individuals, and those institutions may have very different properties than do the individuals who compose them. Furthermore, the interaction among institutions itself creates a system at the second level, one which may have very different properties than the institutions that compose it. Hence constitutionalism is a system of systems.' Adrian Vermeule, *The System of The Constitution* (OUP, 2011) 27.
[53] Jürgen Habermas, 'Constitutional Democracy: A Paradoxical Union of Contradictory Principles?' (2007) 29 *Political Theory* 766.
[54] See how the Brazilian Supreme Court (STF) decided on the constitutionality of the Amnesty Law (Law n. 6.683/1979), where the argument of pacific transition was largely used and won by a 7-2 majority (STF, ADPF 153, Rel. Min. Luiz Fux, Dje 06/05/2010).
[55] Diário da Assembleia Nacional Constituinte, DOU 02/02/1987, p 5.
[56] See Carlos Michiles et al, *Cidadão Constituinte: A Saga das Emendas Populares* (Paz e Terra, 1989).
[57] See Barbosa (n 37) 218, 221, 235.
[58] See Jefferson O Goulart, 'Processo Constituinte e Arranjo Federativo' (2013) 88 *Lua Nova* 185; Júlio Aurélio Vianna, *A Carta da Democracia: O Processo Constituinte da Ordem Pública de 1988* (Topbooks,

the late 70s onwards, Brazilians were living in a moment where years of accumulated learning and progress towards democracy could bear good fruit. There was a 'creative and participatory potential that was dammed',[59] building in anticipation of its moment of release.[60] Procedural rules of the Constituent Assembly aimed at sparking a dialogue with the citizenry were widespread, such as the possibility of submitting suggestions, holding public hearings, proposing popular amendments to the Constitution,[61] and all of them strongly broadcast nationwide.[62] In the end, the paradox of the old regime and those 'political bargains' with this experience of popular groups in dialogue with the Constituent Assembly originated the Constitution that is, by far, the most dynamic and democratic ever in Brazilian history.

Since the promulgation of the Constitution in 5 October 1988, however, congressmen and the government have pursued several strategies to alter some of its core principles with the clear purpose of 'correcting' the so-called 'excesses' of that 'overly democratic' moment of constitution-making. Those strategies have nonetheless met strong resistance, which may signal that that pluralistic moment may have played a role in raising the stakes for any constitutional change that would reverse some of those democratic breakthroughs.[63] The 1988 Constitution, with its 250 articles (and 97 articles of the Temporary Constitutional Provisions Act) has already been amended 99 times through the regular procedure of amendment[64] and six times through the procedure of constitutional revision in 1993.[65] However, most of those 99 regular constitutional amendments and

2008); Marcos Nobre, 'Indeterminação e Estabilidade: Os 20 Anos da Constituição Federal e as Tarefas da Pesquisa em Direito' (2008) 82 *Novos Estudos CEBRAP* 97.

[59] Paixão (n 47) 164.

[60] In the previous years of the Constituent Assembly, massive popular movements accelerated this process, such as: (a) the strikes and demonstrations in distinct regions of Brazil, especially in the region of ABC on the outskirts of São Paulo; (b) the campaign for a wide, general, and unrestricted amnesty in 1979, which, after some comings and goings, resulted in the Law n. 6.683/1979; (c) the Diretas Já (*Direct Elections Now*) in 1983/1984, which gathered more than one and a half million people all over the country, though its results were frustrated by Congress. There was, accordingly, an accumulated popular pressure, which exploded during the Constituent Assembly. See Paixão (n 45) 165; Domingos Leonelli & Dante de Oliveira, *Diretas Já: 15 Meses que Abalaram a Ditadura* (Record, 2004); Alberto Tosi Rodrigues, *Diretas Já: O Grito Preso na Garganta* (Fundação Perseo Abramo, 2003); Flamarion Maués & Zilah Wendel Abramo, *Pela Democracia, contra o arbítrio: A Oposição Democrática, do Golpe de 1964 à Campanha das Diretas Já* (Fundação Perseu Abramo, 2006).

[61] See Barbosa (n 37) 230; Michiles (n 56).

[62] Paixão (n 47) 164.

[63] *See* Juliano Zaiden Benvindo, 'The Seeds of Change: Popular Protests as Constitutional Moments' (2015) 99 *Marquette Law Review* 364.

[64] See n 6.

[65] The Brazilian Constitution and the constitutional doctrine in Brazil have used the concept of 'constitution revision' in a much less radical perspective than the comparative constitutional law literature. Instead of the premise that the constitutional revision 'departs from [presuppositions of the constitution] and is inconsistent with its framework, thereby disrupting the continuity of the legal order' (Richard Albert, 'Amending Constitutional Amendment Rules' (2015) 13 *International Journal of Constitutional Law* 667), in Brazil, it is used to designate a change in the constitutional order as the result of a 'fast track' procedure of amendment that is normally less rigid than the regular one.

those six revision amendments did not structurally affect the democratic feature of the Constitution's rules and principles.[66] Important subjects related to social security,[67] public servants,[68] telecommunications,[69] reelections,[70] among others, were subject of constitutional amendments, but all of them resulted from regular amendment procedures of Article 60 of the Constitution. On the other hand, all those attempts designed to 'correct the excesses' of the 'overly democratic' Constitution through special and simplified procedures of amendments failed in the end.

In the constitutional revision of 1993, a special procedure of amendment that took place five years after the promulgation of the Constitution of 1988,[71] the movements in this direction were stronger and could impact some of those achievements of the Constituent Assembly of 1987/1988. Naturally, it was much easier to promote such changes, because it only required an absolute majority of the members of Congress in a unicameral session. Although the government and some political parties were willing to implement structural changes,[72] particularly in an environment of economic crisis and neo-liberal policy, there was a great resistance from many left-wing political parties and sectors of the civil society.[73] In addition, some contingencies related to a corruption scandal involving some congressmen in 1994[74] and the very turbulent coordination of the voting sessions dispersed the ongoing works.[75] The outcome, despite voices claiming the need of revision in favour of governability,[76] was a tremendous failure.

According to Article 3 of the Temporary Constitutional Provisions Act of the Brazilian Federal Constitution of 1988, 'The revision of the Constitution shall be effected after five years as of its promulgation, by the vote of the absolute majority of the members of the National Congress in a unicameral session.' All the other attempts of constitutional revision were the product of proposals for constitutional amendment, but none has succeeded so far.

[66] A possible exception is the Constitutional Amendment n 95 (Brasil, Emenda Constitucional n 95, de 15 de dezembro de 2016), which, for the next 20 years, will limit the annual growth of public spending to the inflation of the previous year. This amendment may particularly affect the social core of the Constitution of 1988. Richard Albert has, for instance, argued that this is an example of 'constitutional dismemberment,' which 'seeks to transform the identity, the fundamental values or the architecture of the constitution'. See Richard Albert, *Constitututional Dismemberment and Amendment*, (2018) 43 *Yale Journal of International Law* 1, 40–42.

[67] Brasil, Emenda Constitucional n 20, de 15 de dezembro de 1998; Emenda Constitucional n 47, de 5 de julho de 2005.

[68] Brasil, Emenda Constitucional n 41, de 19 de dezembro de 2003.

[69] Brasil, Emenda Constitucional n 8, de 15 de junho de 1995.

[70] Brasil, Emenda Constitucional n 16, de 4 de junho de 1997.

[71] See n 63.

[72] The changes were mostly directly to affect labour and social security rights.

[73] See Barbosa (n 37) 266.

[74] The so-called 'Anões do Orçamento' (*Budget Dwarves*) scandal, related to the use of parliamentary amendments to the annual budget to defraud the Treasury by deviating money through some bogus companies, fake charities, and construction companies. The president of the Chamber of the Deputies, and other ten congressmen either had their mandates revoked or resigned. See Timothy Joseph Power and Matthew MacLeod Taylor (eds), *Corruption and Democracy in Brazil: The Struggle for Accountability* (University of Notre Dame Press, 2011) 2–3.

[75] Barbosa (n 37) 284–319.

[76] ibid, 323.

Nevertheless, the argument in favour of adopting a special procedure for constitutional amendment was kept alive in the following years. The claims for changing the constitutional text to promote governability appeared in distinct opportunities. Right after the failure of 1993, the government and some congressmen reawakened the desire to propose a constitutional amendment that would allow for a special 'fast track' procedure. In 1994, Representative José Serra presented the Proposal for Constitutional Amendment n 192/1994,[77] which had similar rules to the failed constitutional revision of 1993 but established a period of four months of deliberation and preserved the unamendable clauses as set out in Article 60, §4 of the Constitution.[78] In the subsequent years, other proposals with the same goal[79] were presented, regardless of which party was in power. In 1995, in the Federal Senate, the Proposals for Constitutional Amendment n 25 and 30[80] set out a procedure of joint deliberation in both Houses, keeping nonetheless the same quorum of the 1988 Constitution. In 1997 and 1998, at the Chamber of Deputies, the Proposal for Constitutional Amendment n. 478[81] aimed to foster 'constitutional revisions' every five years. The Proposal for Constitutional Amendment n. 554/1997,[82] later attached to the Proposal for Constitutional Amendment n. 157/2003,[83] also sought to create a new 'Constituent Assembly' through a 'fast track' procedure for constitutional amendments to discuss, specifically and exclusively, matters related to political rights, the political system, the division of competences, and the tax system. In 2007, the Proposal for Constitutional Amendment n. 193, later attached to the Proposal for Constitutional Amendment n. 384/2009,[84] included a plebiscite in order to discuss exclusively the tax system, the federal budget, the organisation of powers, and the political system.[85]

[77] Brasil, Proposta de Emenda Constitucional, n 192, Dep José Serra, DCN 17/01/1995, p 734, Col 2.

[78] See n 6.

[79] See Proposta de Emenda à Constituição n 25 (Sen. Humberto Lucena, DCN2, 11 de maio de 1995, p 8026); Proposta de Emenda à Constituição n 30 (Sen. Sérgio Machado, DCN2, de 19 de maio de 1995, p 8480); Proposta de Emenda à Constituição n 62, Dep. Saulo Queiroz, DCN1, de 7 Junho de 1995, p 12404); Proposta de Emenda à Constituição n 463/1997 (Dep. Inocêcio Oliveira, DCD, de 4 de Junho de 1997, p 14551); Proposta de Emenda à Constituição n 478/1997 (Dep. Inocêcio Oliveira, DCD, de 23 de outubro de 1997, p 24819); Proposta de Emenda à Constituição n 554/1997 (Dep. Miro Teixeira, DCD, de 13 de dezembro de 1997, p 41684); Proposta de Emenda à Constituição n 71 (Sen. Delcídio do Amaral, DSF, de 3 de setembro de 2003, p 26040; Proposta de Emenda à Constituição n 157 (Dep. Luiz Carlos Santos, DCD de 26 de setembro de 2003, p 50457); Proposta de Emenda à Constituição n 193 (Dep. Flávio Dino, DCD, 11 de dezembro de 2007, p 65361).

[80] Proposta de Emenda à Constituição n 25 (Sen Humberto Lucena, DCN2, 11 de maio de 1995, p 8026); Proposta de Emenda à Constituição n. 30 (Sen. Sérgio Machado, DCN2, de 19 de maio de 1995, p 8480).

[81] Proposta de Emenda à Constituição n 478/1997 (Dep Inocêcio Oliveira, DCD, de 23 de outubro de 1997, p 24819).

[82] Proposta de Emenda à Constituição n 554/1997 (Dep Miro Teixeira, DCD, de 13 de dezembro de 1997, p 41684).

[83] Proposta de Emenda à Constituição n 157 (Dep Luiz Carlos Santos, DCD de 26 de setembro de 2003, p 50457).

[84] Proposta de Emenda à Constituição n 193 (Dep Flávio Dino, DCD, 11 de dezembro de 2007, p 65361).)

[85] For a detailed explanation of these distinct Proposals for Constitutional Amendment, see Barbosa (n 37) 326–48.

Attempts to change the procedure for constitutional amendment as set out in Article 60 of the Constitution are thereby embedded in Brazilian constitutional culture. Year after year, similar proposals are subject of discussion either at the Chamber of Deputies or in the Federal Senate. However, the examples above demonstrate that, despite being part of the government agenda, they simply recede from prominence after a period of time, without achieving effective impact.[86] Even when they might seem to have provided a solution for matters that, otherwise, would hardly be changed, the historical outcomes of those proposals circumventing the rules of the game are clearly disappointing. Moreover, even when there was a great popular support for the change, those proposals were unable to push ahead with major constitutional amendments. In a sense, constitutional thresholds and institutional constraints have worked somehow against those efforts to break with the precommitments undertaken during the Constituent Assembly of 1987/1988.

This is the institutional and constitutional background that was behind those mass protests of June 2013. If we analyse them without considering all this historical development, we lose numerous nuances that a diachronic perspective of Brazilian constitutionalism offers. Brazilian constitutionalism, even in moments of crisis, has proved rather resilient to formal proposals aimed at circumventing the procedures for constitutional amendment as originally set out in the 1988 Constitution. The inability of President Dilma Rousseff's government to react to those mass protests by passing a sort of 'fast track' procedure of constitutional amendment to change the political system, as strongly supported by the population, adds thereby to this conclusion. Those constitutional precommitments, either as the outcome of that pluralistic moment of constitution-making or the very bargains that have 'imprinted an undemocratic character on the state and on political parties and weakened political representation',[87] as Hagopian posits it, are, at least formally, mostly intact for better or worse.

B. Mass Protests of 2013 in a Comparative Perspective: Constitutional Moments in a Systemic Analysis

The mass protests of June 2013 were indeed intriguing. More than one million people stormed many cities in Brazil in a clear social catharsis. It was also a sensible moment for protest: the matches of the FIFA Confederations Cup were happening while the streets outside the stadiums were thronged with thousands of people from across the nation. Violence naturally erupted and the police reaction, with rubber bullets and tear gas to scatter the crowd, was disastrous, especially in the first days of those movements. All this mixture of social catharsis, violence and

[86] ibid, 329.
[87] Hagopian (n 40) 149.

the FIFA Confederations Cup was explosive. In the beginning, the initial cause was the hike in public transport fares, but, in the end, the general agenda prevailed. Corruption, human rights in general, political system, decrying inflation, poor allocation of public funds, privatisation of government services, all different agendas were raised, many of them conflicting with each other. The New York Times argued that 'Brazil now seems to be pivoting toward a new phase of interaction between demonstrators and political leaders with its wave of protests',[88] and many saw in those demonstrations the sign of a new political culture in Brazil, with new actors and new demands for rights.[89]

Nevertheless, the outcomes of these mass protests might have been rather disappointing, at least at first impression. Although some political leaders immediately attempted to respond to those protests, nothing structural seems to have changed. Then-President Dilma Roussef, following other similar past constitutional proposals,[90] quickly claimed on national TV the need of a 'fast track' procedure for constitutional amendment with a plebiscite for the purpose of promoting a political reform. The idea reemerged that the regular procedures of constitutional amendments as set out in Article 60 of the 1988 Constitution were far too rigid to make changes possible. Yet, once again, this proposal failed. At the beginning of the reform process, Congress reacted by saying that a plebiscite would not be possible because of the complexity of the subject and that it would be best as a referendum, instead.[91] Then, as things calmed down, the issue disappeared from the public debate for a period. After Dilma Roussef's reelection in 2014, one of her agenda items was again this subject of political reform. The idea of a plebiscite and possibly through a sort of 'fast track' procedure of constitutional amendment could naturally come up again. Still, her second term was abruptly ended by an impeachment procedure,[92] and reactions against this agenda were noticeable.[93] Especially with a Congress more conservative than the previous one, which is paradoxical in the wake of those mass protests,[94] the outcome was similar to those previous failed attempts to change the rules of the game for a specific purpose.

[88] Simon Romero, 'Thousands Gather for Protests in Brazil's Largest Cities' (*The New York Times*, 17 June 2013) www.nytimes.com/2013/06/18/world/americas/thousands-gather-for-protests-in-brazils-largest-cities.html?_r=1& accessed 3 February 2018.

[89] See André Singer, 'Brasil, Junho de 2013, Classes e Ideologias Cruzadas' (2013) 23 *Novos Estudos CEBRAP* 97; Ilse Scherer-Warren, 'Manifestações de Rua no Brasil 2013: Encontros e Desencontros na Política' (2014) 27 *Caderno CRH* 417.

[90] See last section *supra*.

[91] See Boadle (n 4).

[92] See Juliano Zaiden Benvindo, 'Abusive Impeachment? Brazilian Political Turmoil and the Judicialization of Mega-Politics' (*International Journal of Consitutional Law Blog*, 23 April 2016) www.iconnectblog.com/2016/04/abusive-impeachment-brazilian-political-turmoil-and-the-judicialization-of-mega-politics/ accessed 3 February 2018.

[93] See Fernanda Krakovics et al., 'Congresso já Reage à Ideia de um Plebiscito proposto por Dilma' (*O Globo*, 28 October 2014) http://oglobo.globo.com/brasil/congresso-ja-reage-ideia-de-plebiscito-proposto-por-dilma-14381463 accessed 3 February 2018.

[94] Benvindo (n 2).

Hagopian's thesis would then prove true, at least when extended to these recent events in Brazil. This structure of entrenching the existing Constitution and political configuration could be interpreted as a protection of the elites. In the end, as she said, 'it is more likely that the features limiting democracy in Brazil will outlive the political pacts that produced or reinforce them'.[95] The mass protests of 2013, even though many regard them as an expression of democracy and social participation, were beaten by the structural reality of Brazilian political institutions. In addition, signs of strategic behaviour by the elites to capitalise on this moment to promote their agendas were largely present, after all.

As those movements progressed, specific claims such as the cancelling of bus fares increased to a generalised, diffuse, and unfocused agenda – a process strongly encouraged by the press and the new media – making those movements easily ripe for co-option. That environment of social catharsis validated any claims, and consequently the elites could seize control of the movement in general while reaffirming their traditional values.[96] It is no wonder that, right after those events, the following elections for the Brazilian Congress in 2014 were characterised by the expansion of the conservative right. Religious, military, rural, and other typically conservative groups won more seats in Congress than any other period after the transition to democracy, clearly contradicting the original purpose of those protests. The elites, although threatened by these movements, could thereby keep untouched or even expand their power and influence.[97]

Nevertheless, when this conclusion is examined more broadly, the outcomes of those mass protests of June 2013 might not necessarily be a feature of a country that is historically bound to 'clientelism, regionalism, and personalism'.[98] History is filled with examples of mass protests whose subsequent outcomes fell short of expectations. This is particularly true when it comes to elections, for example. In 1968, de Gaulle and his right-wing coalition won a landslide victory in the French Parliament after those famous mass demonstrations that May.[99] Although one could argue that those events 'transformed the popular image of socialism in France',[100] it also proved that, notwithstanding the spontaneity and the good ideas of those protests, in the end, de Gaulle was able enough to circumvent the opposition and guarantee his victory.[101] Despite the economic meltdown in 2007/2008 and many protests such as Occupy Wall Street in 2011 in the streets

[95] Hagopian (n 40) 166
[96] Benvindo (n 2).
[97] ibid.
[98] Hagopian (n 43) 16.
[99] See André Barjonet, *La révolution Trahie de 1968* (Éditions John Didier, 1968); Andrew Feenberg & Jim Freedman, *When Poetry Ruled the Streets: The French May Events of 1968* (State University of New York Press, 2010); Serge Berstein, Pierre Birnbaum & Jean-Pierre Rioux, '1968–1969: Une Nouvelle Trahison des Élites?' in Serge Berstein, Pierre Birnbaum and Jean-Pierre Rioux (eds), *Hors collection Sciences Humaines* (La Découverte, 2008) 300.
[100] Feenberg & Freedman (n 99) xxi.
[101] Douglas Kellner, 'Foreword' in Feenberg & Freedman (n 99) xvii.

of New York and other American cities, the following American congressional elections were marked by the growth of polarisation between Republicans and Democrats. There was also the expansion of right-wing political groups connected to movements such as the Tea Party,[102] which also took advantage of the public ire over the Wall Street in order to defend a radical programme of fiscal austerity and expand the attacks on marginalised groups and minorities.[103] More recently, in 2011 Spain underwent a right-wing takeover of its Parliament despite thousands of students – the 'indignados' – protesting against the economic crisis.[104] Indeed, this consequence might have raised the doubts whether those protests could pose the central questions regarding Spain's economy and politics, rather than '[focusing] upon abstract and purely political notions of "real democracy"'.[105]

Therefore, although the links between mass protests and subsequent political changes in democracies have been much discussed by legal scholars and political scientists,[106] it seems that the paradoxical outcomes of those popular uprisings cannot be explained by directly connecting them to a history of 'clientelism, regionalism, and personalism'.[107] Other reasons are also plausible, and how elites will bargain their positions – even though according to distinct degrees of effectiveness – should be analysed from a broader systemic perspective whereby individual interactions may not necessarily correspond to how institutions, and even more broadly, constitutionalism behave.[108] Brazil notoriously has a history of elites blocking much of the transformation of political and

[102] See Peter Dreier, 'Occupy Wall Street and the Tea Party' (*The Huffington Post*, 21 October 2011) www.huffingtonpost.com/peter-dreier/occupy-wall-street-and-th_1_b_1025828.html accessed 3 February 2018; David Lawder, 'On Anniversary, Tea Party Vows to Move U.S. Congress to Right' (*Reuters*, 27 February 2014) www.reuters.com/article/2014/02/28/us-usa-politics-teaparty-idUSBREA1R01G20140228 accessed 3 February 2018.

[103] See Jeffrey Juris & Maple Razsa, 'Occupy, Anthropology, and the 2011 Global Uprisings' (*Cultural Antropology*, 27 July 2012) www.culanth.org/fieldsights/63-occupy-anthropology-and-the-2011-global-uprisings accessed 3 February 2018.

[104] See Greig Charnock, Thomas Purcell & Ramon Ribera-Fumaz, '¡ Indígnate!: The 2011 Popular Protests and the Limits to Democracy in Spain' (2012) 36 *Capital & Class* 3–11; Eva Anduiza, Camilo Cristancho & José M Sabucedo, 'Mobilization through Online Social Networks: The Political Protest of the Indignados in Spain' (2014) 17 *Information, Communication & Society* 750.

[105] Charnock, Purcell and Ribera-Fumaz (n 104) 9.

[106] See Alfredo Saad-Filho, 'Mass Protests under 'Left Neoliberalism': Brazil, June-July 2013' (2013) 39 *Critical Sociology* 657; Jack A Goldstone, 'Understanding the Revolutions of 2011: Weakness and Resilience in Middle Eastern Autocracies' (2011) 90 *Foreign Aff.* 8; Lisa Anderson, 'Demystifying the Arab Spring: Parsing the Differences between Tunisia, Egypt, and Libya' (2011) 90 *Foreign Aff* 2; Barbosa (n 35); Charnock, Purcell & Ribera-Fumaz (n 102); Francis LF Lee, 'The Perceptual Bases of Collective Efficacy and Protest Participation: The Case of Pro-Democracy Protests in Hong Kong' (2010) 22 *International Journal of Public Opinion Research* 392; Guillermo A O'Donell, 'Delegative Democracy' (1994) 5 *Journal of Democracy* 55; Anduiza, Cristancho and Sabucedo Michalis Psimitis, 'The Protest Cycle of Spring 2010 in Greece' (2014) 10 *Social Movement Studies* 191; Wolfgang Rüdig & Georgios Karyotis, 'Who Protests in Greece? Mass Opposition to Austerity' (2014) 44 *British Journal of Political Science* 487.

[107] Hagopian (n 43) 16.

[108] See Vermeule (n 52) 27.

economic institutions.[109] In addition, it is an evident strategic behaviour of those groups that have traditionally benefited from entrenched institutions to do whatever it takes to seize control of any movement that may threaten their positions and privileges.

Paradoxically, though, perhaps it was somehow this strategic behaviour of the elite combined with other opposing actions of distinct social groups that provided some gains and benefits both at the institutional and constitutional levels. Perhaps, without this pluralism of positions, institutional constraints and constitutional thresholds would be much more fragile and flexible to adapt to the interests of a specific group. For example, despite the fact that congressmen may be defending their very political interests and therefore acting against the idea of a 'fast track' procedure for constitutional amendment, in the end, this can render it necessary to follow the 'rules of the game'. This would include a much greater debate over the desired changes, which, in turn, would exactly correspond to what is expected for a constitutional amendment.[110] Interactions, some controversial at the individual level, may yield coherence and consistency at the institutional level, whose interactions can or cannot bring about similar effects at the constitutional level.[111]

This leads us to the conclusion that what is at stake is the very paradoxical nature of the negotiation between constitutionalism and democracy, and how pluralism plays a special role in paving the ground for strengthening constitutionalism and its institutions. Those movements, such as the Brazilian mass protests of June 2013, the demonstrations of May 1968 in France, the Occupy Wall Street in New York in 2011, the 'indignados' in Spain in 2011, can be a clear sign of this increasing pluralism that might, in the long run, engender results that, at first sight, are unpredictable, even though the immediate outcomes may have been a democratic regression and expanded polarisation. This is because the way interactions take place varies constantly and the results, if apparently frustrating at first blush, might engender positive outcomes from a broader dimension of systemic analysis. The constitution, as a form of precommitment, will be followed and changed by distinct prosaic factors, many of them stemming from the strategic behaviour of the elite and other social groups, but also from other forms of interactions taking place at the institutional level. Therefore, people and institutions will work well together, bringing forth the positive effect of the learning curve of democratic life, as long as pluralism at all levels is kept alive. Those protests might not have immediately brought about effective changes in constitutionalism and political institutions. Still, this argument may present just one side of the story.

[109] Hagopian (n 43) 6.
[110] See Albert (n 66).
[111] See Vermeule (n 52).

C. The Other Side of the Story: The Learning Curve of Democratic Living

If we shift focus, maybe we can tell the other side of the story. True, most of the frustrating outcomes of those social uprisings stem from the strategic behaviour of political elites. Particularly regarding those Brazilian mass protests of June 2013, the political inertia, especially in Congress, was a consequence of a direct strategic intervention of elites, facilitated by the fact that those protests exploded in an unfocused, leaderless, and generalised way. One could also argue that the disappointing results were also a symptom of a series of factors such as the left-wing neoliberalism, the power of the right-wing media, the growing expectations of a dynamic country, and the atrophy of the political system of representation.[112] Many of these arguments would validate not only Hagopian's arguments, but also those arguments mentioned by who clearly sustain that the mass protests of June 2013 and the following effort to change the Constitiution by circumventing the rules of the game have anything even remotely resembling the Constituent Assembly of 1987/1988.[113]

However, if we examine those protests from a systemic perspective, the other side of the story emerges. By focusing on some institutional constraints and constitutional thresholds as well as on the historical background discussed above, the argument changes in focus. As previously mentioned, during those mass protests of June 2013, there was a huge popular pressure for change, and particularly change of the political system. On the other hand, Congress has since remained relatively divided on how these changes should come about. If they support some changes, there are many possible controversies on how to promote them. For example, the idea of making the change through a sort of 'fast track' procedure of constitutional amendment, as it has been attempted several times in Brazilian history, naturally has many supporters in Congress and in the streets, but, as history shows, this might be more difficult than planned. In the end, this pluralistic conflict of opinions might bring about a change in the political system as a result of a stronger dialogue.

Furthermore, those protests, even though not immediately yielding the desired outcomes, have showcased how fundamental aspects of democracy such as freedom of speech and political expression are vital to the integrity of institutions. They might also have demonstrated that the constitution, with its thresholds and constraints, can serve as a tool for or impediment to political change. In other words, they might have revealed the pedagogical value of democracy and constitutionalism, how institutions and individuals behave during periods of crisis, and how history – indeed, constitutional history – plays a special role during those moments. These aspects impact how the interactions at all levels take place,

[112] See Alfredo Saad-Filho (n 106) 657.
[113] See Introduction *supra.*

and can enhance the 'performative meaning'[114] that constitutional democracy produces over time.

The results of protests as such are obviously unpredictable, for constitutional democracies are continuously challenged and put at risk. In fact, as previously mentioned, Brazil currently appears to be heading in the opposite direction of most of the claims raised during those protests, with clear signs of democratic regression.[115] Peter Kingstone and Timothy Power, in this regard, argue that, 'in the "hangover" following Dilma's impeachment, Brazil is divided against itself and is currently confronting the deepest political and economic challenges of the New Republic', even though '[doing] so drawing on vital sources of strength'.[116] The scenario is thereby more blurred than expected. For this reason, a distinct approach must be undertaken to seriously understand Brazil, 'focusing – as they say – on micro-level variables and the nuances and complexities among them', which would 'avoid the common tendency to see only the negative or the positive'.[117]

One such interesting micro-level variable is how the constitution has behaved under the severity of a critical moment. Thus far, the Brazilian Constitution, whose rate of amendment is one of the highest in the world,[118] has nonetheless not been strongly affected in its core principles.[119] Moreover, since the 1988 Constitution, formal constitutional change in Brazil has conformed to the procedures of constitutional amendment as articulated in its Article 60. Up to the present, the efforts to implement a sort of 'fast track' procedure of amendment have all failed. On the other hand, despite the immediate setbacks following those mass protests of June 2013, especially after the diffuse and general agenda gained momentum, it would be one-sided and misleading to conclude that the protests simply sparked a movement towards democracic regression. Positive outcomes have also emerged from that context, especially because those demonstrations, at least in their origins, were aimed at bringing about effective changes in distinct areas. As Ricardo Mendonça and Selen Ercan contend, those 'protests have generated an awareness of difference, exposing the existence of silenced controversial issues in a public sphere often inhospitable to disagreement'.[120] Through both constitutional

[114] Habermas (n 53) 775.

[115] See Daly (n 14).

[116] See Peter R Kingstone and Timothy J Power, 'Introduction. A Fourth Decade of Brazilian Democracy: Achievements, Challenges and Polarization' in Peter R Kingstone and Timothy J Power (eds), *Democratic Brazil Divided* (University of Pittsburgh Press, 2017) 22.

[117] Kingstone & Power (n 116) 22.

[118] See Tom Ginsburg & John Melton, 'Does the Constitutional Amendment Rule Matter at All? Amendment Cultures and the Challenges of Measuring Amendment Difficulty' (2015) 13 *International Journal of Constitutional Law* 686.

[119] See Juliano Zaiden Benvindo, 'The Brazilian Constitutional Amendment Rate: A Culture of Change? (*International Journal of Constitutional Law Blog*, 10 August 2016) www.iconnectblog.com/2016/08/the-brazilian-constitutional-amendment-rate-a-culture-of-change/ accessed 2 February 2018.

[120] Ricardo Fabrino Mendonça & Selen A Ercan, 'Deliberation and Protest: Strange Bedfellows? Revealing the Deliberative Potential of 2013 Protests in Turkey and Brazil' (2015) 36 *Policy Studies* 279.

thresholds and democratic practice, Brazilian constitutionalism has performatively strengthened over the years,[121] even if this has taken place as 'two steps forward, one step back'.[122]

The pluralistic procedure of constitution-making during the Constituent Assembly of 1987/1988 and the democratic achievements printed on the Constitution of 1988 as a result of this procedure have gained a 'performative meaning' and yielded, over time, a stability that is unprecedented in Brazilian history. Despite the frustrating outcomes and the political crisis in the aftermath of those events, some important features of those mass protests of June 2013 follow this trajectory of an increasing curve of democratic living and capture this 'performative meaning' the recent Brazilian history has provided. Certainly, those political bargains retained privileges and interests of the elite and weakened political representation. Still, in a systemic analysis,[123] when this characteristic is combined with the increasing democratic curve of popular mobilisation from late 1970s onwards, which was represented during the Constituent Assembly of 1987/1988 and somehow also in those mass protests of June 2013, the outcome can be more democracy and not the other way around. Therefore, both moments – and many other moments in between – are part of a greater process of constitution-making and constitutional living. Both moments are part of this 'constitutional moment' we are still living and which must be preserved and remembered as a way to defend Brazil from falling further into the path of a 'democratic decay'.[124]

III. Conclusion

Brazil is challenging the historical barrier that usually traverses the history of many countries in Latin America. The rising pluralism Brazil has experienced since the movements in the late 1970s against the civil-military dictatorship, and which has echoed in the Constituent Assembly of 1987/1988, the 1988 Constitution and even the popular demonstrations such as those of June 2013 are evidence of this constitutional moment. The years of democratic life have showed that Brazilian people are more actively involved in the destiny of Brazil and more conscious of their rights and of the mechanisms to protect them. Through a learning process that yielded some empowerment at the grassroots level to a more pluralistic distribution of political and economic power,[125] Brazil has indeed achieved important democratic progress over the years (though much remains to be done).

Naturally, as the current events show, threats to the democratic integrity of Brazilian constitutionalism and institutions are widespread. Therefore, it is more

[121] Habermas (n 53) 775.
[122] Kingstone & Power (n 116) 22.
[123] Vermeule (n 52).
[124] See Daly (n 14).
[125] See Acemoglu & Robinson (n 30) 460.

important than ever to enhance the mechanisms of democracy and the design of institutions[126] to cope with rising polarisation.[127] In addition, the future is uncertain, and changes can rapidly occur in a direction that undermines many of the core principles that have long characterised Brazilian democracy. As an 'in-between' country filled with 'in-between' institutional constraints and constitutional thresholds, Brazil is clearly struggling, day by day, to climb up the rungs of development. Perhaps in a few months or years, for example, this historical background of constitutional thresholds is affected by the approval of a 'fast track' procedures of constitutional amendment for promoting political reform or any other subject. Perhaps history will show that, to transform the elite's behaviour, this solution, in the long run, may strengthen pluralism despite the side effects of jeopardising some constitutional guarantees and stability, working thereby as a second-best argument.[128] There is no guaranteed solution, and many of our assurances may fall short of our highest aspirations in the end.

The Brazilian Constitution of 1988 and the subsequent strengthening of Brazilian democracy is thereby not simply the result of one single moment of constitution-making, such as the Constituent Assembly of 1987/1988. At that moment, we could observe the conjunction of different factors which have, little by little, strengthened pluralism over time. Some institutional turning points have since begun to take shape, and a learning curve of democratic life become more visible. As an 'in-between' country, this history of achievements and regressions, of growing pluralism and challenging polarisation, is nothing other than a sign that democracy is a daily struggle in continuous need of care, whose core principles demand permanent vigilance. From this experience, comparative constitutional law may learn that enhancing pluralism while combatting polarisation may be a central method to incrementally consolidate democracy and preserve the precommitments achieved with difficulty during the constitution-making process.

It is not an easy endeavour, though. The stakes, after all, are inherently high and the entrenched extractive institutions will do whatever it takes to maintain their status quo. The recent political events in Brazil – where, from an increasing polarisation, Brazilians ended up electing a President with an evident authoritarian mindset[129] – are evidence of this phenomenon. Hopefully Brazil will overcome this challenge. True, this reality may prove that the pace of democratisation in Brazil is still 'two steps forward, one step back',[130] which is certainly not the ideal. Yet, it is one that at least points out that it is by enhancing the 'performative meaning'[131] of the Constitution that Brazilian democracy will be able to survive and endure.

[126] See Adrian Vermeule, *Mechanisms of Democracy* (OUP, 2007).
[127] See Steven Levitsky & Daniel Ziblatt, *How Democracies Die* (Crown, 2018).
[128] Vermeule (n 52) 14–37.
[129] See Benvindo (n 22).
[130] Kingstone & Power (n 116) 22.
[131] Habermas (n 53) 775.

4

Constitutional Unamendability in Latin America Gone Wrong?

YANIV ROZNAI*

I. Introduction

National Constitutions often impose limitations on the formal constitutional amendment power, in order to protect certain constitutional provisions, values, rules, symbols, or institutions. In this chapter, I refer to these limitations as 'constitutional unamendability'.[1] Constitutional unamendability has become a central theme in comparative constitutional law. Latin America especially, provides a fantastic region to examine unamendability as it has a long history of shielding certain constitutional values as unamendable and current burning scholarly discussions and judicial applications of unamendability. Section II of this chapter provides an overview of the spread of constitutional unamendability in Latin America. It reviews both explicit unamendability and tiered design which can be described as a second-order form of unamendability. It then describes the theory and function of unamendability in Latin America. Section III discusses the judicial enforcement of these types of unamendability. It would demonstrate that nowadays unamendability is not merely declarative but legally enforceable in court. This provides constitutional unamendability with great value as a legal mechanism that can protect the constitutional order from abusive constitutionalism. However, as Section IV would demonstrate, recent cases raise the question

* Senior Lecturer, Harry Radzyner Law School, Interdisciplinary Center (IDC) Herzliya. The data on Latin American Constitutions used for this chapter appears in the appendix of Yaniv Roznai, *Unconstitutional Constitutional Amendments – The Limits of Amendment Power* (Oxford University Press, 2017). The main idea for this chapter was shaped through a joint study with Professors Rosalind Dixon and David Landau on constitutional unamendability and presidential term-limits. All mistakes are my own, of course. Comments are welcome: yaniv.roznai@idc.ac.il.

[1] Richard Albert, 'Counterconstitutionalism' (2008) 31(1) *Dalhousie Law Journal* 37–44. On different forms of unamendability, see Richard Albert and Bertil Emrah Oder, 'The Forms of Unamendability' in Richard Albert and Bertil Emrah Oder (eds), *An Unconstitutional Constitution? Unamendability in Constitutional Democracies* (Springer, 2018) 1.

whether constitutional unamendability has gone wrong. In several cases, instead of guarding the democratic order against leaders trying to release themselves from constitutional limitations, constitutional unamendability has recently been (mis?)used by courts as a tool that allows incumbents a way to overcome constitutional restrictions imposed upon them. This, as I highlight in the conclusion, calls for rethinking the proper application of the doctrine.

II. The Spread of Constitutional Unamendability in Latin America

A. Explicit Unamendability

Whereas the existence of explicit unamendable provisions became prevalent and most noticeable after World War II, with the famous German 'eternity clause' as a prime example for such an explicit limitation on the power to amend constitutions, it was actually in Latin America where such constitutional mechanisms were prevailing in national constitutions since the early nineteenth century.[2] Few examples will illustrate this spread of explicit unamendability.

At first, explicit unamendability appeared in the form of a statement implying the eternity or the everlasting character of a specific constitutional value or institution. For example, in Argentina, the Constitution of 1826, Article II, stated that '(The Argentine Nation) shall never be the patrimony of any Person or Family.' A similar declaration appeared that very same year in the Constitution of the Bolivian Republic, which stated in Chapter I, Article II that 'Bolivia is, and always shall be, independent of every foreign domination, and cannot be the patrimony of any person or family whatsoever.'

Whereas such constitutional provisions may be regarded as more declarative or expressive than functional, a different – more explicit – form of unamendability is the one which clearly prohibited the legislature from amending certain constitutional subjects. Consider Ecuador, for example. The Constitution of Ecuador of 1843 stated in Article 110 that 'The power of Congress to reform the Constitution does not extend to the Third Article and discusses the form of government',[3] and the Constitution of 1851 provided in Article 139 that 'The power of the National Assembly to amend this Constitution shall not ever extend

[2] For a comparative and historical review see Richard Albert, 'Constitutional Handcuffs' (2010) 42(3) *Arizona State Law Journal* 663 and Yaniv Roznai, 'Unconstitutional Constitutional Amendments: The Migration and Success of a Constitutional Idea' (2013) 61(3) *American Journal of Comparative Law* 657; Michael Hein, 'Entrenchment Clauses in the History of Modern Constitutionalism' (2018) 86 The Legal History Review 434.

[3] Art. 3 provided that 'The government of the Republic of Ecuador is popular, elected, representative, alternative, and responsible, and is distributed to its exercise in three branches, legislative, executive, and judicial branches; each shall be exercised separately, and within the limits assigned to it by this Constitution; can never be together in one person.'

to Article 11, which speaks of the religion of the state or to vary the requirements of Article 12'.[4] Such explicit unamendability repeated itself in the Constitutions of 1852,[5] 1861[6] and 1869.[7]

The constitutional protection of certain constitutional principles, rules or institutions, considered to be fundamental to the constitutional order, spread through Latin America during those years. To name just a few examples, in Mexico, the Constitution of 1824 stated in Article 171 that 'The Articles of this Constitution and of the Constituent Act, which establish the liberty and independence of the Mexican Nation, its religion, form of government, liberty of the press, and division of the Supreme Power of the Confederation, and of the States, shall never be altered.' This was an attempt to declare, inter alia, that the compact between the different sovereigns of the confederation was irrevocable.[8] In Venezuela, the Constitution of 1830 stated in Article 228 that 'The authority possessed by Congress to modify the Constitution does not extend to the form of government, which shall always continue to be republican, popular, representative, responsible, and alternate,' and the Constitution of 1858 limited the amendment power, in Article 164, to 'any alteration of the form of government, which shall always be republican, popular, representative, responsible, and alternative'. In Peru, the Constitution of 1839 stated in Article 183 that 'The form of a popular representative government consolidated as unity, responsible, and alternative, and the division and independence of the legislative, executive, and judicial powers is unalterable'; and in Panama, the Constitution of 1841 limited, in Article 163, the amending power of Congress 'to vary the form of government, which it provides and which will always be popular, republican, representative, elective, alternative, and responsible nor which extends to destroy the freedom of the press.' The Bolivian Constitution of 1839, in Article 146, protected from 'The power of Congress to reform this Constitution', Article 1 according to which 'The Bolivian nation is free and independent, and its government is a popular representative' and Article 2 'The name Bolivia

[4] Article 12: 'The government of Ecuador is republican, popular, representative, elective, and responsible alternative.'

[5] Article 143: 'The power of Congress to reform the Constitution, there never will be extended to Article 13 of Title III, which refers to the religion of state.'

[6] Article 132: [a constitutional reform …] 'can never alter the bases contained in Articles 12, 13 and 1.' Article 12: 'The Religion of the Republic is Catholic, Apostolic, Roman, to the exclusion of any other. The political authorities are obliged to protect and enforce it'; Article 13: 'The Government of Ecuador is popular, representative, elective and responsible alternative'; Article 14: 'The Supreme Power is divided into Legislative, Executive and Judicial. Each exercise the powers assigned to him by this Constitution not to exceed the limits which it prescribes.'

[7] Article 115: [regarding constitutional reform] … The reform shall be valid if the majority of voters approve it, voting by "Yes" or "No"' But the bases contained in Arts. IX, XIV, and XV can never be altered.' Article IX: 'The religion of the Republic is Catholic Apostolic Roman …'; Article XIV: 'The government of Equator is republican, elective, representative, alternate, and responsible'; Article XV: 'The supreme power is divided into legislative, executive, and judicial. Each is to exercise the functions which the present Constitution assigns to it, without overstepping the bounds prescribed thereby.'

[8] Mr Payne, in his speech at the House of Reps. On the 'Annexation of Texas', Appendix to the Congressional Globe, 28th Cong 2d Sess, of Jan 1845, at p 169.

is unalterable'. A few years later, the Constitution of 1843 stated in Article 82 that 'The power which the Chambers possesses for reforming the Constitution does not extend to the form of Government, or to the independence proclaimed by the Republic.' In Brazil, the Constitution of 1891 stated in Article 90(4) that 'Proposals tending to abolish the republican federal form or the equality of representation of the States in the Senate may not be made the subject of consideration by the Congress', and the early Colombian Constitutions of 1821,[9] 1830,[10] 1832[11] and 1843[12] have all declared that the form of government was beyond the constitutional amending power.

Explicit constitutional unamendability remained a recurring design in modern constitutions in Latin America. Thus, for example, In Guatemala, the Constitution of 1965 stated in Article 267 that 'any Article referring to the principle of non-re-election of the president of the Republic may never be made' and the Constitution of 1985 in Article 281 explicitly shielded from amendments Articles 140,[13] 141,[14] 165 (paragraph g),[15] 186[16] and 187,[17] nor can any question relating to the republican form of the government, to the principle of the non-re-electability for the exercise of the presidency of the Republic be raised in any form, and neither may the effectiveness or application of the Articles that provide for alternating the tenure of the presidency of the Republic be suspended or their content changed or modified in any other way.

It thus appears clear that a primary constitutional rule protected as unamendable by some Latin American constitutions is the presidential term limit. As a lesson from past constitutional abuses, this unamendability is a design mechanism in response to a problematic history of military coups, authoritarian rule, and leaders' efforts to seize control of the state.[18]

[9] Article 190: '… But the provisions contained in Section 1 of Title I and in Section 2 of Title II may never be amended [Sec 1, Title I: the Colombian nation; Sec 2, Title II: government of Colombia].'

[10] Article 164: 'The power of Congress to amend the Constitution shall not include the power to change the form of government, which shall always be republican, popular, representative, and responsible.'

[11] Article 218: 'The power of Congress to amend this Constitution shall never extend to the Articles in Title III, which concern the form of government.'

[12] Article 172: 'The power of Congress to amend this Constitution shall never extend to the Articles in Title III, which relate to the form of government.'

[13] Article140: 'Guatemala is a free State, independent and sovereign, organized to guarantee to its inhabitants the enjoyment of their rights and liberties. Its system of government is republican, democratic, and representative.'

[14] Article 141: 'sovereignty is rooted in the people who delegate it for its exercise to the legislative, executive, and judicial organs. Subordination among them is prohibited.'

[15] Art 165(g): 'the Congress will have the power to refuse to recognize the president of the Republic if his constitutional term is expired, but he continues in the exercise of his office. In such a case, the Army will automatically fall under the authority [depender] of the Congress.'

[16] Article 186 deals with prohibitions against running for the positions of president or vice president of the Republic.

[17] Article 187 concerns the prohibition of re-election.

[18] See generally, Harry Kantor, 'Efforts Made by Various Latin American Countries to Limit The Power of the President' in Arend Lijphart (ed), *Parliamentary versus Presidential Government* (Oxford University Press 1992), 101, 102.

B. Second Order-Unamendability: A Tiered Design

Returning to Ecuador, explicit unamendability is found in more recent constitutions. According to the Constitution of 1967: 'Ordinary Congress can discuss any proposed constitutional amendment … However, Congress may not introduce any change to replace the republican form of the government or the democratic form of the State of Ecuador' (Article 258), and the Constitution of 2008 states that 'In no case shall amending the Constitution, laws, other legal and regulatory frameworks, or actions by the government endanger the rights recognized by the Constitution' (Article 84). That very Constitution also provides different procedures for 'amendment', 'partial reform' and 'total reform' (Articles 441–444), a tiered constitutional design that implies another, different, type of unamendability – a second order unamendability.

The term 'second order unamendability' was coined by Richard Albert, and refers to the distinction between the procedures for constitutional amendment and for revision or for partial and total revision.[19] Revision, as Albert explains, usually requires a more onerous process of a constituent assembly or a constitutional convention with far-reaching popular participation than amendment.[20] In other words, according to this second order unamendability, the amendment of certain constitutional values, institutions or rules is not completely prohibited but requires a different, heightened procedure, approximating the invocation of primary constituent power, most commonly through some kind of a new constituent assembly or popular involvement of the people.[21] Dixon and Landau describe a constitutional design where different constitutional values or provisions necessitate different procedures for change as a 'tiered constitutional design'.[22] A tiered constitutional design allows the update of the constitutional text while preserving the core – or more fundamental values – of the constitutional order by making their amendment more difficult: 'The rigidity of these provisions may protect the stability of certain aspects of the constitutional order, thus preserving the value of the Constitution as a focal point and precommitment device and perhaps defending against forms of constitutional change that pose a threat to the democratic order.'[23]

[19] On the distinction see generally, Richard Albert, 'Amendment and Revision in the Unmaking of Constitutions' in David Landau and Hanna Lerner (eds), *Edward Elgar Research Handbook on Comparative Constitution-Making* (Edward Elgar, forthcoming 2019).

[20] See eg Richard Albert, 'American Exceptionalism in Constitutional Amendment' (2016) 69 *Arkansas Law Review* 217, 231.

[21] For elaboration on this approximation to the primary constituent power see Yaniv Roznai, 'Constituent Powers, Amendment Powers and Popular Sovereignty: Linking Unamendability and Amendment Procedures' in Richard Albert, Xenophon Contiades and Alkmene Fotiado (eds), *The Foundations and Traditions of Constitutional Amendment* (Hart Publishing, 2017) 23.

[22] Rosalind Dixon and David Landau, 'Tiered Constitutional Design' (2018) 86 *George Washington Law Review* 438, 448–49.

[23] ibid, 476.

This tiered design has been, for example, a repeated design in the constitutions of Costa Rica. The Constitution of 1847 stated in Article 187 that '… the whole of the Charter cannot be repealed, except when the Republic is been reorganized, and it is found that the general laws of the nation require an absolute reform', thereby making a distinction between a partial reform and a total replacement. Similarly, the Constitutions of 1859 (Article 141); 1869 (Article 148), 1871 (Article 135), and 1949 (Article 196) have made a similar distinction, stating that 'The general reform of this Constitution can be affected only by a Constituent Assembly convoked for the purpose.'

In Bolivia, the Constitution of 2009 establishes in Article 411(1) that 'The total reform of the Constitution, or that which affects its fundamental premises, or affects rights, duties and guarantees, or the supremacy and reform of the Constitution, shall take place through an original plenipotentiary Constituent Assembly, put into motion by popular will through a referendum,' and in Guatemala, the Constitutions of 1945 (Article 206) and 1956 (Article 245) have both included a second order unamendability by providing different provisions for amending certain provisions. Likewise, the Constitutions of Nicaragua of 1858 (Articles 103–104), 1893 (Article 156), 1905 (Article 119), 1911 (Articles 163–164), 1950 (Articles 326–328), 1947 (Articles 334–338), and 1987 (Articles 191–195), have set different procedures for a partial reform and a total (or absolute) reform. A similar procedural distinction between reform and amendments appears in the Constitutions of Paraguay of 1940 (Article 94), 1967 (Articles 219–231), and 1992 (Articles 289–290).

Very often, national constitutions drifted between first order and second order unamendability. Venezuela, for example, in its Constitution of 1961, distinguished in Articles 245 and 246 between amendments and reform. The Constitution of 1999 also includes a 'three-track design', according to which a distinction exists between an amendment, a reform, and a complete transformation: 'The purpose of an amendment is to add to or modify one or more Articles of the Constitution, without altering the fundamental structure of the same' (Article 340); 'The purpose of constitutional reform is to effect a partial revision of this Constitution and replacement of one or more of the provisions hereof, without modifying the fundamental principles and structure of the text of the Constitution' (Article 342). In other words, whereas amendment involves a minimal alteration, a constitutional reform is more comprehensive and may comprise the partial revision of the Constitution and the replacement of one or more of the provisions that do not alter the structure and principles of the constitutional text.[24] Finally, 'The original constituent power rests with the people of Venezuela. This power may be exercised by calling a National Constituent Assembly for the purpose of transforming

[24] See Opinion No 53, 3 February 2009, the Supreme Court of Justice of Venezuela (Constitutional Chamber).

the State, creating a new juridical order and drawing up a new Constitution.' (Article 347). The Constitution also includes an explicit 'eternity clause': 'The government of the Bolivarian Republic of Venezuela and of the political organs comprising the same is, and shall always be, democratic, participatory, elective, decentralised, alternative, responsible, and pluralist, with revocable mandates (Article 6).

A tiered constitutional design, or a combination of first-order and second-order unamendability, allows for a clever balance between constitutional rigidity and flexibility; allowing the Constitution to change with changing economic, social or political circumstances while preserving the core values of the constitutional order.[25]

C. The Theory and Function of Unamendability

There are several theories behind constitutional unamendability,[26] the central one rests on a distinction between primary (or 'original') and 'secondary' (or 'derived') constituent power. The basic idea is that the primary constituent power, which belongs to 'the people', is the power to replace the Constitution with a new one, that is, creating a new constitutional order. This power is external and above the constitutional order. In contrast, the secondary constituent power is a constitutional organ created by the primary constituent power and holds only a limited power to amend the constitution. It may amend the Constitution but as long as it does not destroy it or replace it with a new one – an act belonging to the primary constituent power. Accordingly, to preserve the primary constituent power of the people themselves, there are inherent limitations on the constitutional amendment power.[27] Understood through this prism, constitutional unamendability is not undemocratic but in contrast – it is a means for protecting the people's constitution-making power by providing a sphere in which it is reserved for the people to resume their power as constitution-makers, in a way.[28] This justification is manifested, for example, in the jurisprudence of the

[25] See Yaniv Roznai, 'Constitutions, rigid(entrenched)/flexible', in Rüdiger Wolfrum, Frauke Lachenmann, and Rainer Grote (eds), *Max Planck Encyclopaedia of Comparative Constitutional Law* (Oxford University Press, 2018).

[26] For an analysis, see Po Jen Yap, 'The Conundrum of Unconstitutional Constitutional Amendments' (2015) 4(1) *Global Constitutionalism* 114; Yaniv Roznai, 'Towards A Theory of Constitutional Unamendability: On the Nature and Scope of the Constitutional Amendment Powers' (2017) 18 *Jus Politicum – Revue de Droit Politique* 5.

[27] See Joel I Colón-Ríos, *Weak Constitutionalism: Democratic Legitimacy and the Question of Constituent Power* (Routledge, 2012); Yaniv Roznai, *Unconstitutional Constitutional Amendments – The Limits of Amendment Powers* (Oxford University Press, 2017).

[28] See Yaniv Roznai, 'Necrocracy or Democracy? Assessing Objections to Constitutional Unamendability', in Richard Albert and Bertil Emrah Oder (eds), *An Unconstitutional Constitution? Unamendability in Constitutional Democracies* (Springer, 2018) 29.

Constitutional Court of Venezuela, according to which explicit unamendability can only be modified through a national Constituent Assembly, by which the whole structure and principles enshrined in the Constitution can be changed. According to the Court, constitutional unamendability restricts only the limited, secondary constituent power; it does not – and cannot – apply to 'the people' in their capacity as holders of the primary constituent power.[29] Joel Colón-Ríos is correct in his observation that this distinction between constituent power and a more limited amendment power coupled with the recognition of the extra-positive nature of constituent power (with its ability to break constitutional rules and procedures) demonstrates how influential the constitutional theory of Carl Schmitt was – and still is – in Latin America.[30]

The protection of core values of the constitutional order, through first order and second order unamendability, demonstrates that a main function of unamendability is a foremost preservative. Certain features of the constitutional order should be regarded as sacred to the constitutional order, so connected to the constitutional identity, and – as in the protection of term limits – open to abuse considering prior experience, that they should be protected and shielded against amendments.[31]

However, there is another, not less important function of unamendability: to express constitutional values. Constitutional unamendability, Richard Albert forcefully argues, fulfils an expressive function. It expresses the symbolic value of the unamendable principle, rule or institution to the constitutional order. It manifests, to both domestic and external audiences, what are the most imperative or cherished constitutional values.[32] Consider, for example, the Constitution of Cuba that declares the socialist character of the Cuban Revolutionary Constitution to be 'untouchable' or 'irrevocable'.[33] This is the 'ultimate expression of importance that can be communicated by the constitutional text'.[34]

But is unamendability, with its functions, merely *declaratory* or can it be enforced in courts?

[29] Supreme Court of Justice of Venezuela (Constitutional Chamber), Opinion No 53 (3 February 2009); Opinion No 17 of the Supreme Court of Justice of Venezuela (19 January 1999). See Joel I Colón-Ríos, 'Carl Schmitt and Constituent Power in Latin American Courts: The Cases of Venezuela and Colombia' (2011) 18(3) *Constellations* 365, 369–72.

[30] Colón-Ríos., ibid, referring, of course, to Carl Schmitt, *Constitutional Theory* (Jeffrey Seitzer tr, Duke University, 2008).

[31] On the functions of unamendability see eg Yaniv Roznai, 'Unamendability and The Genetic Code of The Constitution' (2015) 27(2) *European Review of Public Law* 775; Albert, 'Constitutional Handcuffs' (n 2).

[32] See Richard Richard, 'The Expressive Function of Constitutional Amendment Rules' (2013) 59(2) *McGill Law Journal* 225.

[33] On the history and surrounding circumstances of this unamendability see Yaniv Roznai, 'Unamendability in the Region', in Richard Albert, Derek O'Brien, and Se-Shauna Wheatle (eds), *Oxford Handbook of Caribbean Constitutions* (Oxford University Press, forthcoming).

[34] Albert and Oder, 'The Forms of Unamendability' (n 1) 9.

III. The Judicial Enforcement of Constitutional Unamendability

A. Enforcing First-order Unamendability

As noted in the first part of this chapter, constitutional unamendability was very common in the nineteenth century constitutions throughout Latin America. However, Latin American constitutions in the nineteenth century institutionalised mainly a weak-form of judicial review whereby even when courts were granted the power to review the consistency of legislation with the Constitution and in case of inconsistency to declare unconstitutionality, such declarations had no legal effect on actions of the Congress, which was usually given the final word on any question of constitutional interpretation.[35] In light of this weak-form model of judicial review of primary legislation, it seems evident that constitutional unamendability was not to be enforced in courts and regarded as primarily declarative or as guidance to the constitutional amenders.

Nonetheless, with the rise of strong judicial review in Latin America, even constitutional amendments have become the subject of judicial scrutiny, mainly *vis-à-vis* any unamendable provisions.[36] In Latin America, Juliano Zaiden Benvindo notes, 'supreme courts have become more powerful and socially trusted as a legitimate body for determining the boundaries of constitutional change'.[37] A paradigm example would be Brazil.[38]

The Brazilian Constitution includes unamendable clauses (*cláusulas pétreas*), listed in Article 60(4) of the 1988 Constitution: 'No proposed constitutional amendment shall be considered that is aimed at abolishing the following: (a) the federalist form of the National Government; (b) direct, secret, universal, and periodic suffrage; (c) separation of powers; (d) individual rights and guarantees.' These are considered to be the basic constitutional principles of the Brazilian constitutional order. As Eneida Desiree Salgado notes, 'These entrenched clauses represent the essence of a hard constitutionalism. They reflect the heart of political

[35] Joel I Colón-Ríos 'A new typology of judicial review of legislation' (2014) 3(2) *Global Constitutionalism* 143, 145–47.

[36] See ibid, 148–62.

[37] Juliano Zaiden Benvindo, 'Brazil in the Context of the Debate Over Unamendability in Latin America' in Richard Albert and Bertil Emrah Oder (eds), *An Unconstitutional Constitution? Unamendability in Constitutional Democracies* (Springer, 2018) 345, 347.

[38] For elaboration, see Benvindo, ibid; Conrado Hübner Mendes, 'Judicial Review of Constitutional Amendments in the Brazilian Supreme Court' (2005) 17 *Florida Journal of International Law* 449; Luciano Maia, 'The Creation and Amending Process in the Brazilian Constitution' in Mads Andenas (ed), *The Creation and Amendment of Constitutional Norms* (BIICL, 2000) 54; Valentina Rita Scotti, 'Constitutional Amendments and Constitutional Core Values: the Brazilian Case in a Comparative Perspective (2018) 5(3) *Revista de Investigações Constitucionais* 59, 66–71.

decisions that demanded a new constitutional moment, a refounding of the state. (…) The permanence of the immutable spine in the Constitution depends on the respect for the rules of constitutional reforms, normally ensured by judicial review.'[39] The Brazilian Constitution provides the Supreme Federal Court with authority to invalidate 'federal or state law or normative acts' (Article 102, I, a). Does this authority extend to review also constitutional amendments vis-à-vis the *cláusulas pétreas*? Since 1993, the Supreme Federal Court declared that it possesses an inherent power to review the constitutionality even of constitutional amendments approved by Congress, through a concrete or abstract review of constitutionality.[40]

This authority, according to the Brazilian Supreme Federal Court, was deductive from the very idea of constitutional supremacy and normative hierarchy. When a conflict arises between the *cláusulas pétreas* and an ordinary constitutional amendment, the latter can be declared unconstitutional, null and void:

> Constitutional amendments … not being original constitutional norms, are not excluded from the ambit of a successive or repressive control of constitutionality. National Congress, when exercising its derived constituent power, and performing its reforming function, is legally bound by the original constituent power, which has laid down, besides circumstantial entrenchment to reform, an immutable clause, immune to parliamentary revision. Explicit material limitations, defined by paragraph 4 of Art. 60 of the constitution constrain reforming power conferred upon the legislative. The immutability of such thematic nucleus, eventually violated, may render legitimate an abstract normative control and even a concrete control of constitutionality.[41]

And indeed, regarding itself as guardian of the Constitution, the Supreme Federal Court has been actively enforcing the unamendability and supervising formal constitutional change, often with a broad interpretation of the unamendable provision. The Supreme Federal Court, in the words of Benvindo, 'has increasingly made use of its power to declare null and void constitutional amendments without even raising doubts on the legitimacy of such a task, interpreting it as an evident consequence of its very existence.'[42]

[39] Eneida Desiree Salgado, 'Brazilian Legislators at Work: Constitutional Amendments as Electoral Strategy' (2017) 16(2) *Election Law Journal* 325, 328.

[40] See Yaniv Roznai and Letícia Regina Camargo Kreuz, 'Conventionality Control and Amendment 95/2016 – A Brazilian case of unconstitutional constitutional amendment' (2018) 5(2) *Revista de Investigaciones Constitucionales* 35.

[41] ADIMC 466/ 91 DF, cited in Roznai, *Unconstitutional Constitutional Amendments* (n 27) 205. See also ADIMC 981/93 PR: 'Revisions and amendment, as procedures to introduce constitutional changes, are expressions of an instituted constituent power, thus, limited by nature. The revision … is subject to the limits established by … the constitution. Constitutional changes deriving from a revision are subject to judicial control and scrutiny, as regard the petrous clauses', ibid.

[42] See Benvindo (n 37) 361; See also Michael Freitas Mohallem, 'Immutable Clauses and Judicial Review in India, Brazil and South Africa: Expanding Constitutional Courts' Authority' (2011) 15(5) *International Journal of Human Rights* 765.

This demonstrates that constitutional unamendability can be a useful bar against a constitutional change that aims to undermine the core values of the constitutional order, protected by unamendability.

Not in all countries in Latin America have courts taken upon themselves the authority to review constitutional amendments. In Mexico, the Supreme Court has held that the constitutional amendment power is beyond the scope of constitutional control, and that it shall not apply limitations on the amendment power.[43] Judicial review of amendments raises difficult questions of legitimacy as it shifts the locus of constitutional change from those elected political branches to the judiciary

An extreme case that demonstrates the enforceability of unamendability, but one that also raises many questions concerning its legitimacy and usefulness, comes from Honduras.

The 1982 Honduran Constitution limited presidents to only one lifetime term in office, prevented any attempt to amend the no-reelection rule by embedding it in an unamendable provision, and moreover provided that anyone attempting to change the term limit would 'cease' to hold office and be barred from doing so for the subsequent ten years.[44] The unamendability of the presidential term-limits played a central role in the removal from power of President Manuel Zelaya in 2009. After winning election, Zelaya contemplated the option of replacing the 1982 constitution. His opponents contended that the aim behind this sought replacement was to evade the unamendable provision, although Zelaya did not explicitly state that he sought presidential reelection. After Zelaya continued to advance his plan to conduct a 'non-binding consultation' on whether to call a Constituent Assembly in spite of judicial decisions barring the consultation, the military arrived at his house shortly before the vote was to be held and put him on a plane to Costa Rica.[45] While the legality of the Zelaya removal is contentious, the story demonstrates that the use of constitutional unamendability may be a successful stop sign, even if risky.

[43] See the working paper by Mariana Velasco Rivera, 'Unconstitutional Constitutional Amendments in Mexico: The Failure of the Guardians of the Constitution and its Implications for Constitutional Hyper-Reformism' (15 January 2016), https://ssrn.com/abstract=2989394 and the presentation by Héctor Fix-Fierro and Francisco Tortolero, 'Challenging the sovereign: Judicial Review of constitutional amendments in Mexico' (Presented at the Round Table Unconstitutional Constitutional Amendments, 26.04.2010), www.youtube.com/watch?v=_i4SMq97oHU.

[44] Article 239 of the Constitution contains a prohibition on presidential re-election and also stipulates that anyone who 'violates' the no-re-election rule or who 'proposes its reform' shall 'cease immediately' in their public posts and will be prohibited from serving in office for 10 years. In addition, Article 374 declares that the no-reelection provision can under no circumstances be amended. Moreover, according to Article 42(5), citizenship may be lost by 'inciting, promoting, or supporting the continuation or reelection' of the president.

[45] For elaboration on this, see Andrew Friedman, 'Dead Hand Constitutionalism: The Danger of Eternity Clauses in New Democracies' (2011) 4(1) *Mexico Law Review* 77, 82–83; Frank M. Walsh, 'The Honduran Constitution is Not a Suicide Pact: The Legality of Honduran President Manuel Zelaya's Removal' (2010) 38 *Georgia Journal of International and Comparative Law* 339; Marco Cáceres di Iorio, *The Good Coup: The Overthrow of Manuel Zelaya in Honduras* (CCB Publishing, 2010).

B. Enforcing Second-order Unamendability

Judicial review of amendment where the Constitution includes a first-order unamendability seems natural or at the very least seems reasonable. As Aharon Barak notes, 'Judicial review is a natural mechanism for protecting eternity clauses in the constitution. Judicial review provides (legal) "teeth" to the eternity clause. In this respect, there is no substantive difference between a regular statute that violates the Constitution and an amendment to the Constitution that violates the eternity clause. Just as judicial review is recognized in the first case … it should also be recognized in the second case.'[46] Likewise, when the Constitution includes a second-order unamendability, providing for a tiered constitutional design, it would appear natural for a court to supervise the process, making sure that constitutional changes are taking place according to the correct procedures. Whereas in such cases, the court would have to examine the content of the amendment, such a review is more like a procedural review; a semi-procedural review, if you like.[47]

The Colombian example is an interesting one, in that respect. Colombia has a long history with judicial review of constitutional amendments, dating back to the 1950s.[48] Yet, it is under the 1991 Constitutional that fascinating constitutional development occurred as the court developed its 'Constitutional Replacement Doctrine'. The Colombian Constitution of 1991 does not include any unamendable provisions and restricts the powers of the Constitutional Court to review constitutional amendments 'only for errors of procedure in their formation' (Articles 241 and 379). Nonetheless, the Constitution provides various methods for a formal change: it can be reformed by Congress, a Constituent Assembly, or a referendum (Articles 374–78). However, the multiple procedures allowed the Constitutional Court to develop a wide definition of the concept 'errors of procedure' when reviewing constitutional amendments. In opinion C-551/03, the Court noted that the constitutional amendment power does not extend to the *replacement* of the Constitution with a different one, and when it substitutes the Constitution, it acts in ultra vires. This procedure and substance are intertwined. It is only the constituent power, acting through extraordinary mechanisms such as a Constituent Assembly that can constitute a new constitution.[49] As the court stated, in another case, 'Congress derives its power to reform the Constitution from the constitution itself. It has a derivative or secondary status as a constituent force. Therefore, it can reform or amend the Constitution, but it cannot replace it or substitute it for

[46] Aharon Barak, 'Unconstitutional Constitutional Amendments' (2011) 44(3) *Israel Law Review* 321, 333.

[47] See Ittai Bar-Siman-Tov, 'Semiprocedural Judicial Review' (2012) 6(3) *Legisprudence* 271. See also Colón-Ríos, *Weak Constitutionalism* (n 27), 134: 'in the context of constitutional reform, procedure and substance overlap with each other'.

[48] See Mario Alberto Cajas Sarria, 'Judicial review of constitutional amendments in Colombia: a political and historical perspective, 1955–2016' 2017(3) *The Theory and Practice of Legislation* 245.

[49] Sentencia 551/03, 09.07.2003.

another constitution. If Congress crosses the line between amending the Constitution, and replacing it, it violates its constitutional powers and competence. If that happens, the Court can overturn Congress' decision, not on the grounds of content review, but based on the fact that a branch of government has ignored its constitutional competence, and therefore, violated constitutional procedural rules.'[50] Modifying an essential clause that transforms the nature of the constitutional regime can be considered a 'constitutional substitution', a change that can only be decided by a Constitutional Assembly convened extraordinarily to review the constitutional regime. This has come to be known as the constitutional replacement (or 'substitution') doctrine.[51]

Accordingly, the Court reviews the constitutionality of constitutional amendments on a regular basis. Very often it upholds the amendments,[52] but sometimes it declares the constitutional change to be an unconstitutional replacement.[53] In recent years, the doctrine has been applying in various instances. For instance, in Decision C-285 of 1 June 2016, the Court invalidated a constitutional provision that introduced a new judicial council in charge of managing the judicial branch, and in Decision C-373 of 13 July 2016, the Court invalidated a constitutional provision that created a new Tribunal in charge of prosecuting and trying criminal acts committed by members of Apex Courts, including Constitutional Court's Justices.[54] Moreover, the Court has been highly involved in the Colombia Peace process.[55]

[50] Opinion C-1040/05. See also judgment C-588/2009 in which the Court invalidated an amendment which granted tenure to certain employees of the Public Administration without passing the necessary merits exams. The Court held that this amendment replaced the principle of equality and the principle of merit which are essential elements of the Constitution.

[51] On this doctrine see generally, Carlos Bernal, 'Unconstitutional Constitutional Amendments in the Case Study of Colombia: An Analysis of the Justification and Meaning of the Constitutional Replacement Doctrine' (2013) 11 *International Journal of Constitutional Law* 339; Gonzalo Andres Ramirez-Cleves, 'The Unconstitutionality of Constitutional Amendments in Colombia: The Tension Between Majoritarian Democracy and Constitutional Democracy' in Thomas Bustamante, Bernardo Gonçalves Fernandes (eds), *Democratizing Constitutional Law: Perspectives on Legal Theory and the Legitimacy of Constitutionalism* (Springer, 2016), ch 10. See also Juan F González-Bertomeu, 'The Colombian Constitutional Court's Doctrine on the Substitution of the Constitution', this vol at ch 5.

[52] See eg decisions C-094-17; C-112-17; C-290-2017, in which the Court upheld some provisions of an amendment to the judicial branch.

[53] For an elaboration, see González-Bertomeu (n 51). For instance, In Judgment C-1056/2012, the Court declared that an amendment prescribing that rules about conflict of interests of congressmen would not be applicable in the discussion and passing of constitutional amendments was a constitutional replacement. The Court held that this amendment infringed basic constitutional principles concerning the respect of public morality in a democracy. In Judgment C-10/2013, the Court declared that an amendment modifying certain rules concerning the distribution of income from mining taxes between administrative regions was not a replacement of the Constitution.

[54] On these decisions see Mario Cajas Sarria, 'The Unconstitutional Constitutional Amendment Doctrine and the Reform of the Judiciary in Colombia' (1 September 2016) *ICON Blog*, www.iconnectblog.com/2016/09/the-unconstitutional-constitutional-amendment-doctrine-and-the-reform-of-the-judiciary-in-colombia/.

[55] In the Judgments C-579 of 28 August 2013 and C-577 of 6 August 2014, the Constitutional Court held that the amendment of the 'Legal Framework for Peace' did not replace the Constitution and declared its conditional constitutionality. On these cases, see Carlos Bernal-Pulido, 'Transitional

Perhaps most famously, the constitutional replacement doctrine played a central role in the presidential term limit cases. In the first case, President Alvaro Uribe, who held power from 2002 amended the Constitution to change the single lifetime term limit and allow a single consecutive reelection, an amendment that was challenged before the Court. In its decision C-1040/05 regarding presidential re-election, the court upheld the amendment, permitting Uribe to run for a re-election and win a second term in 2006.[56] However, another attempt to amend the Constitution again in order to allow a possible third term, was again challenged before the Court. Only this this time, in judgment C-141/2010, the Court in a 7–2 vote blocked the attempt, holding that allowing a third consecutive term would constitute a substitution of the Constitution and thus an unconstitutional constitutional amendment. A third consecutive presidential term, the Court emphasised, would undermine the system of checks and balances and would affect the entire constitutional order.[57] Uribe complied with the decision and was replaced with Juan Manuel Santos at the end of his second term in 2010.

This case demonstrates, again, that constitutional unamendability may function as a useful mechanism to hinder, if not even completely stop, constitutional changes that would undermine the constitutional-democratic order, what has become to be known as 'abusive constitutionalism', following David Landau's influential article.[58]

Justice within the Framework of a Permanent Constitution: The Case Study of The Legal Framework For Peace in Colombia' (2014) 3 *Cambridge Journal of International and Comparative Law* 1136. More recently, in judgment C-699-16, the Court upheld the fast-track amendment that modified (and eased) the procedures to amend the Constitution, in order to implement the peace agreements in a swift way; in judgment C-332-17, the Court invalidated the prohibition for Congressmen to make changes to amendments introduced by the executive branch and aimed at implementing the Peace Agreement; and in judgment C-630-17, the Court endorsed an amendment that established that certain components of the peace agreement cannot be changed by forthcoming presidential administrations. See Gonzalo Ramírez-Cleves, 'The Colombian Constitutional Court Rules that the Peace Agreement is Mandatory for Three Presidential Terms' (26 October 2017) *ICON Blog*, www.iconnectblog.com/2017/10/the-colombian-constitutional-court-rules-that-the-peace-agreement-is-mandatory-for-three-presidential-terms/; Vicente F Benítez R, 'Judicial Review of Peace Amendments in Colombia: Towards Supraconstitutional Rules and Plurality Opinions?' (31 October 2017), *ICON Blog*, at: www.iconnectblog.com/2017/10/judicial-review-of-peace-amendments-in-colombia-towards-supraconstitutional-rules-and-plurality-opinions. In judgment C-674-17, the Court upheld the institution of a Special Jurisdiction for Peace whose main objectives is to prosecute and try former FARC guerrillas' combatants. The amendment also included a provision by which third parties (ie non-combatants) who indirectly participated in the armed conflict (such as entrepreneurs or politicians who funded illegal armed groups) had to be tried by the Special Jurisdiction for Peace. Nonetheless, the Court invalidated this provision, and these third parties can be tried by this jurisdiction only on a voluntary basis. In judgment C-020-18, the Court held that an amendment establishing funds aimed at financing some expenditures to implement the peace agreement does not infringe the Constitution. I thank Vicente F Benítez R for assistance with these judgments.

[56] On this decision see Manuel Jose Cepeda Espinosa and David Landau, *Colombian Constitutional Law: Leading Cases* (Oxford University Press, 2017) 342.

[57] See Espinosa and Landau, ibid, at 351; David Landau, 'Institutional failure and intertemporal theories of judicial role in the global south' in David Bilchitz and David Landau (eds), *The Evolution of the Separation of Powers: Between the Global North and the Global South* (Edward Elgar, 2018) 31, 35.

[58] David Landau, 'Abusive Constitutionalism' (2013) 47(1) *University of California Davis Law Review* 189.

C. Judicially-made Unamendability

As elaborated in previous sections, many Latin American Constitutions adopted constitutional unamendability either in its strong form of unamendability or its second-order form of tiered design. These two forms, as I have demonstrated, provided courts in Latin America with legal anchoring for conducting judicial review of constitutional amendments, putting into practice Carl Schmitt's theoretical presuppositions that the power to 'amend' the Constitution clearly cannot be used in order to abolish the constitution.[59] However, what if the Constitution does not include unamendable provisions?

Even in the absence of any explicit limits, some courts in Latin America have ruled that the amendment power is inherently limited by implicit limits,[60] or have made *obiter dicta* statements in this spirit, as the Supreme Court of Justice in Costa Rica stated, in an *obiter*, constitutional amendments cannot violate 'the essence of fundamental human rights.'[61]

In Argentina, generally, the Court regards itself as competent to adjudicate the process of amendments.[62] The Constitution of 1994 includes a tiered design as it allows for a total or partial reform of its contents that must be declared by at least two-thirds of the members of Congress and must be carried out by a special Constituent Assembly created for that purpose (Article 30). When initiating a reform, Congress must specify which provisions demand revisions and no additional amendments can be introduced by the Assembly. In the *Rios* case of 1993, the Supreme Court stated in an *obiter dictum* that 'the authority of a constituent convention is limited solely to the review of those matters submitted to them for resolution and *within the principles of the Constitution*' [emphasis added].[63] In other words, it imposed implied unamendability upon the convention's power, according to which it must act within the Constitution's basic principles. As Raúl Gustavo Ferreyra stated, 'a constitutional amendment is a process producing a change in the content of a system, but without producing its destruction, since continuity is kept'.[64] While no constitutional amendment was thus far invalidated on substantive grounds, an amendment was invalidated on procedural grounds. In the *Fayt* case of 1998, a District Court partially invalidated a constitutional amendment enacted by a constituent assembly as part of the 1994 amendments to the constitution, requiring justices who reached 75 years of age on the court to be

[59] Schmitt (n 30) 150.

[60] See Joel Colón-Ríos, 'Beyond Parliamentary Sovereignty: The Doctrine of Implicit Limits To Constitutional Reform in Latin America' (2013) 44 *Victoria University of Wellington Law Review* 521.

[61] Res 2010-13313 Supreme Court of Justice of Costa Rica (Constitutional Chamber).

[62] See Ileana Gomez, 'Declaring Unconstitutional a Constitutional Amendment: The Argentine Judiciary Forges Ahead' (2000) 31 *The University of Miami Inter-American Law Review* 93.

[63] 'Rios', [1994-C] LL 46, 48.

[64] Raúl Gustavo Ferreyra, 'Argentine Constitutional Development – Creation and Application of the Federal Constitutional System in Focus' (2006) 54 *Ahrbuch des Öffentlichen Rechts der Gegenwart* 713, 736.

reappointed by the same supermajority process that was required for their original appointment. The Court ruled that the assembly exceeded its delegated mandate as the amendment detracted from the lifetime appointment of justices (which was part of the original constitutional text), and the enabling law had not expressly authorised the assembly to modify their lifetime appointments.[65] More recently, the Supreme Court overruled *Fayt* in the *Schiffrin* case, in which it reaffirmed the holding that it has oversight over the work of the constituent assembly on procedural grounds, but declares it should exercise that oversight with a high level of deference, given that the assembly is an expression of popular sovereignty. Eventually, it disagreed that the Assembly acted outside its purview when it introduced the quasi-forced retirement norm.[66]

In Peru, the Constitution of 1993 does not include any unamendable provisions. Yet, in a series of cases decided in 2005 regarding 'reform of the pensionary system', the Peruvian Constitutional Tribunal declared that it is competent to invalidate constitutional amendments that violate *principios juridicos* or basic legal principles and *valores democraticos basicos* or basic democratic values. While upholding the amendment at issue, the Court refuted the argument that the control of a constitutional reform bill could be seen as a 'non-justiciable political question'. It found that such a proposition yields under the consideration that the Court, as the main guarantor of the Constitution, has to ensure that the supreme norm is not, in itself, violated by amendments that could harm basic legal principles and basic democratic values on which it is based, as this is against the established procedures for constitutional reform.[67] In another case in 2005, the Court emphasised the material limits of a reform, that being what it considered the fundamental principles that give identity to the Constitution, namely the principles of human dignity, the republican form of government, the democratic rule of law, people's sovereign power, or any other evaluative component that the Charter recognises as a fundamental matter.[68]

Thus, in Latin America, one can find different types of constitutional unamendability: explicit unamendability – which was originally declarative but increasingly enforced in courts; second-order unamendability that refers to a tiered constitutional design, also subject to judicial semi-procedural scrutiny, and an evolving notion of implied limitations, according to which constitutional reform procedure must be exercised within the fundamental principles of the constitutional order. Constitutional unamendability provides courts with a powerful tool to be involved in constitutional change, and even completely stop certain formal constitutional

[65] 'Fayt', Suplemento de Derecho Constitucional, LL, 18 de Agosto de 1998, 1, 8–9. This decision was affirmed by the Appellate Court, but on different grounds.

[66] CSJ 159/2012 (48-S) CSI. I thank Daniel M Brinks and David Law for this information.

[67] Opinion No 050-2004-AI/TC, 004-2005-PI/TC, Sentencia No. 007-2005-PI/TC, and Opinion No 009-2005-PI/TC (03.06.2005), para 3; Anibal Quiroga León, 'Los Excesos del Tribunal Constitucional Peruano: A Propósito Del Control Concentrado De La Constitución' (2005) 3(2) *Estudios Constitucionales* 29, 38.

[68] Opinion No 0024-2005-PI/TC, (02.11.2005), para 12.

changes. It proved to be a useful tool in preserving the democratic constitutional order. Yet, this powerful tool may also be utilised not to limit governmental power and to preserve the constitutional order but in contrast to allow leaders to pursue a constitutional change they are unable to achieve through formal constitutional means. It is this trend that gives rise to the question, has constitutional unamendability gone wrong?

IV. Constitutional Unamendability Gone Wrong?

As noted above, a central question regarding limits to constitutional change in Latin America surrounds the issue of presidential term-limits. This is because, perhaps naturally, when the Constitution limits the ability of presidents to continue in office they seek to replace or amend it.[69] And, indeed, in countries such as Venezuela, Colombia, Ecuador, Bolivia, Costa Rica, Honduras, Nicaragua, and Paraguay, incumbent presidents have lately led efforts to ease or remove presidential term limits, and constitutional courts in the region have, in turn, been frequently called upon to rule on the constitutionality of such efforts.[70]

As noted earlier, in Colombia, the Court famously held that President Uribe could amend the Constitution to seek a second consecutive term in office, but not a third. The Colombia example demonstrates how constitutional unamendability (in this case, the 'constitutional replacement doctrine') can be a useful tool against presidential attempts to eliminate presidential term-limits. And in Honduras, it is partially due to the ex-ante prohibition on amending presidential term limits that has led to the outset of Zelaya. Certainly, judicial application of constitutional unamendability doctrines has played a major role in the constitutional change of term limits in Latin American in recent years.[71]

However, constitutional unamendability has not only blocked attempts to remove presidential term limits. In recent years, constitutional unamendability has been (mis?)used in order to remove presidential term limits, declaring them to be unconstitutional constitutional norms. In countries such as Nicaragua,[72]

[69] On the recent trend in Latin American countries to change national constitutions to allow presidential re-election see Javier Corrales and Michael Penfold, 'Manipulating Term Limits in Latin America' (2014) 25(4) *Journal of Democracy* 157; Elena Martínez-Barahona, 'Constitutional Courts and Constitutional Change: Analysing the Cases of Presidential Re-Election in Latin America,' in Detlef Nolte and Almut Schilling-Vacaflor (eds), *New Constitutionalism in Latin America. Promises and Practices* (Routledge, 2012) 289–309. See generally, Gabriel L Negretto, *Making Constitutions: Presidents, Parties, and Institutional Choice in Latin America* (Cambridge University Press, 2013).

[70] See David Landau, Yaniv Roznai and Rosalind Dixon, 'Term Limits and the Unconstitutional Constitutional Amendment Doctrine: Lessons from Latin America' in Alexander Baturo and Robert Elgie (eds), *Politics of Presidential Term Limits* (Oxford University Press, forthcoming 2019).

[71] See ibid. In some instances, such as in Bolivia, Ecuador, and Venezuela, courts have held that attempts to ease or eliminate presidential term limits do not necessarily violate basic constitutional principles and do not require a special, demanding process for the formal change.

[72] Decision 504 of 2009 (Constitutional Chamber, Supreme Court).

Honduras,[73] Costa Rica,[74] and Bolivia,[75] courts have in fact declared presidential term limits to violate constitutional rights, such as the right to vote, and accordingly as unconstitutional constitutional norms, issuing judicial decisions removing them from the Constitution and thereby allowing incumbents to run for reelection when they would not otherwise be able to do so.[76]

Consider a 2009 decision of the Constitutional Chamber of the Supreme Court of Nicaragua. After winning the presidency in 2007, Daniel Ortega, the incumbent president, sought possible reelection in 2011. However, a constitutional provision, added to the Constitution as an amendment in 1995, prohibited consecutive reelection, and limited presidents to serving only two terms in their lifetimes. Since Ortega had already served as president in the 1980s, these two restrictions prohibited his re-election. Unlike Honduras, the presidential term limit was not protected with constitutional unamendability. Nonetheless, Ortega simply lacked the required supermajority in Congress to push for a constitutional amendment that would remove the term limit. It is here that constitutional unamendability and the 'unconstitutional constitutional amendment doctrine' came 'to the rescue'. Ortega challenged before the Constitutional Chamber of the Supreme Court the term limit itself, arguing that this amendment (added to the 1987 constitution in 1995), was an unconstitutional constitutional amendment. The Court held that the constitutional amendment violated the rights of 'electoral suffrage' of both voters and those who are being elected in addition to the principle of equality by treating those who had already been elected differently from those who had not. The court emphasised people's sovereignty and their right to make a free choice as to their representatives. Due to its violation of the core principles of the original 1987 Constitution, the amendment that added term limits was declared to be unconstitutional and void.[77]

In Costa Rica, the Constitution includes a second-order unamendability as it distinguishes between a partial amendment (Article 195) and a general amendment (Article 196), without defining what would constitute a partial or a general amendment. It is this distinction that became central in the term limit decision of 2003. The 1949 Constitution of Costa Rica included a non-reelection rule according to which a president could not be reelected unless eight years have passed since the end of the first term of office. In 1969, the legislative assembly amended the Constitution and prohibited any presidential re-election. The amendment has passed as a partial amendment. In 1999, President Oscar Arias Sanchez announced that he would seek to run for election in 2002 and would attempt to revise the Constitution in a manner that would allow him to run

[73] Decision of 22 April 2015 (Constitutional Chamber, Supreme Court).

[74] Decision 0771-2003 (Constitutional Chamber, Supreme Court).

[75] Decision 2017/84 (Plurinational Constitutional Tribunal).

[76] This trend was recently explored in more details in David Landau, 'Presidential Term Limits in Latin America: A Critical Analysis of the Migration of the Unconstitutional Constitutional Amendment Doctrine' (2018) 12(2) *Law & Ethics of Human Rights* 225.

[77] Decision 504 of 2009, 19 October 2009.

again for office. After failing to advance a constitutional amendment that would remove the term limit, Sanchez' supporters challenged the constitutionality of the amendment. At first, in a decision of 2000, the claim that the 1969 amendment was unconstitutional was rejected. However, after the membership in the Constitutional Chamber had changed, increasing the numbers of known supporters of reelection, another challenge was brought to the Constitutional Chamber in 2003. This time, in a 5 to 2 vote, the Constitutional Chamber held that the 1969 amendment that imposed an absolute ban on reelection was unconstitutional. Thus, in that case, the court declared that a constitutional amendment prohibiting the reelection of resident was adopted in a wrong procedure. Since it limits fundamental rights of voting and elections it should have been adopted under the general reform procedure (Article 196) and not the partial reform procedure (Article 195). Accordingly, the amendment is unconstitutional.[78]

Michael B Wise notes that 'the very different approach taken by the majority … in 2003 from its approach in 2000, coming directly after the change in composition of the Chamber, suggests that the magistrates may have reached the decision with their eyes set on a desired political result. The elaborately constructed rationale of the decision further suggests that the court was determined to reach a result allowing former President Arias to run again.'[79]

Regardless of whether one agrees with the courts in these two examples from Nicaragua and Costa Rica, which use constitutional unamendability to remove presidential term limits, at the very least these decisions are to some extent reasonable as they examine constitutional amendments enacted by the limited secondary constituent power vis-à-vis the original constitution. But unamendability went completely wrong with a decision from Honduras in 2015.

In Honduras, in 2015, facing presidential term-limits, President Juan Orlando Hernandez sought to find a way to relax or remove these limits. As the term limit was protected by unamendability, amending the Constitution was not an option. And, remembering the lesson from the Zelaya episode, proposing to have a new constitution was also likely to be considered as unconstitutional. Hernandez' allies from the ruling National Party filed a case to the Supreme Court claiming that the constitutional provisions concerning term limits were unconstitutional. In response, the Constitutional Chamber of the Supreme Court accepted the challenge, and held that the one-term limit, the unamendable provision and the provision prohibiting attempts to change the term limit were unconstitutional and 'inapplicable'. This decision allowed Hernandez to run for reelection, and to win reelection in 2017. Without this judicial decision, Hernandez had no other legal way to remove the term limits. This decision, Albert correctly remarks, brought

[78] Resolution No 2003-02771 (4 April 2003). For an overview see Michael B Wise, 'Judicial Review and Its Politicization in Central America: Guatemala, Costa Rica, and Constitutional Limits on Presidential Candidates' (2010) 7 *Santa Clara Journal of International Law* 145, 172–76.

[79] Wise, ibid., at 176–77.

about a fundamental change to the core of the constitution.[80] It left the country without any term limits. The decision of the court is highly dubious. Radim Dragomaca asked the following question: 'if the Constitution establishes some part of itself as being unchangeable, and this provision can be said to be addressed to both the legislature and the courts … does it also limit the power of the courts to change the meaning of that provision through interpretation? Does it require the judge to use a different and more restrictive method of interpretation than s/he would otherwise use?'[81] Ostensibly, it appears to me that if certain constitutional principles or provisions are considered unamendable, this logically means that courts cannot interpret them in a manner that modifies their core so as to change the constitutional identity. This does not mean that courts cannot interpret these provisions or principles. Surely, courts retain the legal power to interpret and reinterpret constitutional provisions, even unamendable ones. What courts seemingly cannot do is change the essence of the core of the Constitution and its basic principles, because such an action requires resorting to the primary constituent power. Therefore, the Court decision in Honduras violated the unamendable provision, removing a core principle form the constitution. This, I claim elsewhere, was 'an unconstitutional change by the court'.[82]

It is important to mention the political context that predated the court's decision. In 2012, the National party, which dominated elections after Zelaya's removal, had replaced four of the five members of the Constitutional Chamber of the Supreme Court, after a dispute over decisions the Chamber had issued on another matter. The 'packing' of the Constitutional Chamber was likely illegal, since it relied on impeachment powers that the Congress did not possess in the text of the 1982 Constitution at the time. Nonetheless, it was this 'packed' chamber that issued the unanimous 2015 decision invalidating the presidential re-election.[83]

Most astonishingly, as noted earlier, the primary theory behind constitutional unamendability is the distinction between primary and secondary constituent powers. But in the Honduran case it is the court, a constituted organ that violates a constitutional provision that appeared in the original constitution and was enacted by the primary constituent power. This was not a constitutional

[80] Richard Albert, 'Constitutional Amendment and Dismemberment' (2018) 43(1) *Yale Journal of International Law* 1, 68–9.

[81] Radim Dragomaca, 'Constitutional Amendments and the Limits of Judicial Activism: The Case of the Czech Republic' in Willem Witteveen and Maartje DeVisser (eds), *The Jurisprudence of Aharon Barak: Views from Europe* (Wolf Legal Publishers, 2011) 198.

[82] Yaniv Roznai, 'Unconstitutional Constitutional Change by Courts' (2018) 51(3) *New England Law Review* 572–73.

[83] Apparently, one justice of the Chamber allegedly attempted to change his vote the following day, which would have transferred the case to the Plenary of the Supreme Court. However, this attempt was not allowed on the grounds that the vote already taken was final. See Corte de Honduras abre las puertas a reeleccion presidencial, Milenio, at www.milenio.com/internacional/Corte-Honduras-puertas-reeleccion-presidencial_0_505749431.html.

amendment, and accordingly the court's decision cannot be based on 'constitutional unamendability'. Accordingly, Landau, Dixon and I, claim that the Court's reasoning was problematic in key respects.[84]

The trend of using constitutional unamendability to remove term limits continued recently with a decision of 2017 by the Bolivian Constitutional Court. Relying on the argument that presidential term limits violate international human rights law, the Court held that the term limits existing in the 2009 Constitution are unconstitutional.[85]

V. Conclusion

Since the early nineteenth century, constitutional unamendability has spread throughout Latin America. From a declarative mechanism describing the core values of the constitutional order to an enforceable legal mechanism in court, unamendability has become a forceable tool to preserve the constitutional order and its core principles against attempts to undermine the democratic order.

Of course, in the context of the region, one of the most important protections was that of presidential term limits. Constitutional changes to term limits may pose a grave risk of erosion of liberal democracy. Allowing indefinite reelection may threaten the liberal democratic order to a point where the political field is gradually shifting towards incumbents, potentially allowing a regime to become a hybrid democracy or a 'competitive authoritarian'.[86]

Considering this risk to the democratic order, constitutional unamendability has proven to be a useful tool against the use of constitutional change tools to undermine democracy and the constitutional order. However, the power to declare constitutional norms unconstitutional is great and 'with great power comes great responsibility'. The judicial review power of constitutional amendments allegedly provides courts with the final say over constitutional values. It makes the courts the final arbiters of society's values. This power should be used with care.

[84] See David Landau, Rosalind Dixon and Yaniv Roznai, 'From an Unconstitutional Constitutional Amendment to an Unconstitutional Constitution? Lessons from Honduras' (forthcoming 2019), *Global Constitutionalism*. The court also held that domestic constitutional norms could be set aside if they conflict with fundamental norms of international human rights law, but it made little effort to justify or ground this assertion in Honduran constitutional law. For different senses of how an original constitution may be unconstitutional based on case studies from the United States, South Africa, Canada and Mexico see Richard Albert, 'Four Unconstitutional Constitutions and their Democratic Foundations' (2017) 50 *Cornell International Law Journal* 169.

[85] Tribunal Constitucional Plurinacionl, Sentencia Constitucional N. 0084 of 2017, Nov. 28, 2017. See Sergio Verdugo, 'How the Bolivian Constitutional Court Helped the Morales Regime to Break the Political Insurance of the Bolivian Constitution' (10 December 2017) *ICON Blog*, www.iconnectblog.com/2017/12/how-the-bolivian-constitutional-court-helped-the-morales-regime-to-break-the-political-insurance-of-the-bolivian-constitution/.

[86] See eg Stevern Levitsky and Lucan A Way, 'Elections Without Democracy: The Rise of Competitive Authoritarianism' (2002) 13(2) *Journal of Democracy* 51.

Unfortunately, recent decisions from Latin America demonstrate that even this judicial review power can often be misused not as a 'counter-majoritarian tool' that limits governmental power but as a tool used by the government itself, and incumbents to enhance their powers. Indeed, what is most astonishing in the cases from Nicaragua, Honduras, Costa Rica, and Bolivia is that constitutional unamendability, as a legal mechanism, provided leaders with a legal tool to achieve a goal they could not otherwise have achieved through judicial decisions.[87] Through the courts, incumbents were able to overcome explicit constitutional limitations imposed upon their powers.

This trend, especially in circumstances of 'court-packing', thus necessitates a rethinking about the doctrine and its applicability. We need to recalculate the route. There are several options to consider: (1) Denying the application of the doctrine; that is, not allowing courts any power to review amendments. I fear that the disadvantages of this would outweigh the advantages. The fact that a legal power can be misused does not mean it should not exist at all. Rather it should be better guided. (2) It is here that Dixon and Landau's proposal of 'transnational anchoring'[88] may be of use. In other words, a judicial decision on which changes infringe core constitutional principles in liberal democratic orders can be anchored in comparison with the constitutional practices of other liberal democratic systems. The more widespread a constitutional norm or institution is, where the vast majority of democracies share a certain constitutional practice, this tends to suggest that the practice is in fact fundamental to – or part of the institutional 'minimum core' – of constitutional democracy and accordingly courts should lean toward protecting it from repeal, under constitutional unamendability.[89] This might limit the misuse of the doctrine. Of course, this solution carries its limits, especially once the misuse of the doctrine is further migrated to a large number of democracies. (3) Clear guidance to judges on how to exercise judicial enforcement of unamendability might assist in narrowing judicial discretion. Elsewhere, I have provided clear guidance to courts on how, I believe, judicial review of amendments should be conducted in light of the theory of unamendability.[90] Following clear and relatively narrow guidance may provide a point of reference, or at the very

[87] As Landau demonstrates, in these various case studies, the judicial challenge to the term-limit was 'promoted by allies of the incumbent and clearly served his interests'; Landau (n 76) 243.

[88] Rosalind Dixon and David Landau, 'Transnational Constitutionalism and a Limited Doctrine of Unconstitutional Constitutional Amendment' (2015) 13(3) *International Journal of Constitutional Law* 606.

[89] Landau (n 76) 243: 'in making decisions as to whether a given constitutional change affects fundamental constitutional values or the basic structure, judges ought to consult transnational practice. .... It may have suggested, for example, that reforms in presidential regimes wholly eliminating term limits or stretching them beyond two terms were traditionally unusual by regional and international standards and thus should have been viewed with particular suspicion.'

[90] Roznai (n 27), ch 8.

least a basis to critically evaluate judicial decision's applications of constitutional unamendability.[91]

Finally, the most important lesson to be learned is that comparative constitutional studies should continuously study the contextual application of constitutional doctrines, especially in light of the migration of constitutional ideas. Often, the application of doctrines may not accord with established usage. It is up to us, as constitutional scholars, to discover, criticise and open these usages for a discussion. It is my hope that this chapter will be the beginning of such discussion for the proper application of constitutional unamendability, in Latin America and more globally.

[91] In Sentencia C-285 de 2016, Justice Alejandro Linares wrote a dissenting view, disagreeing with the majority's decision striking down a constitutional amendment that sought to modify the judicial branch structure on the argument that the proposed modification infringed essential basic features of the Colombian Constitution, such as judicial autonomy. Justice Linares opined that the amendment did not repeal any essential features. Moreover, he considered that the unconstitutional constitutional amendments theory adopted by the Court is not precise enough, and it allowed ample room for judicial appreciation which, in his view, was tantamount to a political, non-principled decision. In this specific context, the judge observed that several scholars in Comparative Constitutional Law, have proposed certain models to restrain the current – almost unlimited – power of the Court when it comes to the identification of the basic pillars of the Colombian Constitution. I thank Vicente F Benítez Rojas for this information.

PART II

Judicial Review of Constitutional Amendment

5

The Colombian Constitutional Court's Doctrine on the Substitution of the Constitution

JUAN F GONZÁLEZ-BERTOMEU[1]

I. Introduction

The defence of substantive limits on constitutional change has mainly taken two roads. One has been able to claim that certain constitutional provisions cannot ever be changed, though they might be restricted or suspended under some conditions. This position ('intangibility') has a textual basis in the German Basic Law as well as several other constitutions, including a host of Latin American ones. A second road has been to claim that, ex ante, any provision can be amended, though the Constitution's essential structure either cannot or can only be amended following a more restricted procedure. In other words, this position claims that a 'normal' process of constitutional change cannot 'substitute' or 'replace' the Constitution. Courts have taken an active part in discussions around these limits.

The notion of substitution or replacement – or close relatives – has been invoked in such different countries as Ireland, Italy, and India, to mention a few.[2] In Latin America, it has been employed in politically salient decisions in the past 15 years or so by the Colombian Constitutional Court (the rubric 'substitution' is its own). This chapter concerns itself with this notion, and critically analyses the Court's invocation of it. The Court has taken pains to present the substitution doctrine on procedural grounds regarding both the Constitution's amendment provisions and the Court's authorisation to supervise changes, and this chapter

[1] Thanks to Paulina Araiza Lozano for her research assistance, Bradley Hayes for his editing suggestions, and Jamal Greene and Francisca Pou for their helpful comments. Thanks also to participants at SELA 2017, Quito, Ecuador.

[2] Sudhir Krishnaswamy, *Democracy and Constitutionalism in India. A Study of the Basic Structure Doctrine* (New Delhi, OUP, 2010); Gary J Jacobsohn, 'An unconstitutional constitution? A comparative perspective' (2006) *International Journal of Constitutional Law*; Yaniv Roznai, *Unconstitutional Constitutional Amendments* (OUP, 2017); Riccardo Guastini, *Estudios de teoría constitutional* (Fontamara, 2013).

reviews that attempt. Yet, the doctrine also deals with substantive questions about the nature and content of the (Colombian) Constitution, the activation and limits of constituent power, and judicial review in a democracy. This chapter engages these questions as well. Given both the Court's current use of the doctrine and the renewed discussions of constituent power in the region, these are all timely questions.

Although this chapter objects to the Court's use of the doctrine, the Constitutional Court remains, by and large, an admirable institution that has played a crucial role in shoring up Colombia's democracy. This chapter targets one aspect of its decision making with the aim of strengthening the institution, currently in need of relegitimisation. The criticism is limited to the Court's *substantive* review of constitutional changes; its genuinely procedural review is still fundamental.

The next section (II) describes the substitution doctrine and the context within which it emerged. Section III advances a critique based on the Constitution's text and the likely expectations at the 1991 assembly. Section IV discusses some implications of the Court's doctrine, and section V briefly addresses constituent power and judicial review, in Colombia and beyond. Section VI concludes.

II. Constituent Power and the Substitution Doctrine

Judicial discussions of the limits of constitutional reform have not been exceptional in Colombia, not least because of the confluence over the years of multiple processes of constitutional change and a constitutional adjudication body with an ample mandate.

A. The Supreme Court

One central antecedent (though not the first) is the Supreme Court's decision of 9 October 1990, upholding the call for the constitutional or constituent assembly that eventually produced the 1991 Constitution. In 1990, a student-led civic movement adopted as its rallying cry the notion of a participatory constitutional assembly to pacify the country through law. However, under the 1886 Constitution, then in force, constitutional changes could only be introduced by way of a so-called legislative act (*acto legislativo*), a special statute passed by several readings, consecutive legislatures, and a special majority (Section 209). The students distributed an unofficial ballot in support for an assembly that many voters cast during a legislative election. Right afterward, the V. Barco administration agreed to include a now-official ballot during the presidential election, and a majority supported the call for an assembly.[3] Through a decree regulating

[3] In May, 1990, the Supreme Court certified this process.

an already-declared state of siege, the new administration of C Gaviria put the process into motion by calling an election to select delegates and regulating, and setting limitations to, the assembly.

Then the top adjudicator, the Supreme Court intervened as the body in charge of overseeing emergency decrees.[4] The key question was whether an assembly was (constitutionally) authorised to meet and operate. The Court started by saying the answer was not to be found solely on the Constitution's text but also in the decree's stated aim, and its actual possibility, of achieving long-desired peace in the country, itself a goal of utmost importance. It added that crises often stem from the existence of overly rigid amendment rules, thus imperiling fundamental values and the republican and democratic system of government. For the Court, it was necessary to channel the people's demand for institutional renewal.

The Court went on to say that, as sovereign, the Colombian people retained constituent power. Thus, at any time it saw fit, the people could give themselves a new constitution without being bound by the requirements of the text in force. Quoting a decision from 1957 (a time of 'irregular' constitutional change), it argued that this power did not derive from the Constitution but from 'revolution, a state of necessity … and the people's exercise of their always latent sovereignty …'.[5] The exercise of constituent power was the maximum expression of political will, and, as such, it escaped any limitation set by the law.

This rationale had concrete repercussions. Since a majority had agreed to the call for an assembly, and delegates to it would be democratically elected, this meant the people was behind it, and hence that it would be boundless. Intriguingly, the Court struck down several limitations on the future assembly imposed by the decree for violating the Constitution, including a list of topics the assembly was allowed, and restricted, to consider, and the Court's own power to review the newly-drafted constitution.[6] (It escaped the majority that its own language on the para-constitutional nature of constituent power made this last outcome nonsensical from a legal standpoint – the imposed limitations surely could not violate the *existing* Constitution.) The decision was narrowly adopted by a majority of 14 justices, with 12 against it. It was a politically savvy move on the part of the former, since the process of constitutional change was in full swing.

A decade earlier, in 1978, the Supreme Court had blocked a legislative act setting up a constitutional assembly to consider several reforms.[7] The Court said Congress had 'full capacity to reform the Constitution via a legislative act', but it was not allowed 'to reform it to change the content and reach of its own powers'.[8]

[4] Decision 138-1990, Supreme Court of Colombia [1990]. See also Esteban Restrepo, 'Entre el 5 de mayo de 1978 y el 9 de octubre de 1990' in Marcela Castro (ed), *Gaceta Judicial: 130 años de historia jurisprudencial colombiana* (Bogotá Uniandes/Temis, 2017) 382–405.

[5] ibid.

[6] The Court also upheld what it viewed as democracy-enhancing regulations.

[7] Restrepo (2017).

[8] Gaceta Constitucional N° 7, 18 February 1991, 138.

Only the people as the possessor of original constituent power – the exercise of which seemed to have been left out of the Constitution – could do so.

B. New Constitution and Court

Reacting against the rigidity of the previous constitution, the so-called National Constituent Assembly of 1991 created three main avenues for change – the so-called legislative act, a more flexible alternative to the one that had hitherto existed;[9] the referendum; and the constitutional (or 'constituent') assembly.[10] The mechanisms were regulated in six long sections or articles (374–79),[11] but it suffices to point out two issues. First, they seem to contain one explicit substantive stipulation. A legislative act that touches upon certain subject matters, including fundamental rights, shall be submitted to a referendum if a given number of citizens so request it (377). Secondly, Section 379 establishes that a legislative act, the call for a referendum, the popular consultation itself, and the call for the assembly may only be declared unconstitutional 'when the requirements established in this title [ie the six sections] are violated'.[12]

Under the new constitution, the Constitutional Court took over as the main constitutional adjudicator with a boosted mandate. Section 241, devoted to the

[9] In terms of the initiative to introduce a bill, the number of debates, and (depending on the quorum) the majority required.

[10] These are in some cases combined.

[11] '374. The Political constitution may be reformed by Congress, a Constituent Assembly, or by the people through a referendum. 375. The Government, ten members of Congress, twenty percent of councilors or deputies, or citizens totaling at least five percent of the electoral rolls in force may introduce legislative bills. The bill will be discussed in two ordinary and consecutive session periods [...] 376. By means of a law approved by the members of both chambers, Congress may direct that the people with their vote decide if a Constituent Assembly should be called with the jurisdiction, term, and makeup as set forth by said law. It is understood that the people will convoke the Assembly, if they approve it by at least one-third of the electoral rolls. The Assembly must be elected by the direct vote of the citizens in a separate election […] 377. The constitutional reforms must be submitted to a referendum approved by Congress when referring to the rights recognized in Chapter I of Title II and to their guaranties, to the procedures of popular participation, or to Congress, if so requested, within the six (6) months following the promulgation of the legislative act, by five percent of the citizens who make up the electoral rolls. The reform will be understood to be defeated by a negative vote of the majority of the voters as long as at least one-fourth of those on the electoral rolls participate. 378. Upon the initiative of the government or the citizens under the terms of Article 155, Congress, through a law approved by the majority of members of both Chambers, may submit to a referendum a bill of constitutional reform which the same Congress would include in the law. […] 379. The legislative acts, the convocation to the referendum, the popular consultation, or the act of convocation of the Constituent Assembly may be declared unconstitutional only when the requirements established in this title are violated. Legal action against these acts may be filed only within one year following their promulgation […]' (my emphasis.) Constitution of Colombia 1991. All translations of the Constitution adapted from constituteproject.org.

[12] ibid.

Court's role, assigned it several functions, the following concerning amendments (my emphasis):

1. Decide on the actions of unconstitutionality brought by citizens against measures amending the constitution […] exclusively for errors of procedure [vicios de procedimiento] in their formation.
2. Decide, prior to a popular expression of opinion, on the constitutionality of the call for a referendum or a constituent assembly to amend the constitution, exclusively for errors of procedure in their formation.

It bears mentioning that, between 1991 and 2016, the Constitution received 41 reforms involving 127 sections – none made through an assembly.[13]

C. Substitution

In the approximately 25 years since its creation, the Constitutional Court has issued many decisions involving processes of constitutional change. In around 16 of them,[14] it has invoked or discussed at some length the substitution doctrine, saying an amendment can change though never substitute or revamp the Constitution. It introduced the doctrine in July 2003, though only in 2005 did it (partially) strike down an attempted amendment for seeking to substitute the Constitution.[15] As recently as in May 2017, it struck down a key aspect of the package embedding the peace negotiations between the government and the FARC guerrilla.[16]

The decisions span hundreds of pages, so I shall distill the gist of the Court's criteria instead of proceeding on a case-by-case basis. Also, while the criteria were announced in majority decisions, I treat the Court as a block except for a few dissents. I start with a series of tenets upon which all decisions agreed, and then introduce nuances. Perhaps surprisingly, given the high stakes involved, though probably meant to blur inconsistencies among the decisions,[17] the Court said at different points that its criteria were a work in progress and were tied to the type of action subject to review in each case.[18] At the same time, however, it came to declare that the criteria had remained the same throughout.[19]

[13] María Teresa Garcés Loreda, 'Las 41 reformas a la Constitución' *El Espectador* (Bogotá, 1 July 2016) www.elespectador.com/noticias/politica/41-reformas-constitucion-articulo-640997.

[14] The number cannot be too precise since some cases (not included) mention the doctrine in passing. The following discuss the doctrine at length: C-551-03, C-1200-03, C-572-04, C-970-04, C-971-04, C-1040-05, C-153-07, C-427-08, C-588-09, C-141-10, C-574-11, C-249-12, C-053-16, C-285-16, C-373-16, C-332-17, Constitutional Court of Colombia (hereinafter CCC) (the last two digits identify the year). A review in Diego Mauricio Higuera- Jiménez, 'Análisis dinámico de la línea jurisprudencial respecto de la Sustitución de la Constitución' (2016) *Principia Iuris*.

[15] C-1040-05, CCC [2005].

[16] C-332-17, CCC [2017].

[17] This was the view of dissenting Justice Sierra Porto. C-1040-05, CCC [2005] (dissenting opinion).

[18] A legislative act or a referendum.

[19] Justice Sierra Porto highlighted this tension. C-1040-05, CCC [2005] (dissenting opinion).

In all cases, the reform under scrutiny was being attempted either through a *legislative act* or a *referendum*. This was, for the Court, decisive. The Court claimed that acts and referenda were an exercise of 'derived' constituent power. As such, they were subject to all the limitations, substantive as well as procedural, established in the Constitution. 'Original' constituent power could only manifest itself in a constituent assembly; a duly set up assembly, in principle, was unlimited. In the Court's view, through its regulation of assemblies, the Constitution had sought to channel, though never hinder, the always unruly constituent power, something that could be achieved 'only imperfectly'.[20] The latter seemed to resonate with the Supreme Court's earlier decision on the assembly's powers.

Crucially, the Constitutional Court thus found in the Constitution a two-tiered system of constitutional change, according to which not all reform powers were created equal.[21] For simplicity, I will call *Type-1* instances of change those attempted through *legislative acts* and *referenda*, and *Type-2* instances those introduced through an *assembly*.[22] The Court denied that, ex ante, there were discrete clauses that escaped the possibility of review through a Type-1 change. Unlike some countries – including Germany and Italy but also some in Latin America[23] – that made entrenched clauses impossible to amend, every clause of the Constitution could in principle be subject to change. The fact that every single thing was up for grabs did not mean, however, that everything was up for grabs. For a Type-1 process could not *substitute*, derogate or destroy the Constitution; only a Type-2 process (an assembly) could do so. Otherwise, said the Court, the difference between constituent and constituted power would be obliterated. Only the people as sovereign could adopt the nation's foundational decisions; constituted authorities could only revise the Constitution to adapt it to new circumstances or fix a problem.

The Court's textual basis for the binary categorisation of reforms was defined as much by constitutional silence as by words. In terms of the former, the Constitution did not explicitly say a Type-1 change could totally alter it. In terms of the latter, Section 374, opening the title concerning constitutional change, established that the Constitution could be 'amended' ['*ser reformada*'], not substituted with a new one. The Court adopted different formulations of what could not be subject to change, including the Constitution's 'essential defining elements,' 'identity', 'essential content', 'fundamental principle' and 'basic structure'.

Despite its statements, the Court did not strictly separate reforms introduced by *representatives* from reforms made by *the people* themselves (or in which the

[20] C-551-03, Constitutional Court of Colombia [2003].

[21] The word 'amendment' might evoke, misleadingly, that changes are of a limited nature.

[22] Acting Justice [*Magistrado Encargado*] Uprimny did not agree with this binary distinction. He proposed distinguishing tiers according to the level of people's involvement. The legislative act was the mechanism least inviting of that involvement, the assembly was the one most inviting it, and the referendum was in between. C-572/2004, CCC [2004] (concurring opinion).

[23] Constitution of Brazil 1988 (Section 60), Constitution of El Salvador 1983 (Section 248) and Constitution of Honduras 1982 (Section 374), among them. Ramírez Cleves (2014).

last word is the people's) to give more leeway to the latter.[24] If so, the Court would likely have placed the referendum at least on par with the assembly. Apart from the fact that assemblies *are* representative institutions, their output in Colombia is not subject to popular ratification. While assemblies may certainly be a better forum for deliberation, this is not what the Court put at the forefront.

D. Jurisdiction

The Court still had to circumvent one big obstacle – Sections 241 and 379's ostensible ban on substantive review. The Court's reply, and its mantra throughout, has been that the substantive is formal. The Court claimed that its identity-preserving review involved ensuring that the bodies attempting the constitutional change were authorised to do so (ie, that they had *competencia*). That this did not exceed its mandate was, for the Court, straightforward. In the case of a legislative act passed by Congress, for example, there would be no point in focusing only on whether, say, the required majority had been met if Congress was prevented from passing the act in the first place because it affected the Constitution's marrow. Thus, the Court decided in its favour the (*kompetenz-kompetenz*) issue of authorisation.

The Court claimed to be aware of the perils involved – 'petrifying the Constitution and [succumbing to] the constitutional judge's subjectivism'.[25] To avert these perils, and to dispel worries about possible abuse, the Court emphasised that the difference between amending the Constitution and substituting it was not a matter of degree but categorical. An amendment always conflicts with the existing text. Substituting the Constitution meant something other than changing its clauses; it meant substantively replacing it with a different constitution. So much for the peril of petrification; to minimise subjectivism, the Court held it was incumbent upon the challenger (or the justice invoking the doctrine) to show that the change was of 'such magnitude and importance' that it could be said to have substituted the Constitution.[26]

In 2004, the Court started to develop a 'methodology' to decide this question. The major premise in its scrutiny consisted of carefully articulating the essential defining element that was in principle being replaced. The answer was not to be found 'in a given section of the Constitution [but] rather [in] the whole Constitution understood in light of the essential elements defining its identity'.[27] The element had to be described with all clarity and 'multiple normative references'

[24] This is what such authors as Amar and Levinson have suggested in the US context. Akhil Reed Amar, 'Philadelphia Revisited: Amending the Constitution Outside Article V' (1988) *University of Chicago Law Review* 1043; Sanford Levinson, *Our Undemocratic Constitution* (OUP, 2006). It is also the view of constituent power theorists.

[25] C-1200-03, CCC [2003].

[26] ibid.

[27] C-1040-05, CCC [2005].

that traced its specificities back to the Colombian Constitution.[28] The minor premise involved assessing whether the attempted change indeed replaced the original element. The final analysis hinged on the determination of whether the two elements were indeed incompatible; if so, the amendment had to go. While in other cases the Court described the test differently or enumerated more steps, its structure remained similar. Among the essential elements the Court enumerated (often in dictum) were the separation of powers and the country's identification as a social-democratic state under a republican government (*estado social de derecho*).

The defining elements, said the Court, must be reconstructed by looking at the entire constitutional text. But what text? Since the Constitution was subject to several amendments since it was first enacted, one could entertain the possibility that its identity changed through piecemeal alteration even if each single reform did not substitute it. Suppose that a feature has been deemed essential in the past by looking at the original constitution. Suppose further that several amendments, each pointing in a different direction, have regulated issues that touch upon that feature, though none has been said to substitute it. While it will be hard to conclude that the feature has been replaced with a different one, it might not be so clear anymore that the feature is still defining under the new text, since the disparate clauses may have blurred the original feature. The Court refused to allow this possibility – the identity in question was that of the 1991 Constitution *as enacted*. Only a Type-2 change was able to substitute the Constitution.

E. Internal Critics

Observers including former Inspector-General (*Procurador*) E Maya Villazón and Justice H Sierra Porto, the most clear-eyed of the doctrine's critics, raised doubts about the Court's consistency.[29] In 2003, the Court had hinted that all reforms affecting defining elements entailed a banned substitution. Moreover, to determine whether the Constitution had been substituted, 'it was necessary to take into account the Constitution's principles and values, as well as those in the constitutional bloc [human rights treaties]'.[30] In dictum, it had said the reform powers 'could not be used to substitute the [declaration concerning the country's identity as a] social-democratic state under a republican government (Section 1) with a totalitarian state, a dictatorship, or a monarchy … '.[31] This suggested that a particular clause could indeed be ex ante unamendable, contrary to what the Court said elsewhere in the same opinion. A year later, however, it reached a seemingly different conclusion, one that likely relaxed its criterion.[32] It declared that, by definition,

[28] ibid.
[29] Justices González Cuervo and Linares Cantillo would also become critics.
[30] C-551-03, CCC [2003].
[31] ibid.
[32] C-970-04, C-971-04, CCC [2004].

any constitutional amendment dealt with fundamental issues, since everything in the Constitution was fundamental in nature. Therefore, not everything that affected a fundamental principle was banned. 'Altering' was not the same as 'substituting'.

In 2005, the Court denied that there were inconsistencies in the criteria announced in previous cases.[33] It insisted on the semantic distinction between, on the one hand, substituting a fundamental principle or essential element, something forbidden, and, on the other hand, affecting, altering, and modifying it, something that was allowed. It said that an essential element was not formally enshrined in a single clause but, rather, in a bundle of regulations and principles interspersed in the Constitution that judges had to reconstruct. Going back to the previous example, also dictum in this case, it said a reform could (unduly) substitute the 'social-democratic state' declaration without even altering Section 1. Also, essential principles were not all or nothing but were open to nuances and a 'diversity of formulations, all compatible with the basic defining postulate of the Constitution's identity'.[34] In a dissent, Justice Sierra Porto remarked that the latter made the difference between altering and substituting a matter of degree, thus allowing for subjectivity.[35] The stakes involved in that 2005 decision could hardly have been higher – allowing or not the popular President Uribe to run for one more term.

F. Outcomes

In seven of its 16 or so decisions, the Court said that the attempted reform entailed substitution of the Constitution, at least partially, and blocked it. The first was precisely the 2005 decision.[36] The Court said that one-time reelection did *not* substitute the basic pillars of the social-democratic state or the principle of equality, though it subtly left the door open to change its mind if faced with an attempt to lift the ban on a second immediate reelection. What *did* substitute the Constitution was a relatively minor clause contained in the same package, which gave the Council of State power to pass a specific legislation if Congress did not do so within a set timeframe or the statute was struck down. This impinged on constitutional supremacy, since that body would not be subject to review. In 2009 (and 2012), the Court struck down reform attempts concerning access to civil service.[37] Here, the essential element was the 'regulation of civil service as a career' instead of as a system of open appointment of public servants, which the packages in part introduced.

In 2010, the Court took up the gauntlet it had thrown down earlier, concluding a referendum to allow for a *second* reelection implied the substitution of the system

[33] C-1040-05, CCC [2005].
[34] ibid.
[35] C-1040-05, CCC [2005] (dissenting opinion).
[36] C-1040-05, CCC [2005].
[37] C-588-09 [2009]; C-249-12 [2012], CCC.

of government and the separation of powers.[38] The decision also rested on several procedural violations the Court had detected, and that would have been enough to block the referendum. As a result of this momentous decision (adopted by 7-2, with Justice Sierra Porto joining the majority but dissenting on the substitution doctrine), Mr. Uribe could not run for president a third time. In two decisions announced in 2016 that concerned the same amendment package, the Court said that a reform of the bodies in charge of administering the judiciary and disciplining judges partially substituted the principles of separation of powers, judicial autonomy, and independence.[39]

In May 2017, the Court struck down a significant portion of a reform introducing a 'fast-track' legislative procedure to implement the peace agreement between the government and the FARC guerrilla. The Colombian Congress typically votes a bill in general and then proceeds on a section-by-section basis. Among other points, the reform suspended the section-by-section vote for pieces of legislation implementing the agreement and required the president's authorisation before an amendment. The Court considered that the twin principles of the separation of powers and the equilibrium between them had been substituted.

G. Supreme Court v Constitutional Court

The Colombian Court's insistence on the boundless nature of a constitutional (or constituent) assembly might wrongly be interpreted as in line with the Supreme Court's views expressed in its 1990 decision. One of the crucial differences is that, while the latter sustained its position to *ground* the 1991 assembly's powers, the Constitutional Court was playing defence all along, invoking in dictum the doctrine of constituent power as a shield against what it considered a sweeping Type-1 amendment. Also, only the Supreme Court was referring to an assembly set up *outside* the scope of the existing constitution's regulations.[40]

III. The Double Lock

I turn now to a critical analysis of the Court's use of the substitution doctrine. I start with a low-hanging critique based on the Constitution's text, but one that, as

[38] Reelection was banned altogether in 2015.

[39] C-285-16 and C-373-16, CCC [2016]. In a related case, C-053-16, CCC [2016], it dismissed the action.

[40] See Joel Colón-Ríos, 'Carl Schmitt and Constituent Power in Latin American Courts: The Cases of Venezuela and Colombia' (2012) *Victoria University of Wellington Research Articles* 24/2012; Joel Colón-Ríos, 'Beyond Parliamentary Sovereignty and Judicial Supremacy: the Doctrine of Implicit Limits to Constitutional Reform in Latin America' (2013) 44(3) *Victoria University of Wellington Law Review* 521.

others have noted,[41] might be enough to put the use of the doctrine to rest. In its appeal to the doctrine, the Constitutional Court has bypassed what constitutes a double ban on non-formal review of constitutional changes.[42]

A. Two Levels

There is nothing wrong with a system of constitutional reform that contemplates different routes and makes certain changes exclusive to one of them. There may be two defensible goals behind such a strategy, and the two may be combined. One is to keep key aspects of the Constitution from 'excessive' reform, whatever that means in a concrete instance. A constitution's rigidity is a matter of degree and a society may want to shield some content by making it harder to amend.[43] Alternatively, the goal may be to more actively engage citizens, and not just representative institutions, where central decisions are concerned. The central question in this case is whether the reform mechanism should be attuned to majority sentiment or whether pluralism should be championed as well – there are very good reasons to try to avoid factional and opportunistic reforms. Several countries feature a two-way or multiple-way system,[44] following a logic that commentators have termed 'constitutional escalator'[45] or 'selective rigidity'.[46] Indeed, Colombia *does* have a two-tiered system. When reforms made by a legislative act (a Type-1 change) touch upon such issues as fundamental rights, they must be submitted to a referendum.[47] But this is not the system the Court focused on when announcing its doctrine.

The Court offered two arguments to anchor its limitation of Type-1 events to the Constitution's text. One was that the government only has enumerated powers, and the Constitution does not explicitly say that its fundamental principles can be reformed through a Type-1 change. While, undeniably, the government's powers are enumerated, the argument begs the question. Its conclusion can be reached only if one already accepts the minor premise of the argument – that an authorisation to reform fundamental principles does not already feature in the Constitution. One can conclude that the opposite view stems from what reads as

[41] Apart from the opinions of Justice Sierra Porto and other justices, see Carlos Bernal, 'Unconstitutional constitutional amendments in the case study of Colombia: An analysis of the justification and meaning of the constitutional replacement doctrine' (2013) *Int J Const Law* 11 (2) 339–57; Eloy García, 'La sustitución de la Constitución en el Derecho Constitucional Colombiano' (2016) *Revista de Derecho Político*, UNED, n° 95 229.

[42] Justice Sierra Porto made this point. C-1040-05, CCC [2005] (dissenting opinion).

[43] Víctor Ferreres Comella, 'Una defensa de la rigidez constitucional' (2000) Doxa No. 23 29–47.

[44] Spain, as the Constitutional Court has said, is one. Constitution of Spain 1978, Sections 167–68.

[45] Roznai (2017).

[46] David Landau, 'Abusive Constitutionalism' (2013) 47(1) *UC Davis L Rev* 189; see also Richard Albert, 'Amending Constitutional Amendments Rules' (2015) 13(3) *Int'l J Const L* 655; Roznai (2017).

[47] Constitution of Colombia 1991, Section 377.

a broad authorisation to reform.[48] Alternatively, this conclusion can be implied from Section 377's enumeration of reforms to be subject to referenda. Fundamental rights surely count among the Constitution's fundamental elements, and, if they can be subject to a Type-1 reform, it is because the section reads with that authorisation in the background.[49]

The Court's second argument is the weakest. True, Section 374 says that the Constitution can be 'reformed'. But the section applies to *all types* of reform, including those made through an assembly, which, according to the Court, is allowed to substitute essential features. If we accepted the Court's argument about that section setting a limit, it would follow that an assembly would not be boundless, either. (As I will show, there are some indications of this.)

A look at the 1991 assembly reinforces this argument. There were around 15 proposals touching upon the amendment process submitted to it. Virtually all suggested unlocking the 1886 Constitution's self-established process for reform by adding new mechanisms (typically a referendum and an assembly) and, in most cases, making the process accessible and participatory. Only one explicitly conceived of a difference in the nature or degree of reforms apart from the noted requirement of a referendum. It was submitted by a nonprofit,[50] and it recommended differentiating between a reform of more than 50 per cent of the text, which only an assembly could undertake, and a smaller-scale reform, subject to a different procedure. In April, 1991, the committee in charge voted on an early version of the amendment sections, including the core of what would become Section 377's referendum requirement.[51] During a debate on 8 May 1991, Liberal delegate D Uribe Vargas demanded a different procedure for when rights and liberties were involved. The reply was that such procedure was already incorporated in the draft (the referendum requirement), but that the draft would be made more detailed.[52]

There was a discussion about a proposal to forbid reforms within eight years of the Constitution's enactment. Some delegates claimed that time was needed for the Constitution to take root, and, for this, unnecessary interference was to be prevented. This echoed Madison's insights in Federalist.[53] The proposal was

48 The Court's view is tantamount to interpreting that Congress cannot pass a tax law because it does not have an explicit authorisation to do so, when it has a broad authorisation to legislate and does not face a ban on the matter. See also Bernal (2013).

49 Acting Justice Uprimny considered that (what I call) a Type-1 reform can touch upon the list of topics on Section 377, but never destroy the respective contents. C-572/2004, CCC [2004] (concurring opinion). This interpretation is interesting, but it is not obvious it flows from the text.

50 FUNDESCO.

51 National Assembly, Gaceta Constitucional 52, pp 9–10, 12. http://babel.banrepcultural.org/cdm/search/searchterm/asamblea%20nacional%20constituyente/field/all/mode/all/conn/and/display/200/order/nosort/ad/asc.

52 National Assembly, Gaceta Constitucional 133, p 7. http://babel.banrepcultural.org/cdm/search/searchterm/asamblea%20nacional%20constituyente/field/all/mode/all/conn/and/display/200/order/nosort/ad/asc#49.

53 Alexander Hamilton, John Jay, and James Madison, *Federalist Papers*, http://avalon.law.yale.edu/18th_century/fed49.asp.

rejected outright,[54] since it evoked the previous constitution's chokehold on citizen participation. This is further illustration of the direction of the winds blowing in the assembly. Save for exceptions, the mood was (for better or for worse) to encourage change.

B. The Court's Jurisdiction

Suppose that the Constitution indeed can be construed as creating a two-tiered system like the one the Court defended. Does this mean that, automatically, the Court has a mandate to oversee it? The text limits review to 'errors of procedure' [*vicios de procedimiento*] (241) and makes clear that a legislative act; the call for, and the celebration of, a referendum; and the call for an assembly can only be struck down when 'the requirements established in [the title enumerating them] are violated' (379). Justice Sierra Porto rightly pointed out that these clauses look like clear-cut rules.[55]

Still, the question to consider is whether the issue of the amending body's powers [*competencia*] can qualify as a procedural matter – on the same camp with such issues as whether the required majority has been met.[56] Two arguments suggest that this is not the case. First, the Court reasons from the claimed existence of a two-tiered system to the implication that judicial involvement necessarily follows from it. Yet, even assuming such a system, it is conceivable that the Court is not authorised to oversee it, the same way it is conceivable judges are explicitly disqualified from reviewing an unconstitutional statute save for clear procedural errors. The Court does not pause to think that the enumerated powers argument it made to limit reforms would also limit *itself*.

Secondly, in writing the limitations into the Constitution, many at the assembly were reacting against what they saw as the Supreme Court's abusive supervision of amendments before 1991, including the 1978 decision mentioned above.[57] In the words of delegate Uribe Vargas:[58]

> [B]ehind the spurious arguments made by the Supreme Court, a clear purpose was concealed – to deprive Congress from its constituent power so the Court could become a body with powers above all other public officials …

[54] National Assembly, Gaceta Constitucional 140, p 35. http://babel.banrepcultural.org/cdm/search/searchterm/asamblea%20nacional%20constituyente/field/all/mode/all/conn/and/display/200/order/nosort/ad/asc.

[55] C-1040-05, CCC [2005] (dissenting opinion).

[56] Vicki Jackson has grounded unamendability on process-related reasons. See Jackson, 'Unconstitutional Constitutional Amendments' in Astrid Wallrabenstein, Philipp Dann, and Michael Bäuerle (eds), *Demokratie-Perspektiven* (Mohr Siebeck, 2013); Roznai (2017).

[57] Sierra Porto mentioned this point. C-1040-05, CCC [2005] (dissenting opinion).

[58] The delegate had submitted a proposal detailing the procedural errors the Court could oversee. National Assembly, Gaceta Constitucional 7, p 28. http://babel.banrepcultural.org/cdm/search/searchterm/asamblea%20nacional%20constituyente/field/all/mode/all/conn/and/display/200/order/nosort/ad/asc.

> The only limits the Constitution imposes to Congress in its exercise of constituent power are those explicitly enumerated. To look for intangible clauses, or ideological limitations to reforms, entails an undue invasion on the part of the Supreme Court ...[59]

Admittedly, this was the expressed opinion of only one delegate. But there was no one defending the opposite view – what would become the Constitutional Court's. So, thinking into the future, and with an eye to the past, the assembly explicitly forbade the new Court from reviewing anything but procedural errors. The Court's reply was that reviewing the substance of reforms *did* represent such procedural oversight. It is a perplexing reply, but also an understandable one, as I explain in the last section.

IV. Intangibility and Identity

I deal now with the substitution doctrine's contours.

A. Intangibility

In principle, if we follow (most of) the Court's words, a Type-2 change in Colombia (an assembly) can override any clause or essential element, so the intangibility argument really should have no basis. But the Court attempts to differentiate the substitution doctrine from constitutional intangibility *within the context of Type-1 changes*, and it is in this context that the attempt must be discussed. The argument is that, ex ante, every single clause can be amended, and what cannot be amended are rather the essential elements that derive from the entire Constitution. This is not correct. First, as Justice Sierra Porto noted, there is at least one reference made by the Court to a clause that cannot be amended (Section 1). More important, the argument is self-defeating, for *after* the Court has concluded that the reform of a clause would substitute an essential element, what is left is something akin to intangibility. Unless the Court is asking that its decisions be subsequently ignored, that clause will be impossible to amend *in the direction banned by the Court*. It does not change things that the attempted reform must be confronted with the entire constitution. If the reform consists of adopting a rule to change its exact opposite, now featured in the Constitution, the latter will be at least partially unamendable if the Court blocks the reform resorting to the doctrine.

Take the second reelection case. Most in the majority at the Court concluded that the reform would have substituted the separation of powers. As a result, the clause establishing the president's term limits was made partially intangible. It was

[59] ibid.

still possible to ban reelection altogether, something that happened in 2015,[60] but not to make a renewed attempt at adding a second reelection. A future Court may conclude otherwise, but that is another matter.

B. Identity

The enterprise of identifying a given constitutional text by its central features is not necessarily doomed. A constitution's drafters may have impressed those features upon the text – in its final wording concerning principles and power allocations. It may be entirely plausible to say that, from a substantive viewpoint, some changes will entail a change of that identity. A critical stance regarding the doctrine does not necessarily imply a positivistic view according to which a constitution is merely a set of norms, any modification of which always yields a new constitution.[61]

But the doctrine's problems do not end with this recognition. One of such problems is that, as discussed, it is anything but obvious that the drafters – or the people – intended to preserve those defining features from future reform. Secondly, a constitution, no less than a person, can have multiple, and even clashing, identities. Commentators, for example, rightly note the progressive character of the Colombian Constitution of 1991, which is plain to see, but this coexists with some concessions to neoliberal notions then in vogue.[62]

Thirdly, as the Constitutional Court itself noted in its 2005 decision, essential principles are open to nuances and a 'diversity of formulations'. It stems from this that it should not be possible to find that substitution has taken place except in the clearest of cases, when a reform unmistakably falls outside the scope of an also unmistakably defining feature.[63] This puts under suspicion decisions as those striking down reforms dealing with public servants' career or the body in charge of administering the judiciary. A truly basic feature can hardly be invoked to adjudicate the validity of an institutional reform when more than one design option is admissible.

There is a fourth problem. The Court often enumerates basic defining principles at a quite general level. To infuse them with meaning, it then transcends local specificities and engages with abstract discussions. The more the Court does this, the less clear it becomes that there is something special in the *Colombian* Constitution, apart from cursory references that allow the Court to conclude that an element

[60] The new Section 197 establishes that the reelection ban can only be lifted by a special referendum or an assembly.

[61] Guastini (2013).

[62] Mauricio García Villegas and Rodrigo Uprimny, 'Tribunal Constitucional e emancipação social na Colômbia' in Boaventura de Sousa (ed), *Democratizar a democracia* (Civilizaçao Brasileira, 2002) 298–339.

[63] Rodrigo Uprimny seems to defend this position in an amicus brief submitted to the Court. C-373-16, CCC [2016]. I believe it is also the view of Bernal (2013).

is defining. At times, it appears that the Court implies that there is something akin to a 'true' (liberal democratic) constitution that the Colombian Constitution should mirror.[64] From this, the Court derives a position on the implicit substantive limits of change,[65] with the irrelevance of the actual Constitution as a possible outcome. This may be a problem to the extent that the Court's argument rests on the notion that, by invoking the doctrine, it is preserving the people's original *decision*; it is the Colombian Constitution that should not be substituted.

You and I perhaps agree that your constitution as well as mine should feature certain basic elements – that is, rights protections and democracy-enhancing rules. Yet, this acceptance when referred to basic elements does not automatically turn into a blind approval of a court's invocation of implicit limits and is far from endorsing the string of decisions announced by the Court. First, it is one thing to say that it is much more *desirable* a constitution features them, and it is another to say that those elements *cannot* be reformed. Secondly, if not positively authorised to analyse the content of a reform, a court invoking implicit limits should at least not face a blanket prohibition, which is what seems to happen in Colombia.

In such a scenario, if a court still wants to insist on the implicit limits of change, it must be most careful and transparent. Instead of arguing that the text itself hinders certain reforms, or that its drafters wanted to make them harder to achieve, it should attempt to show that a genuine liberal democratic constitution disallows them. This will be a potentially vulnerable argument, and one that can only have purchase in an extraordinary situation. But it might be worth trying.

V. Constituent Power in Colombia

In this section, I start by analysing the implications of the two-tiered system, and then go on to address the (intractable) issue of constituent power.

A. Two Tiers

With its binary categorisation, the Constitutional Court may inadvertently encourage a maximalist agenda. As Tushnet has noted, the proponents of a change may find the rest of the Constitution acceptable, so they may 'be puzzled at being required to go through an elaborate process of constitutional replacement at the end of which is a "new" constitution identical, save for the [provision in question], to the old one'.[66] According to Tushnet, this can strengthen the incentives to ignore the impediment. But, in the case of Colombia, there is another likely consequence

[64] eg, the Court refers to a true 'liberal democratic constitution.' C-574/2011, CCC [2011].
[65] Guastini (2013).
[66] Mark Tushnet, *Comparative Constitutional Law* (Elgar, 2014) 32.

of repeatedly setting limits to 'modest' reforms – to create incentives to push for, and then try to take over, an assembly to revamp the Constitution. In the hands of a plural composition, an assembly might be an opportunity to boost Colombia's democracy. But things would be very different were the pluralism condition absent. In 2015, the right-wing populist Uribe became the main voice behind a call for an assembly, so one can cast doubts on the wisdom of that choice.

Underlying the sharp distinction between Type-1 and Type-2 changes there seems to be a view that the former are plagued by agency problems common to representative institutions, while the latter allow the people to freely decide and let pluralism flourish. This difference is contingent. An assembly may be a more plural and deliberative body than Congress, since groups excluded from ordinary representative institutions may find a voice in it – this is what happened in 1991. However, a sufficiently popular government may meet the requirements to call for an assembly, with an ensuing limitation to pluralism.[67] Also, as a representative institution, the assembly may face agency issues as well.[68] And, while some Type-1 reforms in Colombia are crowned by direct participation, the assembly's output is not subject to a referendum. Assemblies can be perfectly good constitution-making venues; what does not seem so good is the Court's sharp classification.

B. It's All Derived

Classic theorists of popular sovereignty and constituent power insisted on the people's (or the nation's) inalienable right to change the basic laws of a state to the point of ignoring existing regulations. The Constitution binds the government, not the people.

JJ Rousseau in 1762 stated: '[The legislator], which constitutes the republic, does not enter into its constitution.'[69] J Wilson in 1788 said: '[T]he people may change the constitutions, whenever and however they please. This is a right, of which no positive institution can ever deprive them.'[70] According to Siéyes in 1789: 'A nation should not and cannot subject itself to constitutional forms ….'[71] And according to C Schmitt in 1928: '[The constitution-making power itself] … stands alongside and above every constitution derived from it and any valid constitutional provision […]'.[72]

[67] Uribe did not try this mechanism to get his second reelection. Perhaps he did not anticipate a judgment against the reform or/and the time ran out for him.

[68] David Landau, 'Constitution-Making Gone Wrong' (2013) 64 *Alabama Law Review* 923.

[69] Jean-Jaques Rousseau in Susan Dunn (ed), *The Social Contract* (YUP, 2002) 181.

[70] Kermit Hall and Mark David Hall (eds), *Collected Works of James Wilson, Vol. 1* (Liberty Fund, 2007) 189.

[71] Sieyès in Michael Sonenscher (ed), *Political Writings* (Hackett, 2003) 138.

[72] Carl Schmitt in Jeffrey Seitzer (ed), *Constitutional Theory* (Duke University Press, 2008) 140.

Now, once contained and regulated in a constitution's amendment clauses, the reform power is no longer what theorists referred to as (original) constituent power, and it becomes something else – a choice as to how to change the Constitution *from within*. The Constitutional Court's repeated invocation of an assembly as exercising original constituent power is misguided.[73]

The enormously important question will always remain: Do the people keep that external right continuously, or, as the tamer American Federalists interpreted, is it only reserved for extraordinary circumstances?[74] Regardless, a state's *constitution* itself will not have much say. When, in 1990, the Supreme Court upheld the call for the assembly invoking ideas like those just quoted, it did not stop to analyse whether the existing regulations allowed it. A constitution can, and should, try to channel constituent power, but, at the end of the day, we (or judges) will face one of these two situations: either the amendment regulations do not apply, in which case we have an exercise of original constituent power, or they do, in which case the power is derived. The Supreme Court's decision appeared to conclude the former. The Constitutional Court wants to have it both ways – yes, the regulations apply and yes, in the case of an assembly, it represents constituent power.[75]

Acknowledging that the amendment clauses deal with derived or constituted reform power does not (necessarily) mean that reformers should face substantive limitations. It means, rather, that the formal authorisation to reform is contained in the Constitution, so there should be a strong expectation that the proponents of a change will follow those procedures. The classic theorists wrote within the context of homogenous societies, where it was not particularly difficult to find who the people or their interests were.[76] We do not live, and do not hope to live, in that world anymore. In the circumstances of pluralism we face, a constitution at the same time helps *discover* the people and their interests and *constitutes* them.[77] It also plays a central role normalising political change and preserving the rule of law.

Constituent power will never be tamed altogether. If a constitution prohibited same-sex marriage or freedom of expression and further banned amendments, a genuinely mobilised citizenship would have every (political) right to proceed anyway. Perhaps the 1991 experience illustrates a general point – *the more a reformist movement plans to deviate from established regulations concerning constitutional*

[73] It may have contributed that the Constitution calls the assembly a 'constituent' assembly.

[74] Gabriel Negretto, 'El poder constituyente en la tradición constitucional americana' (2016) 43(3) *Revista Chilena de Derecho*,

[75] Justice Sierra Porto similarly argued that, in Colombia, the Constitution-based reform power is always derived. C-1040-05, CCC [2005] (dissenting opinion).

[76] In the case of Schmitt, this involved a delimitation of friends and enemies. Schmitt (2008); Carl Schmitt, *The Concept of the Political*, Translation, introduction, and notes by George Schwab (expanded edition, University of Chicago, 2007). Larx Vinx, 'Carl Schmitt' (revised 2014), *Stanford Encyclopedia of Philosophy* https://plato.stanford.edu/entries/schmitt/ accessed 31 December 2017.

[77] Stephen Holmes, *Passions and Constraint* (University of Chicago Press, 1995).

change, the stricter the requirement should be that the movement really represents the people. The very notion of 'the people' is of course contested. That is one reason we need amendment rules in the first place – they represent some version of the notion. But it is wrong to say ex ante that the people will *never* be right to do so. Due to the identification difficulties as well as the risk of partisan capture, the condition is that it is a particularly robust version of 'the people.'

C. Enough with Schmitt

If the Court's invocation of constituent power theorists is questionable, its quotations of Schmitt[78] are emphatically problematic.[79] Schmitt distinguished between the 'constitution in the positive sense' and 'constitutional laws'.[80] Prior to 'the establishment of any norm', the Constitution in the positive sense is 'a fundamental *political decision by the bearer of the constitution-making power*'.[81] These decisions are not subject to change following the regular amendment powers.[82] Constitutional laws, in turn, consist of specific individual laws that 'are valid first on the basis of the constitution and presuppose a constitution'.[83]

As Colón-Ríos has claimed, Schmitt's ideas can be used either to limit or block constitutional change.[84] In particular, since he 'denies the possibility of changing the fundamental nature of an established constitution from within',[85] Schmitt's insights come in handy for grounding the substitution doctrine – the Court can close the door to a Type-1 change when it touches upon that nature while still claiming that the people themselves can operate such change. At least two issues make resorting to Schmitt puzzling. First, Schmitt's notions applied to a nation's most fundamental decisions, not to very specific issues of institutional design, however important they may be.[86] Secondly, Schmitt's theory, fashionable as it has become, has illiberal and potentially antidemocratic elements that place it at odds with the circumstances and needs of Colombia and the Court's interpretations of the Constitution.[87] The superiority of the Constitution in the positive sense can lead to the suspension of constitutional clauses if the President unilaterally

[78] C-1200-2003, C-1040-2005, C-588-2009, CCC.

[79] A partially contrasting view is Colón-Ríos (2012).

[80] Schmitt (2008), 75-96, 147-50; Colón Ríos (2012), 7-8; Vinx (2014).

[81] Schmitt (2008), 77 (emphasis in original).

[82] ibid 79.

[83] ibid 76.

[84] Colón-Ríos (2012).

[85] Vinx (2014).

[86] These questions seem to concern 'constitutional laws'. Juan Esteban Jaramillo Giraldo, 'La problemática de los límites al poder de reforma de la Constitución Política de 1999' (2013) 43(118) *Facultad de Derecho y Ciencias Políticas* (Colombia) Abril.

[87] The 1991 assembly's delegate Uribe Vargas said that Schmitt's theory involved 'concepts that are foreign to our constitutionalism'. Gaceta Constitucional N° 7, 18 de febrero de 1991, 139.

considers it important 'to save the constitutional system as a whole'.[88] And, as its name indicates, a sovereign dictator in Schmitt *is* allowed to alter fundamental decisions.[89]

D. Assemblies at the Court

Despite repeated references by the Court to the sovereign and unlimited character of a hypothetical assembly, such an assembly would not be so unlimited (and, perhaps, rightly so). First is the Court's declaration that it would supervise the procedures through which a hypothetical assembly is called and set up, a power one partially finds in the Constitution. With its procedural review, the Court would ensure that what becomes sovereign is the *right* assembly. Secondly, Section 376 establishes that an assembly shall have 'the powers' [*competencia*] that Congress decides to assign it. In other words, Congress can choose to set substantive limitations to the assembly and, in principle, the latter must abide by them. There might be nothing wrong with this. What *is* certainly wrong is the Court's view that such an assembly can still be sovereign. For the Court, an assembly can only be sovereign if Congress so chooses it to be.[90]

Thirdly, in a plurality opinion from 2011, some of the justices who agreed on the Court's outcome had this to say:

> Regarding this possibility [that an assembly is called to write a new constitution], many scholars have established that constituent power is not absolute, unlimited, and sovereign, since it has to abide by a series of limitations already announced by Siéyes …: (i) it has to write a constitution and not something else; (ii) it has to act within a limited timeframe; and (iii) it cannot defraud the will of those represented. Moreover, [the assembly] should take into account all the precommitments in terms of international human rights treaties and the norms of *ius cogens* for it to be able to claim it is establishing a liberal democratic constitution and not something else, circumstances that the Constitutional Court will have to evaluate if the occasion comes.[91]

While this is just dictum in a case decided by a plurality, it seems to indicate that some of the justices would be willing to review the content of a future assembly's outcome.

[88] Seitzer and Thornhill, 'An Introduction to Carl Schmitt's *Constitutional Theory*: Issues and Context' in Schmitt (2008) 27.

[89] eg Schmitt (2008) 110.

[90] Elster has discussed a similar paradox. Jon Elster, 'Forces and Mechanisms in the Constitutional-Making Processes' (1995) 45 *Duke Law Journal* 364–96, 375.

[91] C-574/2011, CCC [2011]. Juan Carlos Henao Pérez was the Justice Rapporteur, joined by Justices María Victoria Calle, Jorge Ignacio Prettelt, and (to some extent) Jorge Iván Palacio. Juan Manuel Sánchez Osorio, 'De la teoría de la sustitución o de los límites materiales a las reformas constitucionales en Colombia' (2013) *Temas Socio Jurídicos* (Colombia), Julio-diciembre.

E. Judicial Review and Change

I have defended judicial review of legislation elsewhere,[92] a project that (under certain conditions) I very strongly believe in. Is the position I hold here compatible with that defence? I believe so. Constitutions contain myriad principles whose interpretation, as Dworkin has claimed, call for a normative discussion that considers, but reaches beyond, the constitution's text or its drafters' intentions.[93] However, these discussions often take place on the assumption that constitutional principles are open to formal change, however difficult this may be, in case of a sufficiently large discrepancy between the people's preferences and a given interpretation. When the substitution doctrine is invoked, it is to *limit* the possibility of such change.

VI. Why it Happened and What to Do

Both the social and political movement that made the 1991 Constitution possible and the Constitution itself are pivotal moments in Colombia's history. Intent on changing an unjust status quo through the rule of law, a pluralist array of forces produced a progressive constitution. The Constitutional Court is the poster child of that movement and sees itself in that way – as the protector of the original spirit of 1991.[94] Many at the Court may have feared the possibility of an assault on the Constitution (and perhaps also their own power) by a factional group; hence the substitution doctrine.

The Court's fear is not misplaced. The 1991 assembly reacted against a regulation it saw as too restrictive of both the people's and representatives' power to change the Constitution. But the ensuing regulation could have been more careful. One may expect the requirements to be stricter and the intervention of the people more crucial the more sweeping a reform can be – this is what the 'escalator' argument holds.[95] The Constitution did not completely follow this path. Nevertheless, the doctrine lacks textual basis, departs from the delegates' deliberations, and is not without normative difficulties. Also, it is not obvious it can find justification via its positive consequences. In some cases, the Court employed it to block things many of us hated (Uribe's second reelection? Please no!), though the decisions might have stood without it. In some other cases, however, the reforms were questionable, but did not threaten liberal democracy. Also, consider the opposite

[92] Juan F González-Bertomeu, 'Against the Core of the Case' (2011) *Legal Theory* 17.2.
[93] Ronald Dworkin, 'Comment' in Antonin Scalia, *A Matter of Interpretation* (Princeton University Press, 1997).
[94] Juan F González-Bertomeu, 'Constitutional Adjudication in Non-ideal Scenarios', JSD dissertation, NYU (2012).
[95] Roznai (2017).

scenario – a conservative constitution that placed some restrictions to change, and an even more conservative Court that expanded those restrictions to block reforms.

Instead of placing gag rules on the possibility of change, the Court should limit itself to 'genuine' procedural violations. Its intervention on that realm is essential and could be compromised if it continues to resort to a type of substantive review that is always liable to abuse. One need only invoke a recently-purged Honduran Supreme Court's decision of 2015. It rendered inapplicable the unamendability of the reelection ban when a similar attempt a few years earlier had resulted in the ousting of the previous president.[96] While the direction of this decision is opposite to the substitution doctrine, the example illustrates the perils involved.

So far, the Court has managed to weather the storms it created when blocking reforms based on the doctrine.[97] Yet, it is playing with fire. The Court has recently suffered a loss of legitimacy, and resorting expansively to the doctrine may not help it regain it. To make matters worse, the Court has employed the doctrine when reforms dealt with issues that were close to home – at least indirectly involving its own powers or the judiciary's – such as in the 2005 decision concerning the Council of State or in the 2016 decisions. The Court must show that its decisions are not outcome-driven, and the substitution doctrine hardly offers a chance to do that. While procedural review will also be contested and liable to subjectivism,[98] the dangers are likely reduced compared to identity-preserving review. Of course, procedural review will not eliminate the risk of ill-advised reforms, but, by ensuring that amendment rules are complied with, it somewhat minimises that risk without the costs the doctrine entails.

My criticism is worlds away from embracing a relativist viewpoint. Weakening or rubbing out some elements of the Colombian Constitution (including the writ of *tutela* and its enumeration of civil, political, and social rights) would be gravely mistaken. Assuming it limits itself to a very critical instance of reform – for example one transferring power to an authoritarian system or depriving citizens of fundamental rights – the Court might do well to block it. In that case, however, it would do better to openly defend its decision on political or normative grounds reaching beyond the text of the Constitution. Other than this, an ill-advised reform otherwise complying with procedural requirements must be countered by head-on mobilisation.

In a non-related article (on mass incarceration in the US), A Gopnik says:

> There's a lovely scene in 'The Castle,' the Australian movie about a family fighting eminent-domain eviction, where its hapless lawyer, asked in court to point to the

[96] Leiv Marsteintredet, 'The Honduran Supreme Court Renders Inapplicable Unamendable Constitutional Provisions' (*Int'l J Const L Blog*, 2 May 2015) www.iconnectblog.com/2015/05/marsteintredet-on-honduras/ accessed 31 December 2017.

[97] Tushnet (2014).

[98] I thank Francisca Pou for this suggestion, which merits further exploration.

> specific part of the Australian constitution that the eviction violates, says desperately, 'It's … just the *vibe* of the thing.' For Stuntz, justice ought to be just the vibe of the thing […][99]

The stakes involved in adjudication concerning constitutional amendments are too high for a decision to be so based. And, yet, one is left with the impression that, in applying the substitution doctrine, the Court seems to be invoking *the vibe of the thing*.

[99] Adam Gopnik, 'The Caging of America' *The New Yorker* (30 January 2012).

6

We the People, They the Media: Judicial Review of Constitutional Amendments and Public Opinion in Colombia

VICENTE F BENÍTEZ-R*

I. Introduction

After more than five decades without presidential reelection, in 2004 the Colombian Congress passed an amendment that allowed President Uribe to run for a second term. The Constitutional Court upheld this constitutional change, concluding that it did not destroy basic essential features of the Constitution.[1] Five years later, Congress proposed an amendment again to allow an additional presidential term. This time, the Court ruled that this proposal destroyed the basic constitutional structure and invalidated the proposed amendment.[2]

Why was one presidential reelection deemed compatible with the Constitution's basic structure, while a second one was struck down if, according to the Court, an additional term does not increase the number of presidential powers?[3] To answer this question, in this chapter I will propose the following thesis: considering the ample discretion involved in the judicial review of constitutional amendments based on implicit limitations on the amendment power, it is likely that extralegal factors such as the public perception of the Constitutional Court play a key role in its decision making.

In other words, one of the main assets of courts is their perception as neutral bodies whose operation is grounded on general principles, rather than

* JSD student at New York University. Constitutional Law Professor at Universidad de La Sabana. I am thankful for the comments of S Issacharoff, L Kornhauser, R Dixon, R Albert, J Ferejohn, P Pasquino, J Gallego-Saade, T Kohavi, J González-Escallón, A Quintana-Cepeda, and Sergio Verdugo. I assume full responsibility for the mistakes this chapter may contain.

[1] Decision C-1040/2005.

[2] Decision C-141/2010.

[3] The doctrinal variation in the Court's reasoning in these two cases is described in Rosalind Dixon and David Landau, 'Transnational constitutionalism and a limited doctrine of unconstitutional constitutional amendment' (2015) 13 I-CON 606, 626–27.

on partisan or capricious motivations. However, when the normative standards applied by courts are indeterminate, they will try to retain popular favour by issuing decisions that, somehow, are in line with public's expectations. As a result, in the face of divisive cases such as the review of amendments – here the law is unclear – courts probably pay attention to public opinion to prevent the loss of their reputation as nonpartisan institutions.

In this context, this chapter aims to analyse the impact of public opinion on the Colombian Constitutional Court when deciding salient cases concerning constitutional amendments. I will demonstrate, by proposing a model, that when there has been a shift in the public's and the media's perceptions of the Court or of its decisions, there has also been a change in its judicial attitude:

		Level of Media Support	
		Reinforced Court	Isolated Court
Level of People's Support	Popular Court	**Scenario 1:** Bold Court without reluctance	**Scenario 2:** 'Second-order' deferral
	Unpopular Court	**Scenario 3:** Bold Court with reluctance	**Scenario 4:** Self-censored Court

Namely I will claim that: (1) when public opinion has supported the Court, it has handed down bold judicial decisions even against the interests of hugely popular governmental policies, and these rulings have been duly complied with; (2) when the people have perceived the Court as a credible institution but the media have largely agreed with governmental interests, it has embraced a relatively self-censored attitude by which it makes decisions that are in line with the government's preferences, and adopts a 'second-order-deferral' strategy; (3) when the Court has been hugely unpopular and its members have thought that the Court will be supported by the media (who still support its institutional reputation, but not the specific outcome), some of its bold decisions have been reluctantly complied with by political actors; and (4) when the members of the Court have realised that the Court is no longer a credible institution, it has assumed a clearly deferential behaviour in favour of executive power, and it has refrained even from taking second-order-deferral strategies.

To support these hypotheses, this chapter will be divided as follows: Section II will develop the idea that public credibility is a key source of judicial legitimacy. Section III will claim that the 'unconstitutional constitutional amendments' theory developed by the Colombian Constitutional Court might undermine this credibility, forcing the members of the Court to consider public perceptions when making decisions. Section IV will propose a model that accounts for the four scenarios described in the matrix described above. In Section V, I will test the model with six cases of the Constitutional Court. Finally, I will propose some conclusions.

II. Judicial Credibility

One of the most celebrated portrayals of the judiciary was made by Hamilton in the Federalist Paper 78: the judiciary is the 'least dangerous' branch because it has 'neither FORCE nor WILL, but merely judgment'.[4] Different from the executive branch (in charge of the force – the sword) and from the legislature (in charge of the will – the purse) the judiciary has only 'judgment' and is highly dependent on the executive branch to enforce its judgments. Additionally, Hamilton believed that, under a limited constitution, the judicial branch ought to have the authority to strike down statutes or regulations when they contravened the Constitution.[5]

But, how can the 'least dangerous branch' be capable of quashing decisions made by popularly-elected and more powerful branches of government? According to Hamilton, judicial decisions should be aimed at upholding the people's view enshrined in the Constitution against their representatives' will contained in statutes or regulations. Similarly, to avoid any encroachment in the executive or legislative domains, the judiciary should remain 'truly distinct from both the legislature and the Executive', that is, it should act based on 'merely judgment', being faithful to the Constitution (ie, people's will), and avoiding the imposition of the judge's personal views over the provisions of the Constitution.[6]

To summarise Hamilton's point: courts can be guardians of the Constitution inasmuch as they faithfully use their judicial judgment to repeal unconstitutional norms. That would also justify their duties in democratic terms and enforce their decisions as an application of the people's will. Conversely, if a court imposes its views (invading the legislative realm), its decisions are not democratic and, therefore, it will be burdensome to enforce them.

Hamilton's words resonate in contemporary constitutional theory. Some scholars have concluded that 'judgment' is a key feature to assure judicial legitimacy. In this sense, the moral strength of any judicial decision stems from 'judgment' understood as the impartial and neutral application and interpretation of legal rules to a particular case.[7] In a similar way, Rawls regarded the US Supreme Court as the 'exemplar of public reason', as it has to justify its rulings in terms of justice or a reasonable variant of it. In that vein, the court cannot build its decisions on its own morality or other comprehensive doctrines, but rather on reasons that reasonable citizens can potentially endorse.[8] In other words, a court must demonstrate that it is the 'forum of principle' rather than the forum of politics.[9]

[4] Alexander Hamilton, *The Federalist Papers* (first published 1788, Palgrave Macmillan, 2009) 236.
[5] ibid 236–39.
[6] ibid.
[7] Alec Stone Sweet, 'Judicialization and the Construction of Governance' in Martin Shapiro and Alec Stone Sweet (eds), *On Law, Politics, and Judicialization* (OUP, 2002) 60–66; James Gibson, Gregory Caldeira and Vanessa Baird, 'On the Legitimacy of National High Courts' (1998) 92 *APSR* 343, 343–45.
[8] John Rawls, *Political Liberalism* (Columbia University Press, 2005) 236.
[9] Ronald Dworkin, 'The Forum of Principle' (1981) 56 *NYUL Rev* 469, 516.

This account makes sense if we analyse the institutional structure of courts, which allows them to produce principled decisions. On one hand, it is normal to find that constitutions contain a series of guarantees of judicial independence that facilitate the issuance of decisions based on principles, different from what happens with the other two branches.[10] On the other hand, given that courts generally do not have mechanisms of democratic accountability, a possible deterrent for preventing the enactment of unprincipled judicial opinions is the reputation of the judge that will be at stake in every important decision.[11]

This description does not mean that judges are mere machines whose mission consists of merely applying the law to a case. Any mechanism of third-party dispute resolution necessarily implies that the dispute-resolver modifies, to some extent, the normative structure that supports her decision. But it is precisely this inevitable judicial creativity which demands that the judge make an additional effort to show that her opinion is grounded in a shared or acceptable normative basis to maintain a perception of neutrality.[12]

When this aura of neutrality is absent because, for instance, a court is seen as a partisan institution whose decisions are driven by whim, it is likely that either its decisions will be met with some degree of disobedience, or that the court will adopt a deferential ruling to deflect any backlash and assure their enforcement. To avoid this dire scenario, one common strategy is relying on predefined and widely accepted principles to render decisions. This sort of depersonalisation of the factors that drive judicial decisions, helps to reinforce the idea that a court is really a forum of principle.

Nevertheless, resorting to this tactic is very problematic in those cases where the normative standards for decision-making are nonexistent, where they are highly contentious or where the court's competence to decide the case is unclear. It is precisely in this point where the Colombian 'unconstitutional constitutional amendment' (or 'substitution') theory – and my claim – comes into the picture: it is a contentious doctrine that was born amidst deep disagreements, and its critics have taken advantage of this situation to argue that its use has undermined the Court's credibility. And to regain its role as the forum of principle, it is likely that the Court has modified its behaviour to meet the expectations of public opinion, as I shall explain.[13]

[10] John Ferejohn and Pasquale Pasquino, 'The countermajoritarian opportunity' (2010) 13 U Pa J Const L 353, 370.

[11] Pasquale Pasquino, 'The New Separation of Powers: Horizontal Accountability' (2015) 7 *IJPL* 157, 158, 164–65.

[12] Stone Sweet (n 7) 60–66; Martin Shapiro, 'The Success 1 of Judicial Review and Democracy' in Martin Shapiro and Alec Stone Sweet (eds), *On Law, Politics, and Judicialization* (OUP, 2002) 160–65.

[13] Since civil society and middle-class sectors have been traditional allies of the Colombian Court, arguably it cares about its public image. See David Landau, 'Beyond Judicial Independence: The Construction of Judicial Power in Colombia' (DPhil thesis, Harvard University, 2014).

III. The Substitution Theory

One of the reasons behind the enactment of the 1991 Constitution was the amendment provision contained in the previous one: Article 218 established that only Congress could amend the 1886 Constitution. In the late 1980s Colombia was in the middle of political turmoil due to terrorist attacks organised by drug cartels against civilians as well the government. Several sectors of society urged for the amendment of the 1886 Constitution, so that some outdated institutions could be reformed to improve public order.

Nonetheless, Congress was reluctant to do so. Some analysts concluded that the path towards the government's modernisation was blocked and, thereafter, massive demonstrations were held in favour of the convocation of a constituent assembly (elected by the people themselves) to draft a new constitution.[14] The Supreme Court of Justice (in charge of judicial review at that time) recognised that, although Congress had an effective monopoly over the power of constitutional amendment, the people were the sovereign and, accordingly, were entitled to repeal the Constitution even by extralegal means.[15]

The framers of the 1991 Constitution were aware of the stalemate created by the previous constitutional text, and attempted to prevent a similar scenario from happening again. To do so, the new Constitution established three amendment mechanisms: legislative act, referendum and constituent assembly.[16] In addition, the Constitution also established that the Constitutional Court would have the power to review the constitutionality of any amendment based *only on procedural grounds*.[17]

From 1992 to 2002, the judicial review of amendments was restricted exclusively to check the compliance of the formal procedures contained in the Constitution. Correlatively, the Court rejected the possibility of examining the constitutionality of any amendment based on substantive criteria.[18] This literal interpretation was also warranted because the Constitution did not include any explicit substantive limitation to the nature of constitutional amendments, unlike some other constitutions such as the German Basic Law.[19]

In 2003, the Court changed this position and held that the constitutional analysis of amendments was not restricted to an examination of compliance

[14] Manuel José Cepeda and David Landau, *Colombian Constitutional Law. Leading Cases* (OUP, 2017) 4–5.

[15] Colombian Supreme Court. Decision 138 (351-E), 9 November 1990.

[16] Article 374.

[17] Article 241.

[18] See decisions C-222/1997; C-387/1997; C-543/1998; C-614/2002.

[19] Yaniv Roznai, *Unconstitutional Constitutional Amendments: The Limits of Amendment Powers* (OUP, 2017); Donald Kommers and Russell Miller, *The Constitutional Jurisprudence of the Federal Republic of Germany* (Duke University Press, 2012).

with procedural requirements, and that the Court was entitled to evaluate amendments on the basis of whether they suppressed implicit constitutional essential features. Drawing on the Indian Supreme Court's case law, the Constitutional Court observed that, although the Constitution does not establish explicit restrictions in the amendment process, it does have certain essential, 'implicit' principles. Consequently, a purported amendment cannot supersede these basic implied features because it would not be an amendment, but a profound constitutional transformation, tantamount to a replacement of the Constitution.[20]

This assertion was supported by two arguments. First, from a textual standpoint, the Court observed that Article 374 of the Constitution only allowed its amendment, and not its repeal or substitution. Therefore, eliminating an essential constitutional feature via amendment would be an *ultra vires* act. Secondly, the Court held that Congress is an institution that represents the people's will, but that cannot be equated to the people themselves. In this sense, Congress has a limited amendment power because it can modify the Constitution, but it cannot repeal it or suppress one of its basic features, because those rights are exclusive to the people themselves. Bearing in mind that in each of the three amendment mechanisms there is a congressional intervention, the Court specified that none of them is able to suppress an essential feature.[21]

This doctrine – which is known as the 'substitution' theory – has been criticised from its very beginning and all criticisms point in the same direction. It opens the door to making unprincipled decisions. More specifically, three critiques have been advanced against it:

- Some scholars argue that the Court is infringing upon the Constitution's plain meaning that restricts the scope of judicial review to procedural analysis, and, accordingly, excludes the examination of substantive issues. Thus, the application of the substitution theory permits unconstrained, substantive judgments which are constitutionally prohibited. In taking this stance, the Court has assigned itself a new (and unconstitutional) power.[22]
- The second problem has to do with the lack of objective criteria to identify the essential constitutional features. Some Constitutional Court's Justices and scholars have contended that, since the Constitution did not explicitly entrench 'eternity clauses', there is no rational way to determine – by means of pre-established and external parameters – which elements can be identified as

[20] Decision C-551/2003.

[21] Decision C-141/2010. Two accounts of the substitution theory in English in: Carlos Bernal-Pulido, 'Unconstitutional constitutional amendments in the case study of Colombia: An analysis of the justification and meaning of the constitutional replacement doctrine' (2013) 11 *I-CON* 339; Mario Cajas-Sarria, 'Judicial review of constitutional amendments in Colombia: a political and historical perspective, 1955–2016' (2017) The Theory and Practice Of Legislation 1 www.tandfonline.com/doi/full/10.1080/20508840.2017.1407397 accessed 9 January 2018.

[22] Sandra Morelli, 'Algunas consideraciones sobre el tratamiento del poder de reforma constitucional en la sentencia C-551 de 2003' in Javier Celis (ed), *Reforma de la Constitución y control de constitucionalidad* (Pontificia Universidad Javeriana, 2006) 445–500.

essential constitutional elements.[23] A variation of this argument maintains that the identification of these essentials is tantamount to the creation of *supra*constitutional rules.[24]

- Lastly, some claim that the final word regarding proposed amendments to the Constitution is in the Court's hands, and this situation is profoundly antidemocratic. Bickel observed that one possible (but quite difficult in the American context) response to the countermajoritarian difficulty could be amending the Constitution to override any judicial deviation of the Supreme Court.[25] However, this possibility is foreclosed when there is judicial review of amendments in light of 'constitutional essentials' discovered by the judge. R Albert has concluded that in such a case there would be a super-countermajoritarian difficulty, because even an amendment whose purpose is to overturn certain judicial ruling will be examined by the very same judge whose decision is at stake.[26]

There is, then, an ongoing jurisdictional, substantive and democratic discussion that surrounds the Court's theory.[27] This doctrinal divisiveness can be used to attack the Court's credibility and thereby impact its behaviour. The lack of a minimum consensus can be easily translated into accusations that the Court's decisions are not justified on sound principles but on arbitrary preferences, thereby creating incentives for a Court's behavioural change.

IV. Applied Judicial Credibility: A Public-opinion-based Model

Before turning to the cases, it is necessary to examine how this idea of credibility and its impact on judicial behaviour have been developed in a well-known model.

[23] Dissenting Justice Sierra-Porto in decision C-588/2009; Dissenting Justice Linares-Cantillo in decision C-285/2016; Gonzalo Ramírez-Cleves, 'El control material de las reformas constitucionales mediante acto legislativo a partir de la jurisprudencia establecida en la Sentencia C-551 de 2003' (2006) 18 *Revista Derecho del Estado* 3, 23; Santiago García-Jaramillo and Francisco Gnecco-Estrada, 'La teoría de la sustitución: de la protección de la supremacía e integridad de la constitución, a la aniquilación de la titularidad del poder de reforma constitucional en el órgano-legislativo' (2016) 133 *Universitas* 59, 74–76.

[24] Vicente F Benítez-R, 'Judicial Review of Peace Amendments in Colombia: Towards Supraconstitutional Rules and Plurality Opinions?' (*Int'l J Const L Blog*, 31 October 2017) www.iconnectblog.com/2017/10/judicial-review-of-peace-amendments-in-colombia-towards-supraconstitutional-rules-and-plurality-opinions accessed 1 November 2017; Vicente F Benítez-R, *Constitución Popular, no Judicial.* (Temis and Universidad de La Sabana, 2014).

[25] Alexander Bickel, *The Least Dangerous Branch. The Supreme Court at the Bar of Politics* (Yale University Press, 1986) 16.

[26] Richard Albert, 'Nonconstitutional Amendments' (2009) 22 *Can JL & Jur* 5, 43.

[27] Fallon has observed that most of the disputes concerning judicial legitimacy arise when courts develop new doctrines that do not 'uncontroversially' stem from the plain meaning of the Constitution's language or the framers' intent. Richard Fallon Jr, 'Legitimacy and the Constitution' (2005) 118 *Harv L Rev* 1787, 1813.

Vanberg has observed that, when a court has strong public support and the public is sufficiently aware of any attempts to circumvent its decisions (ie, a decision's salience), there is a higher probability that the political branches will abide by them. This is so because, if an elected official is reluctant to comply with a court's principled verdict, she is prone to losing the people's support that is essential for advancing effective proposals during her tenure, and for her reelection.[28]

This credibility – also known as 'diffuse support' – is built on an image of judicial impartiality, and yields four possible scenarios pursuant to this account:

(1) Public support and salience: the court has the people's endorsement and the public is aware of the case. In this situation, elected officials will refrain from enacting norms that stray far from the court's preferences. However, should elected officials pass such a law, given the court's popularity, the court will strike it down and congress will not defy the ruling.
(2) Public support and non-salience: although the court is popularly endorsed, the public will not notice the decision's non-compliance. This scenario is likely in low-profile cases. Thus, the political bodies will have no deterrent arising from adverse public opinion to challenging the ruling's enforcement.
(3) No public support and salience: The upper hand is in the politicians' camp. Therefore, the court will censor itself to avoid confrontations. Should the court issue a decision adverse to the interests of elected officials, such officials will try to circumvent it.
(4) No public support and non-salience: like the previous scenario, either the court will try to embrace a deferential attitude or elected officials will ignore its ruling.

Even though the previous model is sensible, I think that it could be adjusted in order to give a more accurate picture of the Constitutional Court's attitudes when reviewing amendments. I turn now to explaining how the model can be modified to account for the Colombian context and, then, I will propose a revised version.

A. Beyond We the People (I): Courts in Times of Abusive Constitutionalism

One assumption of the foregoing model seems to be that public support and salience are enough to assure a relatively bold court and compliant officials. And it is possible that this is the case in countries with well-established democracies. However, in new democracies there may be some traits that disrupt the model's predictions.

[28] Georg Vanberg, *The Politics of Constitutional Review in Germany* (CUP, 2004) 19–60.

In effect, new constitutional courts are now endowed with a wide range of powers that allow their intervention in (and eventual annulment of) political measures. This range of powers usually goes far beyond the traditional competence assigned to courts instituted in mature democracies.[29] Moreover, these transitional regimes sometimes suffer from what in Latin America some have called *caudillismo:* the existence of a charismatic leader with large public support, who tends to perceive that courts are somehow both political and countermajoritarian bodies that impede the implementation of governmental policies.[30]

In this context, there is an incentive for these rulers to curb courts through legal measures because: (a) their popularity produces enough leverage to influence the legislatures' lawmaking against courts; (b) the formal respect of the rule of law helps them to avoid reputational costs; and (c) courts have a broad scope to oversee manifold policy areas of governmental interest.[31] Thus, and contrary to Vanberg's model, a Court's public credibility would not be enough for a court to check a popular government because the public deterrent that prevents elected officers from eluding judicial decisions is no longer effective. Non-compliance with a court's ruling will not affect the politicians' reelection given that, although there is trust in the court, there is also public confidence in the ruler's decisions. Therefore, this defiance will not be interpreted as a disrespect towards a cherished institution (the court), but rather as the implementation of a popular president's policy.

Colombia is a case in point. Despite general acceptance of the Court and its powers, the Constitutional Court assumed a relatively self-censored attitude in the first two major decisions pertaining to judicial review of amendments, in the face of a hugely popular president. Surprisingly, some years later, and with similar rates of popularity in favour of the president and the Court, it halted the possibility of a second presidential reelection.

B. Beyond We the People (II): The Quest for More Allies

If people's support alone does not account for these shifts in the Court's decision-making patterns, what explains them? A first step is to acknowledge that new courts need more allies than the people, such as the media or other prominent actors in the field of public opinion (eg, the legal community, analysts or even religious authorities), particularly when most of the people's views about the court are mediated by these actors. Thus, a court also addresses these elites that

[29] Tom Gerald Daly, *The Alchemists. Questioning our Faith in Courts as Democracy-Builders* (CUP, 2017) 87–92.

[30] Ran Hirschl, 'The New Constitutionalism and the Judicialization of Pure Politics Worldwide' (2006) 75 *Fordham L Rev* 721, 721–28.

[31] This has been called 'abusive constitutionalism'. David Landau, 'Abusive Constitutionalism' (2013) 47 *UC Davis L Rev* 189, 195.

thoroughly read and analyse its decisions and, after that, publish their opinions in media outlets.[32]

It is important to note that these actors are interested in the ruling's outcome, its reasoning, and the credibility of the court as an institution, while the people are not concerned about the legal reasoning behind important cases, rarely pay attention to outcomes (unless it is a notable case), and they usually care about the institutional reputation.[33] Due to the more complex nature of legal and political elites' perception of courts, they can support a court in 'specific' terms (ie, its reasoning and outcome in a concrete decision) and/or in 'diffuse' terms (ie, the court as institution beyond any decision), whereas the people usually hold an institutional opinion.

These elites, in turn, play a key role in building the people's perception of the court's credibility. As Friedman has claimed, the way in which the public at large knows about a court's activity is the same one by which it is informed about anything else: accessing the media that analyse and assess the soundness of the court's job, instead of reading very long technical decisions.[34]

Some empirical studies in the US have explored how expert analyses influence the Supreme Court's diffuse support coming from the people, and have concluded that criticisms against specific decisions – even salient ones – do not greatly impact the people's institutional perception of the Court.[35] Although this type of study has not been conducted in Colombia, for now it is sufficient to say that the specific support (or disapproval) expressed by the media towards single actions of the Court probably does affect the people's diffuse support.[36]

This last hypothesis is relevant because from it follows that, paradoxically, the Colombian Constitutional Court's public diffuse support is inextricably tied to the quality of legal reasons offered by the Court or, what I have called, its role as the forum of principle. Thus, in a similar fashion Fallon has contended that the public acceptance of a court[37] could depend, to a great extent, on the legal/moral legitimacy[38] of the institution which, in turn, is measured and

[32] Rosalind Dixon and Samuel Issacharoff, 'Living to fight another day: Judicial Deferral in defense of the Democracy' (2016) *Wis L Rev* 683, 694–96; Barry Friedman, 'Mediated Popular Constitutionalism' (2003) 101 *Mich L Rev* 2596, 2613; Frederick Schauer, 'Incentives, Reputation, and the Inglorious determinants of Judicial Behavior' (2000) 68 *U Cin L Rev* 615, 629; Michael Wells, 'Sociological Legitimacy in Supreme Court Opinions' (2007) 64 *Wash & Lee L Rev* (2007) 1011, 1032.

[33] Fallon (n 27) 1828 (claiming that diffuse legitimacy is measured in opinion surveys); Wells (n 32) 1032 ('elites do pay attention to reasons as well as results'); Friedman (n 32) 2618 (diffuse support in opinion leaders depends on specific support).

[34] Friedman, (n 32) 2621; Wells (n 32) 1031, 1041. This may be the case in Colombia where decisions related to constitutional amendments are longer than 100 pages.

[35] Fallon (n 27) 1829. See also Nathaniel Persily, 'Introduction' in Nathaniel Persily, Jack Citrin, and Patrick J Egan (eds), *Public Opinion and Constitutional Controversy* (OUP, 2008) 8–10.

[36] See subsection 4.4, and how the Court's involvement in an alleged corruption scandal, affected its institutional credibility.

[37] An institution enjoys sociological legitimacy – which encompasses credibility – 'insofar as the relevant public regards it justified, appropriate, or otherwise, deserving of support for reasons beyond fear of sanctions or mere hope for personal reward'. Fallon (n 27) 1795.

[38] 'Legal legitimacy and illegitimacy depend on legal norms. That which is lawful is also legitimate'. On the other hand, 'When the term is used in a moral sense, legitimacy is a function of moral

assessed by legal/political elites whose examinations are delivered to the people through mass-media. In this sense, as I will try to demonstrate in the following section, the people in Colombia have deemed the Constitutional Court as the forum of principle when they perceive that it is an impartial institution. This impartiality is probably determined, in most of the cases, by how the media evaluate specific decisions or acts concerning an amendment's constitutionality.

To summarise, the information disclosed by the media about a court also can have an important impact on its decisions and, thereby, enhances the idea of judicial legitimacy in transitional contexts, where judicial popularity is not enough. Counting on the endorsement of these potential allies is relevant because: (a) they shape popular opinion; and (b) they can, in and of themselves, be powerful supporters (or detractors) of any court.

C. The Model

Based on the foregoing reasons, it is possible to say that there may be popular courts that, simultaneously, do not have the approval of legal/political elites. In this specific case, it is possible to speak of a popular but 'isolated' court, which will have to face different constraints in comparison with a popular and 'reinforced' tribunal. Similarly, an unpopular and 'reinforced' court will face different levels of pressure than an unpopular and 'isolated' court.

The Colombian Constitutional Court has moved throughout these four scenarios when deciding about the constitutionality of amendments. Pursuant to the gathered data, the specific differences among these four situations when it comes to the Court's attitude are the following:

		Level of Media Support	
Level of People's Support		Reinforced Court	Isolated Court
	Popular Court	**Scenario 1:** Bold Court without reluctance *C-141/2010 (second reelection case)*	**Scenario 2:** 'Second-order' deferral *C-551/2003 (first Uribe's referendum)* *C-1040/2005 (first reelection case)*
	Unpopular Court	**Scenario 3:** Bold Court with reluctance *C-285/2016* *C-373/2016 (judiciary's amendment)*	**Scenario 4:** Self-censored Court *C-699/2016 (Fast-track procedure: peace process)*

justifiability or respect-worthiness. Even if a regime or decision enjoys broad support, or if a decision is legally correct, it may be illegitimate under a moral concept if morally unjustified'. ibid 1794, 1796. According to Wells, in most judicial decisions there is a coincidence among legal, moral and sociological legitimacy. Wells (n 32) 1020.

Each scenario will be contrasted with specific data concerning the Colombian Constitutional Court. For the moment, I will try to describe them separately with the following remarks in mind: (a) from scenario 1 to 4, there is a gradual dilution of the Court's activism, which means that the most favourable judicial setting is Scenario 1, while the least favourable one is scenario 4; and (b) although this model is partially based on Vanberg's,[39] just the people's support is not sufficient to assure bold decisions or its compliance, particularly in the face of charismatic rulers (see scenarios 1 and 2).

Now, let's explore each scenario in detail:

1. Scenario 1: despite the President's popularity, the people's strong diffuse support coupled with the elite endorsement in favour of the Court, will pave the way for a bold decision (no self-censorship) whose reasoning and final outcome (adverse to the President's interests) will be enforced. As described above, the Court's public support is insufficient, given the President's approval and, as a result, it should be accompanied by the media's approval to guarantee the issuance of a bold decision and its compliance.
2. Scenario 2: although the people support the Court, the legal/political elite does not approve of the final outcome (absence of specific support). In addition, the President enjoys widespread public support. In this situation, the court will use a second-order deferral: it will not completely censor itself because it will craft a new theory that will be applied in a more favourable political setting such as the one described in the Scenario 1. Yet, there is a sort of self-restrained attitude because the opinion's disposition benefits the elected officers' interests.[40]
3. Scenario 3: while the media support the Court in diffuse terms and its popular perception is negative, the ruler's credibility is low. Additionally, the members of the Court think that the elite's diffuse endorsement will be sufficient for enforcing a bold decision. This ruling's compliance will face the defiance of elected politicians and public disapproval.
4. Scenario 4: The members of the Court will suspect that the Court's decision will not be complied with because neither the public nor the legal/political elites support the Court. Besides this, the president's popularity is low. The Court will embrace a self-censored attitude, and it will not have the margin to create a new doctrine by a second-order deferral.

The next section will be devoted to applying the proposed scheme to six Colombian Constitutional Court decisions, but before doing that, it is appropriate to present some methodological caveats. First, the influence of public and media opinion cannot be assessed unless the case is significant enough to be noticed

[39] Particularly Scenarios 3 and 4. The low popularity of the Court may be the driving factor behind its behaviour as well as the ensuing attitude of the political branches.

[40] In a second-order deferral a court: (a) pleases the governmental interests in the particular case avoiding backlashes; and (b) creates a new doctrine and postpones its application against the government until a more favourable political landscape arises. Dixon and Issacharoff (n 32) 686, 699–705.

in circles beyond the legal community. Consequently, the six cases deal with the constitutionality of high-profile amendments, and were decided through the substitution theory. They cover the period of 2003–16 because this theory was created in 2003, and, as of December 2016, the Court has applied it continuously.[41] In these cases, there was wide coverage by the media, and members of the public had discernible interests or opinions.[42]

A second methodological issue has to do with the identification of the data regarding the media's and the public's stances on the Court or its decisions. As for the former, I reviewed the news containing opinions given by newspapers, opinion leaders, politicians, public officers and constitutional analysts, six months *before* and six months *after* the Court delivered the decision. I focused on the digital archive of the two main national newspapers in Colombia (*El Tiempo* and *El Espectador*) and on the archive of the weekly political national magazine with the highest circulation (*Semana*). All the data is organised in a spreadsheet according to a set of criteria.[43]

Finally, the people's perception on the Court was gathered from the bimonthly surveys conducted by Gallup-Colombia, which can be publicly accessed.[44] The question asked about the Court is: 'Do you have a favourable or unfavourable opinion regarding the Constitutional Court?' The polls' information regarding the Court's credibility will be analysed with every decision. Let's turn now to the cases.

V. The Influence of Public Opinion on Substitution Cases

A. Uribe's First Referendum: The Substitution Theory was Born (C-551/2003)

Due to the failure of peace negotiations between the FARC guerillas and Pastrana's administration, Alvaro Uribe was elected President in 2002 with an

[41] To control for the turnover of the Court's members as a factor that could determine the changes in judicial behaviour described in this chapter, I decided to look at a set of cases dealing with a similar topic during the periods of rotation. After this analysis, I found that the Court's composition is probably not a key factor that influences its attitude, given that the judicial theses presented by the Court during this period were consistent with respect to this subject matter regardless of the Court's personnel shifts. See appendix, on file with author.

[42] Combining these two elements, the resulting cases addressed issues where the public was expected to have an opinion and, consequently, there was attention from the media. Namely, in four of the six decisions the people had already voted (Section 4.5) or were supposed to vote (Sections 4.1, 4.2, 4.3) for a governmental policy, while in the remaining two rulings the Court reviewed an amendment aimed at combating a prominent corruption scandal (Section 4.4).

[43] The information was sorted out following these categories: (1) Title; (2) publication's type (interview, column, editorial, analysis and description); (3) date of publication; (4) timing regarding the Court's decision (before/after); (5) stance towards the Court's decision (specific opinion) and about the Court (diffuse support); and (6) topics (essentially a summary of the news content).

[44] 'Gallup Poll' (*Gallup*, December 2017) https://drive.google.com/file/d/1BrBx7-FyOqJXRIP-26cJ5lNthm7AWVcNm/view accessed 8 January 2018.

astonishing level of public support. He promised to destroy FARC by military means, and this strategy gave him widespread popularity. However, as the Constitutional Court's General Secretary recognised, relations with Uribe were not going to be smooth. Uribe saw the Constitution and the Court as obstacles for implementing his policies, and he also appointed as Minister of Justice one of the Court's fiercest opponents.[45]

This military-based approach required a significant amount of financial resources and, following the recommendations of the IMF, Uribe proposed 17 constitutional amendments primarily intended to reduce public expenditures. Riding on his popularity (68 per cent in April 2003[46]), he decided to ask Congress for a referendum.[47] However, according to the Constitution, the Constitutional Court must review and approve of the amendments before holding any referendum. Therefore, the success of the amendments depended, to a great extent, on the Court's decision.

Some months before issuing its ruling, the Court called a public hearing to solicit the views of representatives of academia, the government, Congress and some sectors of economy. The result was relatively clear: most of them concluded that the proposed amendments were constitutional. Uribe himself attended the hearing and argued in favour of his amendment package.[48] In the media, economists, risk-rating companies, and most of columnists also opined in favour of the proposed amendments.[49]

One of the few voices against them was that of the Head of the Public Ministry.[50] However, once the Public Ministry gave its opinion to the Court, the Minister of Justice severely criticised it and the government announced a 'Plan B' in case the Court quashed the amendments: Uribe would personally visit multiple cities and would gather citizens' signatures to propose a publicly-endorsed referendum to circumvent this possible setback.[51] Additionally, some days later, the Minister of Justice said that the government was planning to introduce some other amendments to substantially curtail the Court's powers.[52]

In this adverse landscape, the Court issued decision C-551/2003 and decided to uphold 14 out of the 17 proposed amendments. Although several analysts

[45] Sebastián Rubiano 'La Corte Constitucional: entre la independencia judicial y la captura política' in Mauricio García-Villegas and Javier Revelo (eds), *Mayorías sin Democracia* (DeJusticia, 2009) 112.

[46] Gallup (n 44).

[47] Ley 796/2003.

[48] 'Así fue el examen del referendo' *El Tiempo* (Bogota, 6 June 2003) www.eltiempo.com/archivo/documento/MAM-998778 accessed 24 October 2017.

[49] 'Los pro Los Contra' *El Tiempo* (Bogota, 5 June 2003) www.eltiempo.com/archivo/documento/MAM-1000972 accessed 24 October 2017. The list of columnists is on file with the author.

[50] 'Golpe de la Procuraduría al referendo' *El Tiempo* (Bogota, 17 May 2003) www.eltiempo.com/archivo/documento/MAM-994848 accessed 24 October 2017.

[51] 'Si la Corte afecta referendo, habrá convocatoria' *El Tiempo* (Bogota, 25 May 2003) www.eltiempo.com/archivo/documento/MAM-981159 accessed 24 October 2017.

[52] 'Lista la embestida contra las cortes' *El Tiempo* (Bogota, 29 June 2003) www.eltiempo.com/archivo/documento/MAM-1038967 accessed 24 October 2017.

concluded that the decision had been favourable to the government,[53] a significant detail went unnoticed in the media: using a second-order deferral strategy (and perhaps given its popularity in July 2003), the Court announced the creation of the substitution theory but decided to gently apply it in the instant case to avoid any backlash (such as its jurisdiction's reduction) or a possible defiance of its decision through the government's Plan B.

To conclude: since several sectors of public opinion and the government (with its powerful congressional coalition) were rallying behind the amendments, the Court embraced a moderately deferential attitude and postponed the application of the newly-crafted theory until such time as there would be a favourable political setting. Meanwhile, the Court maintained its institutional prestige among the people and the media.

B. The First Reelection Case: The Waiting Continues (C-1040/2005)

In 2005, Uribe's popularity was still high and he continued to develop his military strategy against FARC.[54] His congressional coalition proposed an amendment to repeal the constitutional provision that banned presidential reelection.[55] Once again, the Court had to decide whether this amendment was compatible with the Constitution, but this time the substitution doctrine was employed by opinion leaders to argue in favour or against a new presidential term.

Although Uribe's attitude towards the Court was far less confrontational than that during his first two years in office,[56] his supporters designed alternative plans to circumvent an eventual adverse ruling. His Minister of Justice declared that, should the amendment be struck down, the Government was not going to 'sit back and do nothing'. A congressman proposed to write-in Uribe's name on the ballot in case he was excluded, while another one called for public disobedience against an eventual ruling against reelection.[57]

[53] 'La Corte dejó a salvo grueso del referendo' *El Tiempo* (Bogota, 10 July 2003) www.eltiempo.com/archivo/documento/MAM-10101531/ accessed 24 October 2017.

[54] *Semana* reports that since political surveys were introduced in Colombia, Uribe has scored the highest rates of popularity among Presidents. 'La Aventura de la reelección' *Semana* (Bogota, 19 December 2004) www.semana.com/nacion/articulo/la-aventura-reeleccion/70026-3 accessed 24 October 2017.

[55] The people overwhelmingly wanted Uribe to continue in power. 'Una nítida mayoría' *El Tiempo* (Bogota, 21 June 2005) 21 June 2005. www.eltiempo.com/archivo/documento/MAM-1957821 accessed 24 October 2017.

[56] Rubiano (n 45) 117.

[57] 'Plan B para todos los gustos' *Semana* (Bogota, 18 September 2005) www.semana.com/enfoque/articulo/plan-para-todos-gustos/74904-3 accessed 24 October 2017; 'Corte discute reelección a puerta cerrada' *Semana* (Bogota, 18 September 2005) www.semana.com/noticias/articulo/corte-discute-reeleccion-puerta-cerrada/74949-3 accessed 24 October 2017.

Different from 2003, the media were divided and, interestingly, justified their opinions on the substitution doctrine. A slight majority of analysts backed the amendment (including some economic experts and *El Tiempo*), whereas most of those who disagreed were 'soft contradictors'. In their view, if the Court upheld the amendment 'it was not the end of the world' and the Court's decision should be complied with to maintain its institutional integrity.[58]

Amid this landscape, in a divided decision (C-1040/2005), the Court held that a single reelection did not substitute essential elements of the Constitution, given that some of the external controls on the president remained in place, and because the number of presidential powers was not enlarged. Nonetheless – and resorting once more to a second-order deferral – the Court maintained twice that an amendment that introduces just 'one presidential reelection' was not an infringement of the Constitution, suggesting that an eventual second reelection (ie, for a third presidential term) would be unconstitutional.

This decision resembles Scenario 2.[59] The members of the Court probably knew that the Court was not going to lose its reservoir of institutional credibility from the amendment's soft opponents, and decided to rule in line with the expectations of the executive, several analysts and the public at large. In the meantime, the Court continued with the strategy of quietly laying the groundwork for new implications of the substitution doctrine whose purpose was the future limitation of the executive power, in case an amendment for allowing a new reelection was passed.

This strategy proved to be effective. The Court's credibility was maintained,[60] and even members of the opposition gave positive opinions about the Court, especially after it established some restrictions on Uribe's campaign for reelection.[61] However, the substitution doctrine was still discussed in the press, and despite their triumph, even Uribe's supporters were wary of this theory's future applicability.[62]

[58] Columns on file with author. See, for instance, Roberto Posada, 'El año de la Corte' *El Tiempo* (Bogota, 5 January 2005) www.eltiempo.com/archivo/documento/MAM-1677967 accessed 24 October 2017.

[59] This is the opinion of Roberto Gargarella, 'La Falla de la Corte Constitucional' *Semana* (Bogota, 12 February 2006) www.semana.com/opinion/articulo/la-falla-corte-constitucional/75733-3 accessed 24 October 2017; Juanita León, 'Un paso al centro' *Semana* (Bogota, 12 February 2006) www.semana.com/nacion/articulo/un-paso-centro/76760-3 accessed 24 October 2017.

[60] 'Sin sobresaltos' *Semana* (Bogota, 12 February 2006) www.semana.com/portada/articulo/sin-sobresaltos/75661-3 accessed 24 October 2017.

[61] 'Sigue la desventaja' *Semana* (Bogota, 12 February 2006) www.semana.com/nacion/articulo/sigue-desventaja/76044-3 accessed 24 October 2017.

[62] For instance, María Rueda, 'Y falló la Corte' *Semana* (Bogota, 3 December 2005) www.semana.com/opinion/articulo/fallo-corte/75387-3 accessed 24 October 2017.

C. The Second Reelection Case: The Court Saves the Constitution (C-141/2010)

This case represents scenario 1, of a bold court whose judgments are obeyed. The political landscape was fragmented, and the Court found room and allies to apply the substitution theory (and the implication that the Court had suggested in 2005) against President Uribe. Relying on his enormous popularity, a group of citizens petitioned Congress for a referendum to modify the Constitution to allow a second presidential reelection. As had occurred in 2003, the Court had to verify the amendment's constitutionality before the referendum could take place.

But this time, the political environment was different: the unified front in favour of this amendment was shattered. For starters, Uribe himself was ambivalent about the need for a new term. He had publicly expressed misgivings about staying in power, primarily because he did not want to be remembered as someone who clung to his position, as it was the case with his nemesis, Venezuelan President Hugo Chavez.[63] However, he also defended what he described as the 'state of opinion' which, in his view, was an evolved phase of the rule of law, where the rulers must listen to public opinion instead of focusing on legal technicalities.

In addition, some of his loyal followers (such as the Conservative Party and the Catholic Church), as well as former and current members of his administration, explicitly rejected a new presidential reelection.[64] This time there was no Plan B, and the government pledged to comply with the decision.[65] Likewise, a diverse group of opinion leaders expressed their disapproval of the possibility of a new term: economic analysts, *El Tiempo* (in a shift from its 2005 position), *Semana, El Espectador,* former Justices, constitutional law professors, the vast majority of political/economic analysts, multiple law schools, some international actors, and 35 out of 70 of the former members of the constituent assembly that had drafted the Constitution.[66] Similarly, although members of the public generally still had a positive opinion of Uribe's government, some surveys showed that a significant portion was against the proposed referendum.[67]

In this framework, the Court delivered its decision (C-141/2010) based on the substitution doctrine as well as on the implication of this theory that the Court had alluded to in its 2005 ruling. The Court held, in a divided decision, that a second presidential reelection was unconstitutional because it destroyed basic features

[63] 'Uribe y sus apuntes sobre la reelección' *Semana* (Bogota, 25 February 2010) www.semana.com/politica/articulo/uribe-apuntes-sobre-reeleccion/113604-3 accessed 24 October 2017.

[64] Reportages on file with author.

[65] 'Todo el país está hoy pendiente de la Corte' *El Tiempo* (Bogota, 26 February 2010) www.eltiempo.com/archivo/documento/MAM-3858114 accessed 24 October 2017.

[66] Reportages and columns on file with author.

[67] 'La mayoría de los colombianos preferiría que no hubiera referendo: Datexco' *El Tiempo* (Bogota, 10 January 2010) www.eltiempo.com/archivo/documento/CMS-7074908 accessed 24 October 2017.

of the Colombian Constitution, such as the principles of equality and separation of powers.

After the decision was published, all political actors shared the idea that the decision should be respected. Uribe declared: 'I abide by and respect the honorable Constitutional Court's decision … all citizens must comply with the law and even more the rulers … The law cannot coincide with the rulers' caprice'.[68] Besides the unanimous call for abiding by the ruling, most political analysts recognised the Court as a remarkable, independent and credible institution,[69] and the Constitutional Court's President acknowledged how this wide consensus was positive for the institutional strength of the tribunal.[70]

To return to the model posited in the previous section, the Court's public approval was necessary, but insufficient on its own, to produce this bold decision. Therefore, the Court had also to rely on some other key sources of support to avoid an unfavourable political scenario of non-compliance enabled by a popular President. Nevertheless, the substitution theory was still discussed in the public sphere. Some media leaders – who had approved the decision's outcome – critiqued this doctrine on the basis of its contested character.[71]

D. The Judicial Amendment Cases: The Court Without the People Using a Contentious Doctrine (C-285/2016 and C-373/2016)

April 2015 marks the lowest point in the Court's credibility in its 24 years of existence: in late February 2015, the most damaging corruption scandal in the Court's history took place.[72] Jorge Pretelt – who was by then the Court's President – was accused of having been bribed by a Colombian trust company to overturn a '*tutela*' decision of a lower court that had been adverse to the trust's interests.[73] Most of his fellow Justices, some Congressmen, and President Santos asked for

[68] Non-official translation of 'La participación de los ciudadanos no puede ser contraria a la Constitución: Uribe' *El Tiempo* (Bogota, 26 February 2010) www.eltiempo.com/archivo/documento/CMS-7308927 accessed 24 October 2017.

[69] The Court was named as one of the figures of 2010 by El Espectador. 'Comienza la restauración' *El Espectador* (Bogota, 27 February 2010) www.elespectador.com/articulo190131-comienza-restauracion accessed 24 October 2017.

[70] '¿Quién dice que a la Constitución no se le pueden cambiar los pilares: ustedes nueve?' *El Tiempo* (Bogota, 1 March 2010) www.eltiempo.com/archivo/documento/MAM-3861885 accessed 24 October 2017.

[71] Information on file with author.

[72] 'El día a día del peor escándalo que afronta la Corte Constitucional' *El Tiempo* (Bogota, 20 March 2015) www.eltiempo.com/politica/justicia/escandalo-corte-constitucional-cronologia-de-los-hechos/15434275 accessed 24 October 2017.

[73] According to article 241 of the Constitution, the Constitutional Court is in charge of reviewing some *tutelas* (ie, constitutional complaints). In a similar fashion to the American certiorari, the Court picks, on a discretionary basis, some *tutelas* to review.

Pretelt's resignation while the criminal procedure was conducted. However, he refused to do so, relying on his legal presumption of innocence.[74]

Despite this serious accusation, the general reaction of the media revealed that the Court still had certain institutional prestige among opinion leaders. In this sense, several analysts and public officials observed that the 'most ethical institution' of the government had been tainted, and it was necessary to fix it.[75] To do so, President Santos – who had maintained relative low levels of popularity – proposed two constitutional amendments to: (a) improve the administrative efficiency of the judicial branch with the creation of a new Judicial Governance Council; and (b) improve the effectiveness of the criminal prosecution of high court's Justices (including those of the Constitutional Court) with the institution of a new prosecutorial commission.[76]

In a striking move, in July 2016, the Court quashed these two amendments (decisions C-285/2016 and C-373/2016). Drawing on the substitution theory, it held that since the new administrative scheme allowed the participation of some executive officials, it infringed upon basic constitutional features such as independence and autonomy. As for the prosecutorial commission, the Court concluded that it also breached the basic structure of the Constitution given that, among other things, its members were not democratically elected.[77] One month later, Congress suspended Pretelt from his post. These two events precipitated one of the lowest points in the Court's popularity in August 2016.

Why did this unpopular Court strike down the amendments? A plausible hypothesis is that it perceived that, despite the specific corruption issue, the Court as an institution still had the approval of a significant share of public opinion, and this fact was enough to bolster a decision against the amendments. If this was the case, it was a huge miscalculation: diffuse support was not easily transferable to support specific outcomes.

Most analysts, constitutional law professors and media outlets decried the decision. First, some of them observed that the substitution theory was a largely unprincipled doctrine that could be easily put into the service of partisan enterprises. Several others asserted that the annulment of the amendments reflected the Court's desire to maintain its privileges at the expense of a well-functioning judiciary. Even more seriously, after these decisions, some sectors of public opinion withdrew their support of the institution of the Court.[78]

[74] 'No voy a renunciar a la Corte. Si me voy, nos vamos todos' *Semana* (Bogota, 20 March 2015) www.semana.com/nacion/articulo/el-magistrado-jorge-pretelt-acusa-al-fiscal-de-un-montaje/421620-3 accessed 24 October 2017.

[75] See columns on file with author.

[76] Acto Legislativo 2/2015.

[77] An analysis of these decisions can be seen in: Mario Cajas-Sarria, 'The Unconstitutional Constitutional Amendment Doctrine and the Reform of the Judiciary in Colombia' (*Int'l J Const L Blog*, 1 September 2016) www.iconnectblog.com/2016/09/the-unconstitutional-constitutional-amendment-doctrine-and-the-reform-of-the-judiciary-in-colombia/ accessed 24 October 2017.

[78] See columns on file with author.

But perhaps more importantly, Congress was very reluctant to accept the decisions. Representatives of political parties across the ideological spectrum considered the application of the substitution doctrine to be an encroachment of Congress' powers. In an unprecedented move, a proposal for calling a constituent assembly to amend the functioning of the judiciary was circulated.[79] The rationale for this proposal was that the Court did not want to modify the corrupted judicial structure to which it belonged to and, at the same time, it had closed the doors to a congressional modification.[80]

It is worth noticing that, in this case, the translation of diffuse support into specific endorsement was not a simple task. On the contrary, considering that certain political elites do pay attention to reasons and outcomes, the perception of an unprincipled application of the substitution theory led these elites to rescind their institutional support. Besides this, and following Vanberg, members of Congress saw that attacking the Court was profitable due to its low popularity.

E. Peace Amendments and Fast-track Procedure: The Court Censors Itself (C-699/2016)

The most important political project of President Santos' administration was the achievement of a peace agreement with FARC. After years of negotiations, a far-reaching accord was signed in September 2016, but its successful implementation required the enactment of multiple constitutional amendments. The negotiating parties agreed that the ordinary amendment procedure was burdensome, and any delay in the implementation phase could threaten the agreement. Therefore, they shared the idea that the procedure for amending the Constitution should be eased. Congress passed an amendment (known as the 'fast-track amendment') by which the procedural requirements for passing 'peace amendments' (ie, necessary to implement the pact) were substantially simplified vis-à-vis the ordinary amendment procedure.[81]

Since the fast-track amendment involved a limitation of congressional deliberation and an easing of the ordinary amendment requirements, it provided that this abbreviated procedure could be triggered only if the 'people endorsed' the peace pact. In October 2016 a plebiscite took place, and the agreement was rejected by a narrow margin.[82] Hence, Santos renegotiated with FARC and a new

[79] 'Amenaza del Congreso a la Corte' *Semana* (Bogota, 8 June 2016) www.semana.com/nacion/articulo/consejo-superior-congreso-y-corte-constitucional-en-disputa-por-fallo/476806 accessed 24 October 2017; 'La caída de la Comisión de Aforados en la Corte Constitucional' *Semana* (Bogota, 16 July 2016) www.semana.com/nacion/articulo/reforma-a-la-justicia-se-necesitaria-una-asamblea-constituyente/482055 accessed 24 October 2017.

[80] At the time of writing, this proposal has not been implemented.

[81] Acto Legislativo 1/2016.

[82] A description in English in Julia Symmes Cobb and Nicholas Casey, 'Colombia Peace Deal Is Defeated, Leaving a Nation in Shock' *The New York Times* (New York City, 2 October 2016) www.nytimes.com/2016/10/03/world/colombia-peace-deal-defeat.html accessed 24 October 2017.

accord was reached in November 2016. Some opposition parties (led by former President – and current Senator – Uribe) claimed that the fast-track procedure could not be activated given the absence of people's approval. Despite this, Santos argued that the fast-track procedure could be initiated if Congress – as people's representative – decided to endorse the second agreement, rendering the call for a new plebiscite unnecessary.[83]

Let's recall that the Court's credibility was reduced. Yet, it was called on to decide whether the mere congressional ratification of the agreement could be interpreted as a valid form of 'people's endorsement', which was required to trigger the fast track. The President explicitly asked the Court to uphold the fast track,[84] and some victims 'implored' the Court to endorse it.[85] In more menacing words, FARC said that without fast track, they would return to the mountains to restart their warfare operations.[86] Similarly, a significant number of analysts supported the constitutionality of this amendment. On the other side, Uribe, his coalition, a minor number of columnists, and, arguably, most of the plebiscite voters, rejected the validity of activating the fast-track procedure.[87]

In decision C-699/2016, the Court upheld the fast track, concluding that this procedure was necessary, in a transitional scenario, to attain peace. Likewise, although the Court set forth a series of principles to identify whether this abbreviated procedure could in fact be applied, it avoided to answer this issue, and deferred to Congress its decision. Political analysts on both sides of the political spectrum agreed that the decision was extremely confusing because it did not explicitly answer the question of whether the fast track could be used.[88] The Senate even considered inviting the Court's President to a public hearing to clarify the Court's position.[89] A former Supreme Court Justice suggested that this ambiguity stemmed from the fact that the Court wanted to please all interested parties.[90]

[83] Nicholas Casey, 'Colombia and FARC Sign New Peace Deal, This Time Skipping Voters' *The New York Times* (New York City, 24 November 2016) www.nytimes.com/2016/11/24/world/americas/colombia-juan-manuel-santos-peace-deal-farc.html accessed 24 October 2017.

[84] 'El afán del presidente Santos' *Semana* (Bogota, 5 December 2016) www.semana.com/nacion/articulo/presidente-santos-y-fast-track-corte-constitucional-en-sesion-el-12-de-diciembre/508231 accessed 24 October 2017.

[85] 'La súplica de las víctimas a la Corte Constitucional' *Semana* (Bogota, 8 December 2016) www.semana.com/nacion/articulo/acuerdo-de-paz-victimas-envian-carta-a-la-corte-constitucional/508597 accessed 24 October 2017.

[86] 'Sin Fast track volveríamos al monte' *Semana* (Bogota, no date) www.semana.com/nacion/multimedia/farc-hablan-sobre-refrendacion-del-nuevo-acuerdo-en-el-congreso/507407 accessed 24 October 2017.

[87] Columns on file with author.

[88] Editorial, 'Vía rápida necesaria' *El Tiempo* (Bogota, 12 December 2016) www.eltiempo.com/opinion/editorial/via-rapida-necesaria-editorial-el-tiempo-15-de-diciembre-de-2016/16773338 accessed 24 October 2017. See other columnists on file with author.

[89] 'Colombia en modo 'fast track'' *Semana* (Bogota, 15 December 2016) www.semana.com/nacion/articulo/congreso-avanza-con-el-fast-track/509621 accessed 24 October 2017.

[90] 'La Corte está tomando decisiones políticas: Jaime Arrubla' *Semana* (Bogota, 21 December 2016) www.semana.com/nacion/articulo/jaime-arrubla-explica-fallo-del-fast-track-en-la-corte-constitucional/510112 accessed 24 October 2017.

Thus, while the Court preserved the amendment – endorsing the concerns of the government and an important number of public opinion leaders – it did not take a clear stance as to whether the fast track could be employed to initiate the implementation of the agreement – perhaps to deflect any backlash from those who voted against the agreement.

This explanation is compatible with scenario 4. It is likely that the Court perceived that, given its discredited reputation among the public and the media (ie, its isolation), the safest stance was striving to satisfy to the highest possible extent the expectations of the government, Congress, the opposition and the members of the public who had rejected the first peace agreement. Thereby, compliance with its decision might not face any reluctance by or defiance from Congress or the President.

To attain this result, it was necessary to restrict the bold application of the substitution theory through a self-censored attitude. Had the Court applied the same level of scrutiny used in the judiciary amendments to the fast-track amendment, the amendment would have been quashed. Thus, some analysts shared the idea that the Court modified the strict application of the substitution doctrine to 'save' the amendment.[91] Similarly, this self-censorship is also apparent in the fact that the Court did not create any veiled doctrine to be applied in the future, and also because it simply deferred to Congress to answer the controversial question about the fast track activation.

VI. Conclusions

Judicial credibility is relevant in transitional democracies – such as the Colombian one – where young courts have to struggle against powerful rulers who perceive them as obstacles. Nevertheless, a relevant clarification is appropriate: I am not claiming that, to become a successful and respected institution, the Colombian Constitutional Court should adhere to public opinion in every case. On the contrary, given the contested character of the substitution doctrine, perhaps it should make a greater effort to communicate that its application is not guided by an unprincipled approach and, thus, recover its place as the forum of principle.

Going beyond Colombia, this chapter also attempts to provide an additional tool to analyse the behaviour of young courts and their relationship with public opinion that could be tested in other jurisdictions. By conflating two of the most powerful notions that Positive Political Theory has advanced to explain judicial behaviour (political fragmentation and public credibility[92]), the idea of judicial credibility might contribute a better understanding of courts' behaviour.

[91] See columns of Jaime Castro and Francisco Barbosa, among others. On file with author.

[92] Gretchen Helmke and Frances Rosenbluth, 'Regimes and the Rule of Law: Judicial Independence in Comparative Perspective' (2009) 12 *Annu Rev Polit Sci* 345.

In this sense, I think that it is possible to talk – at least in the Colombian case – of a sort of political metafragmentation that fosters judicial creativity, compliance, and judicial control on the other branches. Instead of taking into account just a horizontal political fragmentation between the executive and legislative branches, it could be productive to focus also on a vertical dimension that accounts for the wider political setting to determine the number and quality of allies a court has. This vertical fragmentation would involve top-down and bottom-up approaches to identifying what the stances of political actors located outside the state's structure are, and assessing how fragmented the political environment is. In any case, more research is required to evaluate the general soundness of this concept.

7

'Resistance by Interpretation': Supreme Court Justices as Counter-Reformers to Constitutional Changes in Brazil in the 90s+

DIEGO WERNECK ARGUELHES AND MARIANA MOTA PRADO

Judges are often accused of manipulating legal interpretation to advance their own political agendas. In doing so, the argument goes, they can create an illegitimate form of resistance to reforms put forward by democratically elected officials, particularly through the use of the mechanism of judicial review.[1] However, judges routinely protect themselves from such charges by framing their decisions as the best interpretation of the legal materials. The better they can do so, the less they can be depicted as using their office to promote their own political and moral preferences.[2] Because we cannot compare how individual judges behave as judges with how they would behave as legislators or constitution-makers, we can only wonder how politically aligned their decisions would be in both scenarios. But what if we could make such a comparison? What would be the implications for the legitimacy of judicial review of legislative decisions?

This paper explores the not so novel idea that a court of law, empowered to strike down or review legislation, may use this power to advance its preferences and reverse institutional changes. The novelty in our analysis is that it builds on the particular case of the Brazilian democratic transition, during which Supreme Court judges employed judicial interpretation to actively resist judicial reforms

+ Earlier versions of this paper were presented in the annual meeting of the Law & Society Association in Seattle (USA), in 2015, and at the Global Symposium on Constitutional Amendment and Replacement in Latin America in Brasília (Brazil), in 2016. The authors would like to thank to Rodrigo M Nunes, Conrado Mendes, Mohammed A Arafa, Andrea Pozas-Loyo, Carlos Bernal Pulido, Juliano Zaiden Benvindo, Richard Albert, David Dyzenhaus, Kent Roach, and several participants in both events for comments and suggestions. We are grateful to Luiz Carlos Penner Costa, Kristen Pue, and Stephane Serafin for excellent research assistance.

[1] eg in the US context, see Cass Sunstein, *Radicals in Robes: Why extreme right-wing courts are wrong for America* (Basic Books, 2005).

[2] Kent Roach, *Supreme Court on Trial: Judicial Activism of Democratic Dialogue* (Irwin Law, 2001).

that had been explicitly enshrined in the new Constitution of 1988. As the constitutional convention of 1987–88 debated these reforms, including an expansion to the Supreme Court's powers of constitutional review and role in the new democracy, the military-appointed Justices voiced their opposition. They were mostly defeated in the political process. After the Constitution was enacted, however, the same military appointed Supreme Court Justices were able to restrict or even reverse these reforms through interpretation. This type of ex post resistance allowed the Justices to achieve what they could not through ex ante resistance to reforms.

While there is a wealth of literature accusing judges of advancing their political preferences, most of this literature relates to cases that are neither related to judicial reforms generally, nor to reforms of the powers of the Supreme Court in particular.[3] By contrast, the substance of the reforms analysed in this paper, combined with the fact that judges opposed the reform in the political arena, seem to dispel any doubt that the Justices were indeed disguising their policy preferences as judicial interpretation. This raises a series of normative questions that we explore in the paper.

In Section I, we explore in detail the Brazilian Supreme Court's resistance to those provisions of the 1988 Constitution that aimed to change the system of constitutional adjudication in Brazil. In this case, the Court was even able to adopt, by judicial interpretation, ideas that had been considered and eventually rejected by the constitution-makers when they designed key features of Brazil's new system of constitutional review. This is an example of 'resistance by interpretation', which raises specific questions of legitimacy that have not been discussed until now in the academic literature.

In Section II, we consider the normative implications of ex post resistance to judicial reform by judges. If a certain group has the power to interpret rules to modify them according to its preferences, without consulting other groups involved, how can the use of such power be considered legitimate? We argue that two features should be present in the process for some kind of legitimacy to be possible: resistance needs to be *explicit* and *reversible*. While the Brazilian case is problematic, we thus conclude that this kind of resistance is not condemnable per se.

In Section III, assuming that resistance by interpretation will be undesirable when it is neither explicit nor reversible, we ask how it can be mitigated or avoided. We explore the pros and cons of reform strategies in preventing and mitigating

[3] The problem may be labelled 'judicial legislation', 'judicial law making' or 'judicial activism', and the literature on the topic has a long history; eg Ezra R Thayer, 'Judicial Legislation: Its Legitimate Function in the Development of the Common Law' (1891) 5 *Harvard Law Review* 172. For an overview of the origins and meanings of the expression 'judicial activism', see Keenan Kmiec, 'The Origin and Current Means of Judicial Activism' (2004) 92 *California Law Review* 1441; Craig Green, 'An Intellectual History of Judicial Activism' (2009) 58 *Emory Law Journal* 1195; William P Marshall, 'Conservatives and the Seven Sins of Judicial Activism', 73 *University of Colorado Law Review* (2002) 1217; Barry Friedman, 'The Birth of an Academic Obsession: the History of the Countermajoritarian Difficulty, Part Five' (2002) 112 *Yale Law Journal* 155.

the possible occurrence of this phenomenon. We illustrate these reform strategies with some of the institutional options that were under discussion at the time of constitutional reform in Brazil.

I. Judges as Counter-reformers: Ex Post, Internal Resistance to Constitutional Reforms in Brazil

Brazil's Supreme Court, the *Supremo Tribunal Federal* ('STF'), has played an expansive and growing role in Brazilian politics in recent years.[4] Indeed, the Court has decided many issues that would most certainly have been considered exclusively political a little more than a generation ago.[5] By contrast, the Supreme Court of the 1990s was often criticised as absent, too timid, or sometimes even downright submissive to elected officials. The only strong stance taken by the Court during this time involved setting aside several innovations in the 1988 Constitution that would have allowed it to act as an effective check on political power.

Many factors must be taken into account to explain this judicial change of heart, from the restraint of the 1990s to the struggle for expanding powers in the last decade. The generational change in the Court's composition from the late 1990s to the early 2000s is one such factor: it was only in 2003 that the last three military-appointed justices retired from the STF. The pre-transitional generation of Justices shared many views on constitutional law, including on the restricted role of the Supreme Court in a democratic regime. These judges survived the democratic transition, maintaining their appointments in the same institution, despite the fact that they had largely built their careers under an authoritarian legal order.[6] Their existing professional values and conceptions would prove to be influential in how the old Justices interpreted the new constitution.[7]

[4] Marcus Faro de Castro, 'O Supremo Tribunal Federal e a Judicialização da Política' (1997) 12 *Revista Brasileira de Ciências Sociais*; Julio Rios-Figueroa and Matthew Taylor, 'Institutional Determinants of the Judicialisation of Policy in Brazil and Mexico' (2006) 38 *Journal of Latin American Studies* 739; Matthew Taylor, *Judging Policy: Courts and Policy Reform in Democratic Brazil* (Stanford University Press, 2008); Matthew Taylor and Luciano Da Ros, 'Os Partidos Dentro e Fora do Poder: a Judicialização Como Resultado Contingente da Estratégia Política' (2008) 51 *DADOS - Revista de Ciências Sociais*; Luis Werneck Vianna and others, 'Dezessete Anos de Judicialização da Política' (2007) 19 *Tempo Social* 39; Ernani Carvalho, 'Trajetória da Revisão Judicial no Desenho Constitucional Brasileiro: Tutela, Autonomia e Judicialização' (2010) 12 *Sociologias* 176; Ernani Carvalho, 'Em Busca da Judicialização da Política no Brasil: Apontamentos Para Uma Nova Abordagem' (2004) 23 *Revista de Sociologia e Política* 127; Luis Roberto Barroso, 'Judicialização da Política, Ativismo Judicial e Legitimidade Democrática' (2010) 12 *Revista Jurídica da Presidência* 3.

[5] Oscar Vilhena, 'Supremocracia' (2008) 4 *Direito GV* 441.

[6] Fabiana Luci de Oliveira, 'O Supremo Tribunal Federal No Processo de Transição Democrática: Uma Análise de Conteúdo Dos Jornais Folha de S Paulo e O Estado de S Paulo' (2004) 22 *Revista de Sociologia e Política* 101; Fabiana Luci de Oliveira, *Supremo Tribunal Federal: Do Autoritarismo à Democracia* (FGV, 2011).

[7] Diego Werneck Arguelhes, 'Old Courts, New Beginnings: Judicial Continuity and Constitutional Transformation in Argentina and Brazil' (Unpublished JSD Dissertation, Yale Law School, 2014).

As we will discuss in greater detail below, during the constitutional convention, these judges expressed their restrictive ideas on the role of their Court in a democratic system in explicit, public manifestations. After these ideas were mostly defeated in the drafting of the new constitution, they resurfaced in the Justices' efforts to promote – by means of judicial interpretation – the very institutional arrangement of relative judicial restraint that had been rejected by the constitutional assembly.

In a dramatic departure from the previous constitutional order, the constitution makers of 1987–88 greatly expanded the number of actors who could challenge the constitutionality of a law before the Supreme Court using the mechanism of abstract review. From 1965 to 1988, the only plaintiff entitled to use abstract review was the attorney general, who had full discretion to decide whether to challenge a given law, but could also be fired at any time, at the president's discretion. Article 103 of the 1988 Constitution revolutionised this state of affairs, opening the doors of abstract review to several different kinds of societal actors: political parties with seats in Congress, state governors, the National Bar Association ('*Ordem dos Advogados do Brasil*'), and national unions.

In a series of cases beginning in the first weeks after the enactment of the new Constitution, the STF started to place severe restrictions on Article 103 by limiting the standing to file *Ações Diretas de Inconstitucionalidade* ('ADIs'), which are a kind of abstract review mechanism filed directly at the Supreme Court level. The most important of these restrictions was the so-called 'subject-matter pertinence' (*pertinência temática*) doctrine, by which the Court distinguished, in Article 103's list of plaintiffs, between 'universal plaintiffs' – who could challenge laws on any topic or subject matter – and 'special plaintiffs,' who could only challenge laws related to their primary institutional activities.

The distinction was consequential. Among the plaintiffs the STF considered 'special,' or not 'universal,' were the national unions and the 'national class associations'. The inclusion of these two non-state, strictly societal actors in Article 103 had arguably been one of the National Constitutional Assembly (the 'NCA')'s most daring measures regarding the standing rules for abstract review lawsuits. By contrast, the STF's doctrine of subject-matter pertinence – a self-conscious exercise in constitutional construction with no explicit textual base – led to a relative restriction of the degree of openness and representativeness of abstract review in Brazil. Article 103 did not prescribe differential treatment between these various actors for a simple reason: this was a deliberate political decision which aimed to build a new, European-style system of abstract review in Brazil. To do so, the NCA explicitly designed a system in which several different social actors should be able

Recent empirical studies on the Court of the 1990s and 2000s have shown that judges appointed by the military regime tend to display more restrained conceptions of the judicial role. Fabiana Luci de Oliveira, 'Justice, Professionalism, and Politics in the Exercise of Judicial Review by Brazil's Supreme Court' (2008) 2 *Brazilian Political Science Review* 93.

to trigger abstract review, and the need for such a change was widely supported within and outside the NCA.[8]

The Court's contradictory opinion regarding abstract review was publicly announced long before these cases were adjudicated. In 1986, the Court sent a formal message to the Afonso Arinos Commission that had been appointed by President Sarney to prepare a draft of the new constitution. Among the many recommendations included in that message, we find the following:

> Regarding the proposal to grant standing, for abstract review challenges of federal and state laws, to certain state entities (from the executive, legislative and judicial branches), or even to certain non-state public and private entities, the Court understands that such standing should remain exclusively with the office of the Attorney-General. If the Attorney-General is perceived as being too bound to the Executive branch, given the presidential power to freely remove the Attorney-General from office, then it is this issue that should be discussed, including the possibility of increasing independence. These, however, are matters to be more safely debated by the Constituent Power itself, and the Court must abstain from making further considerations as they would touch on topics connected to the executive and the legislative branches.[9]

The tone was cautious, but the message was clear: adopting generous standing rules for abstract review was a bad idea. While the STF was unable to persuade the constitution makers on this issue, the Court ultimately obtained what it failed to secure within the constitution-making process by means of judicial interpretation once the Constitution was enacted. The '*pertinência temática*' doctrine and others restricting the standing rules of Article 103 established a different institutional design of abstract review that was more restrictive than what the constitution makers had enshrined in the 1988 Constitution – even if it still allowed for a broader recognition of standing than under the previous 1967 Constitution.

All other things being equal, the broader the number of actors who can potentially be displeased with a given law and decide to challenge it in court, the more opportunities that court will have to shape and develop its own powers.[10] The Court's preferred system would thus reduce the likelihood of controversial political disputes reaching the Justices in a timely fashion, limiting the amount of political power the Court would be able to wield in the new Brazilian democracy.

[8] According to Andrei Koerner and Ligia Barros de Freitas, 'O Supremo na Constituinte e a Constituinte no Supremo' (2013) 88 *Lua Nova* 141, 165–67, even NCA members with conservative views on judicial reform and the Supreme Court displayed a preference for expanding access to abstract review; Ernani Carvalho (n 4) 196. The decision to expand access to social organisations, however, was less consensual. But it was ultimately fuelled by a petition to the NCA, signed by more than 39,000 citizens, asking for the constitution-makers to take the expansion to the next level; Koerner and Freitas 167.

[9] 'Sugestões do Supremo Tribunal Federal à Comissão Provisória de Estudos Constitucionais', published by the newspaper *O Estado de São Paulo* on 3 August 1986.

[10] Tom Ginsburg, *Judicial Review in New Democracies: Constitutional Courts in Asian Cases* (Cambridge University Press, 2003) ch 3.

There are other cases in which the STF used judicial interpretation to restrict clear reforms adopted by the NCA.[11] In particular, when deciding the *Mandado de Injunção n.107*, on 23 November 1989, the Court clearly relinquished powers it had been granted by the new constitution. The *Mandado de Injunção* (usually translated in English as *Writ of Injunction*) was created by Article 5, LXXI of the Brazilian Constitution:

> Art. 5. LXXI – a writ of injunction shall be granted whenever the absence of a regulatory provision impairs the exercise of constitutional rights and liberties, as well as the prerogatives inherent to nationality, sovereignty, and citizenship.

The *Mandado de Injunção* (MI) was incorporated in the Constitution as a new solution to an old problem. Previous Brazilian constitutions had quite a few generous and almost revolutionary provisions for fundamental rights, especially social rights, which unfortunately were never enforced. These provisions almost never made any practical difference: they were not considered self-applicable – and therefore not judicially enforceable – until Congress and the president approved additional legislation.[12] As shown by many scholars of the 1988 Constitution, and acknowledged by several Supreme Court justices over the years, the MI was conceived as an antidote for political omission in implementing fundamental rights.[13]

The MI was not the only device included in the Constitution for this purpose. In detailing the Supreme Court's powers of abstract review of legislation, Article 103, para 2 of the Constitution[14] allowed for the filing of an abstract review suit on the grounds that the government violated the Constitution by *its failure to enact a law* (*Ação Direta de Inconstitucionalidade por Omissão,* or 'ADO'). Although the purpose of the ADO is comparable to that of the MI, the mechanism is different. As an abstract review lawsuit, the ADO can be filed by a select few political actors and institutions, while an MI can be filed by anyone who is in a situation where legislative or presidential omission has 'disabled' the exercise of a fundamental right.

While the Constitution left room for interpretation in defining the boundaries and limits of the ADO and the MI, it was clear from the applicable constitutional provisions that they were *two* distinct mechanisms. Any attempt to interpret them as a coherent system of judicial review of unconstitutional omissions would have to entail some 'division of labor' between the two mechanisms.

[11] Diego Werneck Arguelhes (n 7).

[12] Luis Roberto Barroso, *O Direito Constitucional e a Efetividade de Suas Normas*, 5th edn (Renovar, 2001).

[13] Barroso (n 14); Henrique Fulgêncio and Alexandre Costa, 'O Mandado de Injunção na Constituinte de 1987–1988' (2017) 2 *Revista de Estudos Institucionais* 818, 858.

[14] Constitution 1988 (Brazil), Art 103, para 2: 'When unconstitutionality is declared on account of lack of a measure to render a constitutional provision effective, the competent Power shall be notified for the adoption of the necessary actions and, in the case of an administrative body, to do so within thirty days'.

In the leading case (MI 107), however, the majority of the justices interpreted the MI mechanism in a way that made it almost identical to the ADO, only with different standing rules. Justice Moreira Alves, writing for the majority, reached this conclusion by framing the main problem as one of enforceability of the Court's decisions, based on two assumptions: first, legislating was not the Court's business; secondly, the Court could not force Congress to legislate. All the justices could do, in the end, was signal to Congress or to the president that their inaction was in violation of the Constitution. This ultimately meant that winning in an MI case would only result in a judicial certification that the elected branches were violating a citizen's rights.

The main problem with this position is that it is circular. Because it treats both the MI (which is a mechanism of concrete review of constitutionality) and the ADO (which is abstract review) as equivalent, the MI falls prey to an enforceability problem that would only be applicable to the ADO. As many scholars have since argued, the Supreme Court could have used the MI to create a legal rule *just for the case at hand*, since the mechanism allowed for a lawsuit filed by an individual or limited group of individuals.[15] This option was not available when it came to the ADO, as it is a mechanism of abstract review endowed with *erga omnes* effect; any rules created by the Supreme Court when deciding such a lawsuit would be immediately binding on the whole country. The STF could therefore create rules just for the litigating parties when deciding an MI, even if it could not do so when deciding an ADO. It should come as no surprise that this was precisely the argument made in the concurring opinion of Justice Sepúlveda Pertence, the first civilian-appointed member of the Court. The majority decision on MI 107 found little support in the legal community. Since 1990, it has frequently been cited by scholars as the standard example of how the post-transitional Supreme Court was too timid and refused to fully explore all the possibilities opened up by the 1988 text to enforce the Constitution. Still, the position prevailed until end of the 1990s, when the Court started to haltingly tweak it; and it was only in 2007, that it was finally abandoned.[16] To the extent that a cautious stance may have been warranted at the time, an alternative approach would have been to decide the case in a way that was still cautious enough to protect the Court, such as through the use of 'judicial minimalism'.[17] For example, the Court could have simply asserted that it was still too early to identify the kind of congressional inaction that could trigger judicial review of legislative omissions, or that the STF could not ring the alarm for 'unconstitutional inaction' before a reasonable number of years had passed.

[15] eg Flavia Piovesan, *Proteção Judicial Contra Omissões Legislativas: Ação Direta de Inconstitucionalidade e Mandado de Injunção*, 2nd edn (Editora Revista dos Tribunais, 2003). See also Alice Voronoff, 'Ativismo Judicial e Democracia: Reflexões em Torno do Mandado de Injunção' (2011) 66 *Revista de Direito da Procuradoria Geral do Rio de Janeiro* 29.

[16] Alice Voronoff (n 15).

[17] On the concept of judicial minimalism – Cass Sunstein, *One Case at a Time: Judicial Minimalism in the Supreme Court* (Harvard University Press, 1999).

Instead of pursuing such a minimalistic path, however, a majority of the pre-transitional Justices took a step further and substantively redesigned the system of constitutional review that had just been put in place by the NCA. This approach amounted to nothing less than a judicial override of some of the most important commitments and reforms of the Constituent Assembly's recent break with the past constitutional order. At the end of the day, the Court was relinquishing – that is, more than simply *not using* – a power that the constitution makers had deliberately inserted into the new Constitution.

II. Resistance to Reforms through Judicial Interpretation: Is It Legitimate?

In the previous section, we have seen two examples of how the Brazilian Supreme Court read the new Constitution with old lenses.[18] The new Constitution contained mechanisms like the MI, a citizen's tool against political inaction, as well as greatly expanded standing rules, which aimed to grant access to the Court's abstract review powers to a wide range of social and political actors. Both innovations would have tended to increase the number of actors able to challenge the government, and the Court's clout in national politics. But the Supreme Court had a different system in mind and partly reversed these innovations. The Justices interpreted the Constitution in accordance with their own preferences regarding the Supreme Court's role in Brazil's nascent democratic system, even though they had been mostly defeated during the NCA. The MI became almost useless in practical terms, while the abstract review standing rules were significantly restricted.

In this section, we will analyse these developments and consider their normative implications. As we will argue, the Brazilian case illustrates a unique type of resistance to reforms. Despite courts being outsiders in most cases of judicial review, the substance of these particular reforms – the powers of the Supreme Court – made the Court an internal, self-interested actor. This raises two interesting normative questions. First, can a group legitimately use its power to interpret rules so as to modify the reform according to its preferences, even if its members are not democratically elected? Secondly, is the answer different if these reforms affect the resisting group, and are reversed after the same group participated and was defeated in a reform process?

[18] See Luis Roberto Barroso, *Interpretação e Aplicação da Constituição: Fundamentos de Uma Dogmática Constitucional Transformadora* (Saraiva, 1996) 67); Diego Werneck Arguelhes, 'Poder Não é Querer: Preferências Judiciais Restritivas e Redesenho Institucional no Supremo Tribunal Federal pós-constituinte' (2014) 25 *Universitas Jus* 25.

A. Judicial Interpretation, Democracy and 'Dialogue'

There are three ways to challenge the legitimacy of the Brazilian Supreme Court's re-interpretation of the 1988 Constitution. These largely track the broader debate on the legitimacy of judicial review itself. As we mentioned above, however, our focus here is narrower: namely, how can judges legitimately use judicial review as a form of ex post resistance to reforms they also resisted ex ante?

The first way to challenge the legitimacy of judicial review in these circumstances focuses on the political pedigree of the relevant decision makers: because a democratically elected constitution-making body took the first set of decisions, its preferred blueprint should prevail over the preferences of unelected judges. We will call this 'the democratic challenge'. In short, it suggests that a non-elected body does not have the legitimacy to redesign reforms implemented by a democratically elected one. Since it focuses on the particular actors involved in a particular case, this challenge may not apply to all kinds of ex post internal resistance that have the capacity to redesign reforms. For instance, a bureaucrat who decides to surreptitiously redesign a policy adopted by a minister during its implementation process may not face such a strong democratic challenge, particularly if the minister is also an unelected member of the executive branch in that particular jurisdiction. By contrast, the democratic challenge is especially strong in the Brazilian case: more than not having been elected, Brazilian Supreme Court Justices had been appointed by the outgoing military dictatorship.

The second way of challenging the legitimacy of the Justices' decisions is more outcome-centred. The important question becomes whether the Court's changes improve on the original blueprint. We will call this 'the consequentialist challenge'. There would be many possible criteria for such an assessment, for example the most efficient allocation of fiscal resources or the fairest arrangement from a distributive perspective. In all cases, the assessment is not strictly dependent upon which institution has made the decision: the focus is on a comparison of the substantive outcomes of the two reforms. However, the identity of the decision maker is still indirectly relevant in a democracy, since it remains necessary to determine who should set up the criteria be used to evaluate the reforms. In this sense, 'the consequentialist challenge' eventually takes us back to 'the democratic challenge'.

The third way of challenging the legitimacy of judicial resistance in the Brazilian case focuses on its procedural legitimacy – 'the procedural challenge'. The assumption is that there is nothing intrinsically wrong with accepting multiple sources of authority on constitutional interpretation; judges who second guess legislators might or might not be performing a legitimate task. Instead of asking the 'who' and the 'what' questions, the procedural challenge focuses on the 'how' question: regardless of who is deciding, or what they are deciding, a decision is not legitimate unless certain procedures are followed. By this we do not mean simply following whatever procedural rules are in place. Rather, the procedural challenge relates precisely to the kind of properties such rules should have in order to make the judicial second-guessing of constitutional reforms legitimate.

The most influential example of such a procedural justification is the 'dialogic' interpretation often espoused within the Canadian system of constitutional review.[19] As several Canadian scholars have argued, the fact that neither the Canadian judiciary nor its legislatures can claim final and ultimate authority will tend to improve the quality and legitimacy of their decisions.[20] These dialogic interpretations are built on a set of normative aspirations that, at least according to defenders of this view, are somehow promoted by the Canadian institutional design and judicial decision-making practices. In short, judicial resistance to reforms enacted by Parliament or a provincial Legislative Assembly is considered 'dialogic', and therefore legitimate, when it takes place in a way that is both (i) *explicit*, and (ii) *reversible.*

By *explicit,* we mean that, as it voids a statute or changes the interpretation of a constitutional provision, the Court takes a clear stand against a previous decision by another institution. The decision calls the public's attention to the issue and increases its visibility. By *reversible,* we mean that, even after the Court has struck down a given law, the legislature can keep the discussion open and explore other ways of enacting equivalent measures. Moreover, to do so, the legislature would not be doing anything potentially illegal. Conversely, the more a judicial decision: (i) obscures the controversy and hides the policy change from sight, or (ii) makes it unfeasible for politicians to revisit the issue and try a new approach, either due to features of institutional design or to the judiciary's approach in facing the case, the less 'dialogic' and therefore less legitimate judicial resistance becomes.

The two assumptions are linked in practice, and the combination of both increases the legitimacy of the output of the political and judicial processes. Within a dialogic framework, when the Canadian Supreme Court strikes down a given law passed by Parliament after carrying out a Section 1 analysis of its justifications, it is acknowledging that a different measure might have survived the test. Parliament can then disagree with the Supreme Court's decision and revisit the same discussion, allowing the democratically elected body to potentially reverse the Court. This can be done either by enacting an improved provision, after amassing better empirical and legal justification for rights-restricting measures under Section 1, or by employing Section 33's override mechanism.[21]

[19] eg Kent Roach, 'Constitutional, Remedial, and International Dialogues about Rights: the Canadian Experience' (2005) 40 *Texas International Law Journal* 537.

[20] The main two venues for such dialogues over the meaning of the Constitution in Canada are Section 1 and Section 33 of the Canadian Charter of Rights and Freedoms. Section 1 establishes the possibility of limiting rights, but only 'to such reasonable limits prescribed by law as can be demonstrably justified in a free and democratic society.' And Section 33, the so-called 'notwithstanding clause', allows federal and provincial legislators to immunise a given law against judicial review for a period of five years. This immunisation can be renewed by means of a new legislative enactment after the five years have expired; Roach (n 22). From a broader theoretical perspective; Conrado Hubner Mendes, *Direitos Fundamentais, Separação de Poderes e Deliberação* (Saraiva, 2011).

[21] A brief discussion of Section 33 available at n 23.

In the first scenario, Parliament is trying to convince the Court; in the second, the intended audience is the public in general. In both, however, the fact that the Court's disagreement with Parliament is: (i) explicit, and (ii) reversible gives this conflict of views a dialogic character, as both institutions are expected to improve their arguments at each step. The result is that, over time, both institutions will be increasingly expected to present, not just to one another but to the public in general, the reasons why they believe the law should or should not change on a given issue. These two conditions are not necessarily sufficient for completely legitimising judicial review, but, in their absence, the idea of 'dialogue' loses its force.

The dialogic view above is not without its own critics.[22] Our brief reconstruction of the two underlying assumptions of this sophisticated body of scholarship relied on a stylisation of how Canadian institutions work – an illustration of the argument we are presenting, and by no means a thorough review of the conditions in which dialogue theories were developed. What matters for our purposes here, however, is not Canadian institutions per se, but rather their interpretation by legal scholars in an attempt to assess the legitimacy of judicial review. More specifically, we refer to these theories to draw from their underlying normative assumptions and aspirations on how institutions should work. Whatever its merits to explain and justify judicial review in Canada, this dialogic framework provides us with two important normative benchmarks against which the judicial review of reforms can be assessed in our case: changes made by judges need to be explicit and reversible.

B. Judicial Resistance against Constitutional Changes in Brazil: Was It Legitimate?

Based on the premise that judicial review can be legitimate, if it meets certain procedural requirements, we now turn to an analysis of the Brazilian case. First, the Brazilian Supreme Court Justices did not disagree with the constitutional reforms in a transparent and explicit way, in the terms described above. Instead of vetoing a reform implemented by the legislature, and stating the grounds on which they disagreed with the new constitutional text, they changed its content while pretending they were simply interpreting the legal rules created by the Assembly. The Court did not even discuss the conflicting views on these provisions within the constitutional convention, nor did it present its decision as a continuation of these previous debates, which would have made their decision at least minimally transparent in this respect. Rather, their decision was presented simply as a 'technical' reading of what the constitution makers had created, suggesting that there

[22] eg Rosalind Dixon, 'The Supreme Court of Canada, Charter Dialogue, and Deference' (2009) 47 *Osgoode Hall Law Journal* 235; cf Kent Roach, 'Dialogic Judicial Review and its Critics' (2004) 23 *Supreme Court Law Review* 49.

was just one correct interpretation of the text, and ignoring the lengthy constitutional debates that led to its adoption.

Secondly, the Justices' resistance by interpretation took place in an institutional context in which the legislature's resources to keep the debate open were far from clear. This was mostly due to the move between the formal tracks of constitutional and ordinary lawmaking. The two points of contention (access to abstract review and judicial remedies against political inaction) had been part of the constitution-making agenda, and the Court's decision operated at the level of the constitutional text itself.

Both politically and legally, once read into the constitutional text, the Justices' preferred blueprint was not easily reversible by new rounds of congressional action.

Congress would have needed to resort to the costly procedure of amending the Constitution – which, in Brazil, requires a super-majority of 3/5 of both houses in two different legislative sessions. The amendment path was also much less effective against the Court than against other actors, for two reasons. First, the Brazilian constitution recognises 'eternity clauses', which are interpreted very broadly by the Supreme Court.[23] Secondly, since the Court had adopted a restrictive interpretation of an *expansive* textual provision, any solution would probably have required recourse to more specifically worded rules. This would have narrowed the room for future restrictive interpretations and created higher bargaining costs within the legislative process. The Brazilian Supreme Court's ex post resistance through interpretation, therefore, impaired dialogue instead of promoting it.

C. Judicial Resistance and Judicial Activism: A Smoking Gun?

The Brazilian case study points towards the Supreme Court reversing reforms made by the constitutional assembly – a kind of resistance to reforms by the judiciary that is often branded as judicial activism. Different authors identify different dimensions in their use of this concept.[24] But most versions seem to share a common core: an activist judicial decision is somehow a *deviation* from a clear standard that should have bound the judge *qua* judge – for example the text of the law, accepted interpretative techniques, the separation of powers – and which distinguish the office from that of a legislator.[25] However, distinguishing between

[23] Although the constitutional text does mention that congress cannot deliberate on an amendment that 'tends to abolish' certain features of the constitutional order like fundamental rights and guarantees, universal suffrage and periodic elections, separation of powers, federalism and a republican form of government (Constitution 1988 (Brazil), Art 60, para 4), it was only in 1993 that the Supreme Court officially asserted the possibility of judicial review of amendments on the basis of these provisions. Moreover, it did so in a case involving the creation of a new tax – an interpretive move which required asserting, as a legal matter, that the Art 60, para 4 clauses should be read in expansive ways.

[24] eg Roach (n 2) 106–11.

[25] Stefanie Lindquist and others, 'The Rhetoric of Restraint and the Ideology of Activism' (2007) 24 *Constitutional Commentary* 103; Keenan Kmiec (n 3) and Craig Green (n 3).

law-making and law-interpretation can be daunting in practice, particularly when adjudicating constitutional clauses. Judges accused of 'activism' need only point to the reasonableness of their interpretation of the legal materials – a somewhat low bar, especially in divisive constitutional cases – for the criticism to be considerably weakened. The suspicion of activism might linger on, but there will be no smoking gun.

It is not our goal here to engage with these difficult and multi-dimensional debates on judicial activism. Indeed, the decisions being discussed seem ill fitted for a discussion of the topic. They deal with procedures for constitutional review, and only indirectly with constitutional rights. In these cases, the Court also relinquishes some of its powers, instead of attempting to increase them, such that interpretation was actually used to sustain judicial restraint over the long haul.[26]

Still, the Supreme Court's behaviour in these cases can show us how to make stronger charges of judicial activism, in certain circumstances. Let us assume that, in all these decisions revisiting reforms made by the constitution makers, the Justices could defend the legal (and not political) nature of their decision by pointing, among other things, to existing precedents and the purpose of the constitutional clauses involved. The Justices had nonetheless participated in political debates and had tried to push the constitutional assembly to move in a different direction. This, we believe, should change how we assess their behaviour.

When judges participate in political debates on reform, recommending the creation of some rules and advising against the adoption of others, they reveal their preferences as would-be legislators.[27] We do not need to imagine or guess what their political preferences are, or how they would behave as legislators, as they have openly stated these things. In such a scenario, the claim that judges are simply relying on legal interpretation can be undermined by the judges' previous political engagement on the exact same issue, placing them under a higher level of scrutiny when it comes to accusations of judicial activism. In other words, these judges have given us a smoking gun.

III. Resistance to Reforms through Judicial Interpretation: Can It Be Avoided?

We turn now to a prescriptive question: if resistance by interpretation is not desirable, how to avoid it? Could the Brazilian constitution makers have prevented

[26] Diego Werneck Arguelhes (n 18).

[27] The empirical studies that use an 'attitudinal model' to explain the US Supreme Court's behaviour based on newspaper editorials on nomination and confirmation hearings operate in a functionally similar way; Jeffrey Segal and Harold Spaeth, *The Supreme Court and the Attitudinal Model Revisited* (Cambridge University Press, 2002). However, the situation examined in this paper is much more straightforward: the Justices have publicly expressed their views on the same issues they now have to decide.

this problem? The Canadian debate on democratic dialogue seems to suggest that this is fundamentally an institutional question. As we suggested in Section II, the possibility of reversing the court's decision may come from some openness embedded in judicial interpretation, but it can also be realised in institutional mechanisms that empower the legislature to reverse court decisions (even if temporarily), such as those adopted in Canada. Cognisant of the importance of this institutional dimension, our analysis here will focus primarily on alternative arrangements that could have potentially prevented the problem legislators faced in Brazil.

A. Resistance to Reforms: The Unique Case of Judicial Interpretation

Intentional resistance to reforms by identifiable actors may be driven by different motives. For example, reforms may pose threats to the ongoing viability of existing groups or to the benefits received by them.[28] Intentional resistance to reform can also encompass various strategies and can occur at any stage of the policy process. Facing the risk of oversimplifying, we offer a typology of types of resistance to institutional reform that draws on two relevant dimensions: whether resistance occurs before or after reforms have been implemented, and the position of the resisting actors as insiders or outsiders of the reform process. Based on these two dimensions, this section creates two ideal-type binaries, namely ex ante and ex post resistance, and external and internal resistance, and four categories of resistance to reform, namely ex ante internal, ex ante external, ex post internal, and ex post external.

Beginning with the temporal dimension, resistance can happen at many different stages in the reform process. However, its potential implications seem primarily associated with whether the resistance is taking place before or after the reform is implemented. The assumption here is an intuitive one: there is more room to manoeuvre before institutional change has taken place. After the reform is implemented, any resistance must aim to reverse the change, and is likely to face all the obstacles that any kind of institutional change faces, including systemic and structural obstacles such as path dependence.[29]

Using the implementation of the reform as the focal point, resistance can be split into two categories – ex ante resistance and ex post resistance – according to whether the resistance occurs before or after reform is enacted. This ideal type dichotomy points to different strategies for opposing reform, based on whether the reform must be taken as a fait accompli.

[28] Michael Trebilcock, *Dealing with Losers: The Political Economy of Policy Transitions* (Oxford University Press, 2014).

[29] Mariana Mota Prado and Michael Trebilcock, 'Path Dependence, Development and the Dynamics of Institutional Reforms' (2009) 59 *University of Toronto Law Journal* 341.

Ex ante resistance, which precedes the design and implementation of reform, features groups that may either take active steps to voice their concerns publicly or block modifications in the system surreptitiously. In either case, ex ante resistance may block the adoption of a proposed reform or substantively change its design.

By contrast, ex post resistance takes place once the reform has been adopted and generally aims to undermine its success. This stage in the reform process is important, as 'not only do civil service reforms take time to implement; they require even longer to have an impact'.[30] In this sense, ex post resistance may transpire as the continuation of a failed attempt at ex ante resistance or it may be initiated only afterwards. The former usually occurs when groups who oppose the change have participated, to some extent, in the reform debates, but were ultimately defeated.

There are several ways of undertaking ex post resistance. To the extent that the reformers expect the resisting groups to contribute resources (expertise, information or human capital), these groups can create barriers and obstacles to accessing these resources. If reformers are not directly dependent on resources provided by those resisting reforms, but are still dependent on some kind of resources, resistance may take the form of lobbying to block adequate budgetary allocations. Moreover, those resisting reforms can use negative publicity and spread misleading information, making citizens/consumers hesitant to support, use or benefit from reform efforts. If effective, ex post resistance can destroy a reform by substantially depriving it of resources; by using asymmetry of information to make consumers afraid of using it; or causing the practices of the organisation to change such that the reform no longer threatens the resisting group's interests.

By contrast, the distinction between internal and external resistance relates to the position of the resisting actor vis-à-vis the reforms. This position often correlates to the type of power the actor possesses as well as the manner in which she is expected to participate in the process. Both factors are likely to influence the type of resistance that is exerted.

External resistance comes from stakeholders and interest groups outside of the organisation that is the object of reform. These external actors can be very influential. For instance, the policy goals and behaviour of successful politicians are shaped by interactions with coalitions of supporters, which can be significantly expanded if the insiders supporting reforms can count on the support of outsiders.[31] If we assume that outsiders are self-interested agents trying to maximise their welfare, the survival of institutional reforms is closely tied to the distribution and timing of the costs and benefits that they are expected

[30] Sarah Repucci, 'Civil Service Reform: a Review' (2012) *United Nations University World Institute for Development Economics Research Working Paper No. 2012/90* 6 www.wider.unu.edu/publication/civil-service-reform accessed 6 January 2017.

[31] Thráinn Eggertsson, 'State Reforms and the Theory of Institutional Policy' (1999) 19 *Revista de Economia Politica* 49.

to generate.[32] For example, Williamson has focused on the concept of a 'reform arena', wherein the economic and political interests of stakeholders mediate policy reform within the institutional context of reform.[33]

This approach emphasises the influence of external resistance on the ex ante side of institutional reform; decision making is modelled as a negotiation that is influenced by 'access to and use of information, power relations, perceptions, the timing of policy discussions and by the level and inclusiveness of public debate'.[34] However, it is easy to imagine that this same logic may also apply ex post. Insofar as future decisions, such as resource allocation or role redefinition, will continue to impact reform efforts after enactment, external resistance can persist after the reforms are adopted. For instance, civil service reform involves considerable initial political costs, while political benefits accrue only much later;[35] as such, political will may be vulnerable to external resistance at both the ex ante and ex post stages of reform.

By contrast, internal resistance refers to reform opposition that is carried out by actors within the institutional landscape that is being changed. Internal actors are in a privileged position within the institutional framework that is the object of reform – for example, as civil servants expected to carry out a reform which impacts on their own duties and powers. Internal resistance by these actors may occur due to self-interest – for example, if a reform threatens gains from patronage networks or is expected to result in job losses within an organisation, or if it clashes with established conceptions of these actors' professional role. Resistance can also be a result of uncertainty about the effects of reform on a number of areas, such as the policy goal or the bureaucratic structure.

Based on this typology, there are four categories of resistance to institutional reform: internal ex ante, external ex ante, internal ex post, and external ex post. In each, the stage of reform and position of the resisting actor imply different resistance strategies. While it is beyond the scope of this paper to present a comprehensive list of strategies that may be undertaken in each instance, this typology nonetheless aims to present a useful way of thinking about resistance to reform.

As suggested in the table above, actors adopt different strategies depending on the sources of power available to them, as well as the stage of reform. External actors can first resist reform by appealing to political decision makers and, following the implementation of reform, can continue to resist by influencing the use of these institutions by citizens and the flow of resources to the institution. Internal

[32] Michael Trebilcock (n 28).

[33] World Bank, 'The Political Economy of Policy Reform: Issues and Implications for Policy Dialogue and Development Operations' (2008) *World Bank Social Development Department Report No.44288-GLB* http://hdl.handle.net/10986/7782 accessed 6 January 2017.

[34] World Bank (n 33) 11.

[35] Repucci (n 30) 6.

	Internal	External
Ex ante	Officials operating inside of the institutional framework that may be the object of reform seek to influence political decision makers to alter the reform or prevent it from occurring. *Key strategies*: epistemic influence through control over technical expertise and information; policy advocacy.	Stakeholders outside of the institutional framework that may be the object of reform seek to influence political decision makers to alter the reform or prevent it from occurring. *Key strategies*: interest group lobbying; political mobilisation campaigns
Ex post	Officials operating inside of the institutional framework that has been reformed seek to undermine the implementation of the reform or to influence its operations. *Key strategies*: shaping implementation through bureaucratic autonomy; selective interpretation; policy advocacy.	Stakeholders outside of the institutional framework that has been reformed seek to undermine the implementation of the reform or to influence its operations. *Key strategies*: encouraging a consumer boycott; misinformation; lobbying and political mobilisation to reduce resources to the new institution.

actors may use their expertise to influence the enactment of reform; following the implementation of reform, they can directly shape the operation of the reform, interpret legislation selectively, and continue to advocate for policy changes.

The Brazilian Supreme Court case discussed in Section I is a particular instance of internal ex post resistance. In general, internal ex post resistance through the interpretation and implementation of existing rules is likely to generate gradual and incremental changes that can produce cumulative effectives, resulting in significant changes over time.[36] The difference, in this case, is that the resistance offered by the Supreme Court in reinterpreting reforms that were already implemented resulted in a redesign of the reforms through the selective use of constitutional interpretation and the Court's ultimate autonomy over their implementation. In other words, the Supreme Court created a kind of ex post resistance that produced the effects generally encountered in ex ante resistance strategies – that is, to influence the design of reforms themselves and promoting radical (as opposed to incremental) change.

[36] James Mahoney and Kathleen Thelen 'A Theory of Gradual Institutional Change', in James Mahoney and Kathleen Thelen (eds), *Explaining Institutional Change: Ambiguity, Agency and Power* (Cambridge, 2010), 10–11.

B. Preventing Undesirable Resistance by Judicial Interpretation

The previous section articulates why resistance by interpretation is a powerful strategy to resist reforms, since it can achieve the results of ex ante resistance ex post. As discussed earlier, this strategy is problematic if it is both not explicit and irreversible, as was largely the case in the Brazilian case study. In this context, the most effective strategy may be to try to prevent resistance by interpretation from happening.

Drafting the Constitution in more specific terms could theoretically contribute to preventing ex post judicial resistance, or at least narrow its possible scope. However, the problem that the Brazilian scenario highlights is precisely the difficulty of transforming, from the outside and by means of new legal rules, an institution that has the power to interpret and ultimately redefine its own sphere of competence.[37]

Changing the judges would also be an apt strategy to minimise the risk of resistance by interpretation. However, for a set of complex political, legal and historical reasons, removing the sitting Justices would have been very costly in the Brazilian case. During the transition, the Supreme Court Justices had successfully campaigned to present themselves as non-political professionals who were part of a century-old, honourable institution that had not actively collaborated with the military dictatorship.[38] In such a scenario, placing a change in the Court's composition on the constitution-making agenda could have led to an even stronger ex ante resistance on the part of the Justices. The same could be said of other court-packing proposals, including any attempt to increase the size of the Court so as to dilute the power of the sitting Justices.

This scenario illustrates how promoting an entire package of reforms may not always be politically feasible, and thus incremental and piecemeal change becomes the only option. The dilemma that reformers face, however, is the fact that the component of the reform that is not promptly adopted – for example changing the composition of the court – may be the same feature that will forestall future reforms from being implemented. This creates what one of us had previously described as a 'reform trap': an initial reform is implemented, but the incremental steps are then blocked by the very same initial step taken, not allowing the incremental steps to be implemented later.[39] An alternative would be to invert the sequence, starting by repopulating the court before discussing any substantive or procedural changes in the constitutional powers of the court. However, even this

[37] Ginsburg (n 10) ch 3.

[38] Diego Werneck Arguelhes (n 7).

[39] Mariana Mota Prado, 'The Paradox of Rule of Law Reforms: How Early Reforms Can Create Obstacles To Future Ones' (2010) 60 *University of Toronto Law Journal* 555.

scenario could present significant resistance. If powerful political actors populate the resisting institution, or if these actors are able to recruit outsiders to support their resistance to internal changes, a reformer is left with no alternative but to leave the resisting institution alone.

Another alternative is to wait for the old actors to eventually be replaced on their own, which may help dilute the resistance to reform.[40] Indeed, the gradual change in the Court's composition seems to be one of the main factors that eventually allowed the Brazilian Supreme Court to move away from the restrictive interpretation proposed in the 1990s and embrace a more active role in Brazilian democracy.[41] However, this outcome is uncertain, may take many years to materialise, and a significant amount of irreversible changes may have happened during this time. So, it is not unreasonable to assume that a reformer may prefer not to incur these risks, if at all possible.

Finally, yet another way of pre-emptively mitigating 'resistance by interpretation' is to implement external changes, outside of the resisting institution that affect its modus operandi. This approach can take the form of 'institutional layering', which involves 'grafting of new elements onto an otherwise stable institutional framework'.[42]

Some of the proposals made within the NCA took precisely this form. For example, in the first draft of the Subcommittee on the Judicial Branch, Rep Plinio de Arruda Sampaio recommended the creation of a Constitutional Court *above* the existing Supreme Court. The Supreme Court was to remain basically untouched, but the new and empowered abstract review mechanisms would have been given directly to the new Constitutional Court, which would also be staffed with a new batch of judges.[43] However, even this approach did not succeed in Brazil: although the changes to the Supreme Court's jurisdiction would have been minimal, the sitting Justices nonetheless lobbied strongly against it.[44] They conceived of the proposal as a direct attack on the Supreme Court, and successfully used this discourse to convince outsiders to support their resistance.[45]

By contrast, layering was applied with a large degree of success by Colombia's constitutional drafters in 1991. Aiming to 'change the institutional mission of the judiciary' by reorienting it towards rights adjudication, they established a new Constitutional Court with broad review powers and a more politicised system of appointments.[46] However, the new Court developed a tense relationship with the

[40] ibid.

[41] Diego Werneck Arguelhes (n 7).

[42] Kathleen Thelen, *How Institutions Evolve: the Political Economy of Skills in Germany, Britain, the United States and Japan* (Cambridge University Press, 2004) 35.

[43] Andre Koerner and Ligia Freitas (n 8); Diego Werneck Arguelhes (n 7).

[44] Andre Koerner and Ligia Freitas (n 8).

[45] Diego Werneck Arguelhes (n 7).

[46] Rodrigo M Nunes, 'Ideational Origins of Progressive Judicial Activism: The Colombian Constitutional Court and the right to health' (2010) 52 *Latin American Politics and Society* 67.

existing Supreme Court. In the decade following the new constitution, resistance through interpretation would resurface several times.[47]

Perhaps these issues could have been avoided if Colombia had adopted an alternative form of layering that had also been proposed in the Brazilian case. In the final draft of the Subcommittee on the Judicial Branch, the rapporteur suggested the creation of a Constitutional Chamber *inside* the Supreme Court – a more timid proposal than a new court, but still a form of institutional layering. The Court would still be divided in two chambers, as had traditionally been the case, but only the Constitutional Chamber would have had the power to hear and decide abstract review cases. Most of the eight Justices in the Constitutional Chamber would have been appointed after the Constitution had been enacted. The old Justices would have decided, amongst themselves, who would take the remaining seats.

For several reasons related to the dynamics of the constitution-making process in Brazil, this proposal was also ultimately unsuccessful in the NCA. Supreme Court Justices lobbied against it, and constitution makers – who were already clashing with President Sarney on the scope of the NCA's power to reform the constitutional order – ended up avoiding any measure that could be seen as an attack on the Court or its members.[48] Had it succeeded, however, it would have been a useful tool for preventing ex post resistance by interpretation. The new powers given to the Court – in particular, the ones that the old Justices disagreed with – would be relevant only to the Constitutional Chamber's jurisdiction, where the old Justices were a minority. Moreover, this layering solution was less aggressive towards the sitting Justices than creating a new court, thus reducing the incentives for ex ante resistance on their part.

IV. Conclusion

This paper discussed a special type of ex post resistance to institutional reforms, judicial interpretation, as used by the Brazilian Supreme Court to revert some of the institutional changes adopted as part of the 1988 Constitution. As we have seen, the Court was able to adopt, by judicial interpretation, ideas that had been considered and eventually rejected by the constitution makers when they designed key features of Brazil's new system of constitutional review.

While building inductively from a single case study, the paper describes a problem that is not confined to Brazil. As Tom Ginsburg noted in the Asian context, there are significant difficulties in transforming, from the outside and by

[47] On the 'collision' between the two courts – Everaldo Lamprea, 'When Accountability Meets Judicial Independence: A Case Study of the Colombian Constitutional Court's Nominations' (2010) 10 *Global Jurist*. See also Roberto Gargarella, 'Grafting Social Rights onto Hostile Constitutions' (2011) 89 *Texas Law Review* 1537.

[48] Diego Werneck Arguelhes (n 7).

means of new legal rules, an institution that has the power to interpret and ultimately redefine its own jurisdiction.[49] The concept of 'resistance by interpretation' not only provides a label to describe one possible source of some of these difficulties, but it also helps to understand how this kind of resistance can occur and how it can be tentatively faced.

Solutions may be also not confined to particular countries. Indeed, reformers in a transition context can rely on more ambitious forms of institutional layering, such as creating a new court, or more timid forms of layering, such as creating a new chamber within an existing court, in order to mitigate the risk of resistance by interpretation. While these measures present uncertainties in their own right, the alternative of seeing legitimate and desirable constitutional reforms undone shortly after their implementation seems vastly less palatable.

[49] Ginsburg (n 10) ch 3.

8

The Judicial Review of Constitutional Amendments in Brazil and the Super-Countermajoritarian Role of the Brazilian Supreme Court – The Case of the 'ADI 5017'

ENEIDA DESIREE SALGADO AND CAROLINA ALVES DAS CHAGAS

I. Introduction

For many years, written constitutions have been part of the everyday life of a vast number of countries. The great value that they have achieved over the years has made it important to develop mechanisms for their protection – such as the judicial review – and to establish boundaries for changes in their texts while, at the same time, trying to keep them up to date. These changes are inevitable, since a Constitution represents the idea of law and politics of a society in a determined historical period, which means they cannot be immutable.[1] Constitutional changes can be formal or informal – that is with or without a modification of the written text. Nevertheless, for the purpose of this chapter, the focus will be on the formal changes.

Along with the constitutional reforms is the main idea that they should not alter the core of the Constitution, for this would be the same as making a new one. However, the writing of a new Constitution should only be made by a constituent power, in extraordinary moments through extraordinary political endorsement.[2] Nonetheless what should be pointed out is that judicial review of constitutional amendments is not a settled issue, since amendments are the product of the

[1] Eneida Desiree Salgado, 'O Referendo como Fase Legislativa das Emendas Constitucionais' [2004] *ano 4 n. 15 A & C Revista de Direito Administrativo e Constitucional* 55, 64.

[2] Roberto Gargarella and Christian Courtis, 'El nuevo constitucionalismo latinoamericano: promesas e interrogantes' https://www.cepal.org/es/publicaciones/6162-nuevo-constitucionalismo-latinoamericano-promesas-interrogantes accessed 13 June 2015, 15.

constitutional revision, created by a high consensus of the popular representatives, sometimes together with popular participation, concerning subjects that might involve strong political aspects.

The procedure for a constitutional reform can be rigid or less rigid. In a rigid reform, in some countries, the increasing participation of the Judiciary can be observed. It happens in countries where the courts have already gained certain social status and feel they are apt to take one more responsibility in protecting the Constitution by overseeing its reform procedure.[3] Countries such as India, Colombia, Turkey and – of course – Brazil are known for having courts exhibiting this kind of behaviour.

While considering the judicial participation in the constitutional amendment process, opposing ideas may rise. On the one hand, it could mean another obstacle for the creation of unconstitutional constitutional amendments. However, on the other hand, it could give way to this branch to enforce prerogatives that *a priori* are not designated to it, that is to modify the constitutional text. There is the need, then, to address this phenomenon and rethink possible forms through which the courts could participate in constitutional changes in a more democratic way.

In the Brazilian case, it will be shown that not only the postures of the judges can lead to a mishandling of the Judiciary's prerogatives. The form in which the judicial review system is organised can also propagate actions that are not compatible with the constitutional text.

The constitutional text should be respected since it has a normative force. To deny the normative character of the Constitution is, as affirmed by García de Enterría, to conceive it merely as an occasional compromise by political groups, which could be substituted at any time.[4] On the other hand, to recognise this normative force could imply that the constitutional efficacy should be judicially assured – in other words, adjudicated by a court.[5] Thus, the court should be the one protecting the constitutional text for its own purposes, rather than going beyond it, as occurred in the judicial review of constitutional amendments in Brazil.

The current paper aims to shed a light in the judicial review process of constitutional amendments in Brazil, emphasising its main features and main threats to the rule of law, in particular, to the separation of powers, due to a super-majoritarian posture of the court. With that in mind, the chapter starts with a brief explanation of the procedure for creating constitutional amendments in Brazil, followed with an empirical analytical research of cases that deal with the judicial review of constitutional amendments and how they are subject to some institutional instruments that increase this super-countermajoritarian role. Next, the case regarding

[3] Richard Albert, 'Amending Constitutional Amendment Rules' (2015) 13 *International Journal of Constitutional Law* 655, 669.

[4] Eduardo García de Enterría, *La Constitución como norma y el Tribunal Constitucional* (Civitas, 1985) 175.

[5] Eduardo García de Enterría, *La Constitución como norma y el Tribunal Constitucional* (Civitas, 1985) 176.

the ADI 5017 is chosen for a further substantive analysis where one can get a fuller picture of the consequences of this institutional misuse of powers. The paper closes indicating how this behaviour of the Brazilian Supreme Court (Supremo Tribunal Federal) influences its deliberative functions and suggesting where to look for some practical solutions for the matter.

II. The Amending Process and Judicial Review in Brazil

The judicial review of constitutional amendments can be done controlling the procedure or the content of an amendment. When it is done to control the content, it has as usual basis constitutional rules that are considered to have a more important status than the others to be suppressed, known as eternity clauses (in Brazil, '*cláusulas pétreas*').[6] They are considered substantive limits to the constitutional amendment process with the aim to preserve key elements of the constitutional order, determined by the constituent power.[7] The mere presence of these eternity clauses, however, is not always a guarantee of a judicial review of amendments.[8] Still, judicial review of constitutional amendments in Brazil happens very often.

To better understand what the critics laid out here about the Brazilian approach to judicial review of constitutional amendments, it is deemed necessary to explain its amendment procedure.

Although Brazil is a federative state, the constitutional reforms do not need to be approved by the States' legislative power. Those who can propose an amendment are a third part of the Higher or the Lower Houses, the President, and over a half of the Parliament of the member states. There is no popular initiative.

Formally, for an amendment to be approved in Brazil it needs the consensus of at least three-fifths of Congress (Higher and Lower Houses) with two voting rounds in each House. The proposal of amendments does not need to be sanctioned and can be vetoed by the President. Also, the Constitution cannot be modified in circumstances of political instability, such as when a state of emergency is declared.

The substantive requirements for amendments are in the already mentioned eternity clauses. Alongside them, the Brazilian constitutional scholarship also recognises implicit limits to constitutional amendments. As an example of such implicit clauses, there are the rules of the amendment process and the provision that fixates the eternity clauses.

[6] Article 60, §4º, of the Brazilian Federal Constitution lists the immutable clauses, which are: (i) federalism; (ii) the direct, secret, universal and periodic vote; (iii) separation of powers; (iv) individual rights and guaranties.

[7] Michel Fromont, *Justice constitutionnelle comparée* (Paris, Dalloz, 2013) 252–53.

[8] Norway and the US are examples of countries that have immutable clauses in their Constitutions, but no judicial review of constitutional amendments – Yaniv Roznai and Serkan Yolcu, 'An unconstitutional constitutional amendment – The Turkish perspective: A comment on the Turkish Constitutional Court's headscarf decision' [2012] v. 10 n.1 *International Journal of Constitutional Law* 175, 199/200.

Eternity clauses are one of the examples present in constitutional texts that signalise the tension between constitutionalism and democracy.[9] The existence of eternity clauses can be seen as an anti-democratic restriction made by the past generation to the future ones.[10] Nonetheless, in Brazil the immutable clauses have a solid support; they are broadly recognised as part of the spirit of the Constitution, something that cannot be modified, otherwise, it would deform the constitutional project.[11]

In general, the defence of a judicial review of constitutional amendments is often made as a form to safeguard principles and fundamental rights from abuse from a certain legislative majority, mainly to protect the rights of the minority groups.[12] However, an exacerbated use of its prerogatives by the Judiciary can be sometimes observed. Especially considering that this control is usually exercised in Brazil in an *a posteriori* way,[13] that is after the amendments have been already voted. Besides from being a locus of legal uncertainty, since a constitutional provision may enter into effect and still be challenged a long time after its approval, this repressive judicial review also brings the concern of determining the parameter for a review of provisions that can be considered an already legitimate part of the Constitution.

One of the main distinctions that one might employ within the countries that endorse judicial review of constitutional amendments is between the ones that have a constitutional provision for that review, and the ones in which the Judiciary self-grants this prerogative.[14] In Brazil, this judicial review is a creation of the case law of the Supreme Court, one that the judicial community and society in general largely accept.[15] However, one could agree that it can also be seen as a direct consequence of the interpretation of the constitutional provisions, since the constitutional reform process has formal and substantive requirements. Those requirements make it seem as if their analysis is part of the institutional role of the Supreme Court.

Moreover, it is important to highlight that the amendment prerogative cannot be mistaken for the expression of a constituent power, which is free and

[9] Yaniv Roznai, *Unconstitutional Constitutional Amendments: The Limits of Amendment Powers* (Oxford, Oxford University Press, 2017) 112.

[10] Even though future generations would not actually be totally tied to the past ones, since it would still be possible to activate the constituent power for the building of a new order.

[11] Gilmar Ferreira Mendes and Paulo Gustavo Gonet Branco, *Curso de Direito Constitucional*, 6th edn (Saraiva, 2011) 138.

[12] Yaniv Roznai and Serkan Yolcu, 'An unconstitutional constitutional amendment – The Turkish perspective: A comment on the Turkish Constitutional Court's headscarf decision' 201.

[13] Judicial review of constitutional amendments can be exercised both in an *a priori* approach, ie controlling the draft of the amendment, and in an *a posteriori* approach, ie controlling an already approved amendment.

[14] eg, South-America countries like Ecuador, Colombia and Chile have specific provisions for judicial review of constitutional amendments, while Peru also engages in the practice, but without explicit legal provisions, similarly to the Brazilian experience.

[15] Gilmar Ferreira Mendes and Paulo Gustavo Gonet Branco, *Curso de Direito Constitucional* 1189/1190.

unconditioned. The amendment prerogative comes from a constituted power,[16] one that has fixed constitutional requirements in order to prevent the ordinary legislator from usurping the constituent's determination. That means that amendments are not able to completely alter the social organisation and to change the political values and choices made by the constituent.[17]

What is sought as absolutely indispensable is to establish a strong distinction between constituent politics and constituted – or ordinary – politics, as affirmed by Gargarella. The Constitution should be preserved as a stable, perdurable document, whose modification should be exceptional, through a reinforced political consensus, with special procedures and without replacing the ordinary legislator.[18]

In order to examine the formal requisites for an amendment, it is not necessary for the court to analyse its substance. When it comes to the judicial review of constitutional amendments, the limits that usually challenge the roles of the Judiciary are not the formal ones (ie, a review on the process of amendment), but the substantive ones (ie, a review on the subject to be amended). In that way, any defence of a judicial review of constitutional amendments based on substantive limits should be done in a restrained way, especially not to weaken the important roles of the other democratic players.

Therefore, it is imperative to question the role of the Brazilian Judiciary in the amendment procedure and, at the same time, to rethink the subaltern position of the representative powers and of popular sovereignty in relation to the Constitution and its interpretation. The political decisions, as written in the Constitution,[19] should derive from the people, including the cases in which the constitutional text needs to be defined, for constituent power is the product of the nation's will.[20]

From this perspective, it is not reasonable to reduce the moment of popular participation exclusively to the birth of the Constitution, since such participation should happen at its modifications too. Popular sovereignty does not end in the inaugural moment of the State but continues to be a criterion of legitimacy and validity for the legal rules that are created after the Constitution, as a form of self-determination.[21]

[16] Eneida Desiree Salgado, 'O Referendo como Fase Legislativa das Emendas Constitucionais' 64.

[17] Eneida Desiree Salgado, 'O Referendo como Fase Legislativa das Emendas Constitucionais' 65. This is the main basis for defending implicit substantive limits to amendment procedures. For more see Yaniv Roznai, *Unconstitutional Constitutional Amendments*, 141 ff.

[18] Roberto Gargarella and Christian Courtis, 'El nuevo constitucionalismo latinoamericano: promesas e interrogantes' 14.

[19] Article 1 of the Brazilian Federal Constitution: 'All power emanates from the people, who exercise it through elected representatives or directly, in the terms of this Constitution'.

[20] Emmanuel Joseph Sieyès, *A Constituinte burguesa: que é o Terceiro Estado?* (Norma Azeredo tr, Liber Juris, 1986) 113.

[21] Eneida Desiree Salgado, *Constituição e democracia: tijolo por tijolo em um desenho (quase) lógico: vinte anos de construção do projeto democrático brasileiro* (Fórum, 2007) 43.

One of the alternatives proposed to mitigate this kind of activism by the Brazilian Supreme Court was the Proposal of Constitutional Amendment n 33 (PEC 33). This proposal sought to establish that no decision of preliminary injunction could suspend the amendment and that the final decision, which could declare a constitutional amendment unconstitutional, should be examined by Congress in order to be validated. If Congress expressed a contrary opinion, the controversy should be submitted to a referendum.

Unfortunately, this proposal was not successful[22] and today there is only a bill with a similar theme. The bill n 1360/2015 proposes the necessity of a vote from at least eight judges (out of eleven) for an amendment to be declared unconstitutional by judicial review.[23]

The absence of big proposals and discussions that aim to break the judicial activism of the Brazilian Supreme Court does not imply that this kind of posture should be endorsed. The form with which the judicial review of constitutional amendments is made in Brazil tends to alienate the participation and will of the people and its representatives through a super-countermajoritarian posture of the Court, as will be demonstrated in the next section.

III. The Deficiencies of the System: The Super-countermajoritarian Role of the Brazilian Supreme Court

The Brazilian Supreme Court is an institution with a poor deliberative performance, facilitating what is called here a 'super-countermajoritarian' role. The super-countermajoritarian role is the tendency of the Court to engage in individual reasoning and decisions, even when structured as a collective court. This is a posture that can influence negatively the Court's institutional role,[24] with even worse consequences when dealing with the judicial review of constitutional amendments. As Virgílio Afonso da Silva points out, this kind of behaviour initiates with the type of decision making used by the Court, which is purely aggregative (*seriatim*), and is aggravated by a number of judicial procedures that serve as obstacles to deliberation (some of which are highlighted here).[25]

[22] The amendment proposal n 33 was automatically filed and since then there has been no prospect for its return into the agenda of Congress – 'Câmara dos Deputados, Projeto de Lei e Outras Proposições – PEC 33/2011' www.camara.gov.br/proposicoesWeb/fichadetramitacao?idProposicao=503667 accessed 31 May 2015.

[23] Câmara dos Deputados, 'Projeto de lei e Outras Proposições – PL 1360/2015' www.camara.gov.br/proposicoesWeb/fichadetramitacao?idProposicao=1228722 accessed 11 June 2015.

[24] For some of those consequences see Diego Werneck Arguelhes and Leandro Molhano Ribeiro, '"The Court, it is I"? Individual judicial powers in the Brazilian Supreme Court and their implications for constitutional theory' [2018] v 7 n 2 *Glob Con* 236.

[25] Virgílio Afonso da Silva, 'Deciding without deliberating' [2013] v 11 n 3 *I•CON* 557.

While analysing this distinctive behaviour one can observe the extreme consequences that this kind of approach may cause to the judicial review cases of constitutional amendments. The empirical data of the cases analysed below will help to understand the background of the Court's work and how individual judicial decisions directly influence their outcome. In Brazil, there have already been 100 cases of judicial review of constitutional amendments.[26] From a total of 99 amendments, 31 have been submitted to judicial review. Since there is no deadline for proposing such a revision, it is possible that other amendments could still be subjected to this judicial control.

Although a significant number of these cases was dismissed without a decision on the merits (28 per cent), most of them are still without a final decision (50 per cent) – and with no assured projection for one to be made (only 22 per cent of the cases have had a final merit decision). This happens because a Supreme Court judge – normally the reporting judge of the case – can establish his/her own pace in the duration of a case. The case of the ADI 5017 is a clear example of this, as it will be demonstrated. Some cases against the Amendment n 20/98 – about social security – were initiated in 1999 and are still awaiting a final decision (the processes have already lasted over 19 years).[27]

It is important to highlight that the duration of the cases varies abruptly. Cases with a decision on the merits have taken an average of 2.8 years. The fastest one was resolved in 13 days,[28] while at the same time there are more than 15 cases that have been awaiting a final decision for more than 10 years. Hence, it is clear that the Judiciary also acts in a political way, aiming to directly influence the progress and sequence of important national matters. Therefore, it is recognisable that the Court practices this interference not only with its decisions, but also with its non-decisions, that is, when not proceeding with a case; yet it is clear that even with these non-decisions, it still manages to alter the status quo.

The problem remains, however, with the fact that these 'non-decisions' are often made by a single judge and last for far too long a period of time (in some cases it is an undetermined period), characterising the super-countermajoritarian posture of the court. When it comes to the judicial review of constitutional amendments, this is even more questionable since a single judge can, through a preliminary decision, suspend a constitutional reform democratically voted by Congress. Only one judge is able to paralyse the work made by the representative branch, which he is not originally legitimated to do.

In Brazil, this kind of behaviour is happening too often and is enabled by the presence of certain procedural instruments. These instruments are the preliminary

[26] All data in this chapter about the cases of judicial review of constitutional amendments were collected in the Brazilian Supreme Court's website: www.stf.jus.br. Last update on 27 January 2018.

[27] Brasil, 'Supremo Tribunal Federal – ADI 2096 – Ação Direta de Inconstitucionalidade' www.stf.jus.br/portal/processo/verProcessoAndamento.asp?incidente=1788525 accessed 11 June 2015.

[28] Brasil, 'Supremo Tribunal Federal – ADI 3685 – Ação Direta de Inconstitucionalidade' www.stf.jus.br/portal/processo/verProcessoAndamento.asp?incidente=2367564 accessed 11 June 2015.

injunction in a judicial review, the discretionary agenda-setting of the judges, and the request for a review prior to a decision. All of these mechanisms are related to the timing of the decisions. In these cases, 'the court may dose the rhythm and intensity through which a decision will be made and public contestation will proceed', and this is important because 'the power of prioritizing issues that are urgent in the public sphere might increase the quality and relevance of the public contestation managed by the court'.[29]

Unfortunately, these procedures are not well managed by the Brazilian Supreme Court. The request for review prior to a decision is a faculty that a judge can exercise if she wants to re-study the case before giving her final opinion. Nevertheless, it has been used to paralyse a case for an undetermined period of time – even though there is a 10-day fixed term for resuming judgment.[30] Between the years of 1988 and 2013, these requests made in cases of judicial review (ADI) lasted an average of 1.2 years (429 days). The ones that have not yet been decided have lasted an average of 3.7 years (1,342 days).[31] When dealing with cases of judicial review of constitutional amendments, however, this power has fortunately not been used so far during voting. This means that once the case is scheduled for a final decision, this one is not interrupted. Nonetheless, this pattern can be observed for decisions of preliminary injunctions on these cases. For example, in the ADI 2135 (regarding the amendment n. 19/98), a first request for reviewing a case was posed by one of the judges in 2001 and kept being posed by other judges until the final decision on the preliminary matter in 2007. The same happened in the ADI 2356 (regarding the amendment n 30/2000) with a first request being made in 2002, but the final preliminary decision was only in 2010.

The problems with the preliminary injunctions, by their turn, are even worse in the scenario of judicial review of constitutional amendments. This mechanism offers great judicial insecurity when extending the duration of a case through a temporary decision. Moreover, these decisions have the power to suspend an entire statute or constitutional amendment, with consequences for the entire country. In general, the average time of a preliminary injunction in general cases of judicial review is 6.1 years.[32] Some of the cases dealing with constitutional amendment that are still without a final decision but have a preliminary injunction suspending the effects of these amendments for a long period of time are the ADI 3395 (regarding the amendment n 45/2004) with a preliminary decision since 2006; the ADI 2135, since 2007; the ADI 3854 (regarding the amendment n 41/2003), also since 2007: ADI 2356, since 2010; and the ADI 5017 (regarding the amendment n 73/2013),

[29] Conrado Hübner Mendes, *Constitutional Courts and Deliberative Democracy*, (Oxford University Press, 2013) 161.

[30] Article 134 of the Intern Regiment of the Brazilian Supreme Court.

[31] Joaquim Falcão, Ivar A Hartmann and Vitor P Chaves, *III Relatório Supremo em Números: o Supremo e o tempo* (Fundação Getúlio Vargas, 2014) 94.

[32] Joaquim Falcão, Ivar A Hartmann and Vitor P Chaves, *III Relatório Supremo em Números: o Supremo e o tempo* (Fundação Getúlio Vargas, 2014) 33, 40–41.

since 2013 and with a decision in a peculiar situation of still not being confirmed by the plenum of the Court, as will be explained later on.

Lastly, the agenda-setting made by the reporting judge of the case is also an instrument that can dictate the pace of a final decision. In extreme examples, it is possible to identify judicial review cases that have been waiting for more than 10 years to be put to judgment by the reporting judge.[33] In the end, these cases of judicial review, which often deal with subjects of great social impact, are abandoned for years and mostly by the will of a single judge. And that also happens when the object of these cases are constitutional amendments, where it is also possible to find examples of cases with more than 10 years without a final decision (eg, ADIs 1805, 2096, 3297, 3486, 3653 and 3998). Even worse, some of them have kept the amendment suspended for all these years (see previous examples like ADI 2135 and ADI 3395).

Data shows, thus, that in Brazil constitutional change is a hostage of the misuse of the powers of the Court. All the institutional procedures endorsed in practice increase the power of a single judge in an unbalanced way. This not only brings undesirable consequences to the deliberative functions of the Court but also undermines, in an illegitimate way, the power of the Congress and the People, especially when dealing with cases about constitutional amendments.

From all the examples brought here one can observe that the Brazilian Supreme Court engages in an unsuited practice, the product of a pathological misuse of the legal system and its norms. This behaviour will be further illustrated now with a closer look at the ADI 5017, which has been chosen especially for its even more unique procedural path.

IV. The Case of the ADI 5017 (Amendment n 73/2013)

The judicial case highlighted in this chapter (ADI 5017) can be used as an example of judicial review of constitutional amendments in Brazil. The amendment in question (n 73/2013) aimed to create four new Federal Courts in the Brazilian jurisdiction as a form of updating the Judiciary's structure to the current judicial demand. However, it was not well received by the entire legal community, one reason why it was contested in the Brazilian Supreme Court (*Supremo Tribunal Federal*, or STF, in Portuguese).

The claim made against the 73rd amendment – which originated the case n 5017 – is one of many arguments. Still, most of them were not based on the substantial limits for amendment fixed in the Constitution, which makes them insufficient for a claim of unconstitutionality. The claimant – an association of Federal Attorneys – wanted the amendment to be suspended by the Supreme

[33] Joaquim Falcão, Ivar A Hartmann and Vitor P Chaves, *III Relatório Supremo em Números: o Supremo e o tempo* (Fundação Getúlio Vargas, 2014) 104, 110.

Court on the grounds of: (i) lack of budget allocation for the creation of these new courts; (ii) offence to the principles of efficiency and reasonability; and (iii) violation of the separation of powers – the most important argument.[34] The first two reasons are clearly based on policy issues (ie, issues that require political choices), and so can merely figure as a substantial limit for the amendment or as a matter to be discussed in the Judiciary.

The third reason, on the other hand, alleges a violation of one of the fundamental principles of the Constitution – a substantive limit for an amendment – which is the separation of powers. However, it is important to accentuate that this was not a valid argument – as shown by the opinion of the Prosecutor General's Office. It was alleged that the amendment violated the legislative initiative of the Judiciary in creating and altering its institutional structure, as present in Article 96, II, c, d, of the Constitution. But, as previously shown, there is no amendment initiative for the Judiciary. Moreover, the Constitution, in its original text, has fixed forms for the Judiciary structure, which shows that this is not only a statute matter but a constitutional one as well. Also, there has been another amendment that had the judicial system as an object (n 45/2004) and that has not been declared unconstitutional by the Supreme Court.[35]

Notwithstanding the fragility of these arguments, the president of the Supreme Court (at the time) provided a preliminary injunction to suspend the amendment as requested by the claimant. One of the many problems with an unlimited posture in the judicial review of constitutional amendments is that these suspensions do not have a determined period of time. It means that a single judge in the Supreme Court can paralyse an amendment voted by the two Houses of Congress indefinitely.

Furthermore, this decision needed to be ratified by the Court's plenary, as requested by the legislation and the internal regiment of the Court.[36] Nonetheless, there has been no substantial decision since this one, which characterises years with this amendment suspended by a monocratic decision.[37]

This kind of behaviour of the Supreme Court's judges, which favours an individual approach instead of a collegiate one, corroborates the frequently unconstitutional posture of this Court, as previously shown.

With all that has been demonstrated here, it seems clear that the Brazilian Supreme Court needs a more democratic and deliberative approach.

[34] Brasil, 'Supremo Tribunal Federal – ADI 5017 – Ação Direta de Inconstitucionalidade' www.stf.jus.br/portal/processo/verProcessoAndamento.asp?incidente=4437805 accessed 4 August 2016.

[35] See the case of the ADI 3367 – Brasil, 'Supremo Tribunal Federal – ADI 3367 – Ação Direta de Inconstitucionalidade' www.stf.jus.br/portal/processo/verProcessoAndamento.asp?numero=3367&classe=ADI&codigoClasse=0&origem=JUR&recurso=0&tipoJulgamento=M accessed 4 August 2016.

[36] Article 10, Lei n. 9868/99; Article n 8, I, Article n 21, IV and V, Article n 170, §1° of the Intern Regiment of the Brazilian Supreme Court.

[37] ADI 5017.

V. The Need for a Democratic and Deliberative Judicial Review

The picture of the Brazilian Supreme Court painted here illustrates the need for a more democratic constitutional reform and, consequently, a reform of its judicial review. Clearly, the presence of the Judiciary in this procedure is excessive, as it invades the sphere of participation from other social actors – either the Legislative or the people. Constitutional Courts that insist on this behaviour incur a paradoxical role: trying to protect the Constitution from abuses from a democratic majority while self-abusing their prerogatives.[38]

Supporting a judicial review of constitutional amendments, then, should be made in a restricted manner. In order to avoid great abuses, it would be interesting if the role of this review – which is to defend the most important provisions, such as the immutable clauses – was expressly fixed in the constitutional text. In the event of this not happening, the Court should at least try to remain solely in the analysis of the requirements of the amendment procedure, without determining its subject, since this behaviour is not compatible with the Judiciary attributions.

When proposing possible ways for the protection of constitutional provisions, especially the ones of constitutional reform, Richard Albert mentions the judicial review as a possibility, even though it is not the most advisable one.[39] Nevertheless, for this to be legitimate, it should be present in the constitutional text and be restricted, as much as possible, to the proposals that intend to change the amendment's rules. Not observing that could mean transferring a lot of power to the courts, which seems to produce democratic deficits, as is shown here.[40]

This could mean that sometimes, in exceptional cases, the judicial review of constitutional amendments is necessary. However, it should not be forgotten that this review should be done as a last resource of protection, and it should not be used without constitutional authorisation as a self-amplified version of the judicial competences.

Going beyond judicial behaviour, Richard Albert also brings an alternative to constitutional protection, one without immutable clauses or judicial review of constitutional amendments. According to the jurist, constitutional provisions might be protected through mechanisms that aggregate constitutional design with popular participation. They can be divided into three steps: (i) a predetermined period of latency, when new values and principles cannot be changed; (ii) different

[38] Yaniv Roznai and Serkan Yolcu, 'An unconstitutional constitutional amendment – The Turkish perspective: A comment on the Turkish Constitutional Court's headscarf decision' 197/198.

[39] According to the jurist, the best way to protect a constitutional provision would be through a different range of reforms, divided by difficulty of the procedure and importance of the reformed rule. For more, see Richard Albert, 'Amending Constitutional Amendment Rules'.

[40] Richard Albert, 'Amending Constitutional Amendment Rules' 684.

difficulty stages for different constitutional provisions, based on their importance for the State; and (iii) a multi-phased amendment procedure, which should be subjected to sequential approval through a list of temporal obstacles and a higher quorum (eg, requiring more than one vote for approval or making a referendum in a reasonable period of time).[41] These elements attempt to amplify the democratic space in the constitutional reform, mixing democracy with constitutionalism.

Judicial review of constitutional amendments, without a real predetermined limit, then, is an illegitimate and exacerbated restriction. It denies the people their right to influence their own constitution, since their will can be suspended or ignored by the courts.[42] Therefore, the judicial abuses cannot be neglected and it is still important to seek new possibilities in protecting the Constitution, such as the one proposed by Richard Albert.

When it comes to constitutional reform, not only should the judicial review be restricted, but the Court's behaviour should also be more deliberative. It is not reasonable to have one single judge interfering in this process alone, as it is also mandatory to communicate with society. The power to reform a constitution is one of the constitutive rights of citizenship, since it reflects the most important democratic value: popular choice. Neglecting this right is not just blocking a procedure right, but one of a basic and democratic nature.[43] 'A constitution is a window into the soul of the citizenry, a mirror in which citizens should see themselves and their aspirations reflected, precisely because it is citizens themselves who should give continuing shape and content to their constitutional text.'[44]

VI. Final Remarks

The power to amend a constitution is an extraordinary one and should not be confused with the constituent power. Even so, the people should participate in both moments.[45] Adopting an institutional design is never a neutral choice and what has been observed in Brazil is a great tendency to alienate popular participation in the constitutional interpretation, while privileging judicial intervention. Therefore, it is primordial to rethink the established institutions and their relationship with society in a way that consolidates a more democratic community.

One of the aspects that still needs a further look is the extension of the jurisdiction of the Brazilian Supreme Court, which can interfere in the democratic degree of the Court. The democratic difficulty remains in the accumulation of prerogatives, since this Court is the last court of reveal and appeal, as well as the original

[41] Richard Albert, 'Constitutional Handcuffs' (2010) 42 *Arizona State Law Journal* 663, 712.
[42] Richard Albert, 'Constitutional Handcuffs' 667.
[43] Richard Albert, 'Constitutional Handcuffs' 698.
[44] Richard Albert, 'Constitutional Handcuffs' 667.
[45] Yaniv Roznai and Serkan Yolcu, 'An unconstitutional constitutional amendment – The Turkish perspective: A comment on the Turkish Constitutional Court's headscarf decision' 206.

instance for cases involving authorities of the Republic and a constitutional court, which is responsible for a great number of cases demanding a judicial review. All these functions make the Court accumulate an extraordinary number of cases.

From 1988 to 2009, the Brazilian Supreme Court received 1,222,102 cases. Among these cases, 1,120,597 came from its competence as a court of appeal, 95,306 from acting as an ordinary judge, and 6,199 from judicial review.[46] Consequently, there is a delay in the decision-making process of the Court, one that makes it difficult for it to be always the social deliberator that it should be, as it cannot only focus on the cases with big social impact, such as the constitutional ones.

Another characteristic that undermines a democratic conformity with the judicial review is the fragility of the dialogic mechanisms in this procedure, such as the public hearings and the *amici curie*. For example, the participants in the public hearings are not instigated to engage in a debate and to deliberate, and the judges do not handle the collected information and arguments in a collegiate form, or even in an expressed form, in their written votes.[47]

Regarding public participation, it is opportune to remember the idea of the PEC 33 mentioned before, which not only tries to assure the respect of the constitutional faculties of each of the branches, but also builds an opening for popular participation through consultation. This approach is capable of stimulating the constitutional debate at the democratic arena and of approaching the population about political and constitutional questions.

All in all, it is clear, then, that the democratic gap coupled with the deliberative deficit of the Brazilian Supreme Court needs to be dealt with as a prerequisite to the legitimacy of judicial reviews, especially those over constitutional amendments. Judicial review of constitutional amendments can be considered at least controversial. For that, it demands a bigger adequacy of the Court to the democratic precepts.

Acknowledgements

The authors are grateful to the Academic Publishing Advisory Center (*Centro de Assessoria de Publicação Acadêmica – CAPA*) of the Federal University of Paraná for English-language editing support.

[46] Joaquim Falcão, Pablo Camargo Cerdeira and Diego Werneck Arguelhes, I Relatório Supremo em Números: o Múltiplo Supremo (Fundação Getúlio Vargas, 2011) 21.

[47] Miguel Gualano Godoy, 'As Audiências Públicas e os Amici Curiae influenciam as decisões dos ministros do Supremo Tribunal Federal? E por que isso deve(ria) importar?' [2015] v. 60 n. 3 *Revista da Faculdade de Direito – UFPR* 137, 155.

9

The Role of the Chilean Constitutional Court in Times of Change

SERGIO VERDUGO*

'His advantage over me is that this Constitution – whether I like it or not – is ruling'.
Patricio Aylwin

I. Introduction

In April of 2014, a journalist asked the Chief Justice of the Chilean Constitutional Court (hereinafter, 'the Court'), Marisol Peña, her opinion on whether the Constitution was legitimate. The question was particularly important because of the possibility that the Court could review the constitution-making process that President Michelle Bachelet was promoting at that time. The newspaper reproduced Chief Justice Peña's response:

> I had the impression that that discussion was over. First, because in 1989 [politicians …] achieved important constitutional modifications […] and that reform was approved by a referendum […] The second occasion […] was the 2005 constitutional reform […]. Many of us understood that it was a sort of rebirth, a constitutional moment where all the criticisms, problems, and flaws that had been attributed [to the Constitution] were now in the past […]. I think that it is delicate and serious to subject the country to a complete revision of its constituent pact […] the complete revision of the constituent pact always triggers great political tension. We saw it in Bolivia […].[1]

Although Chief Justice Peña never said that the Court had the power to review Bachelet's constitution-making process, her opposition to the demand for a new constitution triggered doubts, and some claimed that the Court does not, and

* Professor of Constitutional Law, Universidad del Desarrollo, Chile. Email: sergio.verdugo@law.nyu.edu. I thank Christopher Roberts, Marcela Prieto, Vicente Benítez, and José Díaz-de-Valdés for useful comments. The author translated all the Spanish-written texts that this chapter reproduces in English.

[1] La Segunda, 'Marisol Peña, La Defensora de La Constitución' (4 April 2014).

should not, have the power to review Bachelet's process.[2] Until that moment, the Chilean literature had little to say about the possibility of the Court challenging constitutional reforms. The Court had addressed connected issues in a few cases – that I will examine later – but, before Bachelet started to push for a total replacement of the Constitution, Chilean scholars commenting on the demand for a new Constitution had primarily focused on other issues.[3] The literature in English that asks the question of whether the Chilean Court can challenge constitutional reforms is, to my knowledge, non-existent.[4]

This chapter has two purposes. Its first purpose is to summarise and discuss Chile's position on whether the Court can challenge constitutional reforms. A majority of Chilean scholars argue that the Court cannot challenge the Constitution, that it cannot review constitutional reforms on substantive grounds, and that it can only review the procedural aspects of constitutional amendments. Its second purpose is to justify the absence of a judicial doctrine limiting constitutional reform on substantive grounds during Chile's authoritarian and post-authoritarian eras. During those historical periods, lacking a doctrine such as the Colombian 'Substitution' doctrine or the Indian 'Basic Structure' doctrine[5] was useful for removing the authoritarian enclaves of the Chilean 1980 Constitution. The politicians that advanced the democratisation agenda through bipartisan agreements during the post-authoritarian context achieved relevant constitutional reforms that changed the nature of the 1980 Constitution from an authoritarian text to a constitutional document that facilitates representative democracy.[6] Any doctrine protecting the authoritarian core of the original 1980 Constitution would have undermined the democratisation agenda.

Although some scholars complain that the current version of the Constitution needs revisions,[7] future constitutional reforms should not reverse the democratic

[2] eg, Eduardo Chia, 'La Presidenta Del Tribunal Constitucional y Su Oposición a Una Nueva Constitución' (*Red Seca*, 14 April 2014).

[3] The literature is too extensive to cite here. eg, Claudio Fuentes (ed), *En El Nombre Del Pueblo. Debate Sobre El Cambio Constitucional En Chile* (ICSO, Fundación Boll, 2010).

[4] eg, Javier Couso, 'Trying Democracy in the Shadow of an Authoritarian Legality: Chile's Transition to Democracy and Pinochet's Constitution of 1980' (2011) 29 *Wisconsin Intl LJ* 393; Andrew Arato, 'Beyond the Alternative Reform or Revolution: Post Sovereign Constitution-Making and Latin America' (2015) 50 *Wake Forest L Rev* 891; Rachel Kennedy, 'Replacing the Chilean Constitution' (2017) 24 *Constellations* 456; Claudia Heiss, 'Legitimacy Crisis and the Constitutional Problem in Chile: A Legacy of Authoritarianism' (2017) 24 *Constellations* 470.

[5] Possibly the most comprehensive book engaging with these sorts of judicial doctrines in a comparative way, is Yaniv Roznai, *Unconstitutional Constitutional Amendments: The Limits of Amendment Powers* (OUP, 2017).

[6] The 1980 Constitution was an 'authoritarian transformative' document because it planned for a transition to democracy while protecting the political goals of its authoritarian makers. Tom Ginsburg, '¿Fruto de La Parra Envenenada? Algunas Observaciones Comparadas Sobre La Constitución Chilena' (2014) 113 *Estudios Públicos* 1.

[7] eg, Pablo Ruiz-Tagle, 'La Trampa Del Neopresidencialismo: La Constitución "Gatopardo"' in Renato Cristi and Pablo Ruiz-Tagle, *La República en Chile. Teoría y Práctica del Constitucionalismo Republicano* (LOM, 2006); Javier Couso and Alberto Coddou, 'Las Asignaturas Pendientes de La Reforma Constitucional Chilena' in Claudio Fuentes (ed), *En el Nombre del Pueblo: Debate Sobre el Cambio Constitucional en Chile* (ICSO, Fundación Boll, 2010).

achievements of the post-authoritarian era. I argue that, in Chile, a future judicial doctrine aimed to prevent strategies of 'abusive constitutionalism' may be useful to preserve those achievements.[8]

In this chapter, I deliberately avoid using the term 'constituent power,' except when the Court refers to it.[9] Instead, I use the term 'constitution-making' power to emphasise a descriptive and contextualised approach to the power of creating or reforming the Constitution.[10] According to my conceptualisation, sitting politicians hold the 'constitution-making' power; there are authoritarian forms of constitutionalism[11] and authoritarian ways of creating a constitution.[12] Carl Schmitt's theory has influenced the Chilean debate on the 'constituent power',[13] but I do not aim to contribute to this debate, and I do not use the Schmittian theoretical framework. For my contextualised approach, the military Junta had the constitution-making power during the dictatorship, although that power gradually deteriorated between 1985 and 1990 when four relevant events happened: the Court restricted the Junta's lawmaking power by reviewing the organic laws, Pinochet lost the 1988 plebiscite, the 1989 reform eliminated or softened some of the authoritarian enclaves, and a civilian administration was elected. Since 1990, the incoming civilian politicians replaced the Junta and acquired the constitution-making power, but they could only enact constitutional reforms through bipartisan agreements. I identify three possible judicial challenges against the constitution-making power: the ones that target the Constitution, the ones that target specific provisions included in the original constitutional text, and the ones that target a reform seeking to modify constitutional provisions.[14]

The remainder of this chapter proceeds as follows. Section II briefly examines the reforms to the 1980 Constitution and provides some context for readers that

[8] I borrowed the term from Landau, who also explores the possibility of using the doctrine of unconstitutional amendments for protecting democracy. David Landau, 'Abusive Constitutionalism' (2013) 47 *UC Davis L Rev* 189, 231–38.

[9] For a conceptual discussion, see Carlos Bernal's chapter in this book.

[10] Other scholars that follow this kind of approach are Andrew Arato, *Post Sovereign Constitution Making: Learning and Legitimacy* (OUP, 2016); Zoran Oklopcic, 'Three Arenas of Struggle: A Contextual Approach to the Constituent Power of "the People"' (2014) 3 *Global Constitutionalism* 200. The normative idea of a modern constitution is discussed in Pasquale Pasquino, 'Classifying Constitutions: Preliminary Conceptual Analysis' (2013) 34 *Cardozo L Rev* 999.

[11] Mark Tushnet, 'Authoritarian Constitutionalism. Some Conceptual Issues' in Tom Ginsburg and Alberto Simpser (eds), *Constitutions in Authoritarian Regimes* (CUP, 2014).

[12] Gabriel Negretto, 'Authoritarian Constitution Making' in Tom Ginsburg and Alberto Simpser (eds), *Constitutions in Authoritarian Regimes* (CUP, 2014).

[13] Renato Cristi, 'The Metaphysics of Constituent Power: Schmitt and the Genesis of Chile's 1980 Constitution' (2000) 21 *Cardozo L Rev* 1749, 1775; Renato Cristi, *El Pensamiento Político de Jaime Guzmán. Una Biografía Intelectual*, 2nd edn (LOM, 2011) 161; Fernando Atria, 'Sobre La Soberanía y Lo Político' (2006) 12 *Derecho y Humanidades* 47, 53–59; Fernando Atria, *La Constitución Tramposa* (LOM, 2013) 63–64, 84; Renato Cristi, 'Precisiones En Torno a La Noción de Poder Constituyente' in Renato Cristi and Pablo Ruiz-Tagle, *El Constitucionalismo del Miedo* (LOM, 2014) 168–71.

[14] These challenges are of an exceptional nature, and all of them push the judges to solve hard dilemmas. See Nicholas Barber and Adrian Vermeule, 'The Exceptional Role of Courts in the Constitutional Order' (2016) 92 *Notre Dame L Rev* 817.

are not familiar with the Chilean case. Section III discusses the Court's powers to challenge constitutional reforms. Section IV focuses on the few Court's decisions that are relevant for this essay. Section V concludes and briefly presents the reasons that might justify the creation of a Chilean version of the unconstitutional constitutional reforms doctrine.

II. Establishing and Reforming the 1980 Constitution

Following the 1973 coup, the military Junta led by General Pinochet ruled Chile until 1990. The Junta closed all the elected branches of government and attributed to itself the power to enact regulations that could even modify the Constitution that existed at that time: the 1925 Constitution. Although parts of the 1925 Constitution remained formally valid, the Junta had the constitution-making power.

The dictatorship's legitimisation strategy consisted of a narrative claiming to re-establish the rule of law and securing the stability of the economy and the political system. The regime's leaders had promised that, after they could guarantee those goals, they would call for elections and the military will return to the barracks. For the success of this legitimisation strategy, it was useful to have a submissive judiciary with the appearance of independence.[15] The Supreme Court of that time recognised the Junta's powers, it did not investigate human rights abuses, and the dictatorship did not need to intervene the judiciary.[16] The dictatorship was going to last for 17 years and, in the meantime, it suppressed political rights, frequently used emergency powers, and systematically violated human rights.

Key to the regime's legitimisation strategy and the rule of law discourse, the dictatorship enacted the 1980 Constitution. The 1980 Constitution had two parts that operated as 'two constitutions in one'.[17] The first part was 'permanent' because it regulated the institutions that were supposed to operate indefinitely during the post-authoritarian era – for example the Congress and the Electoral Court – although some of them started to function before the return to democracy – for example the Constitutional Court. The second part was 'temporary' because it consisted of sunset clauses regulating the institutions of the dictatorship – for example the Junta – and the itinerary to return to democracy. The temporary part was supposed to cease its effects after the dictatorship finished. The constitutional

[15] About how the judiciary was useful for the dictatorship, see Lisa Hilbink, *Judges beyond Politics in Democracy and Dictatorship: Lessons from Chile* (CUP, 2007).

[16] Jorge Correa, 'The Judiciary and the Political System in Chile: The Dilemmas of Judicial Independence During the Transition to Democracy' in Irwin Stotzky (ed), *Transition in Latin America: The Role of the Judiciary* (Westview Press, 1993); Roberto Garretón, 'Chilean Transitional Justice and the Legacy of the de Facto Regime', *The Role of Courts in Transitional Justice: Voices from Latin America and Spain* (Routledge, 2012).

[17] Robert Barros, *Constitutionalism and Dictatorship: Pinochet, the Junta, and the 1980 Constitution* (CUP, 2002) 169.

itinerary to return to democracy established that in 1988 a referendum was going to decide on whether Pinochet would remain as a 'President' for eight additional years. If Pinochet were to lose the 1988 plebiscite, the Constitution established that the regime should call for presidential elections. Although Pinochet would have preferred a longer dictatorship,[18] in 1980 he accepted this itinerary to secure the Constitution's approval,[19] partly because he did not expect to lose the 1988 plebiscite.[20]

Several constitutional provisions constrained the Junta's power. Among these constraints, the Junta could only modify the Constitution by unanimously approving a reform confirmed by a referendum. It was useful for the Junta to restrain its powers because it was a way to signal a credible commitment with the transition to democracy, it solved coordination issues, and it helped to legitimise the new constitutional system.[21] Robert Barros argues that these constraints created a form of constitutionalism.[22] For him, these constraints were a result of the regime's internal fragmentation and the need to solve interbranch disagreements. The Constitution established a seven-member Court as one of these constraints. Although all the Court's appointment mechanisms were controlled directly or indirectly by the dictatorship, the Court proved to be an independent actor capable of enforcing limits against the Junta, as I will show later.

Many politicians and scholars complained that the Constitution included authoritarian enclaves preventing the establishment of a true democracy,[23] such as the existence of the National Security Council, the non-elected senators, and a provision banning some political ideas. When deciding how to face the dictatorship's constitutional itinerary, the opposition was divided between two rival strategies.[24] The first one rejected the Constitution's legitimacy and advocated for a constituent assembly. The second strategy offered a pragmatic tactic accepting the 1980 Constitution and negotiating more favourable conditions to return to

[18] Darren Hawkins, *International Human Rights and Authoritarian Rule in Chile* (University of Nebraska Press, 2002) 107–08.

[19] Jeffrey Puryear, *Thinking Politics. Intellectuals and Democracy in Chile, 1973–1988* (The John Hopkins University Press, 1994) 129; Pamela Constable and Arturo Valenzuela, *A Nation of Enemies. Chile Under Pinochet* (Norton, 1991) 72.

[20] Constable and Valenzuela (n 21) 304–05.

[21] On the reasons that authoritarian regimes have to constraint their powers, see Tamir Moustafa and Tom Ginsburg, 'The Functions of Courts in Authoritarian Politics' in *Rule by Law. The Politics of Courts in Authoritarian Regimes* (CUP, 2008); Michael Albertus and Victor Menaldo, 'Dictators as Founding Fathers? The Role of Constitutions under Autocracy' (2012) 24 *Economics & Politics* 279.

[22] Robert Barros, 'Personalization and Institutional Constraints: Pinochet, the Military Junta, and the 1980 Constitution' (2001) 43 *Latin American Politics and Society* 5; Barros (n 19).

[23] eg, Grupo de los 24, *Las Propuestas Democráticas Del Grupo de Los 24* (Patricio Chaparro ed, Corporación Grupo de Estudios Constitucionales, 1992); Francisco Cumplido, *¿Estado de Derecho En Chile?* (Instituto Chileno de Estudios Humanísticos, 1983).

[24] Edgardo Boeninger, *La Democracia En Chile. Lecciones Para La Gobernabilidad* (Editorial Andrés Bello, 1997) 364; Óscar Godoy, 'La Transición Chilena a La Democracia: Pactada' (1999) 74 *Estudios Públicos* 79, 102.

democratic rule. Patricio Aylwin, who was later going to become the first President of the post-authoritarian era, championed the second strategy:

> I cannot pretend that General Pinochet recognizes his Constitution as illegitimate, and he cannot demand that I recognize it as legitimate. His advantage over me is that this Constitution – whether I like it or not – is ruling. This is a fact [...] that I abide. How to overcome this impasse while, at the same time, preventing everyone's humiliation? There is only one way: to deliberately avoid the issue of [constitutional] legitimacy [...]. Let's ask ourselves how we can achieve a constitutional text that is acceptable to everyone [...] this requires that we try to search for coincidences [...]. We could [...] achieve agreements to modify the Chilean constitutional regime to accomplish democracy.[25]

Soft-liner rightwing politicians that were part of the dictatorship's supporting coalition shared many of the opposition's demands and agreed to propose a deal to the Junta, which included accepting the Constitution subject to reforms.[26] Although Pinochet rejected the proposed agreement, it was clear that politicians could only achieve constitutional changes with, and not without, the Junta, and that a popular revolt could not defeat the regime.[27] If the dictatorship was going to be defeated, it was going to be under the dictatorship's rules. In the end, Aylwin's approach proved to be the successful way to do so.

Surprisingly, the opposition succeeded in defeating Pinochet in the 1988 plebiscite.[28] The regime was going to call for elections, and the military was going to return to its barracks in March of 1990. In 1989, the opposition and the regime agreed to include modifications to the 1980 Constitution. Both sides had reasons to agree to the 1989 reform. The incoming centre-left civilians could eliminate some of the authoritarian enclaves, and the Junta could enhance the armed forces' autonomy to protect the military career and secure the army's budget,[29] and close two loopholes that had the potential to harm the future rightwing coalition's veto power.[30] Also, the 1989 reform was an opportunity to give the impression that the dictatorship's opponents were legitimising the 1980 Constitution by agreeing to abide by it. The Constitution was the dictatorship's 'masterpiece' and securing

[25] Patricio Aylwin, 'Exposición Del Señor Patricio Aylwin Azócar' in José Polanco Varas and Ana Torres (eds), *Una Salida Político Constitucional Para Chile* (Instituto Chileno de Estudios Humanísticos, 1985) 148–49.

[26] Matías Tagle (ed), *El Acuerdo Nacional. Significados y Perspectivas* (Corporación Justicia y Democracia, 1995).

[27] Mark Ensalaco, 'In with the New, Out with the Old? The Democratising Impact of Constitutional Reform in Chile' (1994) 26 *J of Latin American Studies* 409, 424.

[28] On the impressive organisation of the 'No' campaign, see Eduardo Engel and Achilles Venetoulias, 'The Chilean Plebiscite: Projections Without Historical Data' (1992) 87 *J of the American Statistical Association* 933.

[29] Claudia Heiss and Patricio Navia, 'You Win, You Lose Some: Constitutional Reforms in Chile's Transition to Democracy' (2007) 49 *Latin American Politics and Society* 163.

[30] Patricia Arancibia Clavel, *Carlos Cáceres. La Transición a La Democracia 1988–1990* (Libertad y Desarrollo, 2014) 70–72.

its implementation for the post-authoritarian context was critical.[31] Pinochet's proposal did not include many of the opposition's demands, but the centre-left coalition still gave its 'acquiescence' to the constitutional deal.[32] After all, the reform eliminated or softened some of the authoritarian enclaves. For example, it removed the provision that banned some political ideas, it elevated the number of elected senators (so the non-elected senators had less influence), it raised the number of civilians in the National Security Council (so the military had less control over that Council), and it reduced the necessary legislative quorum to modify the organic laws. The 1989 referendum approved the reform with 85.7 per cent of the votes.

Although many criticisms against the Constitution remained, the 1989 reform prevented those criticisms from influencing the electoral debates[33] and secured the Constitution's authority for the post-authoritarian context.[34] The Junta was dissolved, and the elected centre-left administration was going to rule the country constrained by the constitutional framework designed by the dictatorship. The remaining authoritarian enclaves gave the rightwing coalition a strong veto power over the policies of elected presidents, and the rightwing coalition's consent was necessary to approve additional constitutional reforms. Relevant reforms required bipartisan agreements,[35] and a sort of imposed consensual democracy with high levels of cooperation between competing political parties started to operate.[36] The post-authoritarian political system was an 'incomplete democracy'.[37]

Politicians achieved bipartisan agreements to gradually and incrementally democratise the Constitution by slowly removing the authoritarian enclaves.[38] Amongst other constitutional reforms, the modifications implemented the democratic election of mayors, who were not previously elected, created an autonomous public prosecution agency, and elevated the number of Supreme Court justices to

[31] J Samuel Valenzuela, 'La Constitución de 1980 y El Inicio de La Redemocratización En Chile' (1997) 242 *Kellog Institute for Intl.Studies – Working Paper*.

[32] Carlos Andrade, *Reforma de La Constitución Política de La República de Chile de 1980* (Ed.Jurídica Chile, 1991) 167–69.

[33] Fredrik Uggla, '"For a Few Senators More"? Negotiating Constitutional Changes During Chile's Transition To Demnocracy' (2005) 47 *Latin American Politics and Society* 51, 56–60.

[34] Andrés Allamand, 'Las Paradojas de Un Legado' in Paul Drake and Iván Jaksic (eds), *El Modelo Chileno. Democracia y Desarrollo en los Noventa* (LOM, 1999) 178.

[35] Patricio Navia, 'Living in Actually Existing Democracies: Democracy to the Extent Possible in Chile' (2010) 45 *Latin American Research Rev* 298.

[36] Peter Siavelis, 'Executive-Legislative Relations in Post-Pinochet Chile: A Preliminary Assessment' in Scott Mainwaring and Matthew Soberg Schugart (eds), *Presidentialism and Democracy in Latin America* (CUP, 1997); Detlef Nolte, 'El Congreso Chileno y Su Aporte a La Consolidación Democrática En Perspectiva Comparada' (2003) XXIII *Rev Cien Pol* 43.

[37] The term is from Manuel Garretón, *Incomplete Democracy. Political Democratization in Chile and Latin America* (R Kelly Washbourne and Gregory Horvath trs, The University of North Carolina Press, 2003).

[38] J Esteban Montes and Tomás Vial, 'The Constitution-Building Process in Chile: The Authoritarian Roots of a Stable Democracy' (Intl IDEA, 2005).

make the Pinochet appointees less influential.[39] The most critical reform came in 2005, when constitutional designers agreed to eliminate the non-elected senators, changed the Court's appointment mechanisms, allowed the President to remove the military commanders unilaterally, and eliminated the National Security Council' powers, among other modifications.[40] Most of the rightwing legislators were not willing to continue defending the authoritarian enclaves because it became too politically costly to preserve Pinochet's legacy and because some of those enclaves started to benefit the centre-left coalition by, for example, allowing them to appoint some non-elected senators.[41]

Years later, other political agreements also succeeded in reforming the Congress' electoral system (one of the old centre-left coalition's demands),[42] introducing provisions regulating electoral primaries, implementing the principles of probity and publicity as part of the anti-corruption agenda, and strengthening the autonomy of some territories. I cannot explain all these reforms here. Suffice it to say that the most critical modifications had deepened the democratisation agenda by eliminating the authoritarian enclaves or by implementing provisions supporting the policies advanced by the elected administrations. If the Court had challenged these reforms based on a judicial doctrine aimed to preserve essential cores of the 1980 Constitution, it would have prevented the enactment of useful democratic achievements. Many of these achievements form the core of Chile's democracy, constitution makers should consider them as a starting point for future reforms and politicians should not reverse them.

III. The Chilean Court in Times of Constitutional Change

The Constitution gives the Court an explicit power to evaluate the constitutionality of constitutional reforms (Article 93, Nº 3, of the Constitution). The Court can only review the constitutionality of these reforms using its ex ante review power (and not the ex post review power), if it receives a petition from the

[39] On this last reform, see Lisa Hilbink, 'Un Estado de Derecho No Liberal. La Actuación Del Poder Judicial Chileno En Los Años 90' in Paul Drake and Iván Jaksic (eds), *El Modelo Chileno. Democracia y Desarrollo en los Noventa* (LOM, 1999) 320.

[40] Some complain that the authoritarian enclaves conditioned the constitutional negotiations. Jorge Contesse, '"Las Instituciones Funcionan": La Falta de Diálogo Constitucional En Chile' (2008) 14 *Derecho y Humanidades* 51; Amaya Alvez, 'Forcing Consensus: Challenges for Rights-Based Constitutionalism in Chile' in Colin Harvey and Colin Schwartz (eds), *Rights in Divided Societies* (Hart Publishing, 2012).

[41] Claudio Fuentes, *El Pacto* (Universidad Diego Portales, 2012) 86; Carlos Huneeus, *La Democracia Semisoberana. Chile Después de Pinochet* (Taurus, 2014) 179; Claudio Fuentes, 'Shifting the Status Quo: Constitutional Reforms in Chile' (2015) 57 *Latin American Politics and Society* 99.

[42] See the constitutional discussion of this reform in Lorena Recabarren Silva, 'Reformas Al Sistema Electoral: Múltiples Aristas Del Principio de Igualdad En Sede Constitucional' [2016] *Sentencias Destacadas 2015* 307.

President, from any of the Congress' chambers, or from one-fourth of the chambers' active members. The Court has never stricken down a constitutional reform, and most Chilean scholars believe that the Court's power is limited to the review of procedural issues.[43] Only a few scholars claim that the Court can impose substantive limits to constitutional reforms on grounds such as natural law,[44] essential rights[45] or the republican form of government.[46] Although the Court has never used these arguments, it is important to consider that the post-authoritarian Court has not received significant claims challenging constitutional reforms.[47]

Nevertheless, the Court has played a role in evaluating the constitutionality of the organic laws and their modifications because the Constitution empowered the Court to review this sort of legislation *ex officio* (Article 93, N°1, of the Constitution). The organic laws are not part of the formal Constitution, but some of them are critical for the functioning of constitutional institutions.[48] In reviewing organic laws that specify the organising rules of constitutional institutions (eg, the Congress), the Court has not declared the unconstitutionality of critical parts. Although the Court has challenged minor rules included in some of those legislative bills, such as what happened when legislators replaced the electoral system that was designed by the dictatorship,[49] and when the Court evaluated the constitutionality of its new organising statute of 2008,[50] these types of decisions have not challenged the key modifications of the corresponding organic laws.[51] The Court has not prevented democratisation reforms, and it has even collaborated with the democratisation agenda by giving its advice during the constitutional negotiations of the 2005 reform.[52]

During her second presidency (2014–18), Michelle Bachelet pushed for a total constitutional replacement, but her constitution-making process failed before

[43] eg, Francisco Zúñiga, 'Control de Constitucionalidad de la Reforma Constitucional' (2006) 4 *Est Const* 415; Miriam Henríquez, 'El Control de Constitucionalidad de La Reforma Constitucional En El Ordenamiento Jurídico Chileno' [2011] *Anuario de Derecho Público* 461, 476–77. Also, see José Díaz-de-Valdés, 'Algunas preguntas pendientes acerca del control de constitucionalidad de los proyectos de reforma constitucional' [2007] *Sentencias Destacadas 2006* 145, 168–73.

[44] Cristóbal Orrego, 'Vigencia de Los Derechos Esenciales Que Emanan de La Naturaleza Humana y Su Reconocimiento En El Ordenamiento Jurídico Chileno' (1993) 20 *Rev Chil Der* 59, 63.

[45] Humberto Nogueira, 'Consideraciones Sobre Poder Constituyente y Reforma de La Constitución En La Teoría y La Práctica Constitucional' (2009) 15 *Ius Et Praxis* 229, 262.

[46] Alejandro Silva Bascuñán, *Tratado de Derecho Constitucional*, vol X (Ed.Jurídica Chile, 2004) 264.

[47] The Court has discussed procedural aspects that have not affected the content of constitutional reform bills. STC-269/1997, STC-464/2006.

[48] Sergio Verdugo, 'How to Identify Quasi-Constitutional Legislation? An Example from Chile' in Richard Albert and Joel Colón-Ríos (eds), *Quasi-Constitutionality and Constitutional Statutes* (forthcoming).

[49] STC-2777/2015.

[50] STC-1288/2009.

[51] This is not to say that the Court has not challenged other organic law modifications. In recent years, the Court has challenged important organic law modifications, but those modifications are not connected to critical regulations of key constitutional institutions like the Congress and the electoral organs. I cannot develop this issue here.

[52] Biblioteca del Congreso, 'Historia de La Ley N° 20.050' 29–53.

the Court could have the chance to evaluate it.[53] Before that failure happened, some scholars argued that the Court should not review Bachelet's process because the Court could only review procedural flaws of constitutional reforms,[54] or because the Court should not review the unconstrained 'constituent power' (they used Schmitt's approach),[55] even if that power had followed preestablished constitutional reform rules.[56] During these debates, the prevailing view among legislators was that a total reform to the Constitution was constitutionally permitted.[57]

IV. Judicial Challenges against the Constitution-making Power

This section explores the few cases where the Court has engaged with a challenge against the constitution-making power. Note that the Court enacted all these decisions before Bachelet's constitution-making process, and before the 2005 constitutional reform had eliminated the remaining authoritarian enclaves.

A. Deciding Not to Decide During the Allende Period

The first case in which the Court was asked to review the constitution-making power was before the military coup took place, under the framework of the 1925 Constitution, and during President Allende's Marxist-inspired administration. Allende's coalition did not control the Congress, and the opposition succeeded to approve a constitutional reform restricting the government's power to intervene in the economy as part of a counter-revolutionary strategy.[58] Allende vetoed the reform, but the Congress overrode Allende's veto by a simple majority.

[53] On the failure of Bachelet's process, see Sergio Verdugo and Jorge Contesse, 'The Rise and Fall of a Constitutional Moment: Lessons from the Chilean Experiment and the Failure of Bachelet's Project' (2018) *Int'l J Const L Blog*.

[54] Miriam Henríquez and George Lambeth, '¿Son Válidas Las Modificaciones Al Capítulo de Reforma Constitucional? Una Reflexión Sobre La Autorreferencia Normativa de Alf Ross y Sus Detractores' 13 *Estudios Constitucionales* 153, 163–64.

[55] Atria, *La Constitución Tramposa* (n 14) 91; Fernando Muñoz, '"Chile Es Una República Democrática": La Asamblea Constituyente Como Salida a La Cuestión Constitucional' (2013) *Anuario de Derecho Público* 60, 83–87.

[56] Atria, *La Constitución Tramposa* (n 14) 97–99, 103–09; Pablo Contreras, Domingo Lovera and Ernesto Riffo, 'Proceso (¿)Constituyente(?)' (2015) 23 *Revista de Estudios de la Justicia* 69, 79–80, 85–86.

[57] Contreras, Lovera and Riffo (n 58) 78–79.

[58] Luis Maira, 'Estrategia y Táctica de La Contrarrevolución' in Federico Gil, Ricardo Lagos and Henry Landsberger (eds), *Chile 1970–1973. Lecciones de una Experiencia* (Editorial Tecnos, 1977) 258–74.

The Constitution lacked an explicit rule establishing the required quorum for a congressional override, so the debate focused on what the default rule was.[59] The opposition claimed that simple majority was the default rule, but Allende opposed that interpretation. Allende had the choice to call for a referendum to solve the conflict, but he preferred to bring the case to the Constitutional Court.[60] The opposition claimed that the Court lacked jurisdiction to review constitutional reforms and that the only way to solve the conflict was through a referendum. The opposition also warned the Court that it would not obey the Court's decision should that decision be favourable to Allende.[61]

The Court distinguished two kinds of possible constitutional flaws, the procedural and the substantive ones, and it denied jurisdiction to evaluate both. It first argued that reviewing a reform on the ground of substantive arguments would involve 'usurping the genuine function of the constituent power',[62] and that although challenging a constitutional reform on procedural grounds was the only way the Constitution could give jurisdiction to the Court, the Constitution did not explicitly establish that kind of judicial review power.[63] Also, enforcing procedural limits to constitutional reform might inevitably push the Court to limit the 'constituent power' on substantive grounds indirectly.[64]

Even though it is possible that the Court did not enact a sincere ruling because it probably tried to avoid solving a conflict that was threatening to become violent,[65] this decision included Chile's landmark doctrine on whether the Court could limit constitutional reform. The text of the 1925 Constitution differs from the current constitutional text in that the current Constitution gives the Court an explicit power to review constitutional changes. However, the Court's 1973 ruling is still relevant because some contemporary scholars use it to argue that the 1980 Constitution only added the possibility to review procedural limits and not substantive limits.[66]

[59] Paul Sigmund, *The Overthrow of Allende and the Politics of Chile 1964–1976* (University of Pittsburgh Press, 1977) 168.

[60] Allende probably thought that most of the judges could benefit from his petition. On the Court's composition of that time, see Sergio Verdugo, 'Birth and Decay of the Chilean Constitutional Tribunal (1970–1973)' (2017) 15 *Intl J Const L* 469.

[61] Enrique Silva C., *El Tribunal Constitucional de Chile (1971–1973)* 2nd edn (2008) 38 *Cuadernos del Tribunal Constitucional 1977* 141.

[62] STC-15/1973/20.

[63] STC-15/1973/21.

[64] STC-15/1973/22.

[65] Verdugo, 'Birth and Decay of the Chilean Constitutional Tribunal' (1970–73) (n 62). On this kind of judicial strategy, see Erin F Delaney, 'Analyzing Avoidance: Judicial Strategy in Comparative Perspective' (2016) 66 *Duke LJ* 1.

[66] eg Henríquez (n 45) 473; Sergio Verdugo, 'La Objeción Democrática a Los Límites Materiales de La Reforma Constitucional' (2013) 28 *Actualidad Jurídica* 229, 300.

B. Legitimising the 1980 Constitution

The 1980 Constitution included the infamous Article 8, which prohibited organisations inspired in Marxist doctrines – among other forbidden ideas – and punished individual members of those organisations, giving the Court jurisdiction to solve these cases.

The dictatorship's secretary of the interior asked the Court to use Article 8 against Clodomiro Almeyda, a leader of a socialist faction that was accused of allegedly using radio channels to encourage revolutionary actions against the regime.[67] Almeyda's legal defence argued that Article 8 was 'illegitimate' because, among other reasons, it was part of an 'illegitimate' Constitution. They argued that the people did not properly participate in the constitution-making process and that the Constitution rejected democracy and human rights. Almeyda's argument challenged the Junta's constitution-making power.

The Court rejected Almeyda's argument and upheld the Constitution. It argued that it 'absolutely lacks jurisdiction to decide about the legitimacy of the 1980 Constitution'[68] because it could not review the manifestation of the 'original constituent power'.[69] The Court said that both the 1980 Constitution and the Junta's 'constituent power' were a consequence of the 1973 'institutional rupture',[70] and that the Court could not 'situate [itself] over the original constituent power' because the Constitution was the legal source of the Court's powers. If the Court were to accept the illegitimacy of the Constitution, then, the Court 'would be a legally disqualified body to rule'.[71] The ruling recognised the legitimacy of the 1980 Constitution.[72]

After the 1989 constitutional reform eliminated the infamous Article 8, the Court modified its decision and annulled Almeyda's punishment.[73] Although the Court merely offered a legal reason (ie, the elimination of Article 8), the Court's decision illustrates that the Court was no longer serving the interests of the Junta, but of the group of politicians that were advancing the transition to democracy, who had agreed to restore all the political rights.

C. Advancing the Transition to Democracy

During the 1980s, the Court collaborated with the transition to democracy by reviewing the organic laws that the Junta enacted to regulate the electoral

[67] Eduardo Aldunate, 'Chile' in Markus Thiel (ed), *The 'Militant Democracy' Principle in Modern Democracies* (Routledge, 2009) 70.

[68] STC-46/1987/33.

[69] STC-46/1987/34-35.

[70] STC-46/1987/35.

[71] STC-46/1987/36. This type of argument is not surprising because we cannot expect courts to challenge the legal source of their authority. Barber and Vermeule (n 16) 841–47, 850–53.

[72] Cristi, *El Pensamiento Político de Jaime Guzmán* (n 14) 166–68.

[73] STC-113/1990.

institutions and procedures for the 1988 plebiscite. That plebiscite was a crucial moment for the transition, and although the Junta was expecting the Court to rubber-stamp the organic laws, the Court had other plans. With the leadership of Justice Eugenio Valenzuela, the Court restricted the administrative power to cancel citizens' electoral inscriptions,[74] lowered the requirements for the creation of new political parties,[75] and eliminated some critical rules limiting electoral propaganda, among other rulings.[76] These decisions forced the Junta to remove the contested provisions and modify the organic laws.

The most critical decision was the one reviewing the Electoral Court statute.[77] The constitutional itinerary for the transition established that the Electoral Court was going to start operating after, and not before, the 1988 plebiscite. When reviewing the bill that implemented that part of the constitutional itinerary, the Court declared its unconstitutionality and obliged the Junta to implement the Electoral Court before the 1988 plebiscite took place.[78] The Court's decision directly challenged the 1980 Constitution's 'temporary' part by opposing the literal and originalist interpretative constitutional approach that used to prevail at that time.[79] Pinochet obeyed the Court's decision probably because he believed that he was going to win the plebiscite in any event and challenging the Court's authority would have undermined the dictatorship's constitutional legacy.[80]

The implementation of the Electoral Court was critical for the credibility of the 1988 plebiscite and to signal to the dictatorship's opponents that they had a fair chance to win that plebiscite.[81] Without the Court's decision, the Electoral Court would not have supervised the plebiscite, and it would have made things easier for Pinochet should he have decided to cheat. For these reasons, the Court's decision, along with the other judicial decisions, contributed to ending the Pinochet regime.[82]

D. Avoiding Having to Decide Again

The 1980 Constitution established that the 'former Presidents of the Republic' that served for at least six years could become life-senators. Pinochet had the title of former 'President', and he wanted to become a senator. The reformers of 2005

[74] STC-38/1986.
[75] STC-43/1987.
[76] STC-53/1988. Also, see STC-41/1986.
[77] STC-33/1985.
[78] Also, Carlos Cruz-Coke, 'La Sentencia Del Tribunal Constitucional de 24 de Septiembre de 1985' (1985) 37/38 *Rev Der Publ* 143.
[79] Patricio Zapata, *Justicia Constitucional* (Ed.Jurídica, Chile 2008) 203–09.
[80] Constable and Valenzuela (n 21) 311; Valenzuela (n 33).
[81] Ascanio Cavallo, Manuel Salazar and Oscar Sepúlveda, *La Historia Oculta Del Regimen Militar. Historia de Una Época, 1973–1988* (Editorial Grijalbo, 1997) 477–79.
[82] Eugenio Valenzuela, *Contribución Del Tribunal Constitucional a La Institucionalización Democrática*, vol 30 (Tribunal Constitucional, 2003).

removed this rule but, before that reform could be approved, Pinochet became a senator in 1998. It was a controversial decision because many politicians rejected the idea of having the former dictator as an active political actor. A group of centre-left legislators petitioned the Court to declare Pinochet's inability to be a life-senator, arguing that Pinochet was never a 'President of the Republic' because Presidents are elected – Pinochet was never elected – and because Chile was not a 'Republic' during the dictatorship.

Even though the Court had an explicit power to decide the case (Article 83, Nº 11, of the Constitution), it declared that it lacked jurisdiction on the ground that the petition implied judging the legitimacy of the corresponding constitutional rules.[83] The Court was supposed to 'supervise the strict application of the Constitution' and not to 'violate its essence'.[84] The Court cited the first Almeyda decision to claim that it could not review the 'original constituent power' that had emerged as a consequence of the 1973 coup.[85]

However, unlike the first Almeyda decision, the Court did not enforce the Constitution but declared that it lacked jurisdiction, implicitly delegating the solution to the Senate. If the Court had been committed to the Junta's constitution-making power, it should have rejected the petition claiming the Constitution allowed Pinochet to become a senator, but the Court probably wanted to avoid intervening in the conflict. Even though the Court did not champion the democratisation agenda in this case – for that, the Court should have accepted the petition – allowing the politicians to solve the issue was a compatible approach with the fact that the power to reform the Constitution was in the hands of the political elite that was advancing the transition. Since that elite was divided on this precise issue, Pinochet became a senator. Later, in 2005, the elite decided to remove this authoritarian enclave.

V. Towards a Chilean Unconstitutional Constitutional Reform Doctrine?

Most Chilean scholars state that the Chilean Court can only review constitutional reforms if the reforms violate the procedural limits – as opposed to the substantive limits – and that it lacks the power to review the Constitution. The Court has recognised the authority of the 1980 Constitution, it has never challenged a constitutional reform on substantive or procedural grounds, but it has defied organic laws that implemented original constitutional provisions when it saw that those organic laws could undermine the transition to democracy. By doing that,

[83] STC-272/1998/5-9.
[84] STC-272/1998/6.
[85] STC-272/1998/10-12.

the Court collaborated with the political goal of changing the authoritarian nature of the original 1980 Constitution. Subsequent reforms of the post-authoritarian era have deepened the democratisation of the 1980 Constitution, and the Court has not imposed substantive limits to those reforms. The Court played an active role for the democratisation agenda when the Junta had the constitution-making power, and it played a silent role when the politicians of the post-authoritarian era controlled the constitution-making power by allowing those politicians to implement their bipartisan agreements and gradually eliminate the authoritarian enclaves.

The absence of a judicial doctrine establishing substantive limits to constitutional reform was desirable during the post-authoritarian era because of the need to eliminate the authoritarian enclaves. A judicial doctrine defending the 1980 Constitution's authoritarian basic structure would have slowed down the democratisation of the Constitution because anti-democratic ideas like the 'national security' and the 'protected democracy' doctrines inspired that basic structure. It is not controversial to assume that any acceptable notion of what democracy requires, should conclude that the Chilean political system of 2018 is more democratic than the one of 1980.

In the future, though, there may be good reasons for the Chilean Court to enforce a narrow judicial doctrine limiting constitutional reform on substantive grounds if forthcoming constitutional reformers try to reverse the democratic achievements of the post-authoritarian era. For example, if there is a Chilean president that seeks to become hegemonic by removing presidential term limits in a way that undermines the competitiveness of the political system, the creation of a sort of 'substitution' doctrine might be useful,[86] such as it proved to be useful in Colombia against President Uribe's actions.[87] On the contrary, the lack of a constitutional court willing to enforce a judicial doctrine limiting the president from eliminating term limits may compromise the democratic system if the political opposition is not strong enough to stop that president. The example of the Bolivian Plurinational Constitutional Tribunal, which helped President Evo Morales to remove the limits to reelection in the absence of a competitive opposition, illustrates this danger.[88]

Although a judicial doctrine preserving the Chilean democratic achievements by imposing substantive limits to constitutional reformers is currently non-existent in Chile, using those achievements as Chile's democratic minimum core

[86] Even narrow reasons supporting the use of such a doctrine in the context of a hyper-presidential regime can be helpful against authoritarian impulses. Carlos Bernal, 'Unconstitutional Constitutional Amendments in the Case Study of Colombia: An Analysis of the Justification and Meaning of the Constitutional Replacement Doctrine' (2013) 11 *Intl J Const L* 339.

[87] See Samuel Issacharoff, *Fragile Democracies. Contested Power in the Era of Constitutional Courts* (CUP, 2015) 146–52.

[88] See Sergio Verdugo, 'The Fall of the Constitution's Political Insurance. How the Morales Regime Broke the Insurance of the 2009 Bolivian Constitution.' (2019) 17 forthcoming *Intl J Const L*.

and a starting point for future constitution reformers could be useful for preventing a possible democratic backsliding.[89] Although much more work needs to be done to develop that doctrine's content, I claim that such a doctrine is not inconsistent with Chilean Constitutional Law. First, the Chilean Constitution gives the Constitutional Court the power to review constitutional reforms, without explicitly distinguishing between procedural and substantive limits to constitutional reform. Secondly, the Court could ignore inconsistent past decisions by recognising that, after reformers have eliminated the authoritarian enclaves, the Chilean Constitution is no longer an authoritarian document. The Court released the decisions stating that it cannot impose substantive limits to the constitution makers before the elimination of those enclaves and an originalist argument that ignores those reforms would be unacceptable today. Thirdly, the Court could always look back at the remarkable decisions that it enacted during the 1980s to find additional reasons to enforce democratic principles by flexibly construing the Constitution. These decisions contributed to the democratisation agenda of the 1980 Constitution by limiting the constitution-making power of the Junta and helped to create the conditions for a successful transition to democracy. The following constitutional reforms democratising the 1980 Constitution were possible, in large part, because of those judicial decisions. Therefore, it would make sense for the Court to cite those cases to limit the power of constitution makers that seek to reverse the democratic achievements of the post-authoritarian Chile.

[89] See a useful approach in Rosalind Dixon and David Landau, 'Competitive Democracy and the Constitutional Minimum Core' in Tom Ginsburg and Aziz Z Huq (eds), *Assessing Constitutional Performance* (CUP, 2016).

PART III

Constitutional Reform and Stability

10

The Paradox of Mexico's Constitutional Hyper-Reformism: Enabling Peaceful Transition While Blocking Democratic Consolidation

FRANCISCA POU GIMÉNEZ AND ANDREA POZAS-LOYO*

I. Introduction

Within the conventional mapping of different modalities of constitutional change – replacement, amendment, and interpretation – Mexico exemplifies the reformist strategy taken to an extreme: its 1917 Constitution has been amended, sometimes radically, 706 times.[1] It also illustrates a scenario in which constitutional amendment and democratisation appear to have gone hand in hand: while the rate of amendments was at first moderate, it dramatically accelerated over the last three decades, when political plurality took hold after 70 years of hegemonic party rule.[2] Through continuous, piecemeal reform, the country has progressively incorporated rights, institutions, and regulatory solutions that are part and parcel of the characteristic contemporary Latin American constitutional 'kit', such as a long and robust declaration of rights, instruments of direct democracy, openness to international sources of law, or a multi-faceted system of judicial review.[3]

* Francisca Pou Giménez, ITAM Department of Law, Mexico; Andrea Pozas-Loyo, Instituto de Investigaciones Jurídicas, UNAM, Mexico. We are very thankful to the participants in the Symposium on Constitutional Amendment and Replacement in Latin America held at the University of Brasilia in September 2016 for very enriching comments on a previous draft. We also thank comments by John Ferejohn, Héctor Fix-Fierro and Tom Ginsburg on a preliminary draft at the Seminar on Constitutional Change and Constitutional Efficacy held in Mexico City in November 2015.

[1] We made December 2017 the cutoff date for the count. See 'Sumarios de reformas a la Constitución y Leyes Federales vigentes', available at www.diputados.gob.mx (last accessed 31 January 2018).

[2] María Amparo Casar and Ignacio Marván, *Reformar sin mayorías. La dinámica del cambio constitucional en México 1997–2012* (Taurus, 2014).

[3] Francisca Pou Giménez, 'Constitutionalism old, new and unbound: the case of Mexico' in Colin Crawford and Daniel Bonilla Maldonado (eds), *Constitutionalism in the Americas* (Edward Elgar, 2018).

It could hardly be affirmed, however, that Mexico has been able to consolidate a satisfactory version of democratic-constitutional life, as it can hardly be affirmed that, despite including the characteristic Latin American staples, the country lives under a standard democratic constitutional text. To what extent are the difficulties of consolidating the rule of law, and of attaining a mature constitutional system related to a dynamic of uninterrupted, fragmentary amendments? What is the relationship between the hectic amendment practice and the feeble constitutional life that characterises Mexico?

We argue that, after years of delivering gains, Mexican constitutional reformism is reaching the point of exhaustion. The country is currently trapped in a pattern of constitutional change that we call 'hyper-reformism', which is a particular species of reformism that is now closely associated with the obstacles the country faces in the installation of a recognisable version of rule of law and in the consolidation of constitutional democracy.[4]

Although there are other perspectives for analysing Mexican amendment patterns, in this chapter we focus on the relationships between them and the process of political democratisation and legalisation the country has been experiencing over the last 30 years.[5] We will show that constitutional amendments were first part of a virtuous circle that supported the gradual and largely peaceful transition to democracy. Specifically, during the 1980s and 1990s amendment processes created a space for political negotiation: formal rigidity made governmental commitments credible and gave the opposition parties a guarantee against opportunistic changes by the PRI's (*Partido Revolucionario Institucional*) legislative majority. But reformism had several un-intended consequences on the Constitution itself, both on its content – that became increasingly obscure, convoluted, and incoherent – and on the way politicians started to go about reforming it.

Our point of view is – in contrast with those that consider Mexico's constitutional flexibility mainly a story of success[6] and in contrast with the more favourable views generated by intensive amendment dynamics in countries

[4] We use the term 'hyper-reformism' to systematically account for the pattern of constitutional change in Mexico and take it from the 2015 Symposium 'Constitutional Change and Constitutional Efficacy: Facing Mexico's Hyper-reformism', organised by Tom Ginsburg and Andrea Pozas-Loyo at the UNAM Legal Research Institute in Mexico City. See also Andrea Pozas-Loyo 'A Way Out of Hyper-Reformism? A Project of Constitutional Reorganization and Consolidation in Mexico' *International Journal of Constitutional Law Blog*, 2 March 2016, www.iconnectblog.com/2016/03/a-way-out-of-hyper-reformism-a-project-of-constitutional-reorganization-and-consolidation-in-mexico (last accessed 31 January 2018).

[5] Elsewhere we explore the causes of hyper-reformism, claim that it is a path dependent and identify its mechanisms of self-enforcement: Francisca Pou Giménez and Andrea Pozas-Loyo, 'Self-Reinforcing Hyper-Reformism: The Path Dependent Causes of Mexico's Hectic Constitutional Change' presented at the Symposium on Constitutional Amendment and Replacement in Latin America, Brasilia, September 2016; Francisca Pou Giménez and Andrea Pozas-Loyo, 'Are Constitutional Amendment and Judicial Review Substitutes? Unexpected Lessons from Mexico and Brazil', presented at the Law and Society Annual Conference, Mexico City, June 2017.

[6] Zachary Elkins, Tom Ginsburg and James Melton, *The Endurance of National Constitutions* (Cambridge University Press, 2009), 193–09.

like Brazil,[7] – hyper-reformism is today closely associated with many of the difficulties that Mexico experiences in consolidating a constitutional democracy and the rule of law.

First, as we will see, at the level of the Constitution's *legal* functions, serious problems stem from hyper-reformism (and the constant change, obscurity, disorganisation, and internal inconsistencies that come with it) making it difficult for both citizens and officials to apprehend its mandates and find in it guidance and identifiable reasons for action. This hampers the development and execution of constitutional mandates by legislative and executive means and makes it particularly difficult to build consistent judicial interpretation, all of them central to the adequate functioning of the constitutional system.

Secondly, at the level of the Constitution's *political* functions, hyper-reformism erases the distinction between ordinary and extraordinary law making, and hence the system fails to bestow the benefits derived from not having to address ground rules at any given point. Constant constitutional change alters or impedes the dynamics intrinsic to a healthy democracy, such as the combination of ordinary representative politics with episodes of heightened debate and participation. If legislators ordinarily deal with constitutional reforms, they easily neglect their important role as ordinary-law makers – and vice-versa – and this affects the efficacy of both statutory and constitutional reforms. In addition, when constitutional reforms succeed one another, citizens and NGOs are less likely to oversee and participate in these processes. Hence, hyper-reformism obstructs the adequate development of accountability and participation practices at the constitutional level. Finally, it also damages the integrative function of the Constitution, at a moment when Mexico faces challenges that will be difficult to surmount with a deficit in social cohesion.

Our analysis of the Mexican case may contribute to a debate that, as Elkins, Ginsburg and Melton remark,[8] must be conducted with care and nuance: the debate on the advantages and disadvantages of constitutional longevity. The Constitution of Mexico is already one of the most long-lived in the world, and because of features that assure a sort of 'perpetual motion' at the amendment level, it actually has a very low risk of death and replacement. But unfortunately, at the point we have reached, and given the vicious circle between legal and political dynamics, on the one hand, and constitutional amendment on the other, this is something we should probably not be quick to celebrate.

We divide the analysis into four parts. Section II describes Mexican hyper-reformist patterns, trying to grasp or document the extent of constitutional change through amendment. To this end we provide a combination of quantitative and qualitative dimensions. Section III illustrates some of the effects amendment

[7] Juliano Zaiden Benvindo, 'The Brazilian Constitutional Amendment Rate: A Culture of Change?' www.iconnectblog.com/2016/08/the-brazilian-constitutional-amendment-rate-a-culture-of-change/ (last accessed 31 January 2018).

[8] Elkins, Ginsburg and Melton (n 6) 34.

intensity has had on the text and structure of the Constitution. Section IV then describes how one of the mechanisms that has operated in the country as a positive trigger of reforms – the fact politicians used constitutional reform as a default option for facing credible commitment and coordination problems – created a scenario in which a progressive opening to political plurality seemed palatable for the former hegemonic political force, and thus was conductive to a slow process of democratic transition in the country. Finally, Section V illustrates how, today, hyper-reformism in contrast hampers the adequate fulfilment of the legal and political functions of the Constitution. A brief conclusion will close our chapter.

II. Hyper-reformism: The Intensity of Amendment Dynamics

For normative constitutional theory, constitutional reform is a notion with great conceptual and systemic weight, since it signals the entry into play of a modality of constituent power – 'the derived constituent power' – a particular instantiation of the will of the People, as opposed to that of the representatives who ordinarily govern in their name.[9] For this reason, it is habitually portrayed under an air of extraordinariness: it evokes an exceptional episode, an interruption of ordinary dynamics naturally imagined not to happen very often. The influence the US experience has exerted on legal and political imagination – explained, in part, by the power asymmetries that pervade the political economy of global knowledge[10] – has also nurtured the idea that constitutional amendment is intrinsically rare.

In fact, as the burgeoning field of comparative constitutional studies based on 'large-n' analysis has shown, constitutional amendment is far more frequent than assumed by this theoretical image. Ginsburg and Melton's analysis about amendment dynamics between 1800 and 2010 shows an amazing increase in amendment

[9] See Carlos Bernal, 'Unconstitutional Constitutional Amendments in the Case Study of Colombia: An Analysis of the Justification and Meaning of the Constitutional Replacement Doctrine' (2013) 11 *International Journal of Constitutional Law* 2, 342 (reconstructing the development of this notion and other closely associated ones in the domain of constitutional theory), and William Partlett, 'The Rules and Roles of Democratic Constitution Making Institutions,' paper presented at the Constitution Making in Democratic Orders Conference in Mexico City, August 2016, 1–4 (echoing the distinction between original and derived constituent power and noting that, both in the case of amendment and in the case of replacement, constitution-making is assumed to be different from ordinary politics in terms of popular engagement and in terms of encouraging more deliberative and consensual elite decision-making than ordinary politics). Along the same lines, Gabriel Negretto, 'Replacing and Amending Constitutions: The Logic of Constitutional Change in Latin America', (2014) 46 *Law & Society Review* 749, 751; Walter Murphy, *Constitutional Democracy. Creating and Maintaining a Just Political Order* (Johns Hopkins, 2007), 498; Joel Colón-Ríos, 'The Legitimacy of the Juridical: Constituent Power, Democracy and the Limits of Constitutional Reform' (2010) 48 *Osgoode Hall Law Review* 199, 236.

[10] Daniel Bonilla Maldonado, 'The political economy of legal knowledge,' in Crawford and Bonilla Maldonado (n 3).

rates over time: the number of constitutions amended per year was less than four in 1850, 10 by 1950, 40 in the 1990s, and 30 in the 2000s.[11] In an analysis that covers 18 Latin American countries from 1789 to 2001 – minimalistically computing all amendments enacted in one year as only one amendment – Negretto documents 141 amendments, making 0.28 the mean amendment rate – that is, the mean number of amendments that regional constitutions have endured per year of life.[12]

Certainly, these ciphers give only an approximate sense of the prevalence of constitution amendment processes. The same body of literature clearly suggests that capturing and measuring the 'amount of reform' in any given constitutional system is something fraught with methodological complexity. Calculations in terms of averages hide considerable variability among countries and cause a very different impression when they control for the durability of constitutions – when it is 'rates' that are calculated. But most of all, calculations are typically based on different definitions of what an 'amendment' is: some count by article – so that several changes to the same article count as a single amendment; others by subject matter – so that the number of articles amended is not relevant if they all touch on the same issue; and others by aggregate packages – so that all the changes to constitutional provisions enacted at the same moment in time, or over the same period of time (typically, a year), count as 'one amendment'.[13]

But additionally, most people agree that, to really capture the phenomenon, quantitative assessments must be complemented with qualitative ones, though it is not clear in what exact way.[14] There is no necessary relationship between the quantitative amount of change and its qualitative effects. As we know, a small change in words or syntax can have a huge impact in terms of meaning – legal rules being the meaning of words, not the words themselves. Sometimes the impact is so far-reaching that, as Richard Albert suggests, we should probably stop talking in terms of 'amendments' – a word he suggests reserving for efforts to continue the original constitutional project – and rather talk of 'revisions' or 'dismemberments' – efforts to 'unmake' the Constitution, to change it in radical ways.[15] Conversely, a

[11] Tom Ginsburg and James Melton, 'Does the Constitutional Amendment Rule Matter at All? Amendment Cultures and the Challenges of Measuring Amendment Difficulty' (2015) *International Journal of Constitutional Law* 13 (3), 686. These authors underline that the increase is partly explained by decolonisation, which multiplied the number of constitutions, and so the number of fora where amendment can take place; but only partially, since it does not explain the steep increase from the 1960s onwards.

[12] On a counting that goes from 1946 to 2008, this author calculates a mean number of amendments per constitution of 6, and a mean amendment rate (amendments per year of life of each constitution) of 0.19. Negretto (n 9), 765.

[13] Negretto (n 9), 765.

[14] Elkins Zachary, 'Constitutional revolution in the Andes?' in Rosalind Dixon and Tom Ginsburg (eds) *Comparative Constitutional Law in Latin America* (Edward Elgar, 2017).

[15] Richard Albert, 'Amendment and Revision in the Unmaking of Constitutions' in David Landau and Hanna Lerner (eds), *Comparative Constitution-Making* (Edward Elgar, forthcoming, 2019); Richard Albert, 'Constitutional Amendment and Constitutional Dismemberment' 43 *Yale Journal of International Law* 1 (2018).

considerable amount of formal change may leave core structures and decisions untouched. Juliano Benvindo remarks, for instance, that although the number of amendments passed in Brazil over the last 30 years looks pretty impressive – 92, an average of more than three per year – they have not significantly affected the substantive core of the 1988 constitution.[16] Ginsburg and Melton have struggled to account for the relevance of content variation by coming up with a 'weighted amendment rate' which abandons the assumption – implicit in conventional approaches to amendment rate calculation – that all amendments are equal. This weighted magnitude takes into account both frequency and the 'index of similarity', which compares the contents of a constitutional text before and after an amendment has been passed.[17] Again, however, the strategy has intrinsic limits because assessment of content change is based on the analysis of a list of variables that are insensitive to changes that may look irrelevant from the viewpoint of registered institutional and regulatory choices, but have significant impact in legal or political life.[18]

What can we say, within the limits of these methodological caveats, about Mexican constitutional amendment patterns? From a *quantitative* stance, numbers look imposing. The counting starts at the beginning of the twentieth century, when the Mexican Revolution led to the summoning of the Querétaro Constitutional Assembly and the subsequent approval of the 1917 text, still in force.[19] The amendment formula, enshrined in Article 135, requires the positive vote of two thirds of attending members in each chamber of the federal Congress and ratification by half of the state legislatures.[20] Mexican scholars usually track down amendment evolution by defining 'one amendment' as a change in one article formally enacted

[16] Benvindo (n 7).

[17] Ginsburg and Melton (n 11), 17. On the index of similarity, see also Elkins, Ginsburg and Melton (n 6), 56–57, 222–24.

[18] An example would be a change in the period Congress is in session, or a change in the date the Government must send Congress the Budget bill, which can have an important impact on Executive-Legislative relations, as evinced by the Mexican experience in Eric Magar, 'Los contados cambios en el equilibrio de poderes,' in María Amparo Casar and Ignacio Marván (n 1). Another would be the addition of collective *amparo*, besides the individual one, which may completely alter access to justice and several important dimensions of protection of rights, as shown by the Argentinian experience in Roberto Saba, *Más allá de la igualdad formal. Qué les debe el Estado a los grupos desaventajados?* (Siglo XXI Editores, 2016).

[19] The XIX century was dominated by replacement, not amendment. Thus, after a brief period in which the country proclaimed the Constitution of Cádiz as its own (1812–14, 1820–21), and after an influential constitution-making process in Apatzingán (1814), whose resulting text never entered into force, the country approved several constitutions in a row, in 1824, 1836, 1843 and 1848. Then the pattern changed, and several decades were spent under the formally long-lasting liberal 1857 constitution – which was only intermittently in force because of great political instability. The 1857 Constitution was amended 34 times, O.56 reforms per year. see Flores, I B La Constitución de 1857 y sus reformas a 150 años de su promulgación, *El proceso constituyente mexicano. A 150 años de la Constitución de 1857 y 90 de la Constitución de 1917* 285–324.

[20] At the moment, 32 state legislative bodies. Mexico City was traditionally a Federal District, not a State, and for this rather formal reason it was excluded from the ratification process. This oddity was suppressed with the constitutional amendment on 'Mexico City political reform' published on 29 January 2016.

at a particular moment in time[21] – something that notably underplays the amount of change given the large amount of subsections (and paragraphs within subsections) that many of the articles have today. From 1921 to September 2017, there have been 706 amendments. Figure 1 provides the snapshot, organising amendments by Presidential term.

As we can see, it was from the 1980s onwards, as political pluralism progressively grew after decades of PRI hegemonic political control – and contrary to natural expectations under Section 135's formula – that amendments increase sharply. 70 per cent of the total is post-1982; almost 40 per cent of them passed during President Calderón (2006–12) and President Peña Nieto's (2012–18) presidential periods. In only the first year of his presidency, Peña Nieto promoted six major reforms in the areas of education, telecommunications, energy, antitrust, transparency and the electoral system which touched around 60 per cent of the total number of constitutional sections, besides adding to the Constitution an extraordinarily long, detailed, codified body of transitory provisions, which do not deal with problems of temporal efficacy, as would be expected, but rather develop detailed public policy regulations in all those regulatory fields.

Figure 1 Constitutional amendments by Presidential period (1921–2017)

Period	Reforms	Percentage	Decrees	Words	Increase
1920–1924	8	1.13	2		
1924–1928	18	2.55	5		
1928–1934	28	3.97	12		
1934–1940	15	2.12	10		
1940–1946	18	2.55	10		
1946–1952	20	2.83	13		
1952–1958	2	0.28	1		
1958–1964	11	1.56	9		
1964–1970	19	2.69	8	27 638	
1970–1976	40	5.67	14	28 532	+864
1976–1982	34	4.82	14	29 938	+1406
1982–1988	66	9.35	19	34 916	+4978

(continued)

[21] Héctor Fix Fierro and Diego Valadés, 'Toward the Reorganization and Consolidation of the Text of the Constitution of the United Mexican States of 1917. Introductory Essay' (2015), 12, fn 1. https://archivos.juridicas.unam.mx/www/bjv/libros/9/4050/2a.pdf accessed 23 January 2019. See also Jorge Carpizo, 'La reforma constitucional en México. Procedimiento y realidad' (2011) *Boletín Mexicano de Derecho Comparado* Vol. XLIV, May–Aug 2011, 543–98. The change may be a word or, as we said, a great number of sentences and paragraphs within an article. Mexican scholars habitually also refer to 'amendment decrees', which are the legal instruments that contain all amendments enacted (and officially published) at the same moment in time.

Figure 1 (*Continued*)

Period	Reforms	Percentage	Decrees	Words	Increase
1988–1994	55	7.79	15	36 856	+1940
1994–2000	77	10.91	18	42 802	+5946
2000–2006	31	4.39	17	45 365	+2653
2006–2012	110	15.58	38	54 815	+9450
2012–2017	154	21.81	27	71 572	+16757
Total	**706**	**100.00**	**232**		

Source: Fix Fierro and Valadés (n 21), working with the data available at the Diputados website (www.diputados.gob.mx) and, for 2012–16, our own data, working with the same source.

This figure also registers increases in constitutional length, leaving out transitory provisions. If we do include the transitory provisions – as we should, given the surprising amount of substantive regulation contained in them – the dimension of constitutional growth becomes more transparent: while in January 2010, only five years ago, the Constitution had 78,295 words, in September 2017 it has 126,241 words. In 2010, transitory provisions represented 28 per cent of the constitution; they now make for 43.5 per cent.[22]

What can we say about Mexican amendment patterns from a *qualitative* viewpoint, from a stance attentive to the substantive import of all those changes? The impact of those more than 700 amendments on the normative contents of the Constitution has been, by all accounts, far-reaching. In their 2006 study – which does not reflect the sweeping changes of the last 10 years – Elkins, Ginsburg and Melton already concluded, for the Mexican case, that the cumulative effect of amendments from 1917 to 2006 was more substantial than the change reflected by the approval of the 1917 Constitution – that is: the Constitution was in 1917 closer to the Constitution of 1857 than to its present-day instantiation or version.[23] Available content-based evaluations echo the profundity of changes in all areas, including the creation of dozens of new institutions and the complete redirecting of core constitutional decisions in all areas,[24] and – as we see in the

[22] It is true that contemporary constitutions are often long, the last-wave Latin American ones particularly so: the 1991 Colombian text has 45,111 words, the 2009 Bolivian Constitution has 39,549 words, and the 2008 Ecuador Constitution has 52,649 words. But still, note that the Mexican, is the longest of them all. If we include transitory provisions, it is three times longer than any of them. It is 2.8 times longer than the Colombian, 3.2 times longer than the Bolivian and 2.4 times longer than Ecuador's (our data. We thank Samuel González Cataño for assistance in completing all the counts).

[23] Elkins, Ginsburg and Melton (n 3), 59. According to their calculations, the comparison between the 1917 text and the amended version of 2006 produces an index of similarity of 0.69, while the index of similarity with the 1857 document is 0.87. That is to say: with respect to the scope of topics covered, the 1917 Constitution matches its predecessors in 87% of its content (ibid, p 57).

[24] See Fix Fierro and Valadés (n 21), 13–14, and the various chapters in Casar and Marván (n 2), organising amendment activity in 5 main areas: rights, federalism, separation of powers, the judiciary, the electoral branch and transparency and accountability matters. The studies exclusively map

following section – through developments that go more in the direction of addition or accumulation, than of substitution, with no systematic concern for the maintenance of systemic harmony.

There is a last conspicuous trait, in addition to quantity and quality, we believe must be added to fully portray Mexican amendment dynamics and ground the hyper-reformist diagnosis: the nature of the amending *process*. Though, again, the traditional theoretical reverberations of the notion of 'constitution making' should not define the canon, it seems natural to associate the prospect of changing the Constitution with a moment of political discontinuity of some sort, in terms of inclusion, participation, procedural adequacy, or at least in terms of public opinion mobilisation. In Mexico, however, constitutional reform is just another incidence of ordinary politics. Partly because Article 135 does not require action by special actors outside the ordinary political process, nor special steps, partly because of other political factors that we will later explore, there are really no traces of 'higher law making.'[25] Amending the Constitution in Mexico is legislating by other means: constitutional bills are presented and wait their turn just as legislative bills do; they are lobbied for as easily as ordinary law; and emerge from elite negotiation as much as ordinary law does.[26] Public opinion, and even the legal community, often finds out about amendments once they have already been passed. Occasionally, certain changes become higher profile – but just in the way some statutory bills generate more debate from time to time.

Fast track dynamics is further reinforced by the fact that judicial review of constitutional amendments has been progressively foreclosed by the Supreme Court, in contrast to the situation in Brazil or Colombia, and quite paradoxically in a country that lives under hectic constitutional change. No doubt, among the factors that prompted the Supreme Court of India to develop its bold doctrines on the matter, one can count the frenzied dynamics of constitutional amendment propelled by Indira Gandhi and kept alive after that.[27] In Mexico, in contrast, the Court has closed the door both to substantive and procedural control in all channels of review.[28] It is not that this sort of review is unproblematic – particularly if the Constitution does not contain stone clauses and does not explicitly grant

amendments in the 15 years between 1997 and 2012. The area with the least substantive change is the horizontal division of powers (see Magar, n 14).

[25] Bruce Ackerman, *We the People* (Harvard University Press, 1993).

[26] Even the celebrated 2011 Human Rights reform was a top-down product of elite negotiation. See Natalia Saltalamacchia and Ana Covarrubias Velasco, 'La dimensión internacional de la reforma de derechos humanos: antecedentes hitóricos' in Miguel Carbonell and Pedro Salazar (eds), *La reforma constitucional en materia de derechos humanos: un nuevo paradigma* (2011) (describing how the reform emerged from high-level contacts between politicians, international actors and a few selected civil society organisations).

[27] Gary Jacobsohn, 'An unconstitutional constitution? A comparative perspective' (2006) 4 *International Journal of Constitutional Law* 460; Manoj Mate, 'State Constitutions and the basic Structure Doctrine' (2014) 44 *Columbia Human Rights Law Review* 442.

[28] See CC 82/2001 (no review of procedural or substantive regularity in constitutional controversies); AAII 168/2007 and 169/2007 (no review of procedural regularity in actions of unconstitutionality); and AR 488/2010 (procedural and substantive flaws not ultimately reviewable in *amparo*).

this power to the judges.[29] The point is that the absence of the more complex interaction between courts and legislators this review would produce reinforces a dynamic of quick and unbounded constitutional change.

III. Hyper-Reformism: The Textual Impact of Amendment Dynamics

As seen so far, describing and measuring something so apparently simple as the number of amendments to a country's constitution is less obvious an attempt than one may think.[30] In the former section we have combined three elements to that effect, and we have argued that Mexican dynamics must be described as very intense because of the frequency of amendments, because of their import in terms of substantive change in the constitutional system, and because they derive from a decision-making process that makes amendment just another incident of daily political life.

In what follows, we will briefly illustrate the effects of hyper-reformism on the constitutional text itself, which is a necessary step in order to fully understand the effects the pattern of constitutional evolution has exerted on legal and political dynamics in the country. We are interested in underlining two main aspects: the impact of constitutional amendment on the length and detail of the Constitution, on the one hand, and on the other, its role in producing a text with tensions and incoherencies.

As already reflected in our quantitative presentation in the first section, in Mexico reforms have led to an extraordinarily long and detailed text. Beyond the aggregate number of words, it is the extraordinary detail of specific articles that increases the overall sensation of length in the Mexican Constitution. Article 27, for instance, which famously regulates property, has 3,885 words; Article 41, which deals with elections and political parties, has 4,384 words; Article 122, about the political regime of Mexico City, has 2,864 words; and Article 107, which draws the boundaries of jurisdiction of the federal judiciary, has 3,190 words. The Constitution has only 136 articles, but while some of them occupy four or five sentences,

[29] See Andrea Pozas Loyo 'Los jueces constitucionales latinoamericanos frente al espejo: sobre la procedencia de juzgar la constitucionalidad de una reforma constitucional' in Rafael Rojas, Pablo Mijangos y Adriana Luna (coords), *De Cádiz al siglo XX: Dos siglos de constitucionalismo en México e Hispanoamérica* (México: CIDE-Taurus) and Juan González Bertomeu in this volume.

[30] Note that we are not assessing whether a particular amendment rhythm is excessive, moderate, or insufficient, from an external, systemic viewpoint concerned with maintaining harmony between environmental demands for reform and actual reform. Negretto has this wider perspective in mind when he points out that the idea of formulating a universal standard to capture what would be a 'moderate amendment rate' seems implausible because such a standard would depend on how frequently the Constitution needs to be modified, and this, in turn, 'will vary across cases as a result of extra-constitutional factors, such as the relative stability of the political, social and economic environment' Negretto (n 9), 760.

others are true codifications of entire areas of public policy or integral regulations of state structures. It is, then, actually quite difficult to separate longitude from detail in the overall perception of what the text communicates.

Much of this over-detail and longitude are byproducts of the political dynamics that characterise hyper-reformism. As we will later remark, constitutional reforms have been used to make political commitments credible and shield them from majoritarian tampering, hence the need to include all the details in the political negotiation. A clear example of this is the constitutionalisation of extremely specific political agreements on electoral matters. Consider for instance the provisions in Article 41.III.A.a, stating the following: 'From the run-up to the election campaign until Election Day, the National Electoral Institute shall have forty eight minutes daily, distributed in two to three minutes segments per hour in each radio station and television channel'.[31] Or consider the 890-word long regulation of the transparency agency in sub-section VIII of Article 6, strangely inlaid in the bill of rights, in an article that starts by enshrining the right to information (added 7 February 2014), and that includes dozens of detailed rules touching on the agency's various dimensions of operation. So detailed a regulation naturally touches on several other parts of the Constitution that need to be modified in turn. For instance, to include in Article 6 the provisions that the President and the Senate may use to regulate the agency Commissioners,[32] it was necessary to simultaneously amend Articles 76 and 89, which list in detail the President and the Senate areas of jurisdiction – they now give the former power to 'appoint the commissioners' and the latter power to 'object to the appointments of the commissioners'. And it was necessary to amend sub-sections XXIX-R, XXIX-S, and XXIX-T of Article 73, to give federal Congress jurisdiction to dictate general statutes developing the basic principles regarding transparency, access to State information and data protection, in addition to changing archive regulation to create a National Archive System capable of assuring their homogeneous management at all government levels. And when, in January 2016, a long constitutional amendment conferring a new political status to Mexico City was passed, these sub-sections of Article 6 were among those which had to be amended because the Constitution has traditionally referred to 'the Federation, the States, the Federal District, and municipal

[31] Mexican Constitution, January 2017. This example is taken from Héctor Fix-Fierro, 'Por qué se reforma tanto la Constitución Mexicana', in *Cien Años Cien Ensayos* (IIJ-UNAM, 2016).

[32] The provisions are the following: 'The guarantor institution is composed of seven commissioners. To appoint them, the Chamber of Senators, after conducting a broad consultation with civil society, following the proposals of the parliamentary groups supported by a 2/3 vote of attending members, will select the commissioner who will fill the vacancy, following the procedure prescribed by law.' 'The appointment', then it adds, 'will be open to objection by the President for a period of ten business days. If the President does not object to the appointment in that period, the commissioner's vacancy will be filled by the person selected by the Senate.' But '[i]f the President objects, the Senate will make a new proposal, following the steps of the former paragraph, but under a vote requirement of 3/5 of attending members. If this second option is objected, the Senate, following the steps of the former paragraph, with a vote of 3/5 of attending members, will select the commissioner who will fill the vacancy'.

authorities', instead of using a generic, more 'durable' expression (such as 'all levels of public authority').

We find the same dynamics in countless areas: the hyper-detailed nature of the regulation makes, in turn, further additional and piecemeal reforms necessary, both because it becomes obsolete sooner, and because it naturally touches on countless provisions – contained in constitutional clauses that are, themselves, very detailed – which therefore must be referred to in the amendments even if there was no direct intention of doing so.

Secondly, amendments have generated a constitutional framework full of *lagunae* and internal tensions because, in perfect hyper-reformist style, amendments are not made with an eye on their impact on the pre-existing constitutional body. Certainly, substantive heterogeneity is always reached to some extent in constitutions, which are typically the result of political transaction – and, as has been noted, producing a constitution *ex novo* does not ensure coherence either.[33] Moreover, a certain degree of internal tension is arguably inherent to the constitutions of plural societies, both because they must include a wide range of values and principles in order to have a chance of being accepted and because basic values and rights, outside of their structure and nature, are prone to enter into conflict in the context of specific cases. But in Mexico, the pattern of un-ending, fragmentary change, stirred by political conjuncture, pushed forward by politicians who ostensibly see gains only in what they add to the text – not in what they do to harmonise novelties with the extant clauses – have produced a set of sometimes very troubling inconsistencies and dysfunctions.

We find this in both the 'organic' and the 'dogmatic' part of the Constitution. Let us take some examples. As far as the organic part is concerned, a trait of constitutional evolution in Mexico has been the creation of many independent agencies. While this development is common to many countries, what is characteristic of Mexico is that no less than 13 have been enshrined in the Constitution and, most of them, are regulated there in great detail. They are often called OCAs (*organismos constitucionales autónomos*). For many years, more and more OCAs were added to the Constitution, with nobody accounting for the huge impact their creation has on the pre-existing schemes of the division of power. Even if no explicit changes were made to the corresponding articles, OCA proliferation has detracted powers and functions from the Executive and the Legislative branches, both at the federal and State level, in turn profoundly altering an already very complex federal system.

Over time, conflicts naturally grew between traditional branches and OCAs, and among the latter, but the Constitution offered no channel for solving them because no adjustment had been made to the articles defining who enjoys proper

[33] See Justin Blount, Zachary Elkins, and Tom Ginsburg, 'Does the Process of Constitution-Making Matter?' in Tom Ginsburg (ed) (2012) *Comparative Constitutional Design* 50 (stressing that, for all contemporary emphasis on constitutional design, many factors remain operative in actual constitution making, propitiating heterogeneity).

standing to begin a 'constitutional controversy' before the Supreme Court. Finally, in February 2014, the occasion was taken to amend Article 105 and enlist hypothesis of conflict between 'two autonomous constitutional institutions, and between one of them and the Federal Executive or Congress, whenever they dispute the constitutionality of general acts or rules'. But then an additional sentence was added: 'This will be applicable to the guarantor institution regulated in Article 6' (that is, to the Transparency Agency). What does this last sentence imply? Does non-standing reach other OCAs? Yes, because the first sentence is more encompassing. But the fact that this amendment was passed when the transparency agency was created led amending politicians to add this specific mention that now only creates doubts.[34]

Similar problems derive from the amendment of sub-section II of the same Article 105, which regulates standing on 'action of unconstitutionality' – abstract review. This sub-section, after the 2014 amendments, gives standing to *three* specific OCAs – the National Commission of Human Rights and analogous state institutions, the Article 6 'Transparency guarantor' agency, and the Attorney General's Office – and is *not* complemented with a more general standing clause.[35] This will surely generate new amendments, as soon as the excluded parties discover they cannot defend themselves against certain general statutes and rules.

The domain of federalism is another area in which amendment-associated disorder prevails. José María Serna shows, for instance, that from 1997 to 2014 there were 26 constitutional changes in the constitutional regulation of federalism arguably having been 'predominately motivated … [by] disorder, dispersion, and ambiguity with regard to the different levels of government's competencies, which translate into lack of clarity with regard to their responsibilities and inefficacy in policies'.[36] Fragmentary and constant changes create ambiguity and inconsistencies that in turn motivate more fragmentary reforms.

The bill of rights is in no better shape, even if its heterogeneity and inconsistency do not trigger more reform as systematically because changes typically affect disempowered citizens, not high-ranking public officials and government institutions. A first general problem derives from the great heterogeneity in style of the rights clauses: while some follow the typical abstract pattern and refer to the value that must be protected, others must be thought of as the implied 'negative' face of a bundle of specific rules about what authorities may or may not do.[37] But the most troubling difficulties stem from the fact that there are blatant, open contradictions among certain rules. The number of contradictions increased when, in 2011, the human rights constitutional reform gave constitutional hierarchy to the rights enshrined in treaties without simultaneously getting rid of previous provisions

[34] See Article 105. I, letter (l).

[35] See Article 105. II, letters (g), (h), (i).

[36] José María Serna de la Garza, 'Las reformas al federalismo mexicano', in María Amparo Casar and Ignacio Marván (n 2).

[37] Moreover, some of them find a counterpart in the federalist division of power – ie they are treated as areas of jurisdiction attributed to certain levels of government – and others do not.

incompatible with these. As a result, the Constitution at the moment contains several anti-conventional provisions, such as the one that denies political rights to persons undergoing criminal processes – in conflict with Section 23 of the ACHR and with the right to the presumption of innocence enshrined in Section 20.B.I of the Constitution[38] – the ones allowing Prosecutorial detention for as long as 80 days in some cases – in conflict with Article 7 of the ACHR[39] – or the imposition of community-labour penalties by administrative authorities – incompatible with at least three major international law sources.[40]

IV. Constitutional Change and Democratic Transition

The notably contorted picture offered by the Mexican Constitution, as a text, after 100 years of life is, nonetheless, the end-result of a process that had delivered significant gains for the country in the past. Let's briefly recall how it all started, around the end of the 1970s.

As is well known, after the Revolution and the approval of the Constitution of 1917, Mexico progressively attained a reasonable degree of political stability that had not been enjoyed in the nineteenth century. During those first decades of the century, the Mexican state apparatus grew dramatically and asserted an unprecedented degree of control over people and territory. This was done, however, under the leadership of a single political force, the PRI – previously called the PNR and the PRM – that gradually installed a hegemonic party system which controlled all power resorts and political behaviour at all levels. The political dynamics developed under the PRI effectively suffocated political pluralism in a context in which cooptation of interest groups, power-sharing and strategic circulation of elites replaced the dynamics of contestation and representation, effectively preventing the operation of both democracy and the rule of law.

In the late 1970s and early 1980s, however, the hegemonic party confronted a series of social, political, and economic crises that threatened the stability of the regime. In this scenario, President López Portillo decided to open the political arena (just enough) to the participation of other political forces through constitutional reforms in exchange for a certain degree of cooperation. In 1977 the first of

[38] Article 23 of the ACHR refers to the regulation (not denial) of the right to vote (not the range of political rights referred to in Article 38.II of the Mexican Constitution), and only for persons convicted (not those simply charged with certain counts; the charges could of course have no merit, yet a person can according to Article 38 have already been banned from running for elected office).

[39] See the regulation of the so-called *arraigo* (house arrest) in Article 16 of the Mexican constitution, which is incompatible with the provisions of Article 7 of the ACHR.

[40] See Article 21 of the Mexican Constitution, which contradicts Articles 1 and 2 of the ILO Covenant 29, Article 8 of the ACHR and Article 8.3 of the International Covenant on Civil and Political Rights (exempting community work from being 'forced labour' wherever it is dictated by a *judge* after due proceedings). See, generally, Francisca Pou Giménez, 'Las reformas en materia de derechos fundamentales' in Casar and Marván (n 2).

these reforms took place. President José López Portillo convened a dialogue with opposition parties and associations to discuss a set of constitutional reforms. They all met at the Ministry of Interior and their agreements were constitutionalised. On the one hand, 'the reform was seen by the government as a preventive operation capable of providing a channel for discontent, a place for the "minorities"'.[41] On the other, the opposition movements perceived this reform as a platform from which to further their goals. We believe that the political importance of this reform exceeds its content. It gave the Constitution a role that would later determine its future: it became the space for sealing political negotiations.

In the ensuing years, due to further social and economic crises, the opposition won more spaces. In 1988 the PRI lost the capacity to unilaterally amend the Constitution since it no longer retained the two thirds super-majority in the Chamber of Deputies. As a consequence, the role of the Constitution as the space for sealing political negotiations was reinforced. From then on, constitutionalising the commitments and deals among the three main parties' elites (PRI, PAN and PRD) meant shielding them from future majoritarian defection.[42] In this way, in the early years of the long transition to democracy the Constitution became an extremely successful device for enabling credible commitments between the authoritarian regime and the opposition parties, something that no doubt was critical to attaining a consensual and, to an important extent, pacific change of regime.[43]

Constitutional amendment helped insert and stabilise political plurality in a further sense. As has been remarked, when constitution-making processes – aimed either at replacing or amending a constitution – are multilateral (not controlled by a single political group), there is a tendency to produce institutions that distribute power. The different groups within the constituent body 'face a constraint on the type of institutional framework they can attempt to enact: the other group's veto'.[44] Thus, in Mexico the constitutional framework created over the last decades through a broad, long line of constitutional reforms, has distributed both power and resources, to the great benefit of the three leading political parties. And these benefits are important in explaining the stability and peacefulness of the transition process.

Electoral reforms, for instance, created a system in which Congress is elected through a combination of majoritarian and proportional representation formulae both at the federal and the state level, which in turn has led to an increasingly plural political arena. They also created an enormous and extremely well-funded

[41] José Woldenberg, *Historia mínima de la transición democrática en México* (El Colegio de México, 2012) 20.

[42] Pedro Salazar, 'Sobre la democracia constitucional en México (pistas para arqueólogos)' in *Política y derecho. Derechos y garantías. Cinco ensayos latinoamericanos* (Fontamara, 2013).

[43] Woldenberg (n 38); Francisco Valdés Ugalde, *La Regla Ausente* (FLACSO-IIS-UNAM, 2010).

[44] Andrea Pozas-Loyo and Julio Ríos Figueroa, 'Enacting Constitutionalism. The Origins of Independent Judicial Institutions in Latin America' (2010) 42(3) *Comparative Politics* 298.

electoral branch with probably no peer at the comparative level, in whose context political parties are controlled, but who also have an important say.[45] Similarly, as we have already mentioned, multilateral hyper-reformism has created an institutional framework populated by autonomous agencies, creating or modifying pre-existing institutions to increase their autonomy. Among them we can find the National Human Rights Commission (1992–99), the Bank of Mexico (1993), the National Electoral Institute (1996–2007–14), the National Institute of Statistics and Geography (2005), the National Institute for the Evaluation of Education, the Federal Economic Competition Commission, the Federal Telecommunications Institute, the National Council for Evaluation of Social Development Policy (all in 2013), the Federal Institute for Access to Information and Protection of Personal Data (2014), the Federal Judicial Council (1995–99), the Superior Audit Office (1999–2009–15). Not to mention the reforms directed at the Supreme Court of Justice (1987–94–96–99), that fortify its functions and its independence vis-a-vis the other branches.[46] This immense constellation of bodies has given the three main political forces ample space and opportunities to negotiate the forms and the fora for sharing political presence as well as the economic benefits linked to public offices in Mexico.

This explains why most of the amendments over the last 30 years have been passed with more than the two-thirds majority required by the Constitution[47] and why states have *never* vetoed a constitutional reform.[48] The three main parties together enjoy a super-majority in Congress and strong influence over local legislatures, which is more than enough to keep the 'amendment machine' working.[49] Since 2014 this trend has only got deeper. The bulk of the 90 constitutional amendments passed from 2012 to 2015 were the result of the 'Pact for Mexico,' a high-profile political agreement between the leaders of the three main parties sponsored by the President.[50]

Constitutional amendment, in short, played a central role in the Mexican transition process. It enabled credible inter-party commitments within a scheme that delivered large gains by the three leading parties, thus becoming central to our process of democratic transition.

[45] Javier Aparicio and Jacaranda M Pérez,'Financiamiento público a partidos políticos' in *Grandes Temas para un Observatorio Electoral Ciudadano, Vol. III – Sistema Político Electoral* (IEDF, 2007), 211–32; Pou Giménez (n 3); Ricardo Becerra, Salazar Pedro and José Woldenberg, *La Mecánica del Cambio Social en México* (Cal y Arena, 2000); Lorenzo Córdoba Vianello, 'Las reformas en materia electoral' in Casar and Marván (n 2).

[46] Fix Fierro and Valadés (n 21).

[47] Casar and Marván (n 2) 40. As these authors document, from 1997 to 2014, favourable votes were made 83% of the time by the 3 leading parties.

[48] Remember Article 135 requires approval of at least a majority of the state legislatures for an amendment to pass.

[49] Our goal here is simply to note how a very particular and long-lasting political dynamics helps understand the counter-intuitive scenario in which we have smooth, continuous reform under an amendment rule that requires the approval of more than 15 states. A complete explanation would require an account of the party structure that we cannot provide here.

[50] See Mariana Velasco Rivera, in this volume.

V. Constitutional Change and Democratic Consolidation

Despite its very relevant political role in the recent past, our point of view is that today hyper-reformism seriously impairs the adequate deployment of basic constitutional functions, setting unnecessary and maybe insurmountable obstacles to the construction of a society governed under the rule of law and democratic principles. Let us elaborate on some of these problems.

Normative constitutions – that is, constitutions conceived as enforceable and often directly applicable legal rules – can be attributed to many functions, but two among them seem paramount: legal functions and political functions. Viewed from the viewpoint of the role it plays within the legal system, a constitution is a norm that sets a basic programme for the structuring and management of collective life and provides tools for its own enforcement. We can call this dimension the *legal* function of the Constitution. The Constitution is a key element in a distinctive system of social regulation – the law – which competes with other normative systems that also project demands on people, and aspires to have distinctive advantages over them: advantages because of its origins – who produces legal rules – because of its content – potentially more acceptable in plural societies than the rules of other systems – and because the law aspires to guarantee its own enforcement and dedicates many resources to that end. A constitution, specifically, sets a basic substantive programme for the organisation of collective life. At a preliminary level, its provisions are intended to motivate citizens and authorities and attain a fair degree of self-enforcement. But constitutions also create a large apparatus of legislative and executive structures to implement, develop, and enforce, the substantive programme they set forth. And they create a judiciary, and charge judges with the responsibility of directly enforcing constitutional rules, or of setting in motion processes that operate as a motivational reinforcement for citizens and authorities.[51]

Unfortunately, the now hyper-amended Mexican constitutional text, both for content-dependent and for content independent-reasons – that is, because of its impermanency – works very poorly as a piece of legal machinery. Huge areas of the Constitution, and the text holistically seen – in so far as extraction of a general 'constitutional ethos' is sometimes attempted – are unable to really motivate citizens and public authorities because they do not convey understandable messages, and because, to the extent people know they change all the time, do not constitute for them strong 'reasons for action'.[52] Although it is probably the case that constitutions are poorly known by citizens everywhere, the text of the Mexican

[51] See Juliane Kokott and Martin Kaspar, 'Ensuring Constitutional Efficacy' in Michel Rosenfeld and András Sajó (eds), *The Oxford Handbook of Comparative Constitutional Law* (2012) (mapping different judicial and non-judicial models as methods to assure the efficacy of the Constitution).

[52] Joseph Raz, *Practical Reasons and Norms* (Oxford University Press, 1999).

Constitution is a distinctively mysterious text both for lay citizens and specialists. It is fair to assume that even those that 'feel' subjectively motivated by it, and show appreciation for the Constitution if asked, are moved not by the actual content of the text, but rather by what they imagine this content to be.[53]

This opens great margins for unintended non-abidance by both citizens and public officials and creates difficulties at the level of legislative and administrative 'development' of the Constitution – precisely a dimension that should be well served in a system where the Constitution endures.[54] But where pathologies are perhaps more blatant is at the critical level of constitutional adjudication. A distinctive institutional responsibility of the judiciary is to provide the community with a clarification of what the law says – of what counts as law – constructing narratives about the meaning of the Constitution that can be defended as coherent across time. As we well know, interpretation tasks are never simple due to a wealth of factors.[55] But in Mexico this complexity is multiplied by an amazingly above-average degree of internal constitutional heterogeneity and by the dynamics of perpetual change.

A painful example of this is the amount of time and effort Mexican judges must currently devote to what would be, in Dworkin's terms, mere 'pre-interpretative' tasks: tasks oriented not at ascertaining what the Constitution means in order to resolve conflicts under it, but to ascertaining what the Constitution *is*.[56] This is what happens, for instance, with the brand new Mexican Bill of Rights, after the 2011 reform, for the reasons we described before. The Supreme Court has spent more than three years trying to come up with a scheme capable of making sense of the relative position of national and international sources of rights within the Constitution, paying a very high cost in terms of the internal divisions this has created within the Court, and in terms of failing to provide the guidance the community expected from it. The Court crafted a first 'clarification' ruling in the *Varios 910/2012* case. The criteria set down in this ruling were painfully revisited but confirmed in the *AI 155/2007* case, then disregarded in several cases decided by the Second Chamber in 2013, and finally overruled in the *CT 293/2011* case, that sets criteria which are internally in tension, and that do not fully dissipate doubts about the contours of the Bill of Rights and the relative position of national

[53] People may, for instance, retain a loose sense of what the great social and political deals the 1917 text meant to convey were; a quite radical social conception of property and the separation of church and state would no doubt be among them. In actual fact, amendments to sections 25, 26, 27, together with the economic provisions that the 2013 amendments added to the transitory clauses, have radically altered the property regime, as have the July 2013 amendments to section 24 as far as the constitutional treatment of religion is concerned, though it is very difficult to ascertain in what exact direction.

[54] Elkins, Ginsburg and Melton (n 6), 19–20 (underlining that constitutional endurance promotes the development of ancillary institutions).

[55] Among them, the fact that interpretation can be attempted from many different perspectives, the fact that there are no shared meta-rules about how to choose among the different interpretive methods, and the fact that constitutions are very special rules whose interpretation and application require a special approach.

[56] Ronald Dworkin, *Law's Empire* (The Belknap Press of Harvard University Press, 1986).

and international sources of rights.[57] These cases struggle with problems created to a great extent by irresponsible dynamics of amendments. The transformative potential of changes ends up mortgaged by the un-ending amount of technical talk produced for confronting the problems caused by extreme internal inconsistency. The community cannot yet focus on the task of having the Constitution *enforced* because it is not even clear what the Constitution *says*.

The Mexican Constitution, in sum, offers little guidance and, by the same token, also little constraint. While the degree to which different legal forms are constraining is variable and never absolute,[58] law retains its functionality to the extent that not everything can be convincingly argued in legal terms. Following the rules of the 'game of law' must be perceivably different from following the rules of other social games – violence, exclusion or corruption. In Mexico, by contrast, central traits of hyper-reformism – constitutional obscurity, and the fact that public authorities are often in the position of choosing between abiding the Constitution or changing it – debilitate the position and functionality of the legal system.

The second main function of a constitution is to provide a framework for an adequate expression of the democratic will. We may call this dimension the *political* function of the Constitution. A constitution marks points of equilibrium and division of labour between majorities and minorities, between the government and the governed, and between past, present and future generations. By drawing lines between different kinds of decisions and decision-making processes, it tries to ensure the productive and non-abusive development of the democratic conversation. Thus, the Constitution identifies what issues must be debated giving ample consideration to decisions taken in the past, and which ones are more freely manageable in the present; it distinguishes issues in which non-utilitarian, right-based thinking must prevail from those in which majoritarian political logics is less constrained; it separates questions in which the private judgement of individuals or groups enjoys wider space than those in which the margin is small, and it generally liberates political life from the duty of addressing anything at any point. When citizens and institutional actors respect these lines (ie, when enforcement is attained), discuss where those lines are drawn by the Constitution (ie, when they engage in constitutional interpretation) or should be drawn (ie, when they partake in normative criticism), democratic political life ensues with certain intelligibility and order.

[57] About this judicial saga, see Fernando Silva García 'Derechos humanos y restricciones constitucionales: ¿reforma constitucional del futuro vs. interpretación constitucional del pasado? (Comentario a la CT 293/2011del pleno de la SCJN)' [2014] 30 *Cuestiones constitucionales* 251; Rubén Sánchez Gil, 'Notas sobre la Contradicción de tesis 293/2011', [2014] 21 *Revista Iberoamericana de Derecho Procesal Constitucional* 133 (January–June); and Francisca Pou Giménez, 'Lo que quisiera que la Suprema Corte hiciera por mí: lealtad constitucional y justicia dialógica en la aplicación de la CT 293/2011' in Caballero y Rubén Sánchez Gil (eds), *Derechos constitucionales e internacionales. Perspectivas, retos y debates* (Tirant lo Blanch, 2018).

[58] Jean D'Aspremont, *Formalism and the Sources of International Law. A Theory of the Ascertainment of Legal Rules* (Oxford University Press, 2011).

For instance: if a constitution is rigid, but can be amended, it draws certain lines to the tasks of the judiciary that are democratically enriching. As Rosalind Dixon and Adriane Stone have argued, constitutional amendment is democratically critical because it provides a channel for political majorities to 'respond' to courts even in strong judicial review systems, providing a way for diluting the problem of the judiciary having the last word.[59] In their view, 'political constitutionalists' like Waldron have too easily discarded this argument because they take the US experience as a paradigmatic case, which is in fact, when contemplated from an informed stance, an exceptional constitutional case of what we would call hypo-reformism.[60]

Finally, an additional important political function of constitutions has to do with their capacity to enhance the development of a sense of political *demos* around the constitutional text[61] or, in other words, to deploy an 'integrative function'[62] that can be of critical importance in divided societies. And as several authors have underlined, whether a constitution is successful in this sense may depend on its content, but often depends, crucially, on how the Constitution is made – including how amendments are made – and the extent to which constitution-making processes make people feel the Constitution is 'theirs'.[63]

Unfortunately, none of the dimensions identified by this portrayal of political functionality are well served in the hyper-reformist scenario. For starters, hyper-reformism empowers legislators and judges well beyond the frontiers expected in the context of a constitutional democracy that seeks the sort of equilibriums identified above. In Mexico, for instance, it is very difficult to hold the legislature accountable because of the difficulty of ascertaining what the Constitution says, and because legislative chambers in Mexico simultaneously attempt statutory and constitutional change. It is difficult to say, for instance, whether the 2014 Federal Telecommunications and Broadcasting Act fully respects the Constitution, because it is very difficult to ascertain what is really set forth in the extremely long constitutional transitory provisions on the matter, combined with those in Articles 6, 25, 26, 27 and 28.

The judiciary is, for its part, over-empowered even more. The spectrum of the arguments they can present is as broad and heterogeneous as the Constitution itself.

[59] Rosalind Dixon and Adrienne Stone, 'Constitutional Amendment and Political Constitutionalism: A Philosophical and Comparative Reflection' in *Philosophical Foundations of Constitutional Law* (David Dyzenhaus and Malcolm Thorburn (eds), Oxford University Press, 2016), 95–96.

[60] ibid, 102–06.

[61] Elkins, Ginsburg and Melton (n 6).

[62] Dieter Grimm, 'Integration by Constitution' (2005) 3 *International Journal of Constitutional Law* 193 (nos 2 and 3, Special Issue May 2005); Jan-Werner Müller, *Constitutional Patriotism* (Princeton University Press, 2007).

[63] Stefan Voigt, 'The Consequences of Popular Participation in Constitutional Choice: Towards a Comparative Analysis' in Anne van Aaken, Christina List and Christoph Lutge (eds), *Deliberation and Decision. Economics, Constitutional Theory and Deliberative Democracy* (2003); see Blount, Elkins and Ginsburg (n 33).

Moreover, hyper-reformism debilitates both internal controls within the judiciary and the external supervision of its tasks. For one thing, judges (and the Supreme Court in particular) lack incentives to make the sustained effort necessary for building strong interpretive doctrines under the constraints of integrity: it is foolish to make such an effort if one knows the constitutional provisions these doctrines gloss upon may be replaced tomorrow. By the same token, professors, practitioners and political commentators lack incentives to develop the sort of critical apparatuses that would make the judges feel closely supervised, and hence both their professional tasks and the quality of the public debate are hampered by the difficulties of, again, pointing out what the Constitution says. On the top of that, an incoherent and ever-changing constitution prevents the country from reaping the deliberation-reinforcing benefits of judicial review understood as an institution that, by forcing majorities to pause, on the basis of arguments that articulate the meaning of the Constitution, allows for an overall richer democratic debate.[64]

Nor does it allow for the sort of dialogue between judges and amending majorities that Dixon and Stone have imagined (see above). For even if legislative branches 'respond' to a judicial ruling with an amendment, the Constitution will be the unpredictable result of combining this response with the heterogeneous pool of existing provisions, and judges may easily insist on their previous views by presenting them as derived from a different combination of constitutional ingredients. And while this may happen everywhere, the Mexican over-amended Constitution allows this potentially very rich interaction to proceed with a distinctive degree of arbitrariness. Even if it is true, therefore, that present-day generations in Mexico have the Constitution more at their fingertips than in other countries, in our view this does not translate into gains in terms of obtaining a more robust, healthy democratic or constitutional life.

The Mexican Constitution does not fulfil, either, its potentially very relevant identity-related functions. Its elite-driven constitutional change fails to provide the gains in terms of heightened popular participation and debate that are attained under other patterns of constitutional change.

Note, then, that the problem all along has not been that Mexico lives under a constitution that does not matter. The Constitution has important effects, symbolic and material. The problem lies in the sort of effects it deploys and the sort of obstacles it poses to even the best-intentioned of actors, to play the 'game of law' and the 'game of constitutional democracy'.

[64] We mean to refer to the sort of dynamics that John Ferejohn and Pascale Pasquino, analysing Friedman's argument along those lines, call 'the counter-majoritarian opportunity' in John Ferejohn and Pascale Pasquino, 'The Countermajoritarian Opportunity' (2014) 13 *University of Pennsylvania Journal of Constitutional Law* 353. See also Víctor Ferreres Comella, 'Una defensa de la rigidez constitucional' (2000) 23 *Doxa* 29.

VI. Conclusion

In this chapter, we have shown that in the last 30 years Mexico has exhibited a pattern of constitutional change that can be characterised as *hyper-reformism*, because of the large number of constitutional reforms, because of the scope of the changes involved, and because of the sort of fast-track political process they derive from. We have portrayed some of its different political and legal effects over time, and we have argued that while this pattern was critical for transition to democracy, it now constitutes an obstacle for the consolidation of constitutional democracy.

To conclude, we would like to underline two implications of the analysis. First, we believe that taking patterns of constitutional change as units of analysis enables the evaluation of their effects, regardless of the effects of evaluation of individual reforms – which is the stance constitutional lawyers tend to automatically adopt. We can think of the consequences that the pattern itself has, analytically separate them from the evaluation of the particular consequences of particular amendments, and as a result reach a broader and more encompassing understanding of constitutional realities. In connection with this, we argued that hyper-reformism in Mexico has had negative effects on the consolidation of the rule of law and constitutional democracy even if it paradoxically was central to the transition to democracy. This evaluation captures the effects of the pattern of change on different aspects of the rule of law and reaches conclusions that would have been different had we focused on the effects of individual reforms. We believe, moreover, that this kind of approach could be fruitful in identifying and better understanding the dynamics of constitutional change in other countries. For instance, studying the causes and effects of hypo-reformism (as the one present in the US), or other modalities of hyper-reformism, could enable a better understanding of amendment processes in general, and make some fruitful comparative inferences possible.

Finally, claiming that a pattern exists naturally leads to the inquiry of its causes. As a derivation of our analysis here, the next step in the study of Mexican hyper-reformism must be to strive to produce an account of the mechanisms of reproduction behind this pattern.[65] If, as we have argued, hyper-reformism has become an obstacle for the consolidation of constitutional democracy in Mexico, then understanding those mechanisms is not only an important academic aim, but also a necessary step to transform a troubling reality.

[65] We present an account of these mechanisms in Pou Giménez and Pozas-Loyo, 2016 (n 5).

11

The Political Sources of Constitutional Amendment (Non)Difficulty in Mexico

MARIANA VELASCO RIVERA*

I. Introduction

Amendment difficulty is traditionally understood in terms of institutional design. It is often assumed that amendment difficulty can be read off the text. That is to say, that the formal design of amendment processes necessarily has a direct effect on the possibility of changing the constitutional text – the more formal hurdles there are, the more difficult it would be to amend a constitution and vice versa. This assumption has also led to drawing normative implications regarding the purpose of amendment rules and the impact they must have in the quality of constitution-amending processes. Constitutional amendment rules, in this sense, must guarantee both high quality amendment processes to make sure that popular sovereignty and self-government are most effectively exercised. Accordingly, constitutional amendments must represent the people's fundamental commitments.[1] Within this framework of understanding, constitutional change must be characterised by extraordinary circumstances as opposed to the ordinary circumstances in which ordinary politics and legislation take place.

* LLM '15 and JSD candidate, Yale Law School. I thank Richard Albert, Jack Balkin, Carlos Bernal-Pulido, Joel Colón-Ríos, Raúl Mejía, Francisca Pou-Gimenez, Andrea Pozas-Loyo, Virgilio A da Silva, Eneida D Salgado and Juliano Zaiden Benvindo for comments and conversations on this and/or previous drafts of this chapter. Special thanks to Carlos Velasco and Ángela Zorro for their invaluable help in creating the data set and running the regressions included in this chapter.

[1] See eg Donald Lutz, 'Toward a Theory of Constitutional Amendment' in *Responding to Imperfection – the Theory and Practice of Constitutional Amendment* (Sanford Levinson ed, 1995) 63–87; Bruce Ackerman, 'Higher Lawmaking' in *Responding to Imperfection – the Theory and Practice of Constitutional Amendment* (Sanford Levinson ed, 1995) 66; Richard Albert, 'The Expressive Function of Constitutional Amendment Rules' (2013) 59 *McGill Law Journal* 225.

Prominently, in 1996, Donald Lutz developed a theory of constitutional amendment that is consistent with the mainstream understanding of constitutional amendment and amendment difficulty noted above. According to Lutz, depending on the design of amendment processes, one may predict the amendment rate and understand important aspects of the political system of the country at hand. Different jurisdictions adopt different 'amendment strategies' that respond to a logic in which multiple steps and veto points are supposed to make the Constitution harder to amend. By the same token, amendment difficulty reflects a substantive commitment to popular sovereignty, deliberative processes and/or the distinction of between higher and ordinary laws.[2] There are four types of amendment strategies that, at the same time, give preference to any of the three substantive commitments: parliamentary supremacy, legislative complexity only, legislative complexity plus state approval and legislative complexity plus a referendum.[3] Parliamentary supremacy strategy is the less difficult amendment process and legislative complexity plus a referendum the most. The first strategy, parliamentary supremacy, does not give preference to any of the substantive commitments. The second, legislative complexity (eg, some combination of extraordinary majorities, intervening elections, procedural check points) aims at making the amendment process more deliberative, which also draws a distinction between ordinary and constitutional matters.[4] In addition to deliberation and the distinction between higher/ordinary law, the third strategy is indirectly committed to popular sovereignty. The fourth strategy, by contrast, is directly committed to popular sovereignty for including a referendum.

Lutz categorised Mexico's constitutional amendment formula as a third strategy case, just like the US (which he considers one of the most difficult constitutions to amend). Article 135 of the Mexican constitution requires the vote of two thirds of the present members of both chambers of Congress and the majority of State Legislatures to pass a constitutional amendment. According to Lutz's theory, the formal hurdles provided by Article 135 would ensure constitutional amendment processes in Mexico remain committed to deliberation and popular sovereignty. Yet, in fact, the amendment reality in Mexico is the exact opposite of what Lutz predicts. Since 1917, the Constitution has been amended 706 times,[5] and, as I show in Sections III and IV, amendment processes have been far from committed to deliberation and popular sovereignty.

From 1917 to 1987, it was simple to make sense of a frequent use of the amendment mechanism because the hegemonic *Partido de la Revolución Institucional* (hereinafter PRI) could amend the Constitution on its own (and it did). But after the general election of 1988, the political conditions changed. The once

[2] Lutz (n 1) 263.
[3] Lutz (n 1) 239, 263–64.
[4] Lutz (n 1) 263.
[5] See Cámara de Diputados, *Reformas constitucionales por periodo presidencial* www.diputados.gob.mx/LeyesBiblio/ref/cpeum_per.htm accessed 15 June 2018.

hegemonic PRI lost the ability to amend the Constitution on its own. Since then, the expectation was to see formal veto points to function properly, including those provided by the constitutional amendment rules.[6] Accordingly, the necessary implication was to see a decrease in the constitutional amendment rate. Constitutional amendments, however, not only did not cease to be amended but the amendment rate skyrocketed. From the total 706 amendments, 60 per cent (427) took place between 1988 and 2018; as opposed to 279 reforms adopted between 1917 and 1988. This situation has long puzzled scholars in Mexico. Why, despite its formal amendment difficulty, has the Mexican constitution been so frequently amended over the last three decades?

Mexico's constitutional amendment reality illustrates how the traditional understanding of amendment difficulty is insufficient to understanding the factors that determine formal constitutional change and amendment difficulty.

In this chapter, I propose an alternative account to understand formal constitutional change in Mexico. One that solves the apparent tension between the formal constitutional amendment difficulty and the amendment reality.

In this alternative account, constitutional change should be understood mainly as the product of political entrenchment. Political entrenchment refers to the formal or informal insulation of interests, values, and beliefs of different groups through the institutional means available in a given constitutional order (eg, judicial appointments and ordinary legislation).[7] Constitutional amendment mechanisms, in this context, are just one among other means of political entrenchment. If constitutional amendment mechanisms are just another means of political entrenchment, it follows, formal constitutional change is the result of the efforts of different groups or individuals looking to entrench their interests, values and beliefs directly in the constitutional text.

When constitutional change is understood in terms of political entrenchment, on the one hand, it is no longer necessary to distinguish between higher/ordinary law and constitutional/ordinary politics because constitutional change

[6] See eg María Amparo Casar and Ignacio Marván, *Reformar sin mayorías. La dinámica del cambio constitucional en México: 1997–2012* (Penguin Random House Grupo Editorial México, 2014); José María Serna de la Garza and Isidro de los Santos, *La dinámica del cambio constitucional en México* (IIJ-UNAM, 2018) https://biblio.juridicas.unam.mx/bjv/id/4828 accessed 13 August 2018; Roberto Rives Sánchez and Mexico, *La reforma constitucional en México* (Universidad Nacional Autónoma de México, 2010); Benito Nacif, 'The Fall of the Dominant Presidency: Lawmaking under Divided Government in Mexico' in Roderic Ai Camp (ed), *The Oxford Handbook of Mexican Politics* (Oxford University Press, 2012); Jaime Cárdenas, *Transición política y reforma constitucional en México* (Universidad Nacional Autónoma de México, Instituto de Investigaciones Jurídicas, 1994); Jorge Carpizo, 'La reforma constitucional en México. Procedimiento y realidad' (2011) XLIV *Boletín Mexicano de Derecho Comparado* 555; Héctor Fix-Fierro, Pedro Salazar and Diego Valadés, 'Toward the Reorganization and Consolidation of the Text of the Constitution of the United Mexican States of 1917' (2015) http://comparativeconstitutionsproject.org/wp-content/uploads/Introductory-Essay.pdf?6c8912 accessed 20 August 2017.

[7] Jack M Balkin and Sanford Levinson, 'Understanding the Constitutional Revolution' (2001) 87 *Virginia Law Review* 1045 and Jack M Balkin, *Living Originalism* (Reprint edition, Belknap Press, 2014).

may happen through the different institutional means provided by the constitutional order,[8] not only through formal constitutional amendments. Most importantly, looking at constitutional change through the lenses of political entrenchment makes it easier to understand why formal hurdles for constitutional amendments have little impact on the frequency in which constitutional amendments are adopted.[9] Crucially, in this context, amendment difficulty cannot be read off the text. Instead, whether the amendment mechanism would be used or not, depends on political choices, political conventions, and constitutional culture in particular contexts.[10] In this sense, one might say amendment difficulty is not institutionally determined but politically constructed.

Within this theoretical framework, I argue constitutional amendment remained available for political entrenchment because, even though the political conditions changed after 1988, the political practices of the old regime remained untouched. Mexican politics restructured in such a way that the practices that provided the conditions for the stability of PRI hegemonic regime (ie, centralisation of decision making and party discipline), were adopted by the major political forces after 1988. Just as in the old regime, constitutional decision making is still highly centralised.

Section II of this chapter lays out the political conditions under which constitutional amendment was used during the PRI hegemonic regime. Specifically, the practices that allowed cutting through the mechanisms of separation of powers and, thus the centralisation of the decision making during the PRI-regime. In Section III, I show how after 1988 the practices that allowed the centralisation of decision making during the PRI regime remained untouched after 1988, still allowing to cut through the separation of powers, hence making it possible to continue using the amendment mechanism as a means of political entrenchment. Section IV illustrates the perils entailed by the permanence of old practices in constitution-making processes. As a conclusion, I put forward some of the lessons that can be drawn from the dynamics of constitutional amendment in Mexico.

II. Constitutional Amendment During the PRI Hegemonic Days

Between 1917 and 1987, the Constitution was amended 279 times. The dynamics of formal constitutional in those days were not complicated to understand.

[8] See Jack M Balkin, 'Framework Model and Constitutional Interpretation' (2016) www.oxfordscholarship.com/view/10.1093/acprof:oso/9780198754527.001.0001/acprof-9780198754527-chapter-13 accessed 16 March 2018.

[9] See Tom Ginsburg and James Melton, 'Does the Constitutional Amendment Rule Matter at All? Amendment Cultures and the Challenges of Measuring Amendment Difficulty' (2015) 13 *International Journal of Constitutional Law* 686.

[10] Ginsburg and Melton (n 9).

For most of the years after the enactment of the Constitution in 1917, Mexico lived under the rule of the hegemonic PRI. It has been argued that in the hegemonic days vertical and horizontal mechanisms of accountability did not function properly because the constitutional system was coopted by one party. Accordingly, the President was able to amend the Constitution at will because the PRI had control over the three branches of government, both at the federal and State level.[11] Although constitutional entrenchment rules were in place and formally observed, the power of the President was effectively unbound.

The political conditions in those days were ideal for using the amendment mechanism for political entrenchment when deemed necessary. This situation meant that, should the hegemonic PRI, namely the President, deem it necessary, constitutional amendment would be available for political entrenchment. The political homogeneity of the government cancelled all possibilities of seeing formal veto points working. Benito Nacif describes the political control of the President as follows: '[F]ormally, the Mexican Constitution provided for the separation of the executive and legislative branches of government, but in practice Congress was subordinated to the presidential authority. (…) The Presidency had the ability to deliver "policy shocks" in response to critical situations. Under normal circumstances the chief executive had the power to bring about substantive policy change even when this involved amending the Constitution. Congress had certain influence, but was unable to stop the president.'[12]

According to Jeffrey Weldon the PRI hegemonic regime relied on four necessary conditions: '(1) a presidential system based in the constitution; (2) unified government, where the ruling party controls the presidency and both houses of Congress [ie, PRI hegemony in Congress]; (3) discipline within the ruling party; and (4) a president who is the acknowledged leader of the ruling party.'[13] Naturally, since these are necessary conditions, if any of them cease to exist, he argues, the equilibrium of *presidencialismo* would begin to break down and eventually disappear. Note that from these four conditions only the first is a formal condition; namely, the existence of a presidential system constitutionally established. The other three, also known as the *meta-constitutional powers* of the president, are conditions that depend on political factors (ie, party discipline and distribution of seats in Congress) and internal party politics.

The *meta-constitutional* powers allowed the president to drive the policy agenda, including bringing *policy shocks*[14] in the form of constitutional amendments; 'appoint' and remove governors; and to control not only the legislative and

[11] See Jeffrey Weldon, 'The political sources of presidencialismo in Mexico' in Scott Mainwaring and Matthew Soberg Shugart (eds), *Presidentialism and Democracy in Latin America* (Cambridge University Press, 1997); José Ramón Cossío Díaz, *Cambio social y cambio jurídico* (Instituto Tecnológico Autónomo de México, 2001); Jorge Carpizo, *El Presidencialismo Mexicano*, 16th edn (Siglo Veintiuno, 2002).

[12] See Nacif (n 6) 234.

[13] Weldon (n 11) 227.

[14] See Nacif (n 6).

judicial powers but also the State governments.[15] Accordingly, Weldon claims 'when *presidencialismo* is working efficiently, one should expect most of the presidents' bills to be approved by Congress, and not expect frequent vetoes'.[16] That is to say, the ability of the government to smoothly bring its agenda forward depended less on the constitutional design than on the political conditions that allowed the president to do so (eg, party discipline). The source of power of the president was not the Constitution but 'the extraordinary centralisation of decision making within the party'.[17] That is, the power of the president relied less on the constitutional design of the presidential system than on the internal organisation of the party and the centralisation of power on which it functioned.[18]

The basic problem Weldon points out is a divorce between what the Constitution prescribes and the reality of party politics. In his view, the extraordinary centralisation of decision making within the hegemonic party, which allowed the president to exercise virtually unchecked powers, 'cut across the branches of government, "violating" Article 49, which is supposed to guarantee the separation of powers'.[19] Note that, the most important feature of the PRI regime, the very thing that hampered the division of powers, was party politics, and party discipline based on a system of patronage that resulted in the lack of incentives for government officials and representatives to exercise the formal veto points the Constitution provides.[20] This is the case, for example, of high level public officers and Supreme Court judges. Their political careers depended on a system of patronage controlled at the top of the organisation, thus it was easier to step down whenever the president/party asked them because they knew that as long they stayed loyal they would probably be rewarded later on with a different public post.[21] Loyalty to the regime indeed returned benefits on career prospects.

Given that the centralisation of power is a political question rather than one of design, Weldon suggests that whenever the political order transformed into one of political plurality, *presidencialismo* – and its effects – would definitely disappear and the system of separation of powers would function properly.[22] As the PRI structure became more democratic[23] and the political order more plural, the centralisation of power would break down to finally give an end to *presidencialismo* and a chance for the Constitution to function as it is supposed to. Put differently,

[15] Carpizo (n 11) 190; Weldon (n 11) 225.
[16] Weldon (n 11) 255.
[17] Weldon (n 11) 255.
[18] Weldon (n 11) 255.
[19] Weldon (n 11) 255.
[20] See Alberto Diaz-Cayeros, Beatriz Magaloni and Barry R Weingast, 'Tragic Brilliance: Equilibrium Party Hegemony in Mexico' (2003) https://papers.ssrn.com/abstract=1153510 accessed 7 August 2018.
[21] Weldon (n 11) 254.
[22] Weldon (n 11) 254–55.
[23] For instance, Weldon points out that in 1994 the PRI reformed its nominating procedures to allow local conventions to select candidates running for local posts without interference from the centre. See Weldon (n 10) 257.

once the conditions enabling the meta-constitutional powers of the president ceased to exist, the president would be left only with his constitutional powers, thus the interstice between the Constitution and reality would be narrowed down.

The problem with such an assertion is the underlying assumption that political pluralisation would automatically make the Constitution work properly and make the Mexican polity meet the substantive commitments it enshrines. Weldon's prediction overlooked the fact that political pluralisation neither entailed the disappearance of the PRI as a relevant political force nor the elimination of conventions and practices that became part of the Mexican constitutional culture along the years of one-party rule. Casar and Marván already pointed out that the increasing rate of constitutional amendments cast doubt on the assumption that political plurality and a government without majorities translates into legislative gridlock and, therefore, the end of what they call constitutional reformism.[24] Casar and Marván also point out that constitutional amendments are the result of wide political agreements among the three major political parties (namely, the PRI, the *Partido Acción Acción Nacional* or PAN and the *Partido de la Revolución Democrática* or PRD).[25] Yet, they fall short on giving a nuanced account on the specific conditions that have determined the path of constitutional change in the last 30 years. The next two Sections attempt to do so.

III. Constitutional Amendment After the Fall of the PRI Hegemonic Regime: Old Practices are Hard to Change

Even though, since 1988, the PRI lost the ability to amend the Constitution on its own, the Constitution not only did not cease to be amended but the amendment rate steadily increased as the political landscape became more plural. This situation was unexpected. The political fragmentation and the eventual transition to democracy was anticipated to lead to a new regime with a functional constitutional system of separation of powers and effective constitutional veto points, which would naturally entail a decrease in constitutional amendments. In the context of the political debilitation of the PRI, these expectations were indeed reasonable. As the years went by and the political landscape became even more plural, by 1997–98 onwards, some even expected institutional paralysis due to the political conditions of divided government.[26] However, while some veto

[24] Casar and Marván (n 10) 14.

[25] Casar and Marván (n 6).

[26] Note that regarding constitutional amendments, I understand the government divided since 1988 when the PRI lost the needed qualified majority to reform the Constitution in the chamber of deputies and not since 1997, when they lost the majority of seats in that same chamber. But see Ulises Carrillo and Alonso Lujambio, 'La Incertidumbre Constitucional. Gobierno Dividido y Aprobación

points (such as public confrontation between power branches, presidential veto, constitutional controversies brought before the Supreme Court, and the rejection of judicial nominations)[27] were indeed seen as the PRI lost power, the amendment rate did not drop, but the opposite. Figure 1 shows the increasing number of constitutional amendments between 1917–2018.

Figure 1 Constitutional Amendments by Persidential Term (1917–2018)

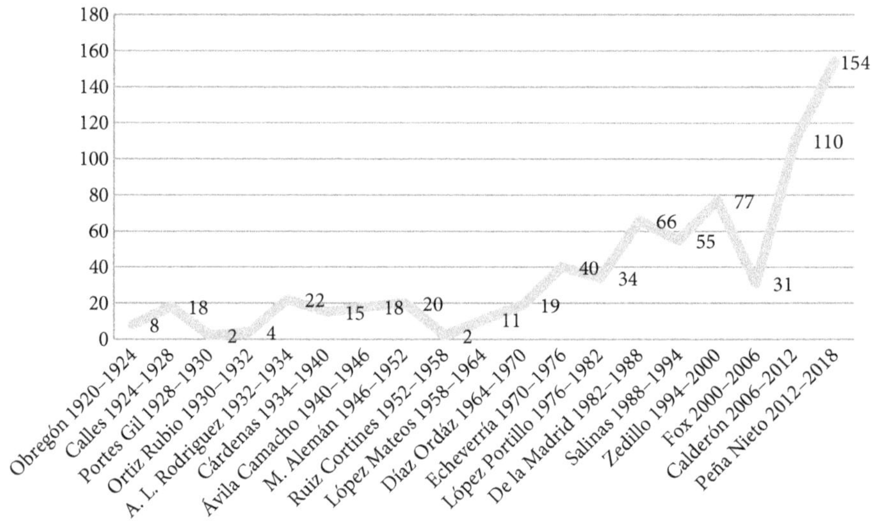

Source: working with the data available at Cámara de Diputados, www.diputados.gob.mx/LeyesBiblio/ref/cpeum_per.htm

The constitutional amendment rate did not drop after 1988 because, even though the political conditions change, Mexican politics restructured in such a way that constitutional amendment remained available for political entrenchment. As described in the previous section, *presidencialismo* relied on four necessary conditions, from which only the unified government ceased to exist – since 1988 no party has had the needed qualified majority to amend the Constitution on its own. According to Weldon's account, the increasing political pluralisation should have ended the centralisation of decision making. Yet, Weldon overlooked the fact that political pluralisation neither entailed the disappearance of the PRI as a relevant

Presupuestal En La LVII Legislatura Del Congreso Mexicano, 1997–2000' (1998) 60 *Revista Mexicana de Sociología* 239; and Casar and Marván (n 6) 31.

[27] See Armand B Peschard-Sverdrup and Sara Rioff, *Mexican Governance: From Single-Party Rule to Divided Government* (CSIS, 2005); Maria Amparo Casar, 'Executive-Legislative Relations: The Case of Mexico (1946–97) in Scott Morgenstern and Benito Nacif, *Legislative Politics in Latin America* (Cambridge University Press, 2002); Nacif (n 10).

political force nor the elimination of conventions and practices that became part of the Mexican constitutional culture along the years of one-party rule.

Crucially, the new structure of Mexican politics relies on the same practices that the PRI-regime relied on, namely centralisation of decision making and party discipline. Accordingly, the exercise of power may go unchecked as well. I make this assertion based on three pieces of evidence. First, the *volume of reforms* between 1917 and 2018; secondly, the restructuring of Mexican politics between 1982 and 1997); and thirdly, the *fast track pattern* in the adoption of constitutional amendments and, the *lack of opposition* by State Legislatures. In the sections below, I first briefly discuss Figure 1 to suggest that the sharp increase of constitutional amendments since 1988 means constitutional amendment is indeed an effective mechanism for political entrenchment. Then, I describe how politics evolved in the political turning point where the PRI lost its ability to amend the Constitution. In particular, I underscore the crucial role that the PRI had in creating the appropriate conditions for constitutional amendment to remain available for political entrenchment. Thirdly, I show the impact that the permanent centralisation of decision making and party discipline has in the quality of amendment procedures.

A. Volume of Constitutional Reforms: Then and After

Looking at Figure 1 we learn several things about formal constitutional change and Mexican politics. First, it shows an increasing trend of amendments to the Constitution in the last century. In total, between 1917 and 2018, 706 constitutional amendments were adopted.[28] Importantly, this figure refers to the number of constitutional articles modified in each Presidential administration, which is different from the number of amendment decrees. Amendment decrees normally include the modification of more than one article. Therefore, the number of decrees would always be less than the actual modifications to the Constitution. In this section I focus on the actual number of modifications because it gives a better grasp of the magnitude of the increasing amendment rate.

Secondly, notably most of the amendments since the enactment of the Constitution in 1917 were adopted after 1988, the year when the hegemonic PRI lost the ability to amend the Constitution on its own. As mentioned in Section II, with regard to the question of amendment difficulty, the period between 1917 and 1988 should not be surprising in that we know the PRI had the ability to amend the Constitution on its own. The increasing number of amendments since 1988 is more noteworthy in that from that year onwards the amendment mechanism could not be used without the cooperation of least two political forces.

[28] Cámara de Diputados, *Reformas constitucionales por periodo presidencial* www.diputados.gob.mx/LeyesBiblio/ref/cpeum_per.htm accessed 15 December 2016.

Yet, 60 per cent (427) of the total 706 amendments were adopted from that year onwards. That is to say, the majority of constitutional amendments since the enactment of the Constitution have taken place via the cooperation of least two political parties. This very fact tells plenty about how Mexican politics restructured after the PRI confronted a serious threat to its hold on power for the first time. But first, we must take a closer look at the increasing number of amendments after 1988 against the backdrop of the PRI hegemonic years.

Between 1988 and 2018, 427 constitutional amendments were adopted, from which 132 were adopted between 1988 and 2000 and 295 between 2000 and 2018. That is, in 30 years the Constitution was amended more times (427 v 279) than during the 68 years during which the PRI was capable of amending the Constitution on its own. Furthermore, even the lowest number of amendments in a Presidential term after 1988 is still a high number against the backdrop of the PRI hegemonic days. The 31 amendments adopted during Vicente Fox's administration are more than those adopted in the nine PRI-hegemonic-administrations between 1929 and 1970; and only fall short by three of those adopted during López Portillo's administration (1976–82). Furthermore, during Calderón's administration alone (2006–2012) 110 amendments were passed, only 30 less than the reforms adopted during Echeverría's (1970–76), López Portillo's and De la Madrid's (1982–88) administrations together (140), which happen to be the three Presidents that most amended the Constitution during the old regime. Finally, between 2012 and 2016, four years into Peña Nieto's administration, the Constitution went through 154 amendments. That is, seven more than Echeverría, López Portillo, and De la Madrid together.

The above numbers suggest one of two things, either the different parties have exactly the same policy goals and agendas of governance, which is extremely unlikely, or that Mexican politics restructured in such a way that each of the political parties have been able to equally entrench their interests directly in the constitutional text. The increasing number of amendments, despite the fragmentation of political power, suggest the answer is most likely the latter. The practical implication of such a reading would simply be that despite the changing political conditions the amendment mechanism remained accessible for the protection of political agendas and interests. The heavy use of the amendment mechanism in different political contexts suggests that constitutional amendment remained an effective mechanism to address political needs. What is more, the increasing rate from 1988 to present day suggests that it has indeed been an effective means of political entrenchment across regimes. This was only possible by the restructuring of Mexican Politics.

B. Restructure of Mexican Politics (1982–97)

The sharp increase in amendments since 1982 precisely suggests a continuity in the use of the amendment mechanism as a means of political entrenchment across regimes. For instance, consider De la Madrid's (1982–88) and Salinas' (1988–94) administrations. This period coincides with the two decades in which the PRI struggled with serious economic crises, legitimacy crises and threats to their hold on power, albeit in different political conditions. While during De la Madrid administration the PRI could still introduce amendments on its own, this was not the case for President Salinas. However, the amendment mechanism remained accessible in both contexts.

When De la Madrid took office, the country was experiencing the most serious financial crisis ever seen in Mexican modern history.[29] Months before his inauguration, López Portillo his predecessor had nationalised banks to avoid economic catastrophe. People across social sectors were upset, public criticism to the government was unprecedented and there were also rumours on calls for violent uprisings.[30] The regime was clearly in the midst of a serious legitimacy crisis due to the economic, political and social turmoil caused by his predecessor's lavish and blatantly corrupted presidency. De la Madrid's government platform consisted in a number of propositions that in general terms aimed at restructuring the economy and, importantly, changing the narrative of the regime. Among said propositions, De la Madrid included the 'National Moral Renovation'[31] to combat corruption and squandering. To materialise the moral renovation against corruption he presented a bill to amend Title IV of the Constitution on Public Servant's Accountability. Among other things, it included new constitutional principles (eg, efficiency and honesty) to rule public service and the modification of the term 'public officer' (*funcionario público*) to 'public servant' (*servidor público*) as a way to transform public service in action. That is, making public service actually serve the public interest instead of serving individual interests (eg, corruption).[32] This amendment was largely symbolic, much like a billboard advertising the government's commitment to the Rule of Law and combating corruption. Clearly, the simple change in how to call public officers was not going to transform the pervasive corruption that had been fuelled for decades precisely by the PRI.

[29] See eg Macario Schettino, 'La peor crisis, dicen' *El Financiero* (21 September 2016) www.elfinanciero.com.mx/opinion/macario-schettino/la-peor-crisis-dicen; Adolfo Gilly, 'USA/MEX: Crisis e integración: La Modernizacion Del Capitalismo Mexicano' *Nexos: Sociedad, Ciencia, Literatura* www.nexos.com.mx/?p=4564 accessed 10 August 2018; Heberto Castillo, 'Ante la bancarrota, la entrega – Proceso' (21 August 1982) www.proceso.com.mx/134138/ante-la-bancarrota-la-entrega accessed 10 August 2018; Alejandro, Alvarez 'Economic Crisis and the Mexican Labor Movement in the 1980s', in Kevin J Middlebrook and University of California, San Diego (eds), *Unions, Workers, and the State in Mexico* (Center for US-Mexican Studies, University of California, San Diego, 1991).

[30] Enrique Mueller, 'La crisis económica que atraviesa México causa una grave crispación en la actividad política' *El País* (Madrid, 1 September 1982) https://elpais.com/diario/1982/09/01/internacional/399679211_850215.html accessed 10 August 2018.

[31] 'La Renovacion Moral que Propone de la Madrid' [1982] *Proceso* www.proceso.com.mx/133015/la-renovacion-moral-que-propone-de-la-madrid accessed 9 August 2018.

[32] See Iniciativa del Ejecutivo, Exposicion de motivos, 3 December 1982, http://legislacion.scjn.gob.mx/Buscador/Paginas/wfProcesoLegislativoCompleto.aspx?q=b/EcoMjefuFeB6DOaNOimNPZPsN-LFqe0s7fey1FqricnNbiZodZlaGwZxDFFrD0chXE4NlnikOFuFNwSQCTBuw==.

De la Madrid's amendments to tackle corruption could have been implemented in ordinary legislation, but amending the Constitution added a symbolic significance and advertising use. The regime, needed to change its narrative. The revolutionary narrative that for decades justified the PRI hegemonic regime was falling apart. Corruption, economic instability, and a general distrust in the government, made it difficult to keep sustaining that the PRI was the only legitimate path for the realisation of the Revolutionary ideals. The discourse surrounding the Title IV amendments and the rest of amendments adopted in De la Madrid's administration indeed marked the change from the official revolutionary discourse to a discourse of the Rule of Law (*Estado de Derecho*).[33] Amending the Constitution, was De la Madrid's political choice for advertising such change.

Even though after the general election of 1988 the PRI lost its power to amend the Constitution on its own, Mexican politics restructured in such a way that constitutional amendment remained available as a means of political entrenchment. For the first time in history the hegemonic party indeed had reasons to fear to lose its hold on power. The PRI not only lost the needed majority to amend the Constitution on its own, it is also widely believed that the government operated an electoral fraud to be able to retain the Presidency.[34] The night of the election and its aftermath plunged the PRI into a legitimacy crisis that needed to be overcome not only to hold onto power for as long as possible but also because the election proved the hegemonic regime was indeed falling apart. The PRI needed to find a new narrative to present itself as truly committed to democratic values, thus a legitimate political option. The question was, how to do it? Should the PRI want to pass any amendment, the weakened hegemonic party had to negotiate with the opposition and vice versa. President Salinas and the PRI found themselves at a political crossroads: it could either resist the inevitable fall of the hegemonic regime and choose other means of political entrenchment or reach out to the opposition and be able to continue using the amendment mechanism for political entrenchment. President Salinas could very well have opted for the former and chosen different means of political entrenchment. In the end, the PRI still controlled Congress to pass ordinary legislation on its own. However, in such a cataclysmic political context, the Salinas' administration opted for focusing its efforts to keep accessing the amendment mechanism even when this necessarily entailed bargaining with the opposition. A cooperating opposition would surely provide a legitimising dose hardly achievable otherwise. Accordingly, many of the opposition's long-standing demands to make the electoral system fair and

[33] The change of narrative is clear from the political platform and speeches of President Miguel de la Madrid (1982–88). See eg Miguel de la Madrid Hurtado, *Los Grandes Problemas Nacionales de Hoy: El Reto Del Futuro* (1a ed, Editorial Diana, 1982).

[34] 'El día en que 'se cayó el sistema' y ganó Salinas' (*El Universal*, 1 August 2018) www.eluniversal.com.mx/colaboracion/mochilazo-en-el-tiempo/nacion/sociedad/el-dia-en-que-se-cayo-el-sistema-y-gano-salinas accessed 9 August 2018.

competitive were conceded[35] – for example, the creation of an independent electoral body in charge of organising the elections and supervising the enforcement of electoral laws. This strategy helped President Salinas both to legitimise his government and party and, to reset the narrative where consensus and cooperation among parties were portrayed as democratic values[36] until these two elements actually became the political convention. In sum, after 1988 the PRI managed to continue to secure a loyal opposition[37] while legitimising itself by using constitutional amendments as billboards of their commitment to democracy.

Note that the opposition in fact considered constitutional amendments were necessary to secure its access to power. Therefore, they had the incentives to seize the opportunity and cooperate with the Salinas' administration. However, the PRI had a bargaining advantage because it was this party, not the opposition, that could opt for ordinary legislation as means of political entrenchment. In this sense, it could therefore be said that between 1988 and 1997 (the year when the PRI lost the simple majority in the Chamber of Deputies), the amendment mechanism remained accessible because the PRI allowed it to be so. Similarly, between 1997 and 2016 although no party had the qualified majority in Congress to pass constitutional amendments, the PRI retained the majority of state legislatures. In this sense, the two-tiered design of the amendment mechanism gave the PRI a bargaining advantage. Even when agreements had been struck at the Congress level, the PRI could veto any constitutional amendment at the state legislatures approval stage. In this context, the fact that after 1988 constitutional amendment remained available as a means of political entrenchment has less to do with the formal difficulty of the amendment process than with a political choice the PRI made and the cooperation of the major political forces, namely the PAN and PRD.[38]

From 1988, the structure of Mexican politics put consensus and cooperation among opposing parties at the centre of the regime. This situation has provided the conditions for constitutional amendment to remain a feasible option for political entrenchment. Crucially, the availability of the amendment mechanism depended (and still depends) both on a political decision to use the mechanism

[35] In fact, the strategy of coopting the opposition was already a long-standing practice. See eg Soledad Loaeza, 'El Partido Acción Nacional: La Oposición Leal en México' (1974) 14 *Foro Internacional* 352; and Francisca Pou and Andrea Pozas-Loyo in this volume arguing that in the midst of political, social and economic instability President López Portillo decided to amend the Constitution granting some of the opposition demands to access Congress in exchange of cooperation.

[36] See Carlos Salinas de Gortari, *México, un paso difícil a la modernidad* (Penguin Random House Grupo Editorial México, 2013); and Ricardo Becerra, Pedro Salazar and José Woldenberg, *La Mecánica Del Cambio Político En México: Elecciones, Partidos Y Reformas* (1 ed, Cal y Arena, 2000) 378 (arguing 'in 1994, after the uprising in Chiapas, the rule of inclusion and consensus became necessary to adequate the legal framework but by 1996 it was unavoidable' (free translation)).

[37] See Soledad Loaeza (n 35).

[38] It took a while to have the cooperation of the two parties. While the PAN immediately started cooperating, it took 7 years for the PRD to capitulate. Yet, the cooperation of the PAN was more than enough to pass constitutional amendments.

and the reproduction of practices that became part of the constitutional culture in the old regime – namely, the centralisation of decision making, and strong party discipline. Accordingly, where these elements are present, even in a context where the cooperation among different political parties is necessary, amending the Constitution remains possible regardless of the design of the amendment rules. The section below shows that in fact there is evidence suggesting practices from the old regime keep reproducing in our days, which explains why the Mexican constitution has continued to be frequently amended despite the formal difficulty of the amendment process.

C. Fast Track Pattern in the Adoption of Constitutional Amendments and Lack of Opposition by State Legislatures

In line with Lutz's theory, Article 135 of the Constitution provides an amendment process with an increased level of difficulty that would seem to promote deliberation, making clear at the same time that constitutional change should be an extraordinary occurrence. Yet, constitutional amendment episodes in Mexico are far from being extraordinary or deliberative. Rather, these processes are characterised by two elements: *fast track approvals* in both chambers of Congress and the *lack of opposition* in State Legislatures when passing constitutional reforms. These two elements evidence that party discipline and centralisation of decision making is still present in constitution-amending processes, and still cuts across the federal and State level separation of powers. Put differently, fast track approvals and the lack of opposition show that like in the old regime party members are willing to align with the decisions made at the top of their party. The implication of these practices, of course, is that the constitutional mechanisms of horizontal accountability (in this case Article 135) would not function properly.

In this section I analyse the constitutional amendments processes from 1997 to February 2017 to show the manifestation of the old regime practices. In doing so I analyse 94 amendment processes (formalised by the same number of constitutional amendment decrees). To do this analysis I created a data set of the time that it takes for a constitutional amendment bill to go through each of all the relevant steps of the constitutional amendment process provided by Article 135 and congressional rules before being adopted. These steps include: (i) the presentation of the amendment bill; (ii) the legislative committee report assessing and proposing a text for the amendment in question (hereinafter report or recommendation); (iii) the discussion and approval of the report by the chamber of congress where the bill was presented (hereinafter chamber of origin); (iv) the reception of the amendment project at the chamber in charge of analysing the project in second turn (hereinafter reviewing chamber); (v) the legislative committee report at the reviewing chamber; (vi) the discussion and approval of the amendment project by the reviewing chamber; (vii) the approval by the state legislatures and formal declaration of the amendment adoption; and (viii) the enactment of the amendment. These eight steps, at the same time, form six stages. Stage 1 indicates the time it takes for the legislative committee to present the report from the moment the amendment bill was introduced. Stage 2 is the time it takes for the full chamber to discuss and approve a legislative committee report from the moment it is presented. Stage 3 refers to time in between the dispatch and reception of an amendment bill from the chamber of origin to the reviewing chamber. Stage 4 indicates the time it takes for the legislative committee to present the report since the reception of the bill. Stage 5 is the same as stage 2 but in the reviewing chamber. Stage 6 represents time in between the dispatching of the bill to the state legislatures and its approval. Stage 7 would be the time between the latter approval and the enactment of the amendment.

i. Fast Track Approvals in Congress

Figure 2 below shows stages 1 to 5. Stages 2 and 5 show the time each chamber of congress spends on discussing a legislative committee report before passing it. These stages show a *fast track* trend on the approval of the legislative committee reports. On average, the chamber of origin takes 2.7 days and the reviewing chamber takes 1.3 days to approve a committee report. Additionally, the middle observation in both cases is 0.[39] These results speak against Lutz's prediction regarding the quality of amendment processes based on the design of rules. The data suggests that far from promoting public deliberation, the design of amendment rules have little effect on the quality of debate and deliberation of constitutional amendments. What is more, stages 1 and 4 strongly suggest that decision making is highly centralised. On average, an amendment bill spends 225 and 187 days in the legislative committee at the chamber of origin and the reviewing chamber, respectively. Note that these numbers do not necessarily correspond to the amount of time a bill is under actual consideration of the committee. Determining the amount of time it takes to draft a committee report would require a separate analysis that is beyond the scope of this article. Yet, the sharp difference between stages 1, 4 and stages 2, 5 allows us to assume that constitutional decision making takes place elsewhere. Specifically, that legislative committees' recommendations are most likely presented when the needed majorities are secured. Thus, the full chamber sessions where public deliberations are supposed to take place, are rather rubber-stamping ceremonies where party members vote as they are told.

[39] I calculated the median to control for outliers. There is one case that spent 6 months in stage 4. As for stage 5, there is one amendment that spent 1 month in this stage, another one 10 days and a handful of cases that spent between 9 and 5 days.

Figure 2 Number of days it takes for an amendment bill to pass each stage of the amendment process in Congress

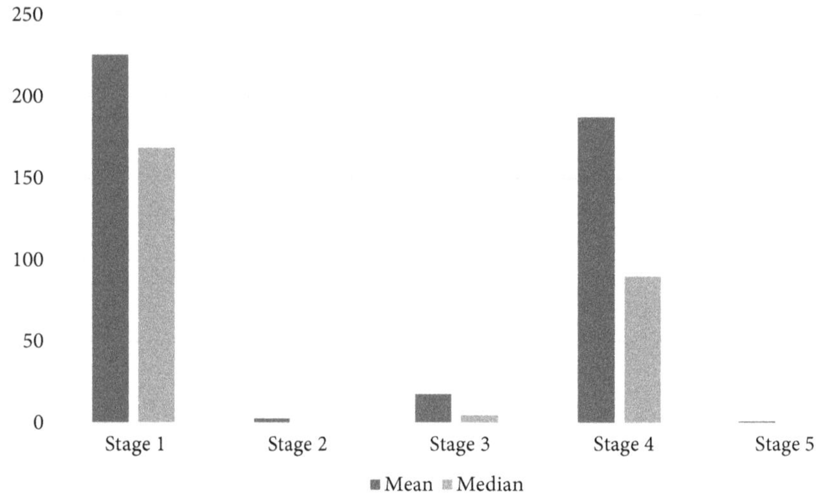

Source: author's own data.

An alternative interpretation of this data could argue that the cause of fast track processes may imply that the constitutional amendments are mostly not substantive or relevant. However, this explanation would not be accurate. The importance of amendments' subject matter has not impeded fast track approvals. There are extreme cases where the drafting, presentation, discussion and approval of the legislative committee's report in both chambers, happen on the same day the amendment initiative is presented.[40] This is the case, for example, of the amendment to Article 4 to include the 'right to sports' and the 'right to nutritious, quality and sufficient food' in 2011. One could attribute the expedite process to the fact that, for politicians, including socioeconomic rights in the Constitution could mean nothing more than the immediate political benefit of populist measures.

[40] Cámara de diputados, *Proceso legislativo reforma constitucional 12 de octubre de 2011 (derecho a la cutlura física y el deporte)* www.diputados.gob.mx/LeyesBiblio/proceso/lxi/142_DOF_12oct11.pdf accessed 30 October 2015; Cámara de diputados, *Proceso legislativo reforma constitucional 31 de octubre de 2011 (derecho a la alimentación nutritiva suficiente y de calidad)* www.diputados.gob.mx/LeyesBiblio/proceso/lxi/144_DOF_13oct11.pdf accessed 30 October 2015.

In addition, there are two cases in which the whole deliberation process only took 2 days: Cámara de diputados, *Proceso legislativo reforma constitucional 20 de diciembre de 2013 (reforma energética)* http://legislacion.scjn.gob.mx/Buscador/Paginas/wfProcesoLegislativo.aspx?q=b/EcoMjefuFeB6DOaNOimNPZPsNLFqe0s7fey1FqrieewCtlZUVdEtexN4AlExWI accessed 30 October 2015; Cámara de diputados, *Proceso legislativo reforma constitucional 10 de Julio de 2005 (facultad del Congreso para expedir leyes generales sobre desaparición forzada)* http://legislacion.scjn.gob.mx/Buscador/Paginas/wfProcesoLegislativo.aspx?q=b/EcoMjefuFeB6DOaNOimNPZPsNLFqe0s7fey1FqrifoPnxmZTvfy5hdt2/SlgBa accessed 30 October 2015.

However, structural amendments are not the exception. Take, for example, the 'energy reform' of 2013, where the Constitution was amended to open the oil industry to private and foreign companies after almost eight decades since the nationalisation of the industry in 1938.[41] After the initiative was presented, it only took two days for both chambers of Congress to pass it and 72 hours to get the approval of the majority of State Legislatures. Note that, the 'energy reform' was part of the so-called '*Pacto por México*' (Pact for Mexico), a written agreement between President Peña Nieto, the (not democratically elected) presidents of the PRI, PAN and PRD – later joined by the Green Party – which went public the day after the former took office on 1 December 2012. The pact ensured that these political parties would respectively vote in favour of several constitutional reforms in Congress. Such an expedite process – despite the complex dimension of the amendment – reflects the absence of a thorough scrutiny by the Congress and State Legislatures. What is more, it shows that the deal made between the heads of the political parties subdued the legislative independence of representatives to partisan interests. The energy reform suggests a greater degree of centralisation of decision making in that, clearly, the needed majorities were secured even before activating Article 135. Naturally, this hampered the possibility of authentic democratic deliberation on the design of new constitutional solutions.

There are also cases where the whole process at the Congress level (both chambers) happens on the same day the legislative committee report is presented to the full chamber of origin.[42] For example, consider the amendment to Article 88, which established a framework to grant the president the power to leave the country up to seven days without previous approval of Congress.[43] Both President Ernesto Zedillo and Vicente Fox faced obstacles put by the Congress to travel abroad to fulfil their foreign policy agendas. In fact, in 2002, there were attempts by the Fox administration to set the agenda to adopt a constitutional amendment on the issue, but the PRI and PRD representatives strongly defended the matter as something Congress should have the power to decide.[44]

[41] See Juan Montes, Laurence Iliff, and David Luhnow, 'Mexico Congress Passes Historic Energy Bill', *Wall Street Journal* (New York City, 12 December 2013) www.wsj.com/articles/SB10001424052702303 932504579254013051981266 accessed 14 January 2015; Dan Molinski and Anthony Harrup 'Mexican Government Presses Ahead With Energy Overhaul' *Wall Street Journal* (New York City, 22 February 2016) www.wsj.com/articles/mexican-government-presses-ahead-with-energy-overhaul-1456181673 accessed 14 January 2015.

[42] Cámara de diputados, *Proceso legislativo reforma constitucional 29 de agosto de 2008 (ausencia del territorio nacional por parte del Presidente)* www.diputados.gob.mx/LeyesBiblio/proceso/lx/111_DOF_29ago08.pdf accessed 15 August 2016.

[43] CPEUM, Art 88. The article establishes the following 'The President of the Republic can leave the national territory for up to seven days, previously notifying his reasons to the Senate or the Permanent Committee, as applicable, as well as the outcome of his activities. For absences larger than seven days, the President shall request a permit from the Senate or the Permanent Committee'. (Translation: Costitute Project.)

[44] Andrea Becerril, 'Descartan senadores y diputados modificar el artículo 88 para facilitar los viajes de Fox', *La Jornada* (Mexico city, 13 April 2002) www.jornada.unam.mx/2002/04/13/006n1pol.php?printver=0 accessed 15 August 2016.

Nothing much happened in those years until June 2008, already under Felipe Calderón's administration, when the amendment was passed in *both chambers* of Congress the very next day the legislative committee presented its recommendation to the full chamber of deputies (by 295 votes in chamber of deputies and 77 in the senate) and received the approval of 17 State Legislatures on August 13.[45]

ii. Absence of Opposition by State Legislatures

Just as fast track approvals of constitutional amendments at Congress level, the absence of opposition by State Legislatures reflects the permanence of centralisation of decision making and strict party discipline. To this day, there are no records of an amendment ever being blocked at this stage of the constitutional amendment process.[46] Not during the PRI hegemonic days, nor after the fall of the old regime. As noted above, after the fall of the hegemony, the PRI never lost control of the majority of State Legislatures.[47] Thus, it is not surprising that State Legislatures remained strictly disciplined – even in those cases where the Constitution has been amended to limiting States' autonomy or divesting them from their competences.[48] Only in three occasions a State Legislature has voted against the adoption of an amendment.[49] First, in 2007 the legislature of Coahuila voted against the electoral reform establishing a system to distribute airtime for political campaigning; then, in 2008, the legislature of Querétaro voted against an amendment adding an age requirement to be a State Governor (Article 116); and, finally, in 2013, the legislatures of Michoacán, Morelos, Oaxaca and Zacatecas, voted against an amendment to Article 24 that defined the concept of 'freedom of worship' as the 'freedom of

[45] Cámara de diputados (n 29).

[46] Casar and Marván (n 6) 38 fn 30.

[47] According to the available data at Congreso de la Unión, from 2000 to 2015 the PRI controlled the majority of State Legislatures. This situation changed with the general election of July 2018, where the newly formed political party *Movimiento de Regeneración Nacional* (MORENA) scored a landslide victory. Besides winning the Presidency, among other things, MORENA won the control of 19 out of 32 State Legislatures. See Congreso de la Unión, *Información historíca* http://www.congreso.gob.mx accessed 15 December 2015; Tom Phillips and David Agren, 'Mexico Election: Historic Landslide Victory for Leftist Amlo' *The Guardian* (2 July 2018) www.theguardian.com/world/2018/jul/02/mexico-election-leftist-amlo-set-for-historic-landslide-victory accessed 12 August 2018; and Carlos Bravo Regidor, 'Opinión | ¿Por qué López Obrador necesita oposición?' *The New York Times* (8 August 2018) www.nytimes.com/es/2018/08/08/opinion-mexico-lopez-obrador-oposicion/ accessed 12 August 2018.

[48] Article 73 is the constitutional provision establishing the Federal Congress exclusive legislative competences and also the most amended article in the Constitution. See Cámara de Diputados, *Reformas constitucionales por artículo* www.diputados.gob.mx/LeyesBiblio/ref/cpeum_art.htm accessed 18 December 2016.

[49] Cámara de diputados, *Proceso legislativo reforma constitucional 26 de septiembre de 2008* www.diputados.gob.mx/LeyesBiblio/proceso/lx/113_DOF_26sep08.pdf accessed 17 October 2016; Cámara de diputados, *Proceso legislativo reforma constitucional 13 de noviembre de 2007* www.diputados.gob.mx/LeyesBiblio/proceso/lx/055_DOF_13nov07.pdf accessed 17 October 2016; Cámara de diputados, *Proceso legislativo reforma constitucional 19 de Julio de 2013* www.diputados.gob.mx/LeyesBiblio/proceso/cpeum/CPEUM_209_DOF_19jul13.pdf accessed 17 October 2016.

ethical convictions, conscience and religion' and forbid acts of public worship with political purposes. Although, one might read these episodes as a positive sign of the willingness of State Legislatures to act independently and in fact be a check on power in constitutional amendment processes, these cases are still outliers.

The practical implication of the persistence of centralisation of decision making and party discipline is that once both chambers of Congress have reached the required majorities, the vote of State Legislatures to adopt a constitutional amendment is a rubber-stamp. To this day, State Legislatures pose no threat for the adoption of constitutional amendments. Just as ordinary legislation, a constitutional amendment is practically enacted once both chambers of Congress have passed it.

IV. The Perils of the Permanence of Old Practices in the Adoption of Constitutional Amendments

Up to this point, I have argued that the increasing number of constitutional amendments in the last three decades suggests that the amendment mechanism is still used as a means of political entrenchment. After 1988, Mexican politics restructured but the practices that allowed for power to go unchecked in the old regime remained untouched. Accordingly, the relevant political forces have been able to bargain and accommodate their different political interests and needs directly in the constitutional text. Ex ante, this situation should not be considered as problematic in that one could interpret a large volume of amendments as a sign of a healthy democracy where representatives are devoted to public good, thus committing to bring forward anything necessary to achieve such an end. However, we know that in Mexico the centralisation of constitutional decision making results in amendment processes that are far from deliberative (see Section III above). In this section I illustrate some of the perils entailed by the permanence of the practices that allowed an unchecked exercise of power during the old days.

The immediate implication of the permanence of the old practices in constitutional decision making is that, like in the old days, power still goes unchecked. Fast track processes and the absence of opposition in State Legislatures secure little or no scrutiny of the amendments and no accountability. As constitutional amendments are not the result of deliberative processes subject to public scrutiny, representatives do not need to articulate coherent public arguments to justify their acts or policy choices.[50] In this context of little accountability, those able to

[50] Monsiváis Carrillo argues that in general government officers and politicians rarely need to articulate coherent public arguments to justify their acts or policy choices. See Alejandro Monsiváis Carrillo, 'Hablar de política. Democracia deliberativa y participación discursiva en México' (2015) 60 *Revista Mexicana de Ciencias Políticas y Sociales* www.revistas.unam.mx/index.php/rmspys/article/view/45379 accessed 19 January 2017.

access the amendment mechanism have been able to change the constitutional text according to their specific interests – even in stark contradiction to the public good. The two examples below show the little effort those with the power to amend the Constitution have to put to be able to achieve their objectives at the expense of justice.

A. The Power to Adjudicate Inter-State Border Disputes: Justice (Un)Served

In 2005, a constitutional amendment eliminated the Supreme Court's power to adjudicate inter-state border disputes to give to the Senate.[51] Seven years later, in December 2012, the very same articles were amended to undo the amendment of 2005.[52] The arguments that were given to justify the urgency of the first amendment made just as little sense as the arguments given to justify the second. First, in 2005, Congress justified the court curbing measure under two arguments: first, that the nature of the disputes was political because no statute set up the standards of adjudication for the Supreme Court to settle this kind of conflicts; and, secondly, that the Senate, as representative of the States, should therefore settle these disputes.[53] Then, in 2012, the reasons given to justify giving the power back to the Supreme Court was that the amendment of 2005 had become dead letter because Congress had not issued a statute to set up standards for the Senate to settle this kind of dispute. In this sense, the best way to proceed was to give said power back to the Supreme Court because, as it turned out, the standards of adjudication to settle these disputes already existed in the first place (the court had the power to settle disputes between powers of different states since 1995). Finally, another reason given was that since the Senate was the body representing the States, it risked having conflicts of interest.

The reasons given to justify the amendments were not only contradictory but also far-fetched. First, on both occasions it was argued that the amendments were necessary because, the body in charge of settling this kind of disputes could not act due to the lack of a statute setting general adjudication standards. Paradoxically, instead of issuing the supposedly needed statute, the legislative body in charge of doing so justified its acts based on the nonexistence of the statute. Secondly, on both occasions it was argued that the body to which the power was being transferred was ideal to settle inter-state border disputes for the same reasons given to

[51] DOF, Decreto por el que se reforman los artículos 46, 73-IV, 76 y 105 de la Constitución Política de los Estados Unidos Mexicanos 2005.

[52] DOF, Decreto por el que se reforman los artículos 46, 76 y 105 de la Constitución Política de los Estados Unidos Mexicanos 2012.

[53] Cámara de diputados, *Proceso legislativo reforma constitucional 8 de Diciembre de 2005* www.diputados.gob.mx/LeyesBiblio/proceso/cpeum/CPEUM_163_DOF_08dic05.pdf accessed 3 October 2016.

take the power away from them in the first place. In 2005 the Senate was the best body to settle these disputes because it represented the States; in 2012, it was not for the same reason. As for the Supreme Court, in 2005 it could not settle these disputes due to the lack of a statute setting adjudication standards; in 2012, it could do so without the special statute. It is hard to believe that on both occasions the best solution possibly imaginable was to transfer the power to another branch of government.

As far-fetched as these justifications may sound, this is the kind of argument that may be given to justify the adoption of constitutional amendments. Both amendments were adopted fast track in Congress and no State Legislature opposed. The fact that the adoption of these amendments went widely unnoticed, illustrates the context of little accountability surrounding constitutional amendments. In this case, the problem is that border disputes are a present issue in Mexico. Border disputes bring questions regarding who is obliged to provide services or the benefits of social programmes, putting the communities living in these areas in situations of uncertainty.[54] Even though the amendments were supposedly adopted due to the urgency of solving three pending cases, the reality is that such disputes have remained unsolved since 1997.[55] In fact, it is not clear if the conflicts are going to be settled at all because there is no record showing the case files returned to the Supreme Court. The last record available in the Supreme Court case files database shows the files were dispatched to the Senate in 2005 in compliance with the third transitory provision of the reform decree of the same year.[56] Notably, the transitory provisions of the reform decree of 2012 did not order the remittance of the files back to the Supreme Court.[57]

B. A Constitutional Amendment to Accept the Jurisdiction of the ICC. It's a Trap!

Now consider the amendment to Article 21 to accept the jurisdiction of the ICC in 2005. In September 2000, toward the end of his term, President Zedillo signed the Rome Statute. The Senate ratified the statute on 21 June 2005,[58] a day after

[54] 'No Son De Aquí Ni Son De Allá: Ante la falta de apoyo de sus autoridades de Calakmul, Campeche, habitantes del Ejido Santa Rosa piden ayuda al gobierno de Quintana Roo' *Noticaribe* (20 March 2018) http://noticaribe.com.mx/2018/03/20/no-son-de-aqui-ni-son-de-alla-ante-la-falta-de-apoyo-de-sus-autoridades-de-calakmul-campeche-habitantes-del-ejido-santa-rosa-piden-ayuda-al-gobierno-de-quintana-roo/ accessed 13 August 2018.

[55] *Controversia Constitucional (Quintana Roo v Campeche)* [pending] SCJN 9/1997; *Controversia Constitucional (Quintana Roo v Yucatán)* [pending] SCJN 13/1997; *Controversia Constitucional (Jalisco v Colima)* [pending] SCJN 3/1998.

[56] See 'Búsqueda Temática' (*SCJN*) www2.scjn.gob.mx/ConsultaTematica/PaginasPub/TematicaPub.aspx.

[57] Decreto (n 52).

[58] The Rome statute came into force on 1 January 2006. For more information about important dates on the adoption process of the statute see Gabriel Mario Santo Villarreal, 'La Corte Penal Internacional',

enacting an amendment to Article 21 to explicitly accept the jurisdiction of the ICC as follows: 'The Federal Executive may accept the jurisdiction of the International Criminal Court, provided that he has obtained the Senate's approval on case by case basis'.[59] Like many other amendments, Congress approved this one fast track and State Legislatures did not oppose.[60]

The issue here is the reason behind explicitly recognising the jurisdiction of ICC when the constitutional system already provided a framework for the adoption and ratification of international treaties (Articles 76-I and 89-X). Article 120 of the Rome Statute explicitly prohibits reservations: every State member recognises the jurisdiction of the ICC because the very objective of the statute is to guarantee the enforcement of international justice, thus the creation of such a court.[61] The timing of the amendment raises questions regarding its impact on the ratification of the Rome Statute. As it was enacted a day before the ratification of the Rome Statute it is not clear, for instance, if the ratification is valid.

The political convenience of passing this constitutional amendment is clear. Mexico could ratify the Statute and get the diplomatic and political benefits of doing so and, at the same time, retain the possibility of shielding the Mexican government from the jurisdiction of the ICC if necessary. Is the constitutional reform of Article 21 a reservation to the statute?[62] What are the effects of such a constitutional provision on the ratification of the treaty? Did Mexico actually ratify the statute? Is this an unconstitutional constitutional amendment? These are questions that remain to be answered. What we know is that the jurisdiction of the ICC raised national sovereignty concerns that made countries like the US not ratify the Rome Statute. Mexico, in fact, shared these concerns. Yet the Mexican government found a way to circumvent the diplomatic costs of not ratifying. The congressional records of the amendment to Article 21 show explicit statements

(*Centro de Documentación, Información y Análisis de la Cámara de Diputados*, 2010) www.diputados.gob.mx/sedia/sia/spe/SPE-ISS-10-10.pdf accessed 16 October 2016.

[59] Free translation. CPEUM, Art 21.

[60] First, the Senate passed the amendment the day after the legislative committee presented its report (14 December 2002). Then, 2 years later, the chamber of deputies passed the amendment by 347 votes the same day the legislative committee presented its report (9 December 2004). Finally, it was approved by the vote of 20 State Legislatures – without opposition – on 4 May 2005 and published by the Executive on 20 June, the day before the Senate's ratification of the Rome Statute. See Cámara de Diputados, *Proceso legislativo reforma constitucional 20 de Junio de 2005* www.diputados.gob.mx/LeyesBiblio/proceso/cpeum/CPEUM_161_DOF_20jun05.pdf accessed 14 October 2016.

[61] The preamble of the Rome Statute states: 'The States Parties to this Statute, (…) Determined to these ends and for the sake of present and future generations, to establish an independent permanent International Criminal Court in relationship with the United Nations system, with jurisdiction over the most serious crimes of concern to the international community as a whole, (…) **Resolved** to guarantee lasting respect for and the enforcement of international justice, (…)'. Rome Statute of the International Criminal Court (adopted 17 July 1998, opened for signature 17 July 1998) UNTS 2187.

[62] See Manuel Becerra Ramirez, 'México Ratifica El Estatuto de Roma Que Crea La Corte Penal Internacional, Después de Reformar La Constitución' (2006) 1 *Anuario Mexicano de Derecho Internacional* https://revistas.juridicas.unam.mx/index.php/derecho-internacional/article/view/186 accessed 16 October 2016.

explaining how the wording of the amendment dealt with the national sovereignty concerns while internationally sending a clear message of Mexico's true commitment to human rights.[63]

In hindsight, in both examples the amendments served very specific interests that are not in line with the reasons given to justify them. In the case of the power to settle inter-state border disputes, the justification was clearly not the social urgency of solving the pending cases or to ensure the separation of powers, as we can see from the fact that the cases remain unsolved. As for the amendment to Article 21, it was precisely by the time of its adoption that drug violence in Mexico started to break out and multiply.[64] Only a year after, in his inauguration address, Felipe Calderón – accompanied by the military – would declare the *war on drugs*. This consisted in the militarisation of the national security strategy. President Calderon appointed military members (licensed or retired) as heads of public security bodies and deployed thousands of military elements to carry out public security functions.[65] This national security strategy entailed terrible consequences. International bodies, such as the Interamerican Commission of Human Rights, have declared 'the disappearance of persons in large swaths of Mexican territory has reached critical levels' and 'the existence of a practice of forced disappearances at the hands of agents of the State'.[66] All this has been systematically denied by the federal government as 'isolated incidents'.[67] Crucially, this is a subject matter that would fall under the jurisdiction of the ICC on crimes against humanity.[68] Yet, it is unclear what would be the effect of Article 21 of the Constitution should the ICC decided to open an investigation. In such a case, the government could potentially argue that Mexico did not ratify the Rome Statute and dodge the jurisdiction of the ICC. In any case, the amendment was advertised as a commitment for the protection of human rights.

[63] See Cámara de Diputados (n 61).

[64] Luis González Placencia, '10 Años de Guerra: Breve Recuento' www.animalpolitico.com/blogueros-phronesis/2016/11/29/10-anos-guerra-breve-recuento/ accessed 1 December 2016. ('En ese contexto, el florecimiento de los cárteles no tuvo precedente. El resultado de la errática política criminal de Vicente Fox multiplicó los grupos criminales y diversificó sus negocios. Algunos de estos grupos se radicalizaron hacia el terror y pusieron su inversión en el secuestro y la extorsión basados en el miedo provocado a la población y en la debilidad de autoridades y policías locales a las que con frecuencia utilizaron – y utilizan – para recaudar sus *impuestos*.')

[65] Comisión Mexican de Defensa y Protección de los Derechos Humanos, '10 años de Guerra: ni se conmemoran ni se olvida', *Animal Político* (Mexico city, 29 November 2016) www.animalpolitico.com/blogueros-verdad-justicia-reparacion/2016/11/28/10-anos-guerra-se-conmemoran-se-olvidan/ accessed 29 November 2016.

[66] Organization of the American States, *Democracy for Peace, Security, and Development* (2009) http://www.oas.org/en/iachr/media_center/PReleases/2016/023.asp accessed 17 October 2016.

[67] Alma E Muñoz, 'Grave Crisis de Derechos En México: CIDH; El Gobierno Refuta Conclusión', *La Jornada* (Mexico city, 5 October 2015) www.jornada.unam.mx/2015/10/03/politica/005n1pol accessed 1 December 2016.

[68] Article 7 of the Rome Statute states: 'For the purpose of this Statute, "crime against humanity" means any of the following acts when committed as part of a widespread or systematic attack directed against any civilian population, with knowledge of the attack: (…) (i) Enforced disappearance of persons'. Rome Statute (n 47).

While in other latitudes these amendments would have been widely covered by the media, they went widely unnoticed in Mexico. This situation only illustrates the context of little accountability surrounding constitutional amendments.

It should be noted that the potential and actual problematic consequences of the amendments analysed here are not necessarily created by the fact that the Constitution is frequently amended. Rather, the real danger is the possibility of exercising unchecked power simply because it allows avoiding accountability. The consequences of being able to get away with political artifices such as the ones described above vary in their gravity. For instance, in the case of the jurisdiction of the ICC, the avoidance of accountability could entail dodging an international trial for crimes against humanity. As for the inter-state border dispute adjudication power, although the consequence is not as grave (criminally speaking), it still leaves entire communities in a situation of uncertainty regarding the provision of basic services and social programmes.

V. Conclusion. Lessons from Mexico's Constitutional Amendment (Non)-Difficulty

In theory, formal amendments signal that the people have spoken. Yet, as shown in the preceding sections, the constitutional amendment reality in Mexico illustrates how this is not necessarily always the case. The permanence of the old practices (ie, centralisation of decision making and party discipline) analysed in Section III, show that new constitutional solutions more often than not, are far from being the result of sustained and considered support or deliberative processes reflecting the nation-wide political consensus.[69]

Mexico's constitutional amendment (non)difficulty, in fact, challenges the scholarly assumption about constitutional amendment rules as effective devices to protect the people's fundamental commitments or *higher law*.[70] It also underscores the limitations that constitutional designers face, particularly regarding the question of formal amendment difficulty as a means to ensuring the quality of constitution-amending processes.[71] Furthermore, it questions the need for distinguishing between higher/ordinary law and constitutional/ordinary politics.

[69] cf Ackerman (n 1) 85; and Lutz (n 1).

[70] For a text discussing the different functions of constitutional amendment rules see Rosalind Dixon, 'Constitutional Amendment Rules: A Comparative Perspective' in Tom Ginsburg and Rosalind Dixon (eds) *Comparative Constitutional Law* (Cheltenham, UK, Edward Elgar, 2011) 96, 98.

[71] See eg Lutz (n 1); Raymond Ku, 'Consensus of the Governed: The Legitimacy of Constitutional Change' (1995) 64 *Fordham Law Review* 535; Jon Elster, 'Deliberation and Constitution making' in Jon Elster (ed), *Deliberative Democracy* (Cambridge University Press, 1998) 111; Arend Lijphart, *Patterns of Democracy: Government Forms and Performance in Thirty-Six Countries* (New Haven, Yale University Press, 1999); Roger D Congleton, Birgitta Swedenborg and ebrary, Inc (eds), *Democratic Constitutional Design and Public Policy: Analysis and Evidence* (MIT Press, 2006) http://site.ebrary.com/lib/yale/Doc?id=10173627 accessed 10 December 2016.

If one understands constitutional change as the result of political entrenchment, such distinctions become of little use to explain formal (or informal) constitutional change. Focusing on the amendment provisions obscures the importance of those actors in charge of putting those rules into play. Instead, it is crucial to understand the political dynamics behind the formal change. As argued in Section III amendment difficulty and non-difficulty is the result of political decisions and conditions that have little to do with the design of the amendment rules. In fact, what the Mexican case shows is that a great deal of amendment difficulty goes beyond institutional design. Amendment difficulty largely depends on elements that are determined by the constitutional culture, such as political conditions, political decisions, political conventions and practices.[72] In Mexico, formal constitutional change dynamics in the last 30 years have been determined by the restructure of Mexican politics and by the permanence of practices that became part of the constitutional culture during the PRI regime. Accordingly, like in the old days, the constitutional amendment mechanism remains as a feasible option for political entrenchment.

Finally, in light of the analysis made in Section IV, it should be noted that the use of the amendment mechanism as means of political entrenchment is not problematic per se. That is to say, amendment reality in Mexico is not problematic only because the Constitution is frequently amended. Rather, as analysed in Section III, the constitutional amendment reality in Mexico is problematic because the permanence of old practices allows formal constitutional change to be the result of unchecked exercises of power.

[72] This, in fact, would be in line with Ginsburg and Melton's thesis in that constitutional amendment relies less on institutional design than in amendment culture. See Ginsburg and Melton, (n 9). In a similar vein see also Vicki C Jackson, 'The (Myth of Un)amendability of the US Constitution and the Democratic Component of Constitutionalism' (2015) 13 *International Journal of Constitutional Law* 575.

12

Subnational Constitutionalism and Constitutional Change in Brazil: The Impact of Federalism in Constitutional Stability

BRENO BAÍA MAGALHÃES*

I. Subnational Constitutionalism and Constitutional Change in Brazil

According to numerous Brazilian lawyers, it is difficult to amend our Constitution.[1] However, this is a classification that requires a thorough investigation and that is not simply justified with abstractions established by the constitutional amendment procedural rules alone.[2] The Brazilian Constitution, until January 2018, had been amended 99 times in its 29 years of existence, which equals an amendment rate of approximately 3.4 amendments per year. Donald Lutz argues that a high amendment rate (higher than 1.25) indicates at least two things: (1) that the Constitution may be about to be replaced, and/or (2) that these constant changes show a disbelief in popular sovereignty (which, consequently, affects its rigidity).[3] In the case of Brazil, that would mean that our current constitution would be close to an end and/or that our constitutionalism is weak and defeasible.

* Master and Doctor in Law by Universidade Federal do Pará (UFPA). brenobaiamag@gmail.com. Professor of Universidade Federal do Pará (UFPA).

[1] Rosah Russomano, *curso de direito constitucional*, 5th edn (Freitas Bastos, 1997) 12; José Cretella jr, *elementos de direito constitucional*, 3rd edn (RT, 2000) 23; Alexandre Moraes, *direito constitucional*, 18th edn (Atlas, 2005) 05 e José Afonso da Silva, *curso de direito constitucional positive*, 32nd edn (Malheiros, 2006) 42.

[2] Astrid Lorenz, 'How to measure constitutional rigidity: four concepts and two alternatives' (2005) 17 *Journal of Theoretical Politics* 339, 343.

[3] Donald Lutz, 'Toward a Theory of Constitutional Amendment' in Sanford Levinson (eds), *Responding to Imperfection* (PUP, 1995) 260.

It is highly unlikely that a constitutional replacement will soon occur in Brazil. Several other factors, in addition to the constitutional amendment rate, are indicative of constitutional endurance.[4] A certain degree of flexibility in amendment rules is one of them. Thus, the high amendment rate of the Brazilian Constitution could be something more than a warning about a possible constitutional replacement, but it still leaves open the question about the value of our constitutionalism.

Among the many factors that may contribute to such a high constitutional change rate in Brazil, we have identified an element that has been rarely explored: absent constitutionalism values in subnational constitutions.

Following a tradition started in the 1891 Constitution, the current Brazilian Constitution granted to subnational entities the ability to self-organise themselves through state constitutions (Article 25[5]). Because it is a constituent power derived from the original, the federal constitution mandatorily imposes limitations. Thus, one of Brazil's constitutionalism main issues is to find the space that can be occupied by state constitutions in the federal system, that is, what rules the state constituents must necessarily follow and what rules they can create freely.

States' ability to organise themselves is something existent in all federations; however, the political decision to allocate such capacity through constitutional documents implies that such documents may be imbued with constitutionalism values. The larger the self-organisation space given to the state constituent power is, the greater the chances of identifying the traits of constitutionalism virtues. On the other hand, a decrease in the organisational capacity of subnational units through rules arising from the federal constitution may be an indication that state constitutions do not follow the principles of constitutionalism, although this does not mean that federalism principles are rejected.

The relationship between subnational constitutionalism and federalism is not necessary because a state does not cease to be federal if it does not allow subnational units to be organised through constitutions.[6] However, the choice of state

[4] Zachary Elkins, Tom Ginsburg, James Melton, *The Endurance of National Constitutions* (Cambridge University Press, 2009) 101.

[5] Art 25. 'The states are organised and governed by the constitutions and laws they may adopt, in accordance with the principles of this Constitution.'

[6] John Dinan, 'The Consequences of Drafting Constitutions for Constituent States in Federal Countries' In Michel Seymour; Alain-G Gagnon (eds), *Multinational Federalism* (Palgrave Macmillan, 2012) 231. As an example, Belgium, India, Nigeria and Canada. In Brazil, municipalities are subnational entities (Art 18), which can self-organise themselves through organic laws (Art 29). Regina Nery Ferrari argues in favour of a constitutional nature of organic laws, only because of its formalities. Her conclusion is based primarily on its alleged rigidity, which must be approved in two rounds of voting by 2/3 of the House of Councilors. She correlates therefore higher quorums of creation and change with the hierarchical superiority of the legal standard. Another feature is the non-necessity of executive sanction for the approval of the organic law. Finally, she argues in favour of a constitutional nature because it is the statute dealing with the organisation of public institutions in the municipality. Regina Maria Macedo Nery Ferrari, *Direito Municipal*, 4th edn (Revista dos Tribunais, 2014) 103.

constitutionalism implies at least that values and virtues inherent in constitutionalism political ideal are present in the subnational constitutions.

Among the values of classic constitutionalism, we can acknowledge the existence of legal rules that constrain political power and the protection of constitutional rights. A constitution committed to the ideals of constitutionalism offers citizens the possibility to oppose government insurgencies, ensuring spheres of individual freedom and creating procedural rules to make the division of power more efficient. A subnational constitution, although termed a 'constitution', may not meet those requirements. On such occasions, not only it does not create original and diverse institutional rules capable of making the subnational government more efficient but also those constitutions of subnational entities do not impose limitations on the political power of local and federal agents.

The space left for state constitutions in Brazil is greatly reduced by the amount of federal constitutional rules of mandatory imitation and because of the Supreme Court's interpretation of the federal constitution, which has expanded those sets of rules to include the organisational structure of the federal government. These rules undermine subnational entities' degree of autonomy, but they do not contradict the federal character of the Brazilian state. However, the compromise of a subnational entity's autonomy governed by a constitution may indicate the absence of constitutional values.

Local polities' inability to dispose of subnational constitutions as a means of controlling the political power of the federal government or as a platform for the discussion of matters regarding constitutional politics entails the overloading and centralisation of political disputes in the federal constitution. Thus, new institutional experiments, new constitutional rights and changes in the policies involving federal entities will necessarily suppose the proposition of amendments to the federal constitution first. Finally, as a mere imitation of the federal constitution, the subnational constitution does not serve as a veto to such policies, even when they bring about harm to subnational entities (decrease in political power, financial constraints, etc).

This chapter will argue, normatively and not as a simple description, that the absence of constitutionalism values in subnational constitutions (the capacity of a polity to make independent decisions based on self-restraint and the idea that the regional political community can engage in equal footing disputes with the federal government) may be one of the reasons[7] why our federal constitution is very often amended (the national constitution is the main forum to discuss political and social changes), a constitutional feature that, in turn, might point toward a reinterpretation of the supposed rigidity of Brazil's federal constitution.

The supposed rigidity, legislative procedure for approval and organisational matter would be enough to define a constitutional document for Regina Ferrari, regardless of the fulfilment of constitutionalism values; the same goes for state constitutions, as we shall see next.

[7] Not the only one or the most important.

II. State Constitutionalism in Brazil: Formal and Substantive Analyses

A. Labels are Enough: State Constitutionalism Reviewed by Constitutional Scholars

Brazilian constitutional scholars tend to attribute only a formal constitution feature to state constitutions; that is, they identify its existence simply by the shape and structure that it takes and not through the functions, values and virtues[8] it should play in regional politics, leaving aside the normative question about compliance with those values.

Anna Candida Ferraz,[9] for instance, believes that the derived constituent power differs from the original one for being limited and complementary. According to Ferraz, in a federation, only a constitutional document could allocate power among the set of subnational institutions (state legislative, executive and judiciary), so she argues that the autonomy of federal entities can only be guaranteed by a subnational constitutional document. Although the entitlement of the power to create a state constitution resides in the local polity, it will not always be able to exercise such power. In normal conditions, it will usually be created by an assembly or a constitutional convention, but it may also be created by anomalous agents, whose creative legitimacy would be indirect (as tacitly ordered by the people of the federal state constituent power).[10]

According to Ferraz, the last scenario occurred when the Brazilian Constitution of 1937 determined that state constitutions were to be imposed by governors and years later when the Federal Constitutional Amendment (FCA) nº 01 to the 1969 Constitution, issued during Brazil's military regime, established the automatic incorporation of its provisions in state constitutions.

As a distinctive formal feature, Anna Ferraz suggests the supremacy of the state constitution with respect to other state laws and notes that it has a central role in the organisation and regulation of governmental structure and its limits.[11]

[8] About constitutionalism virtues, cf Richard Albert, 'The Cult of Constitutionalism' (2012) 39 *Florida State University Law Review* 393.

[9] Anna Candida da Cunha Ferraz, *Poder Constituinte do Estado-Membro* (Revista dos Tribunais, 1979) 61–80.

[10] The exercise of the subsequent constituent power in an anomalous manner is a way of justifying the authoritarian provision of the 1969 Brazilian Constitution. According to Article 200, subnational states were not obliged to adapt their rules but to *incorporate* the amended federal rules. Despite agreeing that this rule would be a measure that limits state autonomy to the point of its elimination, Anna Candida and Manoel Gonçalves consider anomalous agents as a secondary power, and the fact that this decision originates in the federal constitution makes those limitations constitutionally possible. Ferraz (n 8) 103–04.

[11] Ferraz (n 8) 110–29.

Gabriel Ivo,[12] on the other hand, may have expressed more accurately how Brazilian scholars describe state constitutionalism: as the mere exercise of a limited power to organise local authorities. The subordinate nature of state constitutions requires that they follow the organisational model established by the rules directed at the federal government. Given that subnational unities were already established before the enactment of the current Federal Constitution (1988), what is left for state constitutions is only the power to change (adapt) their pre-existing constitutions. It is fair to say that Ivo suggests that the principles to be followed by state constitutions do not mean the reproduction or imitation of the federal model; however, he acknowledges that states' constituent power to establish political bodies must follow the federal design.[13]

Understood as a species of the genus *instituted constituent power*, the subsequent and derived constituent power is given the task of organising the entities that make up the federal state in a limited and compromised fashion. This concept, developed by Manoel Gonçalves Ferreira Filho, is now classic in Brazilian law but does not delve in much more detail about the consequences of a federal constitution that adopts state constitutionalism as a measure of the self-organisation of subnational entities.[14]

Although Brazilian scholars ascribe the name 'Constitution' to the rules governing the autonomy of subnational entities, they do not make clear the consequences stemming from such characterisation. That is, they do not make a big deal about the political decision of the federal constitution to assign state self-organisation through a constitution and the impact it has on the exercise of state autonomy. All of them emphasise the worrying centraliser accent of the Brazilian federation;[15] however, most constitutional lawyers are satisfied in identifying a constitution through its formal features, particularly its origin, that is, they are concerned with the analysis of the consequent and derived constituent power but neglect other factors and the Supreme Court case law.

What is important for the characterisation of a state constitution is its formal process of creating or changing its rules, regardless of their subject and the fulfilment or not of its power-constraining functions. To put it simply, 'constitutional' is the rule created by a particular process, regardless of its subject or content. The study of state constitutions based on an analysis placing their supposed rigidity as its central element blurs the distinction between substantive constitutional functions and formally constitutional rules. This kind of analysis may also show that Brazilian scholars may be willing to accept the existence of state constitutions without constitutionalism.

[12] Gabriel Ivo, *Constituição Estadual* (Max Limonad 1997) 99–113.

[13] Ivo (n 12) 128–56.

[14] Manoel Ferreira Filho, *Poder Constituinte*, 3rd edn (Saraiva, 1999) 109.

[15] Raul Machado Horta, *Direito Constitucional*, 4th edn (Del Rey, 2003) 71 and Oswaldo Trigueiro, *Direito Constitucional Estadual* (Forense, 1980) 62.

B. Constitutions without Constitutionalism: A Paradox?

Formal analysis of the constitutions made by Brazilian authors seems to show that subnational constitutions are enforced independently of their purposes as political documents, that is, the analyses usually do not cover issues relating to the possible purposes and values that state constitutions can meet in the framework of Brazil's constitutionalism and federalism. Thus, two features serve to identify constitutions: their origin (subsequent and derived constituent power) and form (supreme constitutional rules in a subnational space).[16]

On the other hand, the substantive feature of a constitution (national or subnational) is related to the upholding of a political ideal: constitutionalism. A constitution adheres to this political ideal when it upholds substantive principles that limit and shape future government activity. Modern constitutions are concerned with the relationship between the fundamental organs of the state and its institutions, and such a relationship creates a set of limits that allows the freedom of the citizens to prevail and government activity to develop in a more efficient manner. Therefore, a constitution embedded with the ideals of constitutionalism is about limited power.[17]

Although this is not the place to discuss the key subject matters to be included in a constitution and the degree of adherence to a specific programme it entails, the legal rules limiting government, the protection of constitutional rights and the establishment of institutions that serve as a conformation for the exercise of power are the substantive features of a constitution.[18] Thus, from a normative point of view, the absence of constitutionalism values means the absence of a constitution. The Constitution, in this perspective, is a landmark for government policy action.[19]

[16] Elkins (n 4) 38–39 distinguishes between Constitution-as-function (a set of legal rules that meet certain purposes) and Constitution-as-form (written documents that may or may not fulfil such purposes). The distinction is not merely semantic in normative analysis of the Constitution because their main concern is not with the universal concept of Constitution, but with the functions that it must fulfil in a liberal democracy. Thus, a written constitution whose text is not able to frame power relations and impose limits to it shall not be a constitution in its essence or existence, even though termed as one. Karl Loewenstein would classify the latter as nominal or semantic constitutions, establishing degrees of normativity. Loewenstein's classification intends to explain if the normative text of a constitution is in tune or not with the control of government activity, ranging from situations where the government incorporates the Constitution in their practices (normative constitution) to situations where the Constitutions are mere oppression instruments of autocratic governments that use it to stay in power (semantic constitution). Karl Loewenstein, *Teoría de la Constitución* (Ariel 1970) 217–20. We are not claiming that the subnational constitutions in Brazil are semantic, but it is important to show that the existence of formal documents labelled as constitutions does not mean it supports the liberal values of modern constitutionalism.

[17] András Sajó, *Limiting Government* (Central European University Press, 1999) 01–2.

[18] The limitations imposed on governmental action created by constitutions are not necessarily opposed to democracy, since they not only play a negative role (limited power to prevent a course of action) but also have a positive side that enables a democratic government to provide effective means for the distribution and organisation of government functions. Stephen Holmes, *Passions and Constraint* (UCP, 1995) 134.

[19] Jon Elster, *Ulises desatado* (Gedisa, 2002) 122–23.

Formally, therefore, we consider the existence of a constitutional document when we identify a legal written document formally called a 'constitution', edited by a constituent power and that can be altered by qualified amendment procedures; however, paraphrasing Okoth-Ogendo,[20] this does not prevent us from assessing when a constitution does not share the ideals of constitutionalism.

A state constitution embedded with the ideals James Gardner[21] labelled *subnational constitutionalism*, therefore, needs to meet at least three cumulative conditions: (1) it must have a political community that identifies itself as an owner of self-organising powers; (2) it ensures a degree of self-government that allows the polity to make significant decisions about its political institutions and about its personal lives, and (3) the polity should commit itself to self-restraint under the rule of law through the adoption of a written constitution.[22]

However, there is not a logical connection between the defence of constitutionalism and of a federalism that gives subnational entities the power of institutionalisation that serves as a force capable of assigning polities sufficient political means to constrain (by constitutions), particularly federal powers (contestatory federalism).[23]

All federal systems share institutional arrangements that enable the connection between constituent units horizontally and vertically with the federal level. However, such arrangements can vary profoundly in the combination of institutional rules because they respond to different purposes or needs.[24] A federal model may not have as its focus the institutionalisation of a political community by the absorption of its cultural values; the federation could be focused on the creation of an institutional arrangement that effectively implements policies aimed at the cooperation between subnational unities in an interventionist welfare state.[25]

The connection between federalism and subnational constitutionalism also weakens in cases where there is a complete availability of recourse to national policy as a vehicle to address issues of social and political relevance to the subnational polity.[26] The difficulty and the political cost to reform the federal constitution in the US, for instance, transfers to subnational entities the burden of achieving the objectives of state policies in their own constitutions.

[20] HWO Okoth-Ogendo 'Constitutions without constitutionalism: reflections on an African political paradox' in Douglas Greenberg, Stanley Katz N, Melanie Beth Oliviero et al (eds), *Constitutionalism & democracy: The American Council of Learned Societies Comparative Constitutionalism Papers Oxford* (OUP, 1993) 79. The author identifies a paradox in the constitutions of the African continent; they are committed to the ideal of a written constitution but reject the classical notion of constitutionalism because they do not fulfil its main functions in a liberal democratic theory.

[21] James A Gardner 'In Search of Subnational Constitutionalism' *European Constitutional Law Review* 04 (2008) 327. Also, cf Jonathan L Marshfield 'Models of Subnational Constitutionalism' *Penn State Law Review* 115 (2011) 1.157.

[22] John Dinah arrives at a similar set of conditions. Dinah (n 6) 232.

[23] Gardner (n 20) 328.

[24] Arthur Benz; Jorg Broschek 'Federal Dynamics: Introduction' in Arthur Benz and Jorg Broschek *Federal Dynamics: Continuity, Change and the Varieties of Federalism* (OUP, 2013) 02–4.

[25] Gilberto Bercovici, *Dilemas do Estado Federal Brasileiro* (Livraria do Advogado, 2004) 56–57.

[26] Gardner (n 20) 337.

Thus, the decision to incorporate subnational constitutionalism is not an exclusionary choice between the political ideal of constitutionalism and another type of political regime. However, it must be justified by different reasons from the ones used to justify the selection of constitutionalism as the political regime of a federal state. Therefore, the question to be answered in countries such as Brazil that decided to adopt subnational constitutionalism is as follows: what are the normative justifications for decentralising responsibility to structure and limit the subnational government through constitutions? Depending on the federal system created (which may not be of a contestatory type), different results may be achieved with the incorporation of subnational constitutionalism.[27] Therefore, only a substantive and normative analysis can identify the existence or not of subnational constitutionalism in Brazil.

III. Subnational Constitutional Space and the Purpose of Brazilian Federalism

Subnational constitutions, although limited by the parameters set by the federal order, differ in content and scope to accommodate political and cultural goals and specific governmental state institutions.[28] The degree of variation of such subnational constitutional space depends on three factors: the arrangement of the creation of the federation, the symmetry or asymmetry of the federal system and the purposes of the federation.

Federations formed through the unification of pre-existing entities (federation by aggregation) generally provide greater latitude to subnational units than federations created by the transformation of a formerly unitary state (devolutionary federalism) because in the former, they already operate within an institutionally demarcated practice. Entities organised in the first case may have more bargaining power to ensure greater space in the demarcation of their jurisdiction and their constitutional institutionalisation of power before entering the federation; however,[29] a dismembered unitary state may experience difficulty in offering more powers beyond those strictly necessary to achieve the purposes of the federation, which in turn might lead to a suppression of the formulation of demands and bargains of the entities that will soon be formed, which usually end up with residual powers.

A symmetrical federal system that ensures the same power to all units does not allow subnational units to exercise greater self-government space; however, there might be cases where the asymmetry in powers might be relevant.[30]

[27] Marshfield (n 20) 1.165–1.166.

[28] Alan Tarr, 'Explaining Sub-national Constitutional Space' *Penn State Law Review* 115 (2011) 1.113.

[29] Tarr (n 26) 1.135–1.136.

[30] The choice of federalism, for instance, in countries that need to accommodate ethno-national claims of geographically concentrated minorities reduces some issues that could lead to a conflict in the

Finally, the federation purpose may also influence the extent of the subnational constitutional space to be filled. Some federations are designed to provide expression to the ethnic diversity of a population. In such cases, more space for the development of the units would be recommended.[31] If the federation has been created for the protection of a common national identity or to promote administrative efficiency (entities responsible for implementing federal public policy), the subnational units would have less range of powers and less constitutional space.[32] In the latter case, the subnational entities do not constitute a regional government to serve as a stage for discussions about the interests of the local political community before taking it to the national level.[33]

Federalism in Brazil was not set up to respond to deep social fissures among different races, cultures, or religions. Particularly after 1988, there was a political consensus that regional inequalities and the concentration of wealth in some regions of the country were the most important risks of the federal structure. The federation and, consequently, the Federal Constitution of 1988 were marked by federally centralised public policies and limitations on subnational freedom to innovate institutionally through their own constitutions.[34]

The 1988 Constitution gave broad administrative and legislative authority to the Federal Union (Articles 21 and 22). On the other hand, it offered limited institutional opportunities for subnational units to exercise veto powers on the decision-making process in the federal arena. In addition to the wide legislative powers, which cover the main issues related to public policy in the entire country, the federal government has a large capacity to start the legislative procedure (Article 61, § 1) and to control the agenda of the legislative power (Articles 62 and 64 § 1).[35]

This uniqueness of the Brazilian federal arrangement is justified by the emphasis on agency cooperation among entities that provide the means to implement policies created by the federal constitution in order to overcome

national political arena, where national majorities could make unacceptable policies for that portion of the country's population. In addition to geographically established ethnic disputes, federalism allows an ethnic group (considered a *minority* only nationally) to exercise self-rule differently than it would on the national level. Donald L Horowitz 'The Many Uses of Federalism' *Drake Law Review* 55 (2007) 958 and JR Mallory 'The Politics of Constitutional Change', *Law and Contemporary Problems* 45 (1982) 53, James A Gardner 'Federalism and Subnational Political Community' *Harvard Law Review* 127 (2014) 154.

[31] Something that can be better achieved, eg, by assigning asymmetry powers among subnational entities.

[32] Tarr (n 26) 1.137–1.138.

[33] Horowitz (n 28) 958–62.

[34] Celina Souza 'Federal Republic of Brazil' in John Kincaid and Alan Tarr (eds), *Constitutional origins, structure, and change in federal democracies* (McGill-Queens University Press, 2005) 78–82.

[35] On the executive power success to impose its agenda before the National Congress and on the discipline and party cohesion of the House of Representatives (one of the main factors of such presidential success) in the 1988 Constitution, cf Argelina Figueiredo; Fernando Limongi, *Executivo e Legislativo na nova ordem constitucional*, 2nd edn (FGV, 2001).

Table 1 Legislative powers, selected on public policy in the 1988 Constitution

Articles of the Constitution	**Areas of Public Policy in the 1988 Constitution**
Article 21: private material powers of the Federal Union	IX – develop and implement national and regional plans to order territory and economic and social development. XI – (…) telecommunications services, under the law (…). XII – operate, directly or through authorisation, concession or permission: (a) radio broadcasting services, and sounds and images; (b) the electric power services and facilities and the energetic exploitation of watercourses, in conjunction with the states where the potential hydropower is; (c) air and aerospace navigation and airport infrastructure; (d) railway and waterway transport services (…); (e) interstate and international road passenger transport services; XIX – establish a national system of water resources management (…). XX – establish directives for urban development, including housing, basic sanitation and urban transport.
Article 22: Private legislative power of the Federal Union	Union I – civil, commercial, criminal, procedural, electoral, agrarian, maritime, aeronautical, space and labour. IV – water, energy, IT, telecommunications and broadcasting. V – postal service. IX – guidelines of the national transport policy. X – system of ports, lacustrine navigation, river, sea, air and aerospace. XI – traffic and transport. XVI – (…) national employment system and conditions for the exercise of professions. XXIII – social security. XXIV – directives and bases of national education. XXVII – general rules for bidding and contracting, in all forms, to direct public administrations, local and founding of the Union, States, Federal District and Municipalities (…).
Article 24: competing legislative powers of all federal entities	I – tax, financial, penitentiary, economic and urban. VI – forests, hunting, fishing, fauna, nature conservation, soil protection and natural resources, environmental protection and pollution control. IX – education, culture, education, sports, science, technology, research, development and innovation. XII – social security, protection and defence of health. XIV – protection and social integration of people with disabilities. XV – protection of childhood and youth.

Adapted from Arrechte (2012)

regional inequalities.[36] This so-called cooperative federalism emphasises the exercise of concurrent jurisdiction in which each entity has a degree of participation in the implementation of public policies, aimed at a common result in the country's interest. The common political decision is taken at the federal level (National Congress) and is later adapted and performed autonomously by each federal entity.[37]

Brazilian cooperative federalism thus assigns little room for the creation of public policy to be developed by states because they are obliged to follow national decisions. The space granted for differences is only in the manner of their implementation. Moreover, since they do not accommodate ethnic disputes or express the bargaining power of local political communities to obtain more control over central decisions made at the National Congress, state constitutions in Brazil will not have a wide range of self-organisation. A wider constitutional subnational space could endanger the purposes of our federation, which are to standardise the decision on the establishment and financing of public policies and make sure to decentralise their implementation.[38] We should identify next how such a feature of cooperative federalism can affect states' constitutional space.

A. Subnational Federalism Features and Subnational Constitutionalism

A subnational constitution that embraces the ideals of constitutionalism, albeit limited by the principles of the federal constitution, must concede wide latitude to exercise some form of government control to local political communities. The control of government power shaped by state constitutions can be expressed in at least three ways: (a) in the various ways in which the subnational entities can create institutions of political power distribution (self-government); (b) in the creation of mechanisms to control governmental power of other state entities and mainly of the central power; and (c) in the establishment of a system of local constitutional rights, which not only provides a communitarian identification but also represents a means for people to secure their freedoms before local and central governments. By exclusion, a constitution without constitutionalism will not present any of these features. We will examine each of them next.

i. The Self-government of Brazilian State Constitutions

Since the promulgation of the first republican constitution[39] in Brazil, there have been debates about the extension of the now traditional constitutional rule,

[36] Gilberto Bercovici, *Desigualdades Regionais, Estado e Constituição* (Max Limonad, 2003) 149.
[37] Bercovici (n 34) 151.
[38] Marta Arretche, *Democracia, federalismo e centralização no Brasil* (FGV, 2012) 16.
[39] Art 63, da constituição de 1891.

which provides that there are principles of the federal constitution that must be followed by state constitutions.[40]

In our current constitution, the so-called 'sensitive constitutional principles' (*princípios constitucionais sensíveis*) represent the set of rules (Article 37, VII) that unequivocally limit the activity of the state constituent powers. Those principles generically intend to ensure that subnational unities would create republican and democratic institutions, respect human rights and guarantee municipal autonomy. Violations of said principles, moreover, can also give the Federal Union leeway to temporarily intervene in the state's autonomy.

The 'established constitutional principles' (*princípios constitucionais estabelecidos*), on the other hand, are not organised in a single constitutional article, as are the previous ones, but are scattered throughout the federal constitution and include rules that anticipate provisions that the state constitution necessarily must duplicate. As examples, we can mention rules regarding the administrative structure of the state (Article 37) and the organisation of powers, such as the rules governing the state's judiciary power and the rules that states must follow for the election of State Deputies.

The third category of principles, labelled by José Afonso da Silva[41] as 'extensible constitutional principles', encompasses rules that while originally directed at federal institutions, must also be analogically extended to states. Although there is no evidence in the 1988 Constitution that such principles should be reproduced in state constitutions, the Supreme Court has extended obligatory federal constitutional rules to state constitutions through the so-called 'principle of symmetry'.[42]

After analysing 174 Direct Actions of Unconstitutionality (DAU) filed between October 1988 and January 2008, proposing to assess the constitutionality of state laws (47), state constitutions (77) and through the free search in the case law of the Supreme Court by the term 'symmetry' (50), Marcelo Araújo found out that there are specific areas, all related to the separation of powers, that attract the symmetric model required by the Supreme Court.

Most cases related to the application of the principle of symmetry may be included in the category of controversial cases about legislative process. Initially, the court ruled that there was no requirement for the reproduction of the federal legislative process model (DAU 56),[43] but soon after, the Supreme Court changed its opinion on the subject[44] to determine the necessity that rules of the state

[40] Arts 25 da constituição de 1988 e 11 do ADCT.

[41] Silva (n 1) 611. The author, however, suggests that the 1988 Constitution did not reproduce such a set of principles, but at no time does he analyse the Supreme Court case law to prove his point.

[42] Virgílio Afonso da Silva, 'A Strange Kind of Symmetry and the End of Subnational Constitutionalism in Brazil. World Congress of Constitutional Law' (2014) *Oslo Workshop* 2, Subnational Constitutions in Federal and Quasi-Federal Constitutional States; and Marcelo Labanca Corrêa Araújo, *Jurisdição Constitucional e Federação* (Campus Elsevier, 2009) 38–39.

[43] Ruled in 1989, months after the promulgation of the Constitution.

[44] DAU 1201.

Table 2 Themes related to the principle of symmetry according to the supreme court

Thematic area		Number of DAU Proposed	%
1	Invasion of initiative powers in the legislative process	90	51.7%
2	Duties and powers of executive power	46	26.3%
3	Legislature power structure	14	8%
4	Courts of state accounts structure	11	6%
5	Judiciary power structure and competence	11	6%
6	Bodies essential to justice (District Attorney, Public Defender, etc)	2	1%
7	Imposition of provisional measures	2	1%

Table based on Araújo (2009)

legislative process should replicate the federal model, particularly the ones concerning the power to initiate it. Thus, state constitutions that have given to bodies other than those provided for in the federal constitution the power to initiate legislation are unconstitutional.[45]

In its second most frequent occurrence, symmetry serves as a source to guarantee the same powers and prerogatives of the President to State Governors. On those occasions, the Supreme Court argues that the President's appointment power for positions in the administration,[46] judiciary[47] and bodies essential to justice[48] must also be granted to governors.

Finally, with a close incidence degree, are the actions aimed at creating uniformities related to judicial and legislative powers. The Supreme Court ruled that state constitutions could not regulate the number of appeal judges,[49] discipline tenure of state judges or create supervisory bodies of judicial activity.[50]

[45] DAU 89, 1990 (matters related to the employment of public officials must be held within the executive branch powers and not the state constitutions) and DAU 3644, 2009 (the legislative process for structuring bodies of state administration regarding criminal expertise requires the participation of the Executive Power and must not be provisioned by the state constitution).

[46] DAU 578, 2001 (governors should appoint state school principals; therefore, they cannot be elected in balloting conducted by the local community).

[47] DAU 2710, 2003 (governors should freely and solely appoint the Police Chief; the need for class entity approval is unconstitutional).

[48] DAU 1228, 1995 (State Attorney General appointment depends solely on a list submitted by its peers and later selection by the governor; further, the State's Legislative Assembly approval is unconstitutional).

[49] DAU 157, 1995.

[50] DAU 98 and 183, 1997. The case of the unconstitutionally of the External Control Board of the Judiciary established by the state constitution of Mato Grosso is curious for a handful of reasons. The body (State Council of Justice) was regarded as a separation of power violation because it would compromise the judicial autonomy and governance. However, in 2004, the federal constitution was amended to create the National Council of Justice, whose functions and composition resembled the

State constitutions, moreover, should follow the same liability regimes of politicians[51] and the constitutional amendment voting quorum.[52]

The principles extended by symmetry are those that prohibit the creation of different institutional formulas that concern the separation of powers in state constitutions. Thus, the autonomy of states to organise their powers in accordance with the decisions made by the subsequent constituent power is virtually suppressed by compliance with the federal model.

Although regarded by the Supreme Court as a principle, the symmetry required by the court best identifies itself as a hermeneutical criterion capable of identifying federal rules that should (and those that should not) be reproduced by state constitutions.[53] It is not, therefore, a constitutional principle capable of determining the constitutionality of the state constitution based on the absence of symmetry alone: what is unconstitutional is the disrespect of a federal normative model of the separation of powers.[54]

Although used extensively, the Supreme Court did not elaborate more extensively on how the duty of symmetry must be fulfilled by state constitutions, nor did it justify how the principle may affect the self-organisation of states. Moreover, the duty to mimetically follow the federal model implies the 'ripple effect' of state constitutional reforms.[55] The obligation to follow a constantly changing federal model carries the instability of the federal constitution[56] to state constitutionalism, which, lacking the means to limit the power of federal amendment, ends up making their constitutions a mere copy of the federal constitution.

The 'ripple effect' has been empirically tested[57] in a study that concluded that the most significant changes that have occurred in state constitutions were due to the obligation to follow the federal model. Although the changes were different regarding the time of the proposition and the extent of changes, Gabriel Bellon has shown that there is a close correlation between the changes in state constitutions

state agency declared unconstitutional years before. The Supreme Court ruled in favour of the constitutionality of the National Council, confirming that it would not violate the separation of power, as the supervisory body possesses only administrative powers, not interfering with the core activity of the Judiciary, cf DAU 3367, 2005.

[51] DAU 2461, 2005 (Rio de Janeiro's Constitution was declared unconstitutional because, unlike the federal constitution at the time, the decision to recall the State Representative's mandate by his peers should be made by secret votes). In 2013 (CA 76/13), the federal constitution was amended to provide for the open vote in cases of recall by peers of the House of Representatives' mandates. In order to follow the federal amendment (ripple effect), the state Constitution of Rio de Janeiro was amended once again to reestablish the open voting, the same ruled unconstitutional earlier by the Supreme Court (CA to the CA / RJ 55/13).

[52] DAU 486, 1997 (state constitutions cannot create higher quorums of approval compared to the one provided to change the federal constitution).

[53] State constitutions are not obligated to create provisional measures to governors, a power assigned to the President.

[54] Araújo (n 40) 129–30.

[55] Silva (n 40).

[56] We recall, for the readers, the 99 amendments to the federal constitution thus far.

[57] Gabriel Luan Absher Bellon, 'Constituições estaduais pós-1989: processo de emendamento e seus determinantes' (2015) *Dissertação (Mestrado em Ciência Política) Universidade de São Paulo* 74.

with a previous change that occurred in the federal constitution, in particular, regarding matters that are encompassed by the principle of symmetry (separation of powers).[58]

As Maués argues,[59] the idea of separation of powers developed by the Brazilian Supreme Court in such cases is based on a total separation of powers between the branches, giving less importance to checks and balances based on different constitutional arrangements.[60] That is, the reproduction rules extended to state constitutions are copies of the federal constitution because the separation of powers developed by the federal republic represents the concern in reproducing the same division of powers in the states, preventing the creation of alternative forms of checks and balances. Thus, subnational constitutionalism is not seen as an instance for the exercise of the power of self-government of a political community, which means the suppression of the opportunity of relevant political decisions at the state level. Finally, the requirement of symmetry obscures the distinction, at the subnational level, between the powers of the constituent power and of the legislature chamber.

ii. Communal Identity and Senatorial Behaviour in National Politics

State constitutions in Brazil offer no political means to serve as an institution capable of opposing constitutional politics developed at the federal level, in addition to mimicking the federal model, suppressing the self-government of the political community. This is because constitutional politics centre on the federal constitution, causing the irrelevance of state constitutionalism as a forum to discuss issues relevant to the subnational entity (local issues).

The choice of a non-contestatory federalism, granting broad powers of legislative initiative to the federal union and the symmetry required of state constitutions, centralises the discussion and creation of policies while limiting institutional opportunities for subnational entities to exercise veto powers. Furthermore, the votes of regional benches in the Senate (representative of subnational entities) do not show specific federal interests and reflect the decisions of party cohesion.

According to the federal constitution (Article 46), the Senate represents the subnational states and comprises three senators representing each of the 27 states, serving an eight-year term. In the institutional design shaped by the

[58] Another finding concerns the initiative to amend state constitutions. Given that amendments are clearly corrective, the legislature is the institution that proposes most amendments. In the federal case, given that the Constitution is understood as an instrument of the federal government, there is a high rate of constitutional amendments proposed by the presidents. Bellon (n 55) 153.

[59] Antonio Maués, 'O Federalismo Brasileiro na Jurisprudência do Supremo Tribunal Federal (1988–2003)' in Filomeno Moraes and Fernando Luiz Ximenes Rocha (eds), *Direito Constitucional Contemporâneo* (Del Rey, 2005) 65–85.

[60] Virgilio Afonso da Silva also advocates subnational constitutionalism as a suitable place for institutional experimentalism.

1988 Constitution, the Senate works as a second legislative chamber capable of operating as a brake to institutional changes, acting as an additional veto arena, particularly in cases contrary to subnational entities' interests.[61] This is because there are strong federative traits in the Senate, such as: (a) equal representation of states, creating distortions in the proportional representation compared to states' populations;[62] (b) the presence of many former governors in the Senate;[63] and (c) the performance of said House in the fiscal adjustment of the federation.[64] Thus, veto powers exercised by the Senate in constitutional amendment procedures may be considered as *proxies* for communal identity.

In this sense, as a hypothesis, we could argue that proposals for institutional changes that would threaten subnational states' rights would face greater difficulties in approval because senators representing the subnational units would defend the interests of their political communities through their veto power.[65] In other words, the senators could be an indication that the subnational entities have at their disposal a political community that has specific interests that sometimes are opposed to those of the Union.

Recent studies indicate,[66] nevertheless, that the Brazilian Senate behaves as a party and not a federative house because its decisions are based on partisan consistency; that is, senators tend to vote in accordance with how party leaders position themselves in the government political spectrum. Such senatorial action reduces its veto power as a chamber of regional interests.

In an analysis of political parties in the Senate between 1989 and 2009 and its degree of coherence and cohesion in *roll-call* votes, Pedro Neiva[67] confirmed that despite the minor importance of the leaders, in comparison to their role played in the House of Representatives,[68] senators vote consistently with the decision of the party. In another study, Pedro Neiva and Marcia Soares[69] demonstrate that belonging to a party that is part of the government's support base in Congress

[61] Arretche (n 36) 112.

[62] Senators from states whose population amounts to 15% of the country occupy 51% of the seats. Thus, smaller states could veto policies of states representing 85% of the country's population. Ana Luisa Backes, 'Fortalecimento Parlamentar de minorias regionais e suas razões' in Leany Lemos (eds), *O Senado Federal Brasileiro no Pós-Constituinte* (Unilegis, 2008) 64.

[63] In a research that analysed the composition of the Senate from 1991 to 1999, Lemos and Ranincheski found that 33% of senators, on average, had occupied positions in the State Executive (governor or State Deputy). Leany Lemos, Sonia Ranincheski and O Perfil Sócio-Político dos Senadores Brasileiros in Leany Lemos (eds), *O Senado Federal Brasileiro no Pós-Constituinte* (Unilegis, 2008) 105.

[64] Pedro Robson Pereira Neiva; Márcia Miranda Soares, 'Senado brasileiro: casa federativa ou partidária?' (2013) 28 *Revista Brasileira de Ciências Sociais* 99.

[65] Traditionally, bicameralism federalism implies that the upper house would have greater weight when matters of local interest are being discussed at the national decision-making level. This is because in federal states, the Senate has historical influences in the claim made by smaller states in the USA, who wanted equal representation in the Senate. Neiva; Soares (n 62) 98.

[66] Arretche (n 36), Pedro Robson Pereira Neiva. 'Coesão e disciplina partidária no Senado Federal' (2011) 54 *DADOS – Revista de Ciências Sociais* and Neiva; Soares (n 62).

[67] Neiva (n 64) 290–93.

[68] Limongi (n 33).

[69] Neiva; Soares (n 62) 109–11.

remains an important reference for senators' decision-making as well as in matters of specific interest to subnational states, that is, involving federal issues. Moreover, they concluded that governors do not influence senators even in federal or local matters.

Marta Arretche, on the other hand, analysed 62 constitutional amendments adopted in 1988/2009 and determined that 28 of them dealt with federal matters.[70] Of those 28, she concluded that parliamentary cohesion of the senators on *roll-call* votes of those proposed constitutional amendments is similar to that of the House of Representatives and ruled out that pressure from governors or the type of matter in debate would have been able to explain such behaviour.

As examples of constitutional amendments (CAs) that affected regional interests for the worse, we can mention the administrative reforms brought about by CA 19/98 and 43/03, which limited the decision-making autonomy of subnational governments in relation to the salary of the employees and representatives of the three powers. CA 15/96, approved unanimously, hindered the creation of municipalities by states by subordinating their creation to a federal law (to date nonexistent) in an attempt to seek the centralisation of decisions about the subject. CA 14/96 changed the rules regarding federal intervention and states and municipalities' powers regarding education, a reform that continued in CA 53/06 and 59/09. CA 25/00, which replaced CA 01/92 and 19/98 amendments in this specific matter, changed Article 29, VI, to stipulate, more specifically, fixed limits on the city councillor's payments, affecting the spending autonomy of subnational entities. CA 29/00 added in Article 77 of ADCT linking 12 per cent of the revenues of states and municipalities to 15 per cent of health spending.

iii. Constitutional Stability, Rule of Law and State Constitutionalism

As noted above, Brazil has a high amendment rate. Among several possible explanations,[71] we can list the absence of subnational constitutionalism, despite the existence of state constitutions. This is because the latter are not imbued with the values of constitutionalism and fail to provide a framework for making important political decisions in the context of subnational entities and to offer recognition of the political community institutions. The reduced self-organising ability of states centralises the discussion of federative problems and local interests in the federal constitution. Therefore, matters that could be addressed by state constitutions are reallocated to the National Congress.

The hypothesis of constitutional instability due to the absence of subnational constitutionalism can be correlated to a traditional possibility outlined by the political scientists: the excessive constitutionalisation of public policies in the federal

[70] Arretche (n 36) 134–38.

[71] (a) An easy procedure to change the Constitution, (b) agenda-setting powers of the President, and (c) the constitutionalisation of policies.

constitution that should be implemented by subnational units and the concentration of powers in the Federal Union to create them make the federal constitution a necessary instrument for the government in office.[72]

Constitutional changes are welcome since constitutional documents are created to last indefinitely, but the profusion of amendments in a very short period may disclose a weakness of the federal constitutionalism. One of the features of modern constitutionalism was to establish the difference between the exercise of constitutional politics (higher lawmaking) and common or normal politics.[73] The creation of constitutional norms requires a higher degree of democratic consensus and exceptional political manifestations, sometimes revolutionary, to create a legal order. In contrast, decisions on common politics, guided by the dispute of interests and compromise are regulated and allowed by the constitutional norms.[74]

Constitutions treated as milestones for the implementation of common politics and that do not impose themselves as a limitation frame of government activity nor secure the efficiency of the state obfuscate the difference between constitutional and common politics, undermining the rationale for the adoption of constitutionalism as a political ideal. Constitutional changes that occur due to the alternation in government leadership may demonstrate that constitutional rules do not serve to constrain political power, because the officer in chief can change the rules of the game whenever the government agenda changes.

The growing process of Brazilian constitutional reforms began soon after the promulgation of the Constitution, since the first amendment dates back to 1992, suggesting that the same political groups that were present in the constituent assembly considered the constitutional articles as drawbacks since its inception. This informal reopening of the higher lawmaking process demonstrates that those political groups did not consider the constitutional political agreements as permanent but as a mere conjuncture.[75]

As both Maués and Santos have argued,[76] on occasions such as the ones described in the last paragraph, and particularly in Brazil, there is no recognition of constitutional rules as being capable of regulating political conflict; thus, when minority groups in the constituent assembly achieve a political majority later,

[72] Celina Souza 'Regras e contexto: as reformas da Constituição de 1988' (2008) 51 *DADOS – Revista de Ciências Sociais* 792 e Rogério Bastos Arantes; Cláudio Gonçalves Couto 'Construção democrática e modelos de Constituição' (2010) 53 *DADOS* 546.

[73] Bruce Ackerman, *We the people* (Cambridge, 1991) 266–67.

[74] Ulrich Preuss, 'Constitutional Powermaking for the new polity: some deliberations on the relations between cosntituent power and the constitution' in Michel Rosenfeld (ed), *Constitutionalism, Identitity, Difference and Legitimacy* (Duke Universty Press, 1994) 144.

[75] AM Maués, 'Dez Anos de Constituição, Dez Anos de Reforma Constitucional' in Antonio G Moreira Maués (ed), *Constituição e democracia* (Max Limonad, 2001) 13.

[76] Antonio Maués Maués and Elida Santos, 'Estabilidade Constitucional e Acordos Constitucionais: Os Processos Constituintes de Brasil (1987–1988) e Espanha (1977–1978)' (2008) 4 *Revista Direito GV* 349–87.

they alter the promulgated constitution to adapt its rules to their political agendas, with a view to reverting the decisions made at the founding moment.[77]

Constitutional amendments, therefore, are thought of as instruments of the government when the constitutional performance is seen as dysfunctional, that is, when it fails as a structural government institution. Amendments are also used when the problem of dysfunctional constitutional performance is increased by changes in the balance of power.[78] On said occasions, the changes are justified when the institutional performance of the Constitution does not meet the interests of those in office.[79]

Constitutions, such as Brazil's, which have a large proportion of public policies as well as fundamental principles of classic constitutionalism, entail an ongoing process of constitutional amendment. This is because the constitutionalisation of topics that appear as government agendas require constant changes in the constitution.[80] The 1988 Constitution turned public policies into constitutional matters, particularly in the education and health fields, but whose goals and plans are of low durability, because they are dependent on economic and social variables.[81]

Most of those policies are included in the legislative initiative powers of the Union (Article 22), which in turn centralises policy creation in the National Congress with few institutional opportunities for veto coming from subnational entities, and the federal government's plans to change constitutional rules will usually involve federal matters because of the shared competence to implement policies (Articles 23 and 24) between all subnational unities.

The first Fernando Henrique Cardoso (1994–98) government started the biggest change cycle since the promulgation of the Constitution, focusing on fiscal issues, mainly regarding the necessity of an increase in federal revenues and expenditure restraint at all three levels of government.[82] In addition to the fiscal agenda, constitutional amendments were created to promote reformulations in

[77] Arantes and Couto both agree on the point because they suggest that the constant constitutional changes on public policies indicate no consensus on the constitutional rules, able to protect against certain results regarded as intolerable in ordinary political competition. Arantes and Couto (n 70) 558.

[78] As pointed out by Arantes and Couto, Brazilian governments must exercise their policies in the constitutional field to establish their agendas. Rogério Bastos Arantes; Cláudio Gonçalves Couto, 'A Constituição sem fim' in Sérgio Praça and Simone Diniz S (eds), *Vinte anos de Constituição* (Paulus, 2008) 56–7.

[79] Gabriel L Negretto 'Replacing and Amending Constitutions: The Logic of Constitutional Change in Latin America' (2012) 46 *Law & Society Review* 755–56.

[80] Arantes and Couto (n 70) 546.

[81] According to Negretto, detailed constitutional provisions regarding policies tend to become obsolete when there are political and macroeconomic changes, although the author considers this a questionable conclusion. Negretto (n 77) 759.

[82] Analysing constitutional reforms in Brazil from 1988 to 2007, Marcus Melo confirmed that 40% of the amendments had federalism themes, especially on social rights and public policy. The rest of the amendments concerned economic and institutional aspects. See Marcus André Melo, 'Hiperconstitucionalização e qualidade da democracia: mitos e realidade' in Manuel Alcântara and Carlos Ranulfo, *A democracia brasileira* (Editora da UFMG, 2007) 251.

the Brazilian original economic model by breaking state monopolies, allowing for greater openness to private capital, including foreign, as a response to new globalisation paradigms.[83]

The degree and the period of these constitutional changes are also related to changes in the context in which international conjunctures have been incorporated by political elites of different political parties in the constitutional reform agenda. Therefore, excessive constitutionalisation of public policies that falls into the exclusive competence of the Federal Union and that must be conducted by sub-national entities entails constitutional amendments that float at the whim of the changing agenda of governments coming to lead the federal state.[84]

Arantes and Couto suggest that policy-oriented constitutions, such as the Brazilian one, affect the agendas of future governments, possibly limiting the aspirations of the majority in power. The authors estimate that 30 per cent of Brazil's constitutional norms are policies and that the constitutional amendments proposed by the executive are, mostly, related to their change.[85]

IV. Concluding Remarks

Constitutionalism implies the defence of certain values: the constraint of power through legal rules and the protection of constitutional rights.[86] A constitution that upholds constitutionalism[87] should be rigid to differentiate itself from normal politics. That is why to amend a constitution, usually, a super majority is required, but this requirement could be insufficiently capable of drawing a line between regular and constitutional politics in order to constrain power; consequently, there would be no difference between the Constitution and a statute. This could be the case for Brazil.

The way our federal constitution deals with subnational constitutions may be important evidence for explaining constitutional changes. Federal states tend to establish alternate political arenas to deal with local problems.[88] Brazil's federal constitution allows states to create their own constitutions, and one is to assume that the reason this is possible is to provide political means for local polities to protect themselves from the concentration of federal power and to create a more specific bill of rights (constitutionalism values). Nonetheless, federal constitutional features make evident that the presence of states' constitutions does not guarantee that they will endorse constitutionalism.

[83] Souza (n 70) 799–803.

[84] However, the recentralisation of policies may be a way to implement our version of cooperative federalism. Vanessa Elias Oliveira, 'Federalismo e Políticas Públicas: interações e suas consequências' in Daniel Wang (ed), *Constituição e Política na Democracia* (Marcial Pons, 2013) 231.

[85] Arantes; Couto (n 70) 546.

[86] Sajó (n 16).

[87] HWO Okoth-Ogendo (n 19).

[88] Arthur Benz; Jorg Broschek (n 22).

The limitless federal power to create policies affecting subnational entities and to regulate state affairs and the judicial prohibition to create new institutional arrangements due to the obligation of symmetry with the federal constitution show that state constitutions are not the place to discuss constitutional politics in Brazil, so the natural need to express change in political institutions rests exclusively in the federal constitution.[89] Therefore, constitutional changes that affect federal institutions and arrangements are channelled by the centralisation of political disputes in the National Congress. This means that all political changes in Brazil are to be settled in the amendment of the federal constitution, since state constitutions are imitations of the federal one and are subject to judicial review like any other statute.

Constitutionalism incorporates the constraint of power through legal means, and the multilayered structure of federalism is a manner to constrain federal power, whether through the division to create and to enforce policies, or whether to prevent national congress from changing the Constitution as it pleases via amendments. Since those constitutionalism values are not present in Brazilian politics (state constitutions must be symmetrical to the federal one as well as the high amendment rates, particularly in areas that worsen the situation of states), it casts doubts about our constitution's rigidity and the value of our constitutionalism.

[89] Arretche (n 36) 53–62.

13

Legislative Process and Constitutional Change in Brazil: On the Pathologies of the Procedure for Amending the 1988 Constitution

LEONARDO AUGUSTO DE ANDRADE BARBOSA*

I. Introduction

Hannah Arendt once wrote, 'The very authority of the American Constitution resides in its inherent capacity to be amended and augmented'. Arendt argues that 'the most important single notion which the men of the [United States] Revolution adopted' was the belief that founding, developing, and preserving a commonwealth were necessarily interrelated. The founders, following the inspiration of Roman antiquity, did not arrogantly put themselves above all future generations: 'Either they were founders and, consequently, would become ancestors, or they had failed'.[1] Arendt suggests that the Latin word for 'founding', *condere*, contains

* Leonardo Barbosa is an expert in Brazilian constitutional matters and legislative affairs. He has been a legislative attorney with the Chamber of Deputies (the lower House in Brazilian Congress) since 2002, where he has served as chief of staff of the minority leadership, senior adviser for official conduct matters, and, since 2011, as a senior attorney to the Office of the Clerk. Barbosa is also a professor for the master's in legislative studies at the Center for Continuing Education and Professional Development (CEFOR, Chamber of Deputies). His research interests include constitutional history and constitutional rights, election law, international law of human rights (particularly regarding contemporary forms of slavery), and legislative process. He received his LLB from the Federal University of Minas Gerais in 2000, and both his LLM (2005) and SJD (2009) from the University of Brasília. Barbosa was a Michigan Grotius Research Scholar during the 2014 summer and fall terms at the University of Michigan Law School. Acknowledgements: I am much indebted to the comments of the participants in the Global Symposium on Constitutional Amendment and Replacement in Latin America, organised by the International Society of Public Law (ICON-S) in September 2016 at the University of Brasília. I particularly thank Richard Albert and Virgílio Afonso da Silva, respectively chair and discussant of the panel in which I presented the first draft of this chapter, for their invaluable remarks, though they are by no means responsible for any flaws in the interpretations advanced here. Kristin McGuire copyedited this chapter.

[1] Hannah Arendt, *On Revolution* (Penguin Classics, 2006) 194–95.

this very idea. The word 'derives from an early Latin field god, called Conditor, whose main function was to preside over growth and harvest'.[2] A god that is both 'founder and preserver', she notes, points to the intrinsic connection between creation and conservation.

If Arendt's insight is correct, the inauguration of a new constitutional order is not the key – or, at least, the sole key – to its success and legitimacy. A constitution succeeds to the extent that it is able to generate a legal culture in which people trace their political struggles and claims back to the principles enshrined in the constitutional text. The interplay of these struggles and claims with decisions issued by legal institutions reshapes the normative content of the Constitution, reinvigorating or debilitating its authority, depending on the varying outcomes. When people engage in the development of the foundations of their republic by interpreting its 'principles' (in both senses), they are 'keeping its beginning always present'.[3]

This interpretation brings to mind Jacques Derrida's observations in *Declarations of Independence*.[4] Derrida embraces the paradox of a signature that invents the signer, that is, a signature that can be located in time, but is also a 'non-datable process of reappropriation, and making-one's-own', in the words of David Ingram. The 'legitimacy and legality these founding documents have for us today […] was acquired *retroactively*, in the course of being renewed and reinterpreted by *future* generations'.[5] The success of this endeavour can (re)connect the Constitution with its own time, thus preserving its authoritativeness. According to this approach, constitutional change is therefore a way of renewing a commitment to the principles of the Constitution – reaffirming, rather than superseding, it. Its failure, however, can hinder the ability of constitutional law to stabilise normative expectations regarding the exercise of political power and the enjoyment of basic rights.

This understanding of the pliability of the Constitution assumes that the Constitution is more than just a paramount *legal* norm. It presupposes that the attitude of the political community towards the Constitution is one of deference and respect. In order to interpret the Constitution, one has to admit – at least performatively – that he or she is part of a continuous enterprise, a 'self-correcting learning process', that engages the people throughout time in a shared practice, 'meant to bring forth a self-determining community of free and equal citizens'.[6] It would be pointless to augment the foundations of a legal and political enterprise that is alien, idle,

[2] ibid, 195.

[3] Bonnie Honig, *Political Theory and the Displacement of Politics* (Cornell University Press, 1993) 113.

[4] Jacques Derrida, 'Declarations of independence' in Elizabeth Rottemberg (ed), *Negotiations: interventions and interviews, 1971–2001* (Stanford University Press, 2002) 46–54. For a comparison of Arendt's and Derrida's approaches to the American Revolution and the reconcilability of some of their perspectives, cf Honnig (n 3) 109ff.

[5] David Ingram, *Law: Key Concepts in Philosophy* (Continuum International Publishing Group, 2006) 86.

[6] Jürgen Habermas, 'Constitutional Democracy: A Paradoxical Union of Contradictory Principles?' (2001) 29 *Political Theory* 766, 774–75.

or obtuse. Constitutional change often stems from the perception that the constitutional order needs adjustments and improvements. A comprehensive *refusal* of the Constitution, or a de-legitimising approach towards it, is self-defeating, unless one openly advocates the supersession of the Constitution. Sanford Levinson takes this approach in his call for a new constitutional convention, and opens his book, *Our Undemocratic Constitution*, with an account of his view that many provisions of the United States Constitution place 'almost unsurmountable barriers in the way of any acceptable notion of democracy'.[7]

In this chapter, I assume that most reformist discourse and practice in Brazilian constitutionalism develops against a background of criticism (or even cynicism) towards the Constitution's origins; in other words, a denial of the Constitution's normative project. The champions of constitutional reform are not aiming to improve the constitutional order, but rather to undermine its foundations. For that reason, they happily support any legal theory that makes formal constitutional change easier and faster. This echoes a long authoritarian tradition that depicts the Constitution as a mere instrument in the hands of the president, and criticises the 'procedural restraints' that allow the minority in Congress to filibuster proposals sponsored by the government. Back in the 1960s, Pedro Aleixo, the civil vice-president of Costa e Silva, suggested that if a legislative majority is firmly devoted to changing the constitutional text, it is preposterous to prevent it from doing so based on 'procedural restraints', or on conditions whose fulfilment 'depends on a more or less ponderable political minority'.[8]

The 1988 Constitution is the result of a Convention held at the end of the transition from the military dictatorship initiated in 1964. The text was developed through a procedure that included significant popular participation. For the first time, there was no initial draft prepared by notorious constitutional scholars. Breaking with Congress's monopoly of constitutional politics, there was a strong notion that constitution making was not to be treated as a 'predominantly technical task' that should rely on the jurist's 'harmonic sense of balance' in order to achieve a piece of 'architectonic value'.[9] This was not the work of the 'wisest',[10] but a rather chaotic process that ended up embracing a robust set of enumerated basic rights, with an economic model that was perceived by most market players as outdated. Indeed, at the time, Mailson da Nóbrega, a famous Brazilian economist, recognised that the new Constitution would make it harder to administer the economy.[11] Mauro Chaves, a conservative journalist and jurist, wrote an ironic

[7] Sanford Levinson, *Our Undemocratic Constitution: Where the Constitution Goes Wrong (and How We the People Can Correct It)* (OUP, 2006) 6.

[8] Pedro Aleixo, 'Introduction' in Paulo Sarasate, *A Constituição do Brasil ao Alcance de Todos*, (Freitas Bastos, 1967) xxxvi.

[9] Miguel Reale, 'Como deverá ser a nova Constituição' (1985) 60/61 *Revista Brasileira de Estudos Políticos* 9, 11.

[10] Manoel Gonçalves Ferreira Filho, 'Nova perspectiva do processo constitucional' (1985) 60/61 *Revista Brasileira de Estudos Políticos* 129, 142.

[11] Mailson da Nóbrega, 'Nova Ordem' *Folha de S. Paulo* (São Paulo, 6 October 1988) A7.

editorial the day after the enactment of the Constitution in which he takes his readers five years into the future, when the time required to engage in the constitutional revision (deeper reform of the text) has lapsed. In Chaves's imagined scenario, by the time Congress is in charge of making substantial changes to the constitutional text, the Constitution has magically and implausibly improved the county, in a way that has made change itself irrelevant and unnecessary.[12] Chaves, of course, did not expect the 1988 Constitution to do any good to Brazil; on the contrary – his vision was clearly a sort of 'anti-prophecy'.

A constitution is not meant to inspire worship in a religious sense, however it must command respect, or at least respectful dissent. If relevant players in the constitutional scenario perceive it as a mistake or a hurdle to be surmounted, the pressure for constitutional change will grow progressively stronger. The consequences on procedures for altering the Constitution are predictable. The fact that the Brazilian 1988 Constitution has been amended *100 times* in 30 years does not have to do primarily with the fact that the text is all encompassing, too long, and allegedly requires several modifications in order to make any 'plan of government' viable. It has to do with the fact that the Executive branch has consistently sought to regain control of constitutional politics through its congressional base. In order to do so, 'softening' the rules for enacting constitutional amendments proved crucial, as we will discuss below.

II. Legislative Process of Constitutional Reform and its Pathologies

A. A Brief Overview of the Process for Amending the Constitution

The Brazilian 1988 Constitution is a typical 'rigid constitution'.[13] In order to amend the constitutional text, a particular procedure, more demanding than the one applicable to enact ordinary legislation, is required. According to Article 60 of the Constitution, which establishes the standard amendment procedure, a proposal to amend the Constitution [*Proposta de Emenda à Constituição*, henceforth, 'PEC'] may be introduced by: (a) the president; (b) at least one third of the members of the Senate or of the Chamber of Deputies (the lower House of Brazilian Congress); or (c) a joint proposal sponsored by at least 15 of the 27 Legislative Assemblies of the states and of the Federal District, each of them deciding by a simple majority vote. Each House of the Congress discusses and votes upon the proposal in a two-round system, with a three-fifths threshold for approval (308 representatives out

[12] Mauro Chaves, 'Senhores Congressistas' *Estado de S. Paulo* (São Paulo, 6 October 1988) 2.
[13] See James Bryce, *Studies in History and Jurisprudence*, vol 1 (OUP, 1901) 178ff.

of 513 in the Chamber, and 54 senators out of 81 in the Senate). The Chamber and the Senate have to agree on exactly the same text in order to pass the amendment. (This differs from the legislative process of ordinary bills, in which the House that initiates the procedure has the final say on any modifications proposed by the other.) Once the proposal passes both Houses, the Directing Boards of the Chamber and of the Senate enact it into law.

There are both procedural and substantive limitations regarding the amendment process. Procedurally, the Constitution forbids the enactment of amendments during periods of federal intervention, a state of defence, or a state of siege. It also prevents Congress from deliberating more than once, in the same legislative term, on an issue already addressed in a proposal that was rejected or dismissed, on the grounds that the issue has already been decided [*prejudicada*]. As for substantive limitations, the Constitution adopts entrenched clauses (known as '*eternal clauses*'), which preclude changes impairing its 'essential core'. Those clauses encompass the fundamental features of the constitutional design (federalism, separation of powers, and the right to vote in direct elections) and the basic rights.[14]

In 1988, there were two additional alternatives for introducing formal change. Apart from the regular procedure provided for in Article 60, Article 3 of the Temporary Constitutional Provisions Act established that 'the revision of the Constitution shall be effected after five years as of its promulgation, by the vote of the absolute majority of the members of the National Congress in a unicameral session'. This prerogative was available for one time only, and Congress put it to use between October 1993 and May 1994, in the middle of political and economic turmoil. The outcome of the Revision was piddling: Congress managed to pass only six amendments during that period, none of which carried out structural changes within the Constitution.[15] For those who saw the 1988 Constitution as an obstacle to political governance, that failure was particularly frustrating, given the high expectations surrounding the Revision. In their view, the lower quorum and the unicameral proceedings were an excellent opportunity to correct the 'excesses' of the Constitutional Convention of 1987–88, deemed as an all-encompassing document, excessively generous in granting rights, particularly social rights. Conservative scholars and politicians not only mourned the flawed Revision, but also organised attempts to revive the missed opportunity throughout the 1990s and 2000s, so far unsuccessfully.[16] Consequently, the only legal procedure available to modify the 1988 Brazilian Constitution currently in force is the

[14] *See* Virgilio Afonso da Silva, 'A Fossilised Constitution?' (2004) 17 *Ratio Juris* 454.

[15] For a detailed account of the Constitutional Revision of 1993–94, see Leonardo A de Andrade Barbosa, *História Constitucional Brasileira: Mudança Constitucional, Autoritarismo e Democracia no Brasil Pós-1964* (Câmara dos Deputados, 2012) 253–323.

[16] The most emblematic attempt to reintroduce an alternative, less demanding, procedure to amend the Constitution was the PEC n 157/2003. See Barbosa (n 15) 337–48. See also Cristiano Paixão, 'A Constituição Subtraída' *Constituição & Democracia* (Brasília, 5 February 2006) 4.

one prescribed by Article 60, a procedure that – apart from the introduction of the proposal – is completely intra-congressional. Differently from regular legislative process, in which the president has a veto power over bills passed by Congress, there is no presidential veto when it comes to constitutional amendments.

In Brazilian Constitutional law, constitutional amendments are not immune to judicial review. The explicit procedural and substantive limits to constitutional reform prescribed in Article 60, along with the fact that the procedure is completely intra-congressional, with no need of popular or federal ratification, assign a peculiar legal status to the constitutional amendments. If an amendment is *duly* enacted, it becomes part of the Constitution and, therefore, cannot be challenged by judicial review. However, one can *always* call into question the amendment's legitimacy based on the rules of Article 60. It is common for the Federal Supreme Court of Brazil to try cases involving claims of unconstitutionality of constitutional amendments, or even of *proposed* constitutional amendments (given the fact that the Constitution prohibits Congress from even *considering* proposals that threaten any of the entrenched clauses).[17]

By contrast, in US constitutional law, constitutional amendments are commonly 'regarded as the most straightforward way for the people to respond to a Supreme Court decision with which they disagree'.[18] For that reason, the Supreme Court itself has asserted that judicial review of the legitimacy of the procedure involved in the ratification of an amendment to the Constitution 'would have compelled [the] Court to oversee *the very constitutional process used to reverse Supreme Court decisions*' (emphasis added).[19] The view endorsed in this statement depicts the amendment process as a safeguard of popular sovereignty. Constitutional change can trump judicial decisions through a highly demanding procedure, built to certify the true will of the People and to supersede the otherwise unalterable precedent of the Supreme Court. There is substantial – and justifiable – scholarly controversy around the extent of the powers of the Court in those matters,[20] but its

[17] The Brazilian Supreme Court has asserted in several precedents that the Court can hear cases challenging the legitimacy of a constitutional amendment in light of Article 60's rules. See, for instance, BRASIL, Supremo Tribunal Federal, Ação Direta de Inconstitucionalidade n 14, Requerente: Confederação Nacional dos Trabalhadores no Comércio, Requerido: Congresso Nacional e Presidente da República, Relator: Ministro Sydney Sanches, *Diário da Justiça*, Brasília, DF, 18 mar 1994. According to the decision, 'a Constitutional Amendment […] that incurs in a violation to the provisions of the original text of the Constitution can be declared unconstitutional by the Supreme Court, whose primary duty is to protect the Constitution'. BRASIL, Supremo Tribunal Federal, Medida Cautelar na Ação Direta de Inconstitucionalidade n 5316, Requerente: Associação dos Magistrados Brasileiros e outros, Interessado: Congresso Nacional, Relator: Ministro Luiz Fux, *Diário da Justiça Eletrônico*, Brasília, DF, 6 ago 2015. On the possibility of reviewing proposed amendments to the Constitution, still pending deliberation before Congress, see BRASIL, Supremo Tribunal Federal, Mandado de Segurança n 22503, Impetrante: Jandira Feghali e outros, Impetrado: Presidente da Mesa da Câmara dos Deputados, Relator para o acórdão: Ministro Maurício Corrêa, *Diário da Justiça*, Brasília, DF, 6 jun 1997.

[18] Geoffrey R Stone and others, *Constitutional Law*, 6th edn (Aspen Publishers, 2009) 78.

[19] *Goldwater v Carter* 444 US 996 (1979), drawing a parallel with *Coleman v Miller* 307 US 433 (1939).

[20] See Laurence Tribe, 'A Constitution We Are Amending: In Defense of a Restrained Judicial Role' (1983–84) 97 *HLR* 433.

approach to constitutional amendments in this case suggests that the complexities involved in the process of bringing about formal constitutional change in the US grant such political decisions superior legitimacy.

This is obviously *not* the case with constitutional amendments in Brazil. As mentioned above, formal constitutional change in Brazil can develop entirely within the walls of Congress, making an outcome that is per se entitled with superior democratic credentials unlikely. Moreover, despite the many objections raised against the stringent provisions of Article 60 during the Constitution's early years, legislative practice and judicial interpretation have made it progressively easier to fulfil the requisites to change the Constitution, allowing the enactment of approximately 100 amendments throughout the 30 years of the 1988 Constitution. In the following pages, I will explain the procedural artifices that turned the once 'insurmountable' obstacles to enact constitutional amendments into a more feasible enterprise. I will argue that those artifices reinforced constitutional change in Brazil as a matter of 'normal politics', rather than of 'constitutional politics', to use Bruce Ackerman's distinction in a somewhat loose fashion.[21]

B. Bicameralism and Constitutional Reform in Brazil: 'Ping Pong' Procedure and Partial Promulgation of Constitutional Amendments

As mentioned above, in order to pass Congress, a proposed amendment to the Constitution must be approved by three fifths of the members of each House in a two-round system. While the quorum required to amend the Constitution has varied, the idea of a two-round system combined with bicameral deliberation has been consistent in Brazil's constitutional history, particularly after the 1946 Constitution.[22] This means that both Houses of Congress have to approve the *same* provisions in order to pass a proposal. For obvious reasons, this procedural design stimulates narrow, specific, proposals, rather than generic or comprehensive ones. As a consequence, part of Brazilian constitutional doctrine suggests – despite considerable terminological controversy – that formal constitutional change ('constitutional reform') encompasses two different categories: constitutional revision and constitutional amendment. The first refers to modifications that are broader in scope and relate to crucial constitutional issues; the latter describes well-defined, circumscribed changes in the Constitution, which amount to adjustments, rather than substantial modifications, of the text.[23] Given the transitional nature of the rules governing constitutional revision in the 1988 Constitution,

[21] Bruce Ackerman, *We the People: Foundations* (HUP, 1991).

[22] See Art 217 of the 1946 Constitution; Art 51 of the 1967 Constitution; and Art 48 of the 1967 constitutional text, as rewritten by Constitutional Amendment n 1.

[23] Ivo Dantas, 'Constitucionalismo Brasileiro: Ontem, Hoje e Amanhã' (1995) 35 *Revista da Faculdade de Direito da Univesidade Federal de Minas Gerais* 237, 245–46.

the only mechanism currently available for introducing formal change within the text is the constitutional amendment, as provided for by Article 60.

One could suppose – reasonably – that this design was purposeful: the 1987–88 Constitutional Convention not only protected some principles (the 'essential core') from any modifications aimed at their suppression, but also established a procedure that would make broad constitutional change difficult to achieve. From the standpoint of the Convention, the plan was relatively clear: after at least five years of experience with the 1988 Constitution, Congress would be authorised to start a constitutional revision, applying lighter procedural requirements (simple majority, unicameral deliberation) to correct malfunctioning features at large. After that, the amendment procedure itself would be responsible for controlling the breadth of change that could be introduced in the Constitution by Congress. The design of Article 60 suggests, therefore, an *attempt to balance a completely intra-congressional technique of constitutional reform* with a demanding procedure, intended to preserve the fundamental choices of the Convention.

After the enactment of the 1988 Constitution, members of Congress and jurists criticised the procedures outlined in Article 60 as 'too demanding', even 'absurd'. The idea that both Houses of Congress had to agree, by a three fifths majority, with precisely the same wording of a proposal in two rounds, aroused the fear of legislative stalemate, something that had been prevented during the military dictatorship by a special regime designed exclusively for amendments initiated by the Executive branch.[24] Here is the difficulty: in ordinary legislative process, the House revising a bill has the ability to propose amendments, but the final say on the matter rests with the House that initiates the bill. With constitutional amendments, if both Houses do not come to an agreement, the proposal moves back and forth from the Chamber to the Senate, with no resolution whatsoever. Legislative jargon calls this 'phenomenon' *ping-pong procedure*.

As large sectors of institutional politics depicted constitutional change as a precondition to governability in Brazil in the 1990s, solving the *ping-pong* dilemma became crucial; otherwise, government would have to disperse a huge amount of political capital, as it engaged in simultaneous battlefronts within Congress, each aiming at reforming one particular feature of the Constitution. Looking at the first 18 amendments to the 1988 Constitution, passed up until 1998, we will notice that they regularly addressed a single topic, and consisted of only a small number of Articles,[25] making approval by both Houses without modification easier. However, in 1998, during debates on reforms of the public administration and the public pension system (highly controversial topics, and an essential part of the government's agenda at that moment), a Point of Order decided by the Speaker of the Chamber of Deputies provided a solution for ping-pong procedure.[26]

[24] See Barbosa (n 15) 47ff.

[25] EC n 3 is the only amendment that overtly addressed different and unrelated topics. With the exception of EC 10, 14, and 18, the proposals were also limited to one or two provisions.

[26] BRASIL, Câmara dos Deputados, Questão de Ordem n 10130, *Diário da Câmara dos Deputados*, Brasília, DF, 4 dez 1998, 2942.

The Speaker's strategy sought to address the fact that the proposals introduced extensive modifications in controversial issues of the Constitution, and also underwent dozens of amendments in each House of Congress, making it virtually impossible to pass the same text through all the steps of the legislative procedure. The solution allowed those *parts* of the proposal that were able to pass the constitutional threshold to be enacted *separately* from the parts that failed to do so. For instance, if a proposal passed by the Chamber presented five articles, but the Senate agreed only with the first three, and suggested modifications in the other two, then the Senate would be allowed to detach the last two provisions from the original proposal and send them back to the Chamber. The three articles approved by both Houses could be promulgated independently. According to the decision issued in the Point of Order:

> When it comes to constitutional amendments, the correct interpretation of the Constitution requires, by analogy [with the regular legislative procedure], that the part of the amendment approved […] is promulgated by the Directing Boards of the Chamber and the Senate. The deliberation on the part of the proposal pending approval will continue as long as the matter goes back and forth between both Houses [failing to gather sufficient political support]. Once the qualified majority aforementioned [in each House] decides to endorse it, the remainder of the proposal will be promulgated. This interpretation prevents an absurd outcome. 'The absurd is not congenial to the law', as the legal philosophers insist. The proposed interpretation avoids the absurdity of the ping-pong procedure, which threatens to paralyze completely the deliberation on a proposed constitutional amendment.

Between late 1988 and 2008, Congress enacted 36 amendments to the Constitution; and from 2008 to 2016, 45. By comparison, in the 10 years that preceded the adoption of partial promulgation of constitutional amendments (1988–98), Congress enacted only 18 amendments (plus the six amendments passed during the 1993–94 Constitutional Revision). Therefore, in the first decade after the enactment of the 1988 Constitution, Congress passed an average of 1.9 amendments per year; in the following decade, when partial promulgation was already available as an established parliamentary strategy, this average climbed to 3.6 amendments per year; and from 2008 to 2016, it went up to 4.3 amendments per year. In addition to that, all major constitutional reforms passed in the period relied on partial promulgation to succeed, including the administrative reform (EC 19/1998), the pension system reform (EC 20/1998), the tax system reform (EC 42/2003), the Judiciary reform (EC 45/2004), and the end of the secret ballot in some congressional deliberations (EC 76/2013), among many others.

Partial promulgation did address some of the government's concerns, but it was hardly a costless solution. The parallel with ordinary legislative process, particularly with the partial promulgation of the parts of a bill that were not vetoed by the president, is in itself problematic. However, even if we take for granted the argument made in the Point of Order (admitting an analogy between ordinary legislative process and the amendment procedure), there are strong reasons for not allowing partial promulgation without explicit constitutional authorisation.

As Alemán and Tsebelis have observed, the permission for presidents to 'automatically promulgate the nonmodified parts of a vetoed bill' has been rare.[27] Usually, when the president vetoes parts of a bill, the entire bill returns to Congress, including the vetoed parts. After Congress deliberates on the presidential vetoes, the final version of the bill is enacted into law. The reason for the exceptionality of this procedure lies in the many troubles it can generate. In ordinary legislative process, partial promulgation can turn the presidential veto into a real power of amendment, particularly considering the longstanding practice in Congress (under revision since 2014) of not deliberating upon the vetoes for many years.[28] Using this procedure to enact constitutional amendments only magnifies its flaws, the most evident being the risk of compromising the coherence of the proposal, or even significantly altering its meaning.

There are a number of controversies that resulted from using partial promulgation in the procedure for constitutional amendment. In 2004, for example, Congress enacted Constitutional Amendment n 45, introducing major modifications within the judicial branch. Partial promulgation was key to the successful enactment of the proposal into law. One modification in particular was immediately challenged before the Supreme Court.[29] Article 114 of the Constitution enumerates the powers of the Labor Courts. The proposal approved by the Chamber established, in Article 114, I, that Labor Courts should hear and try 'judicial actions arising from labor relations, comprising entities of public international law and of the direct and indirect public administration of the Union, the states, the Federal District, and the municipalities'. The Senate, on its turn, added an exception to this provision, establishing that this prerogative did not comprise the power to hear and try cases involving civil servants of the Union, the states, the Federal District, or the municipalities.

Given the fact that the Chamber and the Senate failed to reach an agreement on the wording of this particular provision, the Directing Boards should have refrained from promulgating it along with the parts of the Amendment that were actually approved by both Houses. However, the Boards argued that the exception to civil servants was a merely explanatory clause, with no legal value. In the Boards' interpretation, the clause only reinforced a principle already established by the Constitution and endorsed by judicial precedent; therefore, omitting it did

[27] Eduardo Alemán and George Tsebelis, 'The origins of presidential conditional agenda-setting power in Latin America' (2005) 40 *Latin America Research Review* 3, 5.

[28] Until this day, there are more than 200 vetoes pending deliberation in Congress, some of them since 2002. In 2013, Congress passed a Resolution reinterpreting the rules governing veto deliberation in order to force a decision on pending vetoes. BRASIL, Congresso, Senado, Resolução n 1 de 2013, Altera a redação dos arts 104 a 106 da Resolução nº 1, de 1970-CN, que dispõe sobre o Regimento Comum do Congresso Nacional, *Diário Oficial da União*, Brasília, DF, 12 jul 2013, Seção 1, 1. For a complete list of vetoes pending deliberation before Congress, check 'Congress's Order of Business' ['Ordem do Dia do Congresso'], at www25.senado.leg.br/web/atividade, accessed 3 January 2017.

[29] BRASIL, Supremo Tribunal Federal, Medida Cautelar na Ação Direta de Inconstitucionalidade n 3395, Requerente: Associação dos Juízes Federais do Brasil e outro, Requerido: Congresso Nacional, Relator: Ministro Cezar Peluso, *Diário da Justiça*, Brasília, DF, 10 nov 2006.

not really change the legal meaning of the provision. The Supreme Court acknowledged the Boards' argument and issued a preliminary injunction, shortly after the enactment of the Amendment, requiring all judges and courts in the country to abstain from interpreting Article 114, I, of the Constitution in a way that recognised the Labor Courts as competent to hear and try cases involving civil servants. The decision on the merits of the case is still pending.

Another example of controversy prompted by partial promulgation of constitutional amendments can be found in the so-called 'PEC of the municipal representatives', a proposal introduced in 2009. In this case, partial promulgation was ultimately refused by the Chamber's Board, but it illustrates how political whims can be at play in the enactment of constitutional amendments. The proposal attempted to reverse a decision of the Superior Electoral Court, which ordered the reduction of almost 8,000 seats throughout the country. (Brazil has approximately 5,500 city councils, and the number of seats in each council ranges from nine to 55.) Local leaderships, dissatisfied with the Electoral Court decision, exerted considerable political pressure on their representatives in the Chamber of Deputies to reestablish the eliminated seats. Because the majority of the representatives were unwilling to support the cost of the measure, they passed as a condition to the reestablishment of the seats a new, more stringent limit on the municipalities' expenditures towards the legislative branch.

The Chamber sent the proposal to the Senate with these two separate provisions. The first allowed the creation of new seats to compensate for the ones eliminated by the decision of the Electoral Court. The second imposed a new limit on legislative branch-related expenditures, applicable to the municipal government throughout the country. The senators, however, had different plans. They approved only the first provision in the proposal, and suggested to the Chamber its partial promulgation, *without* the expenditure limit. The Speaker of the House refused to promulgate the amendment, arguing that the senators had breached the balance of the proposal.[30] Indeed, the proposal was enacted into law only after the senators agreed with the expenditure limit. The incongruous manoeuvre of the Senate could have been successful, however; it depended solely on the position of the Speaker and of the directing Board of the Chamber, whose interests might not be necessarily aligned with those of the majority of the representatives. This scenario amounts not only to a risk of incoherent lawmaking, but also to a serious lack of transparency in the legislative process.

[30] Eduardo Piovesan, 'Câmara Aprova PEC que Aumenta o Número de Vereadores do País' *Agência Câmara* (Brasília, 10 September 2009): www2.camara.leg.br/camaranoticias/noticias/NAO-INFORMADO/139761-CAMARA-APROVA-PEC-QUE-AUMENTA-O-NUMERO-DE-VEREADORES-DO-PAIS.html accessed 23 November 2016. This incident led the president of the Senate to file a lawsuit in the Supreme Court attempting to force the Speaker of the House to promulgate the amendment. BRASIL, Supremo Tribunal Federal, Medida Cautelar em Mandado de Segurança n 27807, Impetrante: Mesa do Senado Federal, Impetrado: Presidente da Câmara dos Deputados, Relator: Ministro Menezes Direito, *Diário da Justiça*, Brasília, DF, 3 jan 2009.

C. Circumventing the Two-Round System

As mentioned above, the enactment of an amendment to the Brazilian Constitution requires a two-round vote in each of the Houses of Congress. The Constitution is silent on the matter of how much time must separate the first and the second rounds, but the Standing Rules of the Chamber (SRCD)[31] and the Standing Rules of the Senate (SRS)[32] have norms regulating the issue. According to Article 202, § 6º of the SRCD, there must be at least five sessions of the Chamber separating the first and the second rounds; the SRS requires a minimum interval of five business days between the two rounds of voting (Article 362).[33]

During the first 20 years of the 1988 Constitution, Congress approved 57 constitutional amendments. 24 of those passed without having complied with either Article 202, § 6º of the SRCD, or Article 362 of the SFS. Parliamentary practice in both Houses has developed ways of circumventing the mandatory interval using motions that, in principle, do not apply to the constitutional amendment procedure.[34] For a long time, the Chamber of Deputies refused to waive the mandatory interval between the two rounds of a proposal to amend the Constitution, unless the floor of the Chamber unanimously assented to the measure. More recently, however, there are at least two examples of motions admitted before the floor of the Chamber requesting the dismissal of the five-session interval.[35]

The topic came to the attention of the Supreme Court at the end of 2009, due to the EC 62/2009, which regulated the judicial execution of the government's debts.[36] The proposed Amendment had passed the Senate in a single night; the

[31] BRASIL, Congresso, Câmara dos Deputados, Resolução n 17, de 1989, Aprova o Regimento Interno da Câmara dos Deputados, Disponível em: http://www2.camara.leg.br/atividade-legislativa/legislacao/regimento-interno-da-camara-dos-deputados/arquivos-1/RICD%20atualizado%20ate%20RCD%2030-2018.pdf accessed 29 November 2016.

[32] BRASIL, Congresso, Senado Federal, Resolução n. 93, de 1970, texto editado em conformidade com a Resolução n 18, de 1989, consolidado com as alterações decorrentes de emendas à Constituição, leis e resoluções, até julho de 2016, Brasília: Senado Federal, 2015.

[33] According to Article 202, § 6º, SRCD, 'The proposal will be submitted to two-rounds of debate and voting, with an interval of five sessions'. Article 362, SRS, determines, 'The interval between the first and the second round will be of, at least, five business days'.

[34] For a detailed account of this parlimentary practice, see Heraldo P Carvalho, 'A Subtração do Tempo de Interstício entre Turnos de Votação de Proposta de Emenda à Constituição de 1988: uma Contextualização de Interesses Segmentados em Detrimento do Direito de Cidadania' (LLM thesis, University of Brasília 2010), 33 and 61–63.

[35] BRASIL, Congresso, Câmara dos Deputados, Requerimento n 8235/2013, *Diário da Câmara dos Deputados*, Brasília, DF, 17 jul 2013, 31593. BRASIL, Congresso, Câmara dos Deputados, Requerimento n 7565/2010, *Diário da Câmara dos Deputados*, Brasília, DF, 15 dez 2010, 51239. Representative Ivan Valente unsuccessfully challenged the latter motion. *See* BRASIL, Congresso, Câmara dos Deputados, Questão de Ordem n 720/2010, Autor: Deputado Ivan Valente, *Diário da Câmara dos Deputados*, Brasília, DF, 15 dez 2010, 51476.

[36] BRASIL, Supremo Tribunal Federal, Ação Direta de Inconstitucionalidade n 4357, Requerente: Conselho Federal da Ordem dos Advogados do Brasil e outros, Interessados: Mesa da Câmara dos Deputados e Mesa do Senado Federal, Relator para o acórdão: Ministro Luiz Fux, *Diário da Justiça Eletrônico*, Brasília, DF, 6 ago 2015.

question, therefore, was if the violation of the mandatory interval prescribed by the SRS amounted to a violation of the two-round system, provided for by Article 60, § 2º of the Brazilian Constitution. Regarding this particular issue, the Court decided, in 2013: 'There is no objective parameter to guide a judicial assessment of the soundness of the political will to reform the Constitution'. Moreover, 'judicial interference in the heart of the political process [...] shall be firmly and unequivocally anchored *in the text of the Constitution*' (emphasis added).

The notion that deliberating on a matter with a couple of hours between the first and second votes suffices the two-round requirement sounds bizarre. In order to make the Court's assertion comprehensible for those not familiar with Brazilian constitutional law, it is important to clarify that the Supreme Court generally refuses to engage in legal interpretation of the standing rules of the Houses of Congress. For that reason, unless a breach of those regulations can be traced back to a breach of the Constitution itself, it is viewed as legally irrelevant to the Court. The right to a due legislative process is depicted as a 'subjective right' held exclusively by Congresspeople, and justiciable only insofar it is based in the Constitution, and *not* solely in the standing rules.[37]

As Frederick Schauer points out, the standing rules governing the activity of legislatures are likely to be ineffective if the only mechanisms available to enforce those rules are internal.[38] This is precisely the case with the legislative process in Brazil, including the constitutional amendment procedure, especially because the ineffectiveness of the procedural rules is usually perceived as a minor issue. Legislative jargon has it that 'the floor of the House is sovereign'. Therefore, a breach of the standing rules, as long as it has the assent of the majority of the House, poses no real legal dilemma. The silent assumption behind this line of thought is that the enactment of laws is a matter that concerns only the representatives. Part of Brazilian constitutional doctrine, however, has insistently criticised this view, on the grounds that it ignores how internal procedural rules of the legislature can work as a general legal guarantee of democratic government.[39]

The standing rules are not mere *interna corporis* regulations, which organise congressional deliberation. By clarifying the necessary steps to turn a suggestion

[37] BRASIL, Supremo Tribunal Federal, Mandado de Segurança n 22503, Impetrante: Jandira Feghali e outros, Impetrado: Presidente da Mesa da Câmara dos Deputados, Relator para o acórdão: Ministro Maurício Corrêa, *Diário da Justiça*, Brasília, DF, 6 jun 1997.

[38] In Schauer's words: 'Yet although these and other external mechanisms are quite plausible, using the courts to perform this function is most common and realistic. And this is not just a matter of a court enforcing the Constitution and being treated as supreme when it does so. It is also a matter of courts being empowered to hold legislatures even to their own subconstitutional rules. If the commands of *Magna Carta* and the rule of law, *inter alia*, demand that legislation be made according to law, then the full range of laws that constitute and constrain the legislative function would be within the purview of a court operating in this fashion'. Frederick Schauer, 'Legislatures as Rule Followers' in Richard Bauman and Tsvi Kahana (eds), *The Least Examined Branch: the Role of Legislatures in the Constitutional State* (CUP, 2006) 477–78.

[39] Marcelo Cattoni, *Devido Processo Legislativo* (Mandamentos, 2000). See also, Leonardo Augusto de Andrade Barbosa, *Processo Legislativo e Democracia: Parlamento, Esfera Pública e Jurisdição Constitucional* (Del Rey, 2010).

into law, the rules make it possible for citizens to keep track of legislative proposals. The more power Congress has to circumvent procedural rules, the less transparent the legislative process becomes. Making the events within the legislature less predictable also reduces the ability of the people to reflect on their representatives' decisions and, ultimately, to influence those decisions through the means usually available in the political public sphere (the press, academia, associations, labour unions, political parties, informal gatherings, etc). In other words, interpreting the standing rules as an ordinary internal matter of legislatures mocks the idea of the rule of law and weakens the connection between institutionalised politics and the public sphere, thus making the legislative bodies less responsive, especially during the decision-making process.[40]

By circumventing the mandatory interval between each round of voting in the constitutional amendment procedure, Congresspeople are suppressing time that is critical for public debate and participation.[41] The two-round system is not simply about providing representatives with a second chance to evaluate their own political options in a matter as crucial as changing the Constitution. It is also, and, I suggest, *primarily* about allowing the political public sphere to take a stand and exert pressure upon institutionalised politics, checking the Legislature's power to alter the basic rules governing our society. While this might seem like a negligible procedural detail, it is an eloquent symbol of the prevailing constitutional mentality in Brazil.

D. Floor Amendments in Breach of the SRCD

Another legislative practice developed to empower Congress leadership at the expense of transparency and predictability in the constitutional amendment procedure is the admissibility of floor amendments to a proposal. In the Chamber of Deputies, Article 202, § 3° of the standing rules provide that a PEC can only be amended in the Special Committee responsible for issuing an opinion on the matter, that is, *before* the proposal moves to the floor for the two-round vote. The committee analyses the germaneness, the constitutionality, and the merits of the proposed amendments, which must fulfil the same initiative requisites as the proposal itself, namely, each amendment needs the support of at least one third of the representatives (which amounts to 171 signatures). This prerequisite ensures that the House will not discuss a matter that fails to gather a certain level of political support.

The main purpose of restricting amendments to the Committee is to reduce the risk of incorporating non-germane or poorly considered provisions during floor deliberation. The Special Committee's opinion delineates the scope of the matter,

[40] Here I take for granted a great deal of assumptions advanced by Jürgen Habermas from *Between Facts and Norms: Contributions to a Discourse Theory of Law and Democracy* (MIT, 1996) ch 8.

[41] I have made this point elsewhere, particularly in Barbosa (n 39) ch 4.

providing the public with a basic idea of all the alternatives currently under consideration within that particular proposal. This procedural design allows anyone to anticipate the possible outcomes of the debate, making it easier for people to assess those outcomes and to organise accordingly, if need be. However, it also restricts the options of the players in charge of negotiating the issue on the floor of the Chamber, to whom flexibility is a valuable asset.

The idea of allowing amendments during the floor proceedings was conceived during deliberations on the reform of the public pension system (PEC n 33/1995). Pension reform was one of the most controversial pieces of legislation drafted during the term of president Fernando Henrique Cardoso, affecting both private and public sector workers. The Special Committee in charge of analysing the matter received 82 amendments, and was unable to issue an opinion in a timely fashion. The Speaker of the House ordered the matter to move to floor deliberation, pending the Committee's opinion. In this situation, the SRCD authorises the Speaker to appoint a Representative who will issue the opinion directly on the floor on behalf of the Committee. The opinion typically submitted to the floor involves a new text, which incorporates the adopted amendments to the original proposal, plus any necessary structural adjustments. This new text is called the 'substitutive proposal' [*substitutivo*]. In the pension reform debate, however, the substitutive submitted to the floor failed to pass the three fifths threshold. This defeat would have prompted a procedural maze (involving deliberating upon each of the amendments to the proposal), costing the government precious time and resources. Faced with imminent disaster, the government came up with the idea of presenting an 'agglutinative amendment'. In practice, the amendment would provide an alternative version of the opinion previously defeated on the floor, reproducing the defeated text with minor modifications, just enough to secure it a 'second chance',[42] which proved crucial to the passing of the PEC.

According to Article 118, § 3º of the SRCD, an agglutinative amendment is the 'result of the fusion of amendments offered to a proposal, or of amendments with the text of the proposal itself'. This 'fusion of texts' implies an agreement that results in a new amendment, based in the 'approximation of the objects of the amendments agglutinated'. From a theoretical perspective, this kind of procedure is not exactly an *amendment*, but rather a technique to foster political agreement and organise deliberation, and one that should be limited to solving simple problems. For instance, take the case of one amendment that proposes free daycare to children below the age of six, and another that suggests granting this right only to children below the age of four. The classical example of an agglutinative amendment would be a text suggesting providing free daycare to children below the age of five.

[42] BRASIL, Congresso, Câmara dos Deputados, Emenda Aglutinativa Substitutiva à Proposta de Emenda à Constituição n 33-C n 6, de 1995, *Diário da Câmara dos Deputados*, Brasília, DF, 30 abr 1996, 11860.

The practice of agglutinative amendments can be quite different from the theory, however. The main artificer of this practice was Nelson Jobim, a former Justice of the Supreme Court, former member of the Constitutional Convention of 1987–88, and the Rapporteur of the 1993–94 Constitutional Revision. According to Jobim, 'Agglutinative amendments [...] are provided for in the Standing Rules of the Chamber of Deputies, according to which there is no outright need of prior amendments to be agglutinated'. What happens in fact is the 'elaboration of a single text', a text that is *formally* based in pre-existing amendments, but not necessarily *related* with them. The agglutinative amendments are defined as '*transaction amendments*' [*emendas de transação*] that originate on the floor of the House in order to make it possible to reach an agreement upon a certain issue'.[43]

The candid definition provided by Jobim is somewhat consistent with parliamentary practice during the Constitutional Convention, but since then stricter parameters have guided the legislative process, including the procedure for amending the Constitution. The Speaker has been consistently refusing agglutinative amendments that covertly attempt to introduce new matter during floor proceedings, despite a number of Points of Order denouncing abuses.[44] Permitting the introduction of new matter on the floor during the deliberation of a PEC would be particularly grave, given the initiative requirements applicable to the proposal *and* to the amendments. Nevertheless, the fact that agglutinative amendments have not yet been employed with this purpose does not mean that they will not be put to this use at some point in the future. It also does not mean that the procedure in itself is appropriate. It is important to emphasise that the rule of Article 202, § 3º only authorises amendments offered *in the Special Committee* and does not discriminate between kinds of amendment.

The core of the argument in favour of agglutinative amendments is that allowing room for congressional leadership to manoeuvre on the floor is desirable. This argument, however, overlooks the fact that the procedural design of both the Constitution and the SRCD indicates otherwise. The *Committee* – which has up to 40 sessions of the Chamber to discuss a PEC – is the place *par excellence* to analyse the matter, to build consensus, and to design alternatives to the original proposal. The floor, on the other hand, should play a more restricted role, endorsing or rejecting proposals already largely structured, and only introducing minor adjustments if need be. Radically reshaping the matter during floor proceedings not only reduces the ability of the public to keep track of the debate, but also increases the chances of technical and legal flaws in the wording and structure of the approved provisions. Obviously, for those negotiating the proposal it is appealing to keep open as many alternatives as possible until floor proceedings are on course. This strategy, however, functions at the expense of transparency and openness to public

[43] BRASIL, Congresso, *Diário dos Trabalhos Revisionais*, Brasília, DF, 9 mar 1994, 1499.

[44] See, for instance, BRASIL, Câmara dos Deputados, Questão de Ordem n 132/2007, Autor: Arnaldo Faria de Sá, *Diário da Câmara dos Deputados*, Brasília, DF, 5 jul 2007, 34474–34480.

criticism, values that are crucial, and even more so when altering the Constitution through a procedure completely endogenous to Congress.

In 2015, the deliberation of a controversial PEC – a proposal that dealt with the reform of the political system,[45] and particularly with campaign financing – relied heavily on agglutinative amendments. The goal of the reformers within the Chamber was to *reverse* a decision of the Supreme Court that banned corporate contributions to political campaigns.[46]

Once again, the Special Committee in charge of analysing the proposal failed to conclude its deliberation on time. Similar to what happened with the pension system reform, the proposal then moved to the floor of the House by order of the Speaker, pending an opinion.[47] On the floor, the rapporteur issued an opinion on behalf of the Committee advancing a 'substitutive proposal' [*substitutivo*] (Article 118, § 4º, SRCD), a text aiming to synthetise all the provisions deserving approval among the various PECs and amendments offered before the Special Committee.

The Chamber may analyse proposals dealing with the same topic together, according to Article 142 of the SRCD. In this particular situation, *more than 100 other PECs* were appended to the main proposal, not to mention the *43 amendments* submitted before the Special Committee. On the floor, Representatives offered *62 agglutinative amendments*, and, to top it all off, passed a motion to vote the proposal Article by Article. The resulting procedure was unheard of. It was not based on the standing rules and it allowed an unprecedented level of uncertainty regarding the alternatives on the table. The text of the substitutive proposal, organised in topics, would work more or less like a pathway to guide deliberation, instead of providing the priority alternative to be considered by the floor (Article 191, II and III of the SRCD). In clear violation of the Standing Rules, agglutinative amendments drafted right before the voting process were given priority over the substitutive amendments. When the floor rejected one of those amendments, it would be covertly redrafted into a *new* agglutinative amendment (with more or less ponderable variations in its wording) and submitted to a new vote, until a version eventually reached the constitutional threshold, ensuring a result as close as possible to the intent of those controlling these rather illogical proceedings.[48]

[45] BRASIL, Congresso, Câmara de Deputados, Proposta de Emenda à Constituição n 182/2007, *Diário da Câmara dos Deputados*, Brasília, DF, 10 nov 2007, 60500.

[46] BRASIL, Supremo Tribunal Federal, Ação Direta de Inconstitucionalidade n 4650, Requerente: Conselho Federal da Ordem dos Advogados do Brasil, Interessado: Presidente da República e Congresso Nacional, Relator: Ministro Luiz Fux, *Diário da Justiça Eletrônico*, Brasília, DF, 24 fev 2016.

[47] BRASIL, Congresso, Câmara dos Deputados, Ato da Presidência de 26 de maio de 2015, *Diário da Câmara dos Deputados*, Brasília, DF, 27 mai 2015, 124.

[48] Apparently, the Speaker had clarified, earlier during the negotiations with party leaders, that, in the event of the rejection of a proposed text, he would discard the remaining alternatives and that issue would be considered moot for the rest of the deliberation. See Representative Chico Alencar's observations in *Diário da Câmara dos Deputados* 28 May 2015, 127 and 131. Nevertheless, defeated in the attempt to reestablish the right of companies to make electoral contributions, the Speaker backed away from the initial agreement and submitted to vote other alternatives to the same topic.

It is easier to understand the implications of this procedure by looking into the deliberation of the provision regulating campaign financing. When it was initially submitted for a vote, the Agglutinative Amendment n 22, read, 'Political parties and candidates are allowed to receive contributions in money or in goods from persons or legal entities [which includes *companies*]; the law shall establish the maximum limits for collection and expenditure of campaign contributions to each elective office'.[49] The text failed to reach the constitutional threshold, and received only 264 'yes' votes.[50] As an alternative, an amendment limiting the right to make campaign contributions to individuals was proposed and rejected;[51] another followed, banning any kind of campaign contribution, from individuals or legal entities other than the government (the so-called 'public funding'), and it was also rejected.[52] Finally, the Agglutinative Amendment n 28 was passed.[53] This amendment reproduced the text of the Agglutinative Amendment n 22, initially *rejected* by the floor, with *one single difference*: it prevented candidates from *directly* receiving money from legal entities. They could only receive contributions from individuals. Political parties, however, remained authorised to receive contributions from both individuals *and* legal entities (and, of course, to pass along the money to their candidates).

As one reads the official journal of the Chamber of Deputies, it becomes clear how confusing the procedure was to the Representatives themselves, let alone to the public. The country's major newspapers reported the setback of the proposal sponsored by the Speaker on Tuesday 26 May 2015, without even considering the strategy that would follow the next day.[54] Even if one could contend, just for the sake of argument, that such procedure was according to the SRCD, it is patent that it was designed in bad faith, in order to obliquely allow the House to vote on the same issue over and over again. By slightly altering the terms of the proposal on the table, Representatives advocating for the reversal of the Supreme Court's decision to ban corporate campaign funding – led by the Speaker of the House – could persist to have things their way. This is neither legal, nor reasonable. Further, it is inconsistent with procedures designed to reform the Constitution, where publicity, transparency, and formality should play a critical role.

III. Conclusion

A proper understanding of the rhythm of constitutional change in Brazil cannot rely solely on *constitutional* design. Neither the breadth of the constitutional text,

[49] Emenda Aglutinativa n 22/2015, *Diário da Câmara dos Deputados* 27 May 2015, 286.
[50] For the result, *see Diário da Câmara dos Deputados* 27 May 2015, 307.
[51] Emenda Aglutinativa n 10, *Diário da Câmara dos Deputados* 28 May 2015, 150.
[52] Emenda Aglutinativa n 32, *Diário da Câmara dos Deputados* 28 May 2015, 183. For the result of the voting, ibid, 189.
[53] *Diário da Câmara dos Deputados* 28 May 2015, 250.
[54] See, for instance, Ranier Bragon and Aguirre Talento, 'Câmara Rejeita as Bandeiras de Cunha para a Reforma Política' *Folha de S. Paulo* (São Paulo, 27 May 2015) A4.

nor the amendment process provided for by it can, alone, explain the vast number of changes introduced in the 1988 Constitution against all predictions made in the late 1980s and early 1990s. The average of 3.6 constitutional amendments passed every year (or almost one amendment every three months), as well as the increasing pace of formal constitutional change throughout the last 28 years, depended heavily on legislative practice and judicial interpretation, coordinated in order to make the requirements to alter the Constitution easier to fulfil.

The current scenario is the result of many different elements, the all-encompassing breadth of the constitutional text being only one of them (and hardly the most relevant): a completely intra-congressional procedure for introducing constitutional change; majorities in Congress generally aligned with the Executive branch and willing to advance its reformist agendas; legislative authorities committed to interpreting the Constitution and the Standing Rules of each House in a manner that makes change easier (and, of course, empowers these authorities vis-à-vis Executive officials); a Supreme Court that has consistently refused to oversee the *procedural* aspects involved in formal constitutional change; and last, but not least, a constitutional mindset marked by a skeptical approach to the fundamental constitutional decisions made back in 1988.[55]

The combination of these factors induces a pathology in Brazilian constitutional democracy. Instead of reinforcing the principles that laid the foundations of the 1988 Constitution, particularly the vibrant interplay between institutional politics and public opinion, constitutional change has been progressively converting the Constitution to a government-oriented document, designed according to administrative imperatives through procedures that lack transparency and hinder accountability. So far, these amendments have not yet involved the straightforward elimination of rights and guarantees, but some of them threaten the underlying conditions for the proper enjoyment of basic rights.[56]

[55] This enumeration aims at the broader institutional context that favoured quick constitutional change in Brazil. There are a number of context-related reasons that were not addressed in this article, but that may help to explain the frequency of constitutional amendments in Brazil without the oversimplifying approach that blames the 'size' of the constitutional text. One of the most important seems to be the federal government's effort to control expenditures at state and local levels after the considerable decentralisation of public services promoted by the 1988 Constitution. Marcus André Melo, 'O Sucesso Inesperado das Reformas de Segunda Geração: Federalismo, Reformas Constitucionais e Política Social' (2005) 48 *Dados* 845, 880.

[56] See, for instance, Richard Albert, 'Constitutional Dismemberment' (2018) 43 *Yale Journal of International Law* 1, 40–42, discussing the impact of a constitutional amendment establishing a Public Spending Cap on the enjoyment of social rights. Constitutional Amendments n 3 and n 45 have also been criticised for concentrating power in the Supreme Court in a way that weakens the rest of the judicial branch and thwarts the ability of citizens to advance their own perspectives on basic rights through the judiciary. Aline Lisbôa N Guimarães and others, 'Jurisdição Constitucional e Concentração do Acesso à Justiça: "A Voz que Vem de Cima"', Série Pensando o Direito, n 15 (Observatório do Judiciário), Ministério da Justiça, 2009, 128, 135: www.justica.gov.br/seus-direitos/elaboracao-legislativa/pensando-o-direito/publicacoes/anexos/15pensando_direito_relatorio.pdf accessed 4 January 2017.

14

Transformative Constitutionalism and Extreme Inequality: A Problematic Relationship

MAGDALENA CORREA HENAO[1]

I. Introduction[2]

Every day, societies around the world and their economies demonstrate greater inequality on a global and local level. Thus, extreme inequality has become a common subject of study. In fact, in recent years there have been numerous studies in the field of philosophy,[3] constitutional law[4] and political economy (by academics[5] as well as by multilateral organisations[6]) that have addressed this issue.

[1] Constitutional Law Professor, Externado de Colombia University, Bogotá.

[2] With my gratitude to the editors of this book, Professors Richard Albert, Carlos Bernal and Juliano Zaiden. To Professor Mauricio Pérez, who provided significant ideas for the development of the first part. And to Professors David Landau from Florida State University College of Law and Federico Corredor, Andres Gutierrez, Diego Gonzalez and Jorge Roa from Externado de Colombia University also, who read the preliminary version of the text and made invaluable comments. In addition, to young scholars Marcelo Lozada, and Manuela Losada from Externado de Colombia University.

[3] Amartya Sen, *Inequality Reexamined* (Oxford, Clarendon Press, New York; Russell Sage Foundation, Cambridge, Harvard University Press, 1992); Amartya Sen, The Idea of Justice (Harvard University Press, London, Allen Lane, 2009); Jeremy Waldron, *One another's equals: the basis of human equality* (The Belknap Press of Harvard University Press, 2017).

[4] Rosalind Dixon and Julie Suk, 'Liberal Constitutionalism and Economic Inequality' (2018) 85 *The University of Chicago Law Review* 369; Samuel Moyn, *Not Enough: Human Rights in an Unequal World* (Belknap Press/Harvard University Press, 2018).

[5] Joseph E Stiglitz, *The Great Divide: Unequal Societies and What We Can Do About Them* (WW Norton Company, 2015); Richard Wilkinson and Kate Pikett, *The Spirit Level: Why More Equal Societies Almost Always Do Better* (Allen Lane, 2009); Anthony B Atkinson, *Inequality: What Can Be Done?* (Harvard University Press, 2014); Ha-Joon Chang, *Economics: The user's guide* (Bloomsbury Press, 2015); Branco Milanovic, *The Haves and the Have-Nots. A Brief and Idiosyncratic History of Global Inequality* (Nueva York, Basic Books, 2011).

[6] In multilateral organisations such as the IMF, the WB, the WEF, ECLAC, agree on the harmfulness that results from inequality for the collective good. See Oxfam International, *Even It Up: Time to End Extreme Inequality.* (Oxfam, GB, 2014); A Berg and J Ostry. 'Inequality and Unstable

In Latin America, some scholars support the idea of a 'transformative constitutionalism', which aims to fulfil the economic promises contained in Latin American constitutions. However, the situation of extreme inequality that persists in these societies seems to challenge the true transformative potential of such constitutional proposals.

This study examines whether extreme inequality is a constitutionally relevant problem by looking into the constitutions of Brazil, Colombia, Peru, Ecuador and Bolivia.[7] In other words, it seeks to determine whether these constitutions identify economic inequality as a central concern, and whether they give institutional actors the tools to ameliorate it.

For that purpose, this chapter is structured as follows: first, it will define extreme inequality, a specific concept determined on the basis of quantitative and qualitative indicators of extreme poverty, inequality, and social mobilisation. Likewise, it defines the concept of an 'economic constitution' in order to establish the set of norms that might bear on the problem of economic inequality.

Based on those foundations, the second part analyses the dogmatic or substantial ingredients of the economic constitutions, looking for principles, rights, liberties, guarantees and mandates where extreme inequality could be recognised as a problem. Finally, the third and fourth parts study the institutional design of these constitutions, or the 'engine room' assembled to achieve the goals set out in the economic constitutions. This includes the powers of the executive and legislative branches, as well as the powers and actions of constitutional judges, based on examination of some of the case law of the five Latin American countries under study.

The analysis concludes that despite the normative power of the Constitution and the value assigned to human rights, extreme inequality has not been identified as a relevant constitutional problem in Latin American constitutions. Thus, Latin American constitutionalism is not yet transformative enough.

Growth: Two Sides of the Same Coin?' in *IMF Staff Discussion Note* (IMF, 2011); CEPAL, Pactos para la igualdad: hacia un futuro sostenible (Thirty-fifth sessions of the CEPAL, 2014).

[7] The selection explains that for 5 out of 6 of the constitutions that have been ratified in the last 30 years, as new constitutions, not including that of Venezuela of 1999 with its reforms, extreme conditions and being outside the constitutional state that had been in place in this country. They have also been selected because, as will be seen, from its substantial contents (norms and/or precedents), may be considered an expression of the transformative constitutionalism. The foregoing is surprising, despite coming from very different political processes. In Brazil (1988) as a formula of transition from a military dictatorship (Guillermo Fárfan. 'Brazil: la constitución de 1988 y las reformas a los sistemas de pensiones' (2014) 19 *Latin American Journal of Social Rights* 31–62; in Colombia (1991) as the Constitution for getting out of the domestic armed conflict and finding peace; and in Peru (1993) as a legitimising norm of a dictatorial government (Enrique Bernales, 'El desarrollo de la Constitución de 1993 desde su promulgación a la fecha' (2013) 18 *Pensamiento Constitucional* 35–46, as well as in Ecuador (2008) and Bolivia (2009) for the political projects of warlords. (Juan Pablo Muñoz, *Movimientos sociales y procesos constituyentes. El caso de Ecuador 2008* (2008)). Also see Franco Gamboa, 'Transformaciones constitucionales en Bolivia. Estado indígena y conflictos regionales' (2010) 157 *Colombia Internacional* 151–188.

II. Two Essential Concepts for the Analysis

To answer the research question, it is necessary to clarify two concepts. First, the concept of extreme inequality. Secondly, the economic Constitution as the gauge that must be used to measure the constitutional relevance of extreme situations of inequality.

A. Defining Extreme Inequality

All societies are unequal to some extent.[8] In the case of market-based societies, it can be argued that some inequality is necessary to assure that individuals have incentives to create value and reap economic rewards. But it is not obvious that the reasons based on the economic efficiency of markets can justify extreme levels of inequality.

Extreme inequality affects many relevant dimensions of human well-being, as a recent study from Richard Wilkinson and Kate Pickett found.[9] They show how more equal societies achieve better results in terms of collective welfare.[10] Additionally, they demonstrate the correlation between income inequality and a myriad of social problems: mental illness and drug use; life expectancy and infant mortality; obesity; low educational levels; teenage pregnancy; homicide rates and propensity to conflictive behaviour; incarceration rates; and, of course lower possibilities of intergenerational social mobility. The authors conclude that, 'our future lies in improving the quality of the social environment in our societies … [and] greater equality is the material foundation on which better social relations are built.'[11]

Nevertheless, definitions of extreme inequality continue to be controversial. The extremes of the income distribution are not always measured with high quality data, because of methodological problems in household surveys used to measure them.

It has not been that difficult to quantify as 'extreme' or 'intolerable' certain living conditions or income ranges; however, the most elusive issue is to determine the point where wealth becomes intolerable, and whether this inequality gap benefits market economies and the democratic life or jeopardises it.

Thomas Piketty is a pioneer in developing new techniques to improve available information about extreme inequality. He has gone into new research sources, like tax returns, to complement the results of household surveys that

[8] Chang (n 5) 301. This can also be found in the OECD database.

[9] Wilkinson and Pikett (n 5).

[10] An economist in Colombia reported some similar findings recently. See Federico Corredor, *El precio de la desigualdad: fragmentación social y desarrollo truncado. El caso de Colombia* (Bogotá: In process of publication, Universidad Externado de Colombia, 2019).

[11] Wilkinson and Pickett (n 5) 272.

systematically underestimate economic inequality.[12] But his findings and suggestions have increased rather than ending debate on these issues.[13]

What is really behind the unfinished disagreement, beyond considerations regarding market efficiency, is the fact that the drive for profit is itself the cornerstone of the economic system, a freedom of liberal states, untouched by later social and democratic developments.[14]

To get around those hard issues, this study does not seek a complete definition of extreme inequality, but rather focuses on the bottom end, starting with indicators of extreme poverty, inequality and social mobility.

B. Indicators of Extreme Poverty (Monetary and Non-monetary)[15]

Poverty indicators measure absolute levels of income or consumption, which are difficult to compare across countries.[16] Nevertheless, the World Bank's indicator of monetary poverty is a well-accepted parameter, which over the years has used different Purchasing Power Parity cut-offs (measured in international dollars) such as $1.90 or $3.10 a day per capita.

Table 1 presents data on the percentage of population that is below the latter in the five Latin American countries under study.

Table 1 Share of population living on less than $3.10 international dollars per day

COUNTRY	2014
Bolivia	12.7%
Brazil	7.6%
Colombia	13.2%
Ecuador	10.2%
Peru	9.0%

Source: World Bank Data is not available for developed countries, but presumably, the result of the calculation would be close to zero.

[12] See Thomas Piketty, *Capital in the 21st Century* (The Belknap Press of Harvard University Press, Cambridge, Massachusetts, London, England, 2014) 345–73.

[13] See Michael Tanner, 'Piketty Gets Its Wrong' *National Review* (23 April 2014); Diana Furchtgott-Roth, 'The Systematic Errors In Thomas Piketty's New Book' in *Real Clear Markets* (22 April 2014); Clive Crook, 'The Most Important Book Ever Is All Wrong' *Bloomerang Opinion* (20 April 2014); Scott Winship, 'Whither the Bottom 90 Percent, Thomas Piketty?' *Forbes* (17 April 2014); Jonathan Finegold, 'An Austrian Take on Piketty' *Economic Thought* (April 2014); Hunter Lewis, 'Thomas Piketty's Sensational New Book' *Mises Institute. Austrian Economics, Freedom, and Peace* (23 April 2014).

[14] A question that was anticipated by John Stuart Mill in 1965. See John Stuart Mill, 'Principles of Political Economy' in *Collected Works v II* (Toronto, University of Toronto Press, 1965) 225.

[15] Indicators presented in this chapter refer to the Latin American countries analysed. And for purposes of comparison, some developed (and less unequal) countries will also be mentioned, though data on inequality within societies, especially when non-monetary aspects are involved, is hard to find.

[16] See Max Roser and Esteban Ortiz, *Global Extreme Poverty* (published online at OurWorldInData.org. Retrieved from: https://ourworldindata.org/extreme-poverty (Online Resource)) Section II.1.

On average, 10 per cent of the population of these five states lives below that minimum poverty threshold needed for survival. But to flesh out the importance of this basic measure, it is helpful to add in non-monetary poverty indicators. One of these is the Human Development Index (HDI) elaborated by the United Nations Development Program, which contains indicators related to education and health, as well as Gross National Income (GNI) per capita.

Table 2 HDI, life expectancy and schooling

COUNTRY	HDI	LIFE EXPECTANCY AT BIRTH	AVERAGE YEARS OF SCHOOLING
US	0.920	79.2	13.2
Germany	0.926	81.9	13.2
Spain	0.884	82.8	9.8
Brazil	0.754	74.7	9.9
Peru	0.740	74.8	9.0
Ecuador	0.739	76.1	8.3
Colombia	0.727	74.2	7.6
Bolivia	0.674	68.7	8.2

Source: UNDP. 2015.

As can be seen in Table 2, there is a strong correlation between the HDI, GNI/per capita and two basic indicators related to health and education: life expectancy at birth and average years of schooling. The average gap between the Latin American countries and the US, Germany and Spain is more than seven years of life expectancy and three and a half years of average schooling.

Another set of non-monetary indicators is shown by the Multidimensional Poverty Index (MPI), developed by The Oxford Poverty and Human Development Initiative. According to this index, the percentage of the population suffering multidimensional extreme poverty is 20 per cent in Bolivia, 10 per cent in Peru, 5 per cent in Colombia, 5 per cent in Brazil and 4 per cent in Ecuador.[17]

C. Indicators of Inequality

Inequality indexes are always a matter of relative patterns of distribution of income, wealth or opportunities.

The first set of indicators measures monetary income inequality. An intuitive approach is to compare the average income of the top and bottom deciles of the income distribution (also known as the 90/10 ratio).

This score is shown in figure 1.

[17] 'Of the 706 million people who are destitute (…) over 8 million live in Latin America'. Sabina Alkire and Gisela Robles, *Global Multidimensional Poverty Index 2017* (Oxford poverty and human development initiative, Briefing 47, 2017) 13, 14.

Figure 1 Ratio of top decile income to bottom decile income

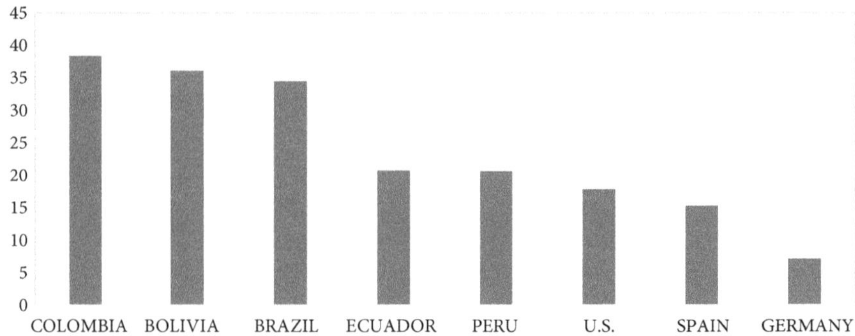

Source: World Bank 2016, last year available according to WILD 3.4.

Inequality is thus far more pronounced in Latin American states than in more developed countries. The three developed countries – Germany, Spain and the US – have ratios between 7 and 18. Two of the Latin American countries in the sample are not too far from the US ratio; Ecuador and Peru are slightly below 21. In contrast, the ratio for Bolivia, Brazil and Colombia goes from 34 to over 38.

A second indicator of inequality on wealth or opportunities is the Gini coefficient, which measures distribution across the whole spectrum and not merely the extremes. In general terms, a Gini coefficient of (1) indicates perfect inequality, while a value of (0) corresponds to perfect equality.

What is most interesting about the Gini coefficient is that it can be constructed for market income and for adjusted income – the latter taking into account the effects of taxes and social spending, that is to say public policies that normally work to lessen inequality. In other words, this allows one to see how unequal a society is and how much the State intervention in the economy contributes to reduce it. Both measures are provided in Table 3.

Table 3 Market income and disposable income GINI coefficients

COUNTRY	MARKET	DISPOSABLE INCOME
Colombia	0.57	0.57
Brazil	0.59	0.54
Peru	0.51	0.50
Ecuador	0.48	0.45
US	0.51	0.39
Spain	0.53	0.35
Germany	0.51	0.29

Source: IMF Database Oct. 2017. Data not available for Bolivia.

The economic outcomes of markets are relatively unfair in most countries; nevertheless, many nations reduce inequality through public policies. For a number of reasons, however, Latin American countries typically do not.[18]

Indeed, market outcomes are not very different in developed countries than in Latin American societies. For example, the Gini market coefficients in the US, Germany and Peru are identical: 51 per cent. The adjusted Gini, however, is very different among these countries. Public policies reduce adjusted Gini coefficients by 12 per cent and 22 per cent respectively, in the US and Germany; Peru's adjusted Gini coefficient is only 1 per cent less than the market index. Even more dramatically, state intervention has zero effect on the high levels of inequality found in Colombia.

D. Coefficient of Social Mobility

A last indicator used to establish extreme inequality is the Social Mobility Index (SMI). Certainly, extreme inequality has much to do with the continuance of wide gaps between the two income groups.

The beta coefficient, within the measurements of social mobility,[19] calculates to which extent the economic success of previous generations determines that of current generations.[20] With a 1 representing maximum immobility, Peru recorded a 0.67, Brazil a 0.69, and Colombia a 0.74.[21]

Similarly, a 2018 study from the OECD entitled 'A Broken Social Elevator? How do we promote Social Mobility,' measured the time it takes 'for those born in low-income families to approach the mean income in their society',[22] and determined that in Brazil and Colombia, it 'would take even nine generations or more' based on current patterns.[23]

[18] Some have argued that redistributive policies are anti-growth. In colloquial terms, they hold that the challenge is to make the pie bigger before we decide how it should be shared. This point of view is disputed in a study published by several economists at the IMF who conclude that countries with redistributive policies tend to grow more than countries that lack them. See Jonathan D Ostry, Andrew Berg and Charalambos G Tsangarides, *Redistribution, Inequality, and Growth*, 1st edn (INTERNATIONAL MONETARY FUND, Research Department, 2014).

[19] See also the gamma coefficient of SMI. For example on Francesca Castellani and Jannet Zenteno, *Pobreza y movilidad social en Bolivia en la Ultima década* (Inter-American Development Bank, Technical Note No, IDB-TN-889, 2015) 16.

[20] Luis Galvis and Adolfo Meisel, 'Aspectos regionales de la movilidad social y la igualdad de oportunidades en Colombia' in *Cartagena: Documentos de trabajo sobre economía regional #196* (CEER, Banco de la República, 2014) 1, 12, 40.

[21] See Maribel Jiménez and Monica Jiménez, 'La Movilidad Intergeneracional del Ingreso: Evidencia para Argentina' in *Documento de Trabajo #84* (Buenos Aires, CEDLAS, Universidad Nacional de la Plata, 2009) 8–10; Viviane Azevedo and César Bouillon, 'Social Mobility in Latin America: A Review of Existing Evidence' in *Working Paper #689* (Washington DC, BID, 2009) 10–15, 20; Javier Núñez and Miranda Leslie, 'Intergenerational income and educational mobility in Urban Chile' (2011) 38(1) *Estudios de Economía* 197–206.

[22] OECD, *A Broken Social Elevator? How to Promote Social Mobility* (June 2018) 26.

[23] ibid, 26.

E. The Economic Constitution

The indicators of extreme poverty, inequality, and social mobility in Latin America surveyed above allow extreme inequality to be recognised. Extreme inequality reduces human development conditions and the probabilities of social and economic advancement. Extreme inequality is made up of many factors, one of them being the inefficiency of public policies adopted in order to curtail it.[24]

In order to study the issue from a constitutional perspective, we must take the economic constitution[25] into account. Such an expression embodies constitutional norms relating to the production, marketing, and consumption of goods and services (economic liberties and rights[26]), as processes to satisfy varied human needs (individual, social, cultural, environmental rights), in a situation of scarce resources (principles of wealth and poverty distribution, private property, environment and sustainable development), where public intervention plays a major role in optimising opportunities and achievements.[27]

The economic Constitution has been part of the history of modern Constitutionalism at key moments[28] – the foundation of the bourgeois liberal state,[29] the development of the social Constitutionalism, and much later on, in 'fiscal' Constitutionalism.[30] It has also been the subject of debate between Kelsen and Schmitt about the very concept of the Constitution as a norm[31] or as a fundamental political decision.[32] Moreover, the economic Constitution has been a determinant to distinguish between the formal and material concepts of the Constitution,[33] or to define its neutrality and rigidity.[34]

[24] 'Inequality is not inevitable. Governments can reduce economic extremes by adopting a package of redistributive measures, including more progressive tax systems that redistribute incomes fairly, and by increasing investment in universal, good-quality and free public services and social protection programs' Winnie Byanyuma. *Rising extreme inequality is a concern for us all* (UNESCO, 16 March, 2016) 269.

[25] See Martín Bassols. *Constitución y sistema económico.* (Madrid, Tecnos, 1988); José María Gimeno, 'Sistema económico y derecho a la libertad de empresa versus reservas al sector público de actividades económicas' (1994) 135 *RAP* 150, 151, 158, 170, 184–87.

[26] Terence Daintith, *The constitutional protection of economic rights* (Oxford University Press and New York, 2004; 2(1) *I.CON* (2004)) 57–61.

[27] Magdalena Correa Henao, 'El orden económico constitucional' in Magdalena Correa Henao, Néstor Osuna Patiño and Gonzalo Ramírez Cleves (eds), *Lecciones de Derecho Constitucional, Tomo II* (Bogotá, Universidad Externado de Colombia, 2018) 634–35.

[28] Jorge Canció Meliá, 'La constitución económica: promesas incumplibles' (2002) 7 *Revista Jurídica Universidad Autónoma de Madrid* 66–78.

[29] Manuel Aragón, *Libertades económicas y Estado social* (Madrid, McGraw Hill, 1995).

[30] Canció Meliá (n 27) 78–95.

[31] Hans Kelsen, *Compendio de Teoría General del Estado* (México, Colofón, 1992) 164–70, 190–93, 217–26.

[32] Carl Schmitt, *La defensa de la constitución: estudio acerca de las diversas especies y posibilidades de salvaguardia de la Constitución* (Tecnos, 1983).

[33] Gonzalo A Ramírez C, *Límites de la reforma constitucional en Colombia* (Bogotá, Universidad Externado de Colombia, 2005); Antonio Cidoncha, *La libertad de empresa* (Madrid, Editorial Civitas, 2006).

[34] Miguel Herrero, 'La Constitución Económica: desde la ambigüedad a la integración' (1999) 57 *Revista Española de Derecho Constitucional. Año 19* 15, 20–26; PAPIER, 'Ley Fundamental y orden económico' in BENDA, *Manual de Derecho Constitucional* (Madrid, 1996) 567.

At present, it is a normative concept composed of various legal sources, among which constitutional norms stand out. It also comprises human rights norms included in the treaties ratified by the states, where rights and liberties that define and give human meaning to the economy and to government intervention are vested in the former.[35] At the same time, these norms are part of the Latin American variation of the 'block of constitutionality'. Hence, their supra-legal rank (Brazil) or constitutional-rank (Colombia, Peru, Ecuador, Bolivia).[36]

This study seeks to establish if the dogmatic contents of the economic constitution in Latin America, and its institutional structure,[37] corresponds to the idea of transformative constitutionalism. In other words, whether or not the normative power of the Constitution and the effectiveness of fundamental rights[38] allow underprivileged groups to expect satisfaction of their primary needs, to be free and to guarantee social progress to some extent. Or whether extreme inequality such as scarcity of life conditions and the lack of social mobility is, or is not, constitutionally tolerable.

III. Substantial Components of the Economic Constitution

We first consider the dogmatic contents of the economic constitution, or the principles, rights and liberties and guarantees that define the fair economic order.

A. Three Fundamental Principles

Every Constitution stresses at least three fundamental principles useful to the understanding of the economic Constitution, as guidelines to interpret its norms.[39]

[35] Mainly the International Covenant on Civil and Political Rights, the International Covenant on Economic, Social and Cultural Rights, the American Convention on Human Rights and the San Salvador Protocol to the American Convention on Human Rights, ratified by the five States under study. In order to limit the extension of this article, it will solely make explicit mention of constitutional norms.

[36] Manuel Eduardo Góngora, 'The Block of Constitutionality as the Doctrinal Pivot of the Ius Constitutionale Commune' in A Von Bogdandy, Eduardo Ferrer Mc-Gregor, Mariela Morales and Flavia Piovesan (eds), *Transformative Constitutionalism in Latin America. The emergence of a New Ius Commune* (Oxford, Oxford University Press, 2017) 235–53. See also H Fix-Zamudio, *El derecho internacional de los derechos humanos en las Constituciones latinoamericanas y en la Corte Interamericana de Derechos Humanos* (Revista Latinoamericana de Derecho, 2004) 141–80.

[37] Karl Loewenstein, *Teoría de la constitución*, 2nd edn, translated by Alfredo Gallego Anabitarte (Barcelona, Ariel, 1986).

[38] Armin Von Bogdandy, 'Ius Constitutionale Commune en América Laina: Observations on Transformative Constitutionalism' in *Transformative Constitutionalism in Latin America* (Oxford, Oxford University Press, 2017) 32–33.

[39] See Luis Prieto, *Ley, principios, derechos* (vol 7) (Madrid, Dykinson, 1998); Herbert Hart, *El concepto de Derecho* translated by Genaro R Carrió, Ed Abeledo-Perro (Buenos Aires, 1990). In the Colombian case see T-079 of 1995, C-445 of 1999, C-690 of 1996 and C-126 of 1998.

They are the principles of constitutional supremacy,[40] *pro personae* or human dignity[41] and *pro libertate.*[42]

When indeed there is a constituent determination to building a constitutional state,[43] the Constitution is given supremacy[44] since it is the critical understanding about what is fair and unfair to the state. Human dignity or the *pro personae* principle is also part of the axis of the constitutional order, which gives a substantial value to the human person and to the guarantee of a dignified existence.[45] And finally, the very liberal *pro-libertate* principle reinforces the meaning of the liberties as well as the economic ones within them.

B. The Liberties and Rights of the Economic Constitution

Economic liberties and rights are the main faculties, rights and guarantees that allow participation of individuals or groups in the productive process, in order to seek economic gain and to allow economic resources to fulfil human necessities and interests (See Appendix 1 'The economic liberties and rights of the Economic Constitution').

In all of the constitutions studied, liberal and market freedom clauses exist. These Constitutions also recognise the typical economic rights to work, to freedom of association, among others. Likewise, special guarantees of labour stability are contemplated for more vulnerable groups of the population. All those rights and freedoms are essential for the functioning of the economy and in order to ensure that people can make a living, live with autonomy and dignity,[46] and advance and prosper.

Social and cultural rights belong to the economic constitution. Their guarantee is one of the main goals of the state, which provides the goods and services that satisfy their content or regulate the markets. These rights are also protected by the Constitutions, although the provisions of the Brazilian, Ecuadorian, and Bolivian constitution on this point are more numerous and diverse than those in Peru and Colombia.

Finally, all of these constitutions include environmental rights as well, although their protection is undoubtedly stronger in the constitutions of Ecuador and Bolivia, than those of Brazil, Colombia and Peru. These norms generally allow

[40] Br Art 5; C art 4; P art 51; E art 424; B art 410, no 2.

[41] Br Art 1, no 3; C. art 1; P art 3; E art. 11, no 8; B art 8, no 2.

[42] Br Art 1; C art 333; P art 59 and 61; E art. 66, no 5, 9, 10, 16 and 17; B art 8, no 2.

[43] Gustavo Zagrebelsky. *El derecho dúctil.* (Madrid, trotta, 1995).

[44] See Josep Aguiló, 'Sobre la constitución del Estado constitucional' (2001) 24 *DOXA* 435–40, 446–49.

[45] See Constitutional tribunal from Bolivia, cases SCP 0487/2014, SCP 0778/2014, SCP 0112/2012.

[46] Colombian Constitutional Court, judgment T-881/02.

the use of natural resources in order to increase productivity, but nonetheless limiting their exploitation in order to ensure sustainable use.

C. Institutional Guarantees

In general, the rights and liberties found in the economic constitution are protected in several ways (see Appendices 2 and 3). All of these constitutions contain the guarantee of 'legal reserve', which requires a law to place limits on the rights and liberties established in economic constitutions.

Property is protected through the requirement of due process and compensation before expropriation is carried out. Furthermore, these constitutions contain provisions giving special value to business as the key to development, and a mandate to preserve free competition.

The social state is also present through the recognition of a social and ecological function of private property. Moreover, the constitutions generally require that budgets cover social expenses and reduce inequality. Social, economic and environmental rights are generally protected through relatively weak mandates of progressive realisation and non-regression.

All of these constitutions also justify many different types of state intervention. Standing out among them are the planning institutions, public budgets, tax system, public utilities regulation, as well as financial and monetary policies.

Finally, there are constitutional mandates on the judiciary to preserve individual and collective interests related to the contents of the economic constitution from infringements of legislative and executive officials.

D. Preliminary Conclusion: Latin American Dogmatic Economic Constitutions Bear on Economic Inequality

Without question, the dogmatic economic constitutions studied here have important differences. However, in each case the dogmatic economic order is not strictly neutral,[47] but instead places key limits on political actors.

This is true, for example, when economic and market freedoms are protected in the constitutions and are established as objectives of state intervention in the economy. And it is true as well when some principles, rights and mandates are defined to improve living conditions and to attend to the most unequal individuals and groups. Finally, it is true when constitutions define the political order as working within a social market economy (Colombia and Peru), or as being a

[47] The constitutions of Ecuador, Bolivia and even Brazil are richer in contents and more pluralist than the Peruvian one. We can place the Colombian constitution between them.

welfare state (Brazil, Ecuador and Bolivia), or in other words as systems where economic justice requires freedoms and competition, as well as a guarantee of basic equalities and opportunities. The substantial economic norms of the Latin American constitutions under study thus include a concept of equality in the *ius constitutionale commune.*[48]

In this sense, it can be argued as a preliminary conclusion that extreme inequality is a relevant constitutional issue.

IV. The 'Engine Room': The Functional Elements of Economic Constitutions

The evaluation of extreme inequality, in the context of the constitutions we have analysed, would be incomplete without a discussion of the functional elements and competences that are set up to realise the desired constitutional economic arrangements; what Gargarella[49] has called the 'engine room' of the Constitutions.

A. Power and Representative Democracy

Once a clause providing state intervention in the economy is inserted into a constitution, it ensures that the legislative and executive powers can define those topics.[50] This conclusion is sustained in the old foundations of the democratic components of the *rule of law*, given the legitimacy they grant to the representatives chosen by the people.[51]

On the one hand, the work done by legislators is public and deliberative; they represent their electors and have the power to define the public interest.[52] On the other hand, the executive has powers to intervene in the economy as an authority legitimised by popular election who presumably has the knowledge to promote the best policies,[53] taking initiatives and technical decisions that do not belong to the sphere of political deliberation.

[48] See Armin Von Bogdandy, 'Ius Constitutionale Commune en America Latina: una mirada a un constitucionalismo transformador' (2015) 34 *Revisa de Derecho del Estado* 18–19.

[49] Roberto Gargarella, *La sala de máquinas de la Constitución. Dos siglos de constitucionalismo en América Latina (1810–2010)* (Buenos Aires, Katz Editores, 2014) 91.

[50] See José Ignacio De Aquino, *El estado de derecho latinoamericano. Integración económica y seguridad jurídica en Iberoamérica* (Salamanca, Ediciones Universidad de Salamanca, 2003) 443–50.

[51] See Emmanuel-Joseph Sieyes, *¿Qué es el tercer estado?: Ensayo sobre los privilegios* (España, Alianza Editorial, 1994); Bernard Manin, *Los principios del gobierno representativo* (Alianza Editorial, 1998) 8–30, 111–14; C Schmitt, *Verfassungslehre* (1928, citado por Dottrina della constituzione, Trad de A Caracciolo, Milán, Giuffrè, 1984) 114.

[52] C art 133; P art 93; E art 127.

[53] See Jean Meynaud. *La elaboración de la política económica* (Madrid, Tecnos, 1969); Catherine Conagham, *Capitalists, Technocrats and Politicians: Economic Policy-making and Democracy in the Central Andes* (Keilog Institute, University of Notre Dame, 1988) 33–48.

That also means that, in the structure of the 'engine room' of the economic constitutions, citizen participation does not have a leading role in economic decision making, despite the principle of popular sovereignty that is also declared in the Constitutions.[54] Instead of the people, it is the executive and the legislative branches that share the main constitutional competences to design and implement whatever is necessary to achieve economic goals.

In the Latin American States under study, the scope of such principles also means that most of the relevant powers are under the jurisdiction of the national political authorities rather than more local actors. This is true both in centralised states (Colombia, Peru, Ecuador and Bolivia[55]) and under a federal system (Brazil[56]).

B. Institutional Design and the 'Engine Room'

Both the formal design and practice of the separation of powers in Latin America casts serious doubt on the adequacy of representation in this context.

It is well known that in Latin America the executive power has more weight than the legislative power.[57] Presidential preeminence is particularly evident in economic matters (see Appendix 4).

Presidents often have exclusive power to initiate legislation over a broad set of issues related to international relations and the national budget; management of the nation's incomes, public finance and the investment of state revenue. The Congress not only lacks initiative in those topics, but its capacity to amend bills presented by the president on budgetary and related matters is often minimal.[58] The same point applies to the competence of the legislature in the approval of international treaties signed by the head of state. The legislative branch often has limited power to make changes,[59] which can only be invoked in certain situations[60] or on certain subjects.[61]

Thus, the checks and balances between the legislative and executive branches are weak and tilted in favour of the latter. Political representation, which should foster the inclusion of criteria of justice in economic policy decisions by means of deliberative and public proceedings, is diluted through an industrial and technocratic design that centralises the development of the economic order around the executive.

[54] Br art. 1, no 2; C art 3; P art 2, no 17; E art 2 and 95; B art 7.

[55] C art 288; P 188, 190; E title V, chap IV; B Third part, title I, chap VIII.

[56] Br Título III.

[57] See Carlos Bernal, 'Direitos fundamentais, juristocracia constitucional e hiperpresidencialismo na America Latina' (2015) 17(111) *Revista Juridica de Presidencia*, Brazilia 15–34.

[58] C arts 346, 351; P Art 79–80; E art 295.

[59] C art 150, no. 14.

[60] Br art 49, no 1.

[61] P art 57; E art 419.

This perspective is complemented if we consider how political parties actually work in Brazil,[62] Colombia,[63] Peru,[64] Ecuador[65] and Bolivia,[66] where presidents often play a predominant role and deliberation is minimal. Broader dysfunctions in democratic systems[67] also play a role here.

C. The Design of the State Undermines Commitments to Economic Inequality

From the above, one could conclude that even if the implementation of the economic constitution suitably appertains to political authorities that are democratically representative, institutional design in Latin America prefers a strong presidency that has a robust technocratic capacity, despite its less transparent decision-making process and its lack of pluralism.

Extreme inequality that involves the noncompliance of constitutional objectives and does not guarantee minimum rights and freedoms, strongly depends on the convictions and concerns of the current President. Since those issues are not one of the executive's preferred policies, they are not included in the political agenda, so they become non-existent.

In other words, extreme inequality is a constitutionally relevant problem, but the institutional arrangements of the constitutions under analysis show that nobody represents the have-nots politically.

V. Can We Expect Something from Constitutional Judges?

If, and as it has been stressed here, it cannot be expected that the executive and legislative powers understand extreme inequality as a constitutionally relevant problem, can we count on judges?

To answer that question, we must first look into the powers they have, and then on how those powers are exercised.

[62] Br Título II, Chap V.
[63] C Título IV, Chap II.
[64] P art 35.
[65] E Título IV, Sección V.
[66] B art 210.
[67] ECLAC's Social Indicators analyse how much democracy and the functioning of institutions is valued by the population. In the states in our sample the valuation of democracy falls in the medium high range. It is considered the best form of government by 75% of Ecuadorians and 71% of Bolivians. The country with the lowest score is Colombia (61%) while Peru and Brazil both have an indicator of 62%. See United Nations ECLAC, CEPALSTAT, *Databases and Statistical Publications. Statistics and Indicators* (2000–18).

A. Do Judges Have a Sufficient Level of Power?

Judicial review varies across the countries being studied, but courts generally enjoy a high level of power to review laws and executive acts for non-compliance with the economic constitution.[68]

The constitutional tribunals studied here have a centralised power to review the constitutionality of laws, decrees, and constitutional reforms abstractly.[69] The tribunals are also competent to exercise the constitutional review of treaties signed by the Head of State, by means of prior control in Ecuador,[70] Bolivia[71] and Colombia.[72] In Brazil[73] and Peru[74] control is exercised after the fact.

In terms of judicial mechanisms to protect fundamental human rights,[75] the courts can decide or revise several forms of safeguarding fundamental rights, such as *segurança, tutela*, and popular actions.[76]

Besides the differences among constitutions, one can easily identify the constitutional norms that determine the competences of the tribunals.[77] None of the constitutions at issue contain express prohibitions on exercising constitutional control over certain matters. Therefore, they have power to review the laws that regulate the economy. In this context, constitutional judges can exercise control over state actions or omissions that increase conditions of extreme inequality.

[68] About the different models of constitutional control in Latin America, see Elena I Highton, 'Sistemas concentrado y difuso de control de constitucionalidad. in Bogdandy, Armin von et al (coords), *La justicia constitucional y su internacionalización. ¿Hacia un ius constitutionale commune en América Latina?* (México, UNAM, Instituto de Investigaciones Jurídicas, Max-Plank-Institut für Ausländisches Öffentliches Recht and Völkerrecht, Instituto Iberoamericano de Derecho Constitucional, 2011) 119–49. And Jorge Roa Roa, 'La Justicia Constitucional en América Latina' in Correa Henao, Osuna Patiño, Ramírez Cleves (see n 27) 449–86.

[69] Br art 102, C art 241, E art 436, P art 202, B art 202.

[70] E art 438, no 1.

[71] In this case however, it is not clear if it is treated as optional or compulsory control. See Nataly Vargas Gamboa, 'Los Tratados Internacionales de Derechos Humanos en la Nueva Constitución Política del Estado Plurinacional de Bolivia' in R Bandeira Galindo, R Urueña and A Torres Pérez A. *Manual: Protección Multinivel de los Derechos Humanos* (Red de Derechos Humanos y Educación Superior (rdhes), 2013) 335.

[72] C art 241, no 10. Constitutional precedent has specified that this control is: (i) prior, (ii) automatic, (iii) integral (formal and material control), (iv) preventative, and (v) has *res judicata* impact. (Constitutional Court C-157 of 2016.)

[73] Br art 102, num 1. See George Rodrigo Bandeira Galindo and Antonio Moreira Maués, 'El caso Brazileño' in R Bandeira Galindo, R Urueña and A Torres Pérez, *Manual: Protección Multinivel de los Derechos Humanos* (Red de Derechos Humanos y Educación Superior (rdhes), 2013) 357.

[74] P art 200. The unconstitutional action on the treaties, can only be filed within the following 6 months after entering into force (Art 100 del Código Procesal Constitucional).

[75] For a complete description of the actions in the region, see Allan Brewer-Carías, *Constitutional Protection of Human Rights in Latin America. A Comparative Study of Amparo Proceedings* (Cambridge, Cambridge University Press, 2009).

[76] Br art 5, no 70, 72; C arts 86, 88; P art 200, no 2; E art 88; B art 128.

[77] Br art 102; C art 241; P art 202; E art 436; B art 202.

B. Finding Case-law about the Problem

Have the Courts used their extensive competences on economic matters in order to confront extreme inequality?

With only one exception,[78] none of the five courts have expressly referred to extreme inequality.[79] To get around this shortcoming, this study makes use of scholarship about jurisprudence and also chooses a random sample of judicial decisions where some kind of economic inequality could be concerned.[80]

The case law can be divided into two classifications: first, those cases where Courts defended centralist[81] or presidential[82] powers to regulate the economy, or legislative measures in favour of free (and concentrated) markets;[83] or conversely, those cases that looked to assure the fundamental contents of economic, social and environmental rights and economic freedoms.

i. The Protection of ESC Rights

One characteristic of Latin American transformative constitutionalism is that the orders to ensure an equality of minimums have come from the national courts, and to a lesser extent, from the Inter-American Court of Human Rights.[84]

[78] That conclusion is determined just after searching the phrase 'extreme inequality' in the databases of the courts. The phrase was used once by the Colombian Constitutional Court. See judgment SU254/13.

[79] This is different from the case of extreme poverty. When one searches for this concept on the databases of the five tribunals chosen, the results are as follows: Br 2 rulings, 48 rulings; C 12 rulings; P the page is not working well; E 3.361 results; B 13 rulings. But this is not the concept this study uses, because the extreme inequality is determined by different causes, and extreme poverty is only one of them.

[80] The main criteria was to match the 'inequality' word, with phrases like 'economic model', 'welfare state', 'material equality', 'mining', 'foreign investment', 'economic and social rights', 'environmental rights', 'freedom of enterprise', and 'social market economy'.

[81] On the FSC (by its Portuguese acronym), see Gretchen Helmeke and Julio Ríos Frigueroa. *Tribunales Constitucionales en América Latina* (México, Poder Judicial de la Federación, 2010). And Francisco Secaf Alves Silveira, *O estado econômico de emergência e as transformações do Direito Financeiro Brazileiro* (Catalogação da Publicação, Serviço de Biblioteca e Documentação, Faculdade de Direito da Universidade de São Paulo, 2018) 223, 249. From the Plurinational Constitutional Court of Bolivia, see DECLARACIÓN CONSTITUCIONAL PLURINACIONAL 0046/2016, Issued 11129-2015-23-CEA, 25 April 2016, DECLARACIÓN CONSTITUCIONAL PLURINACIONAL 0156/2016. Issued 10564-2015-22-CEA, 1 December 2016, Plenary session; DECLARACIÓN CONSTITUCIONAL PLURINACIONAL 0040/2017. Issued 17612-2016-36-CEA, 19 May 2017, Plenary Session. See CCE RULING No. 002-16-SAN-CC CASE Nros. 039-10-AN y 033-12-AN, 6 April 2016, on control measures against informal mining.

[82] See CCE 1 April 2014. Case 0001-14-RC, which passed the constitutional reform in 2015.

[83] TCP. Judgment 5 March 2010 Application for unconstitutionality. Issued NO. 00026-2008-PI/TC and 00028-PI/TC, on planned consolidation of the fishing sector. And judgment 27 September 2005. Issued 0020-2005-Pl/TC and 0021-2005-Pl/TC, on the coca leaf.

[84] Because a direct protection of the social and economic rights has just recently come under debate. See Corte IDH, case *Lagos del Campo v Peru* 31 August 2017, with dissenting vote from judge Humberto Sierra Porto. Also see Elizabeth Salmón and Renata Bregaglio Estándares, 'jurisprudenciales de derechos económicos, sociales y culturales en el Sistema Interamericano' *Derechos Humanos y Políticas Públicas (11)* 383–444.

The cases that stand out the most are those that assure the enforceability of economic and social rights.

In Brazil, the high court declared unconstitutional the future or *ex nunc* tax norms,[85] due to the damage they could generate to government finances, and therefore to social security and health policies.

The Colombian Constitutional Court is a good example in this regard.[86] It has declared unconstitutional rules that breached the principle of equality to the right to social security,[87] and the right to a minimum essential level of subsistence.[88] In addition, it has ensured the rights to labour stability for some groups subject to special protection,[89] as well as the right to water[90] and the protection of natural resources.[91]

The Ecuadorian Constitutional Court has declared unconstitutional limits on the worker's profit as provided by law.[92] Likewise, safeguarding the rights to legal certainty and due process, it has protected the right to social security.[93]

The Plurinational Constitutional Tribunal of Bolivia, from the recognition of the necessity to 'throw out the so-called weak constitutionalism and bring in the "strong constitutionalism"', has extended the Action of Constitutional Protection in order to grant protection to economic and social rights.[94] Moreover, it has upheld legislation that imposes limits and controls on the sugar sector in order to protect 'the prime offer of food supply strategy'.[95]

However, the most useful judgments to understand the power of constitutional judges to face extreme inequality are the 'structural injunctions' or 'structural judgments' ruled under the so-called 'unconstitutional state of affairs'.[96] In these

[85] See Fábio Martins De Andrade, *Modulação em Matéria Tributária: o argumento pragmático ou consequencialista de cunho econômico e as decisões do FSC* (São Paulo, Quartier Latin, 2011).

[86] Where 'using remarkable legal innovations, the Court attempts to implement social rights in a difficult context, despite not counting on legislative or administrative social development'. See Von Bogdandy (n 43) 18–19.

[87] Vid. Pension case of senior officials, CCC C-1354/00; C-258/13.

[88] See judgments C-1433 of 2000, C-1064 of 2001, C-1017 of 2003 and C-931 of 2004.

[89] Jorge M Benítez Pinedo. *El principio de estabilidad laboral reforzada en los pronunciamientos de la Corte Constitucional 1992–2005*. (Bogotá: Universidad Externado de Colombia, 2006).

[90] See judgments A030/18, T-475/17, T-712/14.

[91] See judgments T-384A of 2014 (Yaigojé Apaporis Park and mining), C-035 of 2016 (prohibition on mining in wilderness even with legal exploration permits.) And judgment T-361 of 2017, on delimitation of wilderness areas.

[92] EL UNIVERSO, *El pleno de la Corte Constitucional, en sesión extraordinaria realizada en Quito hoy, miércoles 21 de marzo de 2018, resolvió sobre el caso No. 0053-15-IN y acumulados* (21 March 2018).

[93] CCE judgment no 175-14-SEP-CC, 15 October 2015, Case no 1826-12-EP.

[94] Such as public health (1154/2012); salaries received (SCP 368/2013); the right to water (0052/2012; 0052/2012; 0084/2012; 1027/2012; 1027/2012; 1539/2012; 1941/2012); the access to education (0080/2012); SSCC 0165/2010-R and 0294/2010-R, 2179/2012; 2225/2012; 2234/2012) and the rights of people belonging to high priority or enhanced protection (SSCC 0165/2010-R and 0294/2010-R, 2179/2012; 2225/2012; 2234/2012). Or the right to the access to 'medicinal products for terminally ill patients' (SCP 1746/2013).

[95] PCTB Constitutional judgment SCP 005/2015 – AIA 06/02/2015.

[96] Blanca Raquel Cardenas, *Del estado de cosas inconstitucional (ECI) a la formación de una garantía transubjetiva*, (Bogotá, Universidad Externado de Colombia, 2016) 40–55, 100–19, 447–59; César Rodríguez Garavito, 'Más Allá del Desplazamiento, o Como Superar un Estado de Cosas

kind of resolutions, 'the judges make an important effort to give effectiveness to the constitutions, when confirming the grave and reoccurring disregard for human rights',[97] fixing orders to 'a plurality of powers, bodies or public agencies, the coordinated implementation of public policies (...) along with the elaboration of legislative, executive and also judicial measures (...)'.[98]

Its introduction into the Latin American case law is attributed to the Colombian Constitutional Court, which made use of this formula to confront overcrowding in prisons,[99] to overcome the discrimination in the public health system,[100] and especially, to ensure different rights to victims of internally displaced people.[101] In Brazil, the Supreme Federal Tribunal has recently appealed to the 'state of unconstitutional affairs'[102] in order to attend to the situation of the pressures in the prisons[103] and other cases.[104] Finally, in Peru, the tribunal has extended the safeguard of labour[105] and retirement[106] to all the people that were found in the same situation of the petitioners.

ii. The Protection of Economic Freedoms

It is also useful to review how courts treat fulfilment of the freedoms of property, labour, business and competition, from a liberal or from a 'social market economy' approach.

Liberal judicial decisions were founded in the Brazilian, Colombian and Peruvian cases. The FSC of Brazil applies the general rule that retroactive taxes are

Inconstitucional' in *allá del desplazamiento: políticas, derechos y superación del desplazamiento forzado en Colombia* (Bogotá: Universidad de los Andes, 2009) 435, 441–48.

[97] Néstor Osuna, 'Las sentencias estructurales. Tres ejemplos de Colombia' in BAZÁN, Víctor (ed), *Justicia constitucional y derechos fundamentales. La protección de los derechos sociales. Las sentencias estructurales.* (Colección Konrad Adenauer, No 5, 2015) 92.

[98] César Rodríguez Garavito and Diana Rodríguez Franco, 'Un giro en los estudios sobre derechos sociales: el impacto de los fallos judiciales y el caso del desplazamiento forzado en Colombia' in Christian Courtis and Ramiro Ávila *La protección judicial de los derechos sociales* (Ministerio de Justicia y Derechos Humanos) 359–61, 367–68.

[99] See judgments T-153 of 1998, T-606 of 1998, T-388 of 2013, T-762 of 2015.

[100] See judgments T-760 of 2008 (right to health).

[101] See judgments T-025 of 2004 and follow-up decisions, eg Autos 050/04. Also, SU254/13, the only reference to 'extreme inequality' in all of the Latin American case law explored expressly containing that expression. It is used to refer to the condition that the forced displacement victims find themselves in, which 'imposes the State the obligation to overcome the said condition, adopting affirmative measures in favor, with the objective to guarantee effective and real equality'.

[102] Thiago L Santos Sombra, *The Unconstitutional State of Affairs of Brazil's Prison System: The Enchantment of a Legal Transplantation* (I·CON, 2015).

[103] FSC – Pleno, RE 559.943, Rel Min Cármen Lúcia, j. 12.06.2008, DJE 25.09.2008; FSC – Plenary, RREE 556.664 e 559.882, Rel Min Gilmar Mendes, j. 12.06.2008, DJE 14.11.2008; FSC – Plenary, RE 560.626, Rel Min Gilmar Mendes, j. 12.06.2008, DJE 04.12.2008. See De Andrade (n 93).

[104] STF PLENÁRIO AÇÃO DIRETA DE INCONSTITUCIONALIDADE 5.488 DISTRITO FEDERAL. Judgment 31 August 2016.

[105] See CCP Issued No. 3149-2004-AC/TC. Judgment 20 January 2005.

[106] CCP Issued No. 05561-2007-PA/TC Case ONP. Judgment 24 March 2010.

unconstitutional, in order to protect the rights of contributors.[107] In Colombia, the BITs and FTAs have been declared constitutional, including the clauses that intensely preserve the assets of the investor, with clear unequal treatment towards national competition and privileges over the regulating power of the state.[108] And in Peru, the constitutional court struck down reforms of mining royalties for violating property rights.[109] The Court has also privileged mining companies' rights to carry licences from the state ahead of measures to pledge water sources committed in the licences granted.[110]

The resolutions that follow the social economic market model are those in which Courts are concerned about the restrictions of equality in the exercise of economic freedoms. In Colombia, contrary to the Brazilian jurisprudence,[111] during the financial crisis of the late 1990s, the court declared the formula of calculating interest rates in housing debts[112] unconstitutional.[113] It also guaranteed as fundamental rights some material equality to exercise the freedom of enterprise and free competition,[114] and the consumer's right to be informed.[115]

In Peru, the tribunal struck down administrative standards to reduce tariffs in favour of certain actors, because of the absence of efficiency of such measures.[116]

In Ecuador, the Constitutional Court ruled some reservations regarding certain clauses of an economic treaty unconstitutional because they violated the system of legal sources, legal security and because of the impossibility to determine the competences of arbitral tribunals.[117]

Finally, the tribunal of Bolivia has struck down norms that restrict the exercise of free enterprise due to pending state debts, because of the lack of due process.[118] Regarding property law, steps have been taken to comply with the ordinary fees that guarantee correct setting of boundaries,[119] but in a case of popular action, it prohibited private property constructions that blocked neighbouring farmers from transporting their products.[120] And as a way to defend 'an inclusive

[107] FSC – Plenary, RE 559.943, Rel Min Cármen Lúcia. See De Andrade (n 93).
[108] C-750 of 2008, C-031 of 2009, C-941 of 2010, C-199 of 2012, C-186 of 2016.
[109] CCP. Issued No 0143-2013 PA/TC. Judgment 20 November 2013, Constitutional remedy.
[110] CCP. Issued No. 03932-2015-PA/TC. Judgment 14 March 2017.
[111] Alves Silveira (n 88).
[112] Followed by some remarkable mandates. See David Landau and Julián López-Murcia, *Political Institutions and Judicial Role: An Approach in Context, The Case Of The Colombian Constitutional Court* (Universitas. Bogotá (Colombia) No 119, julio-diciembre de 2009) 22–24.
[113] CCC C-383 of 1999, C-700 of 1999, C-747 and C-995 of 1999).
[114] CCC judgment T-724 of 2003; A- 268 of 2011; A-275 of 2011.
[115] CCC judgment T-136 of 2013; C-313 of 2013; T-670 of 2016; T-543-2017.
[116] CCP, Issued No 03116-2009 PA/TC. Judgment 10 August 2009, Constitutional Remedy.
[117] CCE No 023-10-DTI-CC, CASO No 0006-10-TI. 24 June 2010. See CCE No 009-16-DTI-CC, Case No 0015-16-TI.
[118] PCTBB, judgment 1050/2013. Issued 00322-2012-01-AIC. 28 June 2013.
[119] PCTB, judgment 0059/2015. Issued No 07395-2014-15-AAC. 10 February 2015, Constitutional Safeguard Action.
[120] PCTB, judgment 0801/2013-L. Issued 2011-24639-50-AP. 8 August 2013, Popular Action.

constitutional market',[121] it has ordered municipalities to comply with the construction of a market building that guarantees the rights of both the sellers, as well as the consumers.[122]

All of these decisions potentially alter the balance of power and resources between haves and have-nots, even if they do not refer to extreme inequality as such.

C. Balance and Effects of Judicial Power

An indicative overview of the jurisprudence of the Courts in which the case-law could have been related to the extreme inequality as a problem, shows some results: (i) Widespread decisions that allocate vital requirements of social, economic, cultural and environmental rights. (ii) Institutional guarantees to the market and the liberal dimension of economic freedoms was found in the jurisprudence of Peru and Colombia, which can be explained by the Constitutions they interpret (as in Brazil). (iii) Meanwhile, those three courts have employed structural judgments and the unconstitutional state of affairs formula. (iv) With the exception of the FSC in Brazil, constitutional judges have awarded a fundamental guarantee to some equal exercise of economic freedoms.

This overview also reveals how the imbalances between the substantial ingredients of the economic Constitutions might be (partially) compensated by the judges.[123]

Nevertheless, it is difficult based on this review to have high expectations for constitutional judges facing extreme inequality. On one hand, there are no express decisions about extreme inequality. On the other hand, the decisions that most nearly approximate to the extreme conditions suffered by the people, have not been effective.[124]

There is no doubt about the symbolic power of this jurisprudence[125] and the significance of the temporary satisfaction of basic needs provided to a large number of people. However, it did not transform their lives, nor has it altered

[121] Peter Häberle, 'Seven theses for a constitutional theory of the market' (2006) 5 *European Constitutional Law Journal* 24–27, 34–36.

[122] See PCTB judgment 0443/2015-S1. Issued 08944-2014-18-AP. 8 May 2015. First Section. Popular Action. Judgment Constitutional Plurinational 1560/2014-AP. Issued 05257-2013-11-A. 1 August 2014, Third Section. Popular Action.

[123] A characteristic of the transforming constitutionalism that is not only constructed from the constitutional texts, but from the interpretations of the judges. Von Bogdandy. (n 34) 33–32.

[124] Andrés M Gutiérrez, *El amparo estructural de los derechos* (Madrid, Center for Political and Constitutional Studies, 2018).

[125] Mauricio García, *La eficacia simbólica del derecho. Sociología política del campo jurídico en América Latina* (Bogotá, IEPRI, Debate, 2014) 80, 92.

the established economic distribution criteria and context where the extreme inequality is bred.[126]

Furthermore, case law that intervenes in the economy with social objectives, is seen by some as undesirable because it presumably sets up institutional and political instability, affects the decision making of other powers, breaches some international obligations of the state, or distorts the public budgets.[127] This jurisprudence has also been critiqued for resolutions adopted without sufficient procedural safeguards, and because 'the policies' formed by the judges create perverse incentives against the protected groups[128] as well as dependence that degrades the human condition.[129]

The main reason to dismiss the constitutional judge as the power entitled to challenge extreme inequality is the complexity of the constitutional problem. The causes of extreme inequality[130] cannot be reached by constitutional courts within their competences and capacities, since their reasoning normally focuses on more discrete judicial problems raised by the plaintiffs. This point also explains why there is so much conflicting reasoning to these decisions, which are liberal or egalitarian, centralist or pluralist, depending on the case.

In any case, these interpretations minimise the conception of a fair economic order of the Constitution, reducing the problem of inequality to a social obligation of the state, external to the economic realm.

VI. Conclusions and Remarks

This chapter has aimed to determine whether extreme inequality is a constitutionally relevant problem in Latin America, by studying the economic contents of the Brazilian, Colombian, Peruvian, Ecuadorian and Bolivian Constitutions. The answer should be able to clarify to what extent those constitutions correspond to the ideal of transformative constitutionalism.

[126] This is why within the indexes of democracy, the proportion of citizens who believe in judicial power is very low: 20% in Peru; 33% in Brazil; 36% in Colombia; 39% in Bolivia; and 40% in Ecuador. See United Nations ECLAC, CEPALSTAT, *Databases and Statistical Publications. Statistics and Indicators* (2000–2018).

[127] We have seen it in Colombia with the judgment on the subject of health care (Sebastian Escobar, Luis Mario Hernandez and Cristhian M Salcedo, *El juez constitucional como garante de los derechos sociales en Colombia: una mirada crítica al activismo judicial de la Corte Constitucional colombiana* (2013) 10 Universitas Estudiantes, Pontificia Universidad Javeriana 148).

[128] Mauricio Pérez Salazar, *Economía y fallos constitucionales: la experiencia colombiana durante la vigencia de la carta política de 1991* (Bogotá, Universidad Externado de Colombia, 2004).

[129] Niklas Luhmann, *Teoría política en el Estado de Bienestar* (translated by Fernando Vallespín. Madrid, Alianza, 1993).

[130] Causas de la desigualdad, see Joseph Stiglitz, *El precio de la desigualdad. El 1% de la población tiene lo que el 99% necesita* (Taurus, 2012) 92–105, 174–88.

Extreme inequality in Latin America was characterised by scarce life conditions, lack of basic needs and social immobility where state intervention has not had any effect whatsoever. This is incompatible with many core provisions prescribed by Latin American constitutions: specifically, those that guarantee legal individual or collective positions of economic, social, cultural and environmental rights and freedoms, enforceable to at least essential minimums.[131] Also, those describing mandates from the state, which claim for equal distribution of advancement opportunities, as well as for welfare and improved living conditions.

According to those constitutional ingredients, it has been argued from the start that extreme inequality is a constitutionally relevant problem, as it implies a human rights violation or deprivation and a disregard for constitutional objectives.

Nevertheless, this argument could not be confirmed by the institutional norms of the economic Constitution, due to the weak powers of the Legislative branch to define the political agenda and economic policies, compared to the strong power of the Executive. In addition, the representative system does not guarantee enough pluralism and inclusion of diverse social interests in the parliaments or in the executive branch.

Constitutional judges face similar limitations. Although they have not faced this issue yet in a serious way, they would not be able to solve it anyway. This is why their decisions on economic matters that are understood as ways to face the causes or the consequences of extreme inequality often turn out as being incoherent or insufficient, ineffective or undesirable.

Extreme inequality is a substantial constitutional problem, but the engine room of the economic constitution, designed to acknowledge and challenge extreme inequality, does not work, and there are no legal or factual premises to expect any change. Indeed, it is a problem, but not one that is relevant to the public powers, because of both failures of political representation and because there is no judicial capacity to force change.

Thus, concerning extreme inequality, Latin American constitutionalism is not really transformative. This big conclusion is understandable because that problem surpasses the normative power of constitutions, regardless of the decisions of some brave or reckless judges. Moreover, we must consider the failures of the democratic system (so important and inadequate to face these kinds of problems), where Latin American constitutionalism does not look transformative after all.

Following Law and Veersteg, one can affirm that the constitutional practice of the five countries under study is sham transformative constitutionalism.[132] Sham, because its well-shaped achievements are not able to avoid and control the lack of

[131] Wesley N Hohfeld, 'Some Fundamental Legal Conceptions as Applied in Judicial Reasoning' (1913) 23(16) *Yale Law Journal*; Martin Borowski, *The structure of fundamental rights* (Bogota, Universidad Externado de Colombia, 2003).

[132] David S Law and Mila Versteeg, *Sham Constitution* (California Law Review, 101, 2013) 880–85, 919–34.

political will to take on the big questions around extreme inequality.[133] Sham, for being a constitutionalism that ultimately proves 'compatible with inequality, even radical inequality'.[134] Latin American constitutionalism, in the end, has proven unable to establish even the minimum conditions of a free and equal dignified existence that public intervention must ensure the people.

Abbreviations

B.	Bolivia
Br.	Brazil
BITs	Bilateral Investment Treaties
C.	Colombia
CCC	Colombian Constitutional Court
CCP	Constitutional Court of Peru
E.	Ecuador
ECC	Ecuadorian Constitutional Court
ESCR	Economic, Social and Cultural Rights
FTAs	Free Trade Agreements
GNI	Gross National Income
HDI	Human Development Index
MPI	Multidimensional Poverty Index
OECD	Organization for Economic Co-operation and Development
P.	Peru
PCTB	Plurinational Constitutional Tribunal of Bolivia
SMI	Social Mobility Index
FSC	Federal Supreme Court

[133] This is, the 'aspects related to (…) the wage distribution and the labor market' or to 'the segmentation for production integration and territorial factors, and the sharp inequalities to access assets or property all which perpetuates and strengthens the inequalities and stops progress from having a distributed impact'. See CELADE, *Desigualdades sociales y derechos humanos: hacia un pacto de protección social. Santiago de Chile: Reunión de expertos sobre población, desigualdades y derechos humanos.* (2006) 2.

[134] Moyn (n 4) 213.

Appendices

No. 1

	The liberties and rights of the Economic Constitution														
	Constitutional Rights														
	Liberal market liberties or rights						Typical economic rights								
	Rights with recognition in human right treaties			Rights without recognition in human right treaties											
	The private common and intellectual property rights	Guarantee of acquired rights	Freedom of work	Free enterprise	Free competition	Mandate to the legislator to regulate the consumers' rights	To work	Freedom of association	Collective bargaining	Right to strike	Guarantees of labour stability	Right to the collective property of indigenous and black	Special protection in favour of the peasant population and except Ecuador, rural property is contemplated as a right	Social and cultural rights	Environmental rights
Bolivia	Art. 30, num II, num 11; 56, num II	Art. 394	Art. 46	Art. 47, 308	Art. 405	Art. 75	Art. 46, Chap. 5 section III	Art. 51	Art. 49	Art. 53	Art. 48, num VI; 49, num III	Arts. 394, num III; 31	Art. 30, num II, num 6; 394, num I; 405 and ss.	First part, title II, chapter V, section I, II, chapter VI,	Art. 33; 34; 311, num III; fourth part, title II,

Brazil	Art. 5, num 22, 26 and 28	Art. 5, num 35	Art. 5, num 13	Art. 1; 5, num 13	Art. 170, num 4	Art. 5, num 31	Arts. 6; 7; Title II, Chap. II	Art. 8	Art. 8, num 6	Art. 9	Art. 7, num 20.	Arts. 231; 31	Art. 5	Title II, chapter II; title VIII; title II, chapter II, chapter II, sections I, II, IV, V, VI, VIII; title I, chapter II	Art. 225
Colombia	Art. 58	Arts. 48, 58, 332, 336, 365	Art. 26	Art. 333	Art. 333	Art. 78	Arts. 25, 55, 56	Art. 39	Art. 55	Art. 56	Arts. 45, 46, 47, 53	Arts. 63, 329; Transitory article 55	Arts. 64, 65, 66	Title II, Chap II	Art. 79
Ecuador	Arts. 66, num 22; 322		Art. 66, num 17	Art. 66, num 15		Art. 52, 55	Arts. 33, 326, Cap. VI, Section III	Art. 326, No 7	Art. 326-13	Art. 326-14	Arts. 38, num 2; 39; 46, num 2; 47, num 5; 329; 330; 331; 332	Arts. 57, num 4; 59		Title II, Chap I y II	Art. 10
Peru	Art. 70	Art. 71	Art. 59	Art. 58, 60	Art. 61	Art. 65	Arts. 22, 28	Art. 28, num 1	Art. 28, num 2	Art. 28, num 3	Art. 23	Art. 88, 89	Arts. 88, 89	Title I, Chap II	Art. 2, num 22

No. 2

	Institutional Guarantees								
	The market economy						Budgetary mandates		
	Expropriation, previous trial and compensation	**Special value to the enterprise**	**Promotion of small enterprises and opportunities in the sectors**	**Mandates to preserve free competition**	**Prohibition of law monopolies**	**How to pay public debt**	**Social expenses**	**The social and environmental function of property**	**Social, economic, environmental rights, weaker mandates of progressive realisation and no regression**
Bolivia	Arts. 57, 401				Art. 314		Art. 321, num II	Art. 56, núm I	
Brazil	Art. 5, num 22; 128, num 3 and 4; 184; 243			Art. 170, num 4	Art 177; 220, num 5		Art. 165	Art. 5, núm 22	
Colombia	Art. 58	Art. 333		Art. 333	Art. 336	Arts. 334, 339, 346	Art. 350	Art. 58	Arts. 48, 64
Ecuador	Art. 323, 376				Art. 17, num 3; 281, num 11; 304, num 6; 335		Art. 298	Art. 321	Art. 11, num 8.
Peru	Art. 70	Art. 58	Art. 59	Art. 61	Art. 61		Art. 77		

No. 3

	Institutional Guarantees									
	The Constitution's various types of intervention							Judicial guarantees		
	Types of intervention	The planning institutions	Tax law	Public budgets	The rules on public services	Establishment of a central bank	Financial policy	To the defence and protection of liberties and rights	To preserve as individual	To preserve as collective
Bolivia	Art. 311, 316	Art. 311. num II	Artíc. 323,	Art. 321	Art. 36, No 2	Art. 327	Arts. 330, 331	Art. 132	Art. 22, 128, 129; 130; 132; 218	Art. 14, num III; 24; 31; 34; 130; 132; 135; 218
Brazil	Art. 174	Art. 174, num 1	Art. 150	Art. 165	Art. 175	Art. 164	Títle IV, Chap. I, Sec. IX.	Art. 103	Art. 5	Art. 5
Colombia	Art. 334	Art. 339	Art. 345	Art. 345	Art. 365	Art. 371	Art. 335	Art. 40, num 6; 241	Art. 86, 87	Art. 88, 89
Ecuador	Art. 335	Art. 241	Art. 301	Art. 292	Art. 318	Art. 303	Art. 302		Art. 70, 86, 88	Art. 72, 86, 88
Peru	Art. 58, 59		Art. 74	Art. 77	Art. 58	Art. 84	Art. 77	Art. 200, num 4	Art. 200, num 2	Art. 200, num 5

No 4.

		Bolivia	Brazil	Colombia	Ecuador	Peru
Functions of the president	The power to veto bills for reasons of inconvenience or unconstitutionality		Art. 48, num 5; 66	Art. 165	Art. 138	Art. 108
	To issue regulations that implement laws		Art. 84, num 4	Art. 189, num 11	Art. 147, num 13	Art. 118, num 8
	To nominate or designate office holders with broad powers of economic intervention	Art. 172, num 22	Art. 84, num 1, 14 and 15	Art. 189, num 1	Art. 147, num 9	Art. 172, num 15 and 22
	Legislative initiative	Art. 162, num 3	Art. 61; 84, num 3	Art. 154	Art. 134, num 2; 147, num 11	Art. 107
	Exclusive legislative initiative in issues related to international relations			Art. 164	Art. 261	
	Development plans	Art. 172, num 10		Art. 200, num 3	Art. 147, num 4	Art. 192, num 2
	The national budget	Art. 172, num 11	Art. 84, num 23	Art. 200, num 4	Art. 147, num 8	Art. 78
	Public services		Art. 61, num 1.1.2	Art. 154	Art. 135	
	Decree the investment of state revenues	Art. 172, num 9		Art. 189, num 20		
	The creation, modification or elimination of taxes		Art. 61, num 1.1.2	Art. 154	Art. 135	
	Use emergency economic powers to legislate in this field	Art. 172, num 24	Art. 62; 84, num 26	Art. 215	Art. 140	

INDEX

www.ingramcontent.com/pod-product-compliance
Ingram Content Group UK Ltd.
Pitfield, Milton Keynes, MK11 3LW, UK
UKHW020906190926
475560UK00010B/294

9 781509 923502